Draining the Swamp,
Southern Style

Also by Bruce D. Epperson
and from McFarland

The Moulton Bicycle: A History of the Innovative Compact Design (2018)

Roads Through the Everglades: The Building of the Ingraham Highway, the Tamiami Trail and Conners Highway, 1914–1931 (2016)

Bicycles in American Highway Planning: The Critical Years of Policy-Making, 1969–1991 (2015)

Peddling Bicycles to America: The Rise of an Industry (2010)

Draining the Swamp, Southern Style

North Carolina and Florida Wetlands and the Wright Report Scandal, 1896–1926

BRUCE D. EPPERSON

McFarland & Company, Inc., Publishers
Jefferson, North Carolina

ISBN (print) 978-1-4766-8464-2
ISBN (ebook) 978-1-4766-4244-4

Library of Congress and British Library
cataloguing data are available

Library of Congress Control Number 2021003066

Printed in the United States of America

McFarland & Company, Inc., Publishers
Box 611, Jefferson, North Carolina 28640
www.mcfarlandpub.com

Table of Contents

Introduction 1

1. Sort of a Plan of His Own 13
2. This Country Is Not Good for Anything 30
3. Simply Fundamental Hydraulics 49
4. Land Richer Than the Valley of the Nile 65
5. It Looks Peculiar to Me 81
6. Adventures in Draining the Great Dismal Swamp 102
7. A Damned Lying Statement 120
8. The Best Photographs I Have Ever Seen 134
9. Vacillating and Deficient 148
10. Lamar's Crying Cow 166

Chapter Notes 185
Bibliography 217
Index 225

Introduction

> The Division of Drainage in the Department of Agriculture was organized to assist in developing the full agricultural resources of the Nation through the reclamation of swamp areas. The work of the division is mainly confined to the examination and exploration of latent agricultural possibilities and consequent undeveloped wealth. Thus, its field force, in many instances, is the first to come into possession of knowledge of the real value of certain tracts of land. This knowledge is acquired as a result of the expenditures of public funds. To prevent this peculiar opportunity from being used for speculative purposes, the department has adopted rules prohibiting outside interests in investigations of the department. Every officer and employee must subscribe to these regulations.
>
> —*Final Report into the Florida Everglades Investigation*, August 1912[1]

On February 3, 1912, the House Committee on Expenditures in the U.S. Department of Agriculture convened to investigate accusations that an important report evaluating the feasibility and cost of draining the Florida Everglades prepared by the Department's Office of Experiment Stations, Division of Drainage Investigations, had been suppressed because of the influence of land speculators. Only days before the hearings began, Charles Elliott, the Chief of the Division of Drainage Investigations and his assistant, A.D. Morehouse, had been fired for allegedly shifting a few hundred dollars in expense vouchers from fiscal year 1909 to 1910 to cover a budget shortfall, although the Agriculture Department's Solicitor, George McCabe, admitted that Elliott had actually under-spent his budget for 1909.

Forty-two sessions and seven months later, the committee, named after its chairman, Ralph Moss of Indiana, determined that the so-called "Wright Report" had been withheld, but not because of wrongdoing. It had actually been withdrawn twice: the first time on the eve of publication due to technical errors that may have been due to sloppy engineering, or may have been an attempt to hide discrepancies between the report's optimistic recommendations and its decidedly less rosy field data. The corrected report was then cancelled by the Secretary of Agriculture, James Wilson, due to conflicts between members of the Florida congressional delegation and state officials over Everglades drainage policy. But the seven months of committee hearings had uncovered a veritable horror-show of corruption, self-dealing, misuse of government personnel and property for private gain, the tarring of reputations in order to protect high-level officials, and outright blackmail within the Department of Agriculture and the state governments of Florida and North Carolina. The alleged financial improprieties by Elliott and

Staff of the Drainage Investigations Division, Office of Experiment Stations, 1908. Arthur Morgan, front, second from left. Charles Elliott, front, third from left. Probably John T. Stewart, front, far left. Probably Anson Marston, second row, far right. Photographer unknown (Arthur Morgan Papers, Antioch College, Yellow Springs Ohio).

Morehouse resulted from accounting procedures so inadequate and outdated that it took the committee weeks to figure out what the budget status of one small division was.

The "Wright Report Incident" has been touched on in most major histories of the Everglades, starting with those by Marjory Stoneman Douglas and by Alfred and Kathryn Hanna in 1947 and continuing to the present.[2] None, however, have included the simultaneous malfeasance involving the North Carolina Pocosin wetlands along the west shore of Pamlico Sound that turned out to be at the core of the scandal, and it is mentioned in none of the (admittedly few) histories of the North Carolina coastal plain swamps.[3] While nobody was able to prove that the errors and miscalculations made in the first draft of the report by its author, J.O. (James Oliver) Wright, were done deliberately to justify a drainage project that was inevitably doomed to failure, taking the money of tens of thousands of small homesteaders down with it, Wright was hired by the State of Florida immediately after completing his report at an exorbitant salary. It was also Wright who was shown to have accused his former boss of the financial improprieties that led to his firing. But the hearings did conclusively establish that Wright had spent years preparing federal surveys of proposed bond-financed drainage districts in North Carolina while at the same time accepting stocks, bonds, and cash commissions from the landowners, contractors and even the state, all of whom stood to benefit from the formation of these districts. In a few cases, he defrauded his partners. In others, he was the one defrauded. Most often, the deals were more or less honest, but involved glaring conflicts of interest. On one project, he attempted to recruit Assistant Agriculture Secretary Willett Hays as an investor. On another, he created a dredging company, bought a dredge on credit, put his former assistant at the Division of Drainage Investigations in charge of the outfit, wrote the specifications for the bids on behalf of the North Carolina district, and recommended the winning firm. It was this testimony and evidence that led to his exposure and, ultimately, forced him to resign his Florida position. While the wrongdoing in North Carolina proved to be more egregious than that in Florida, it has been overshadowed because previous writers have been focused on Everglades history.

From the time of statehood, Florida did not own the wetlands within its boundaries. These were owned by the federal government and granted, or "patented" to the state. However, in the chaotic years during and after the Civil War, the legislature gave away much of its current and future patentable land to railroads and railroad subsidiaries. In 1902, Governor William Jennings arranged for the transfer of the last remaining land in the hands of the federal government, three million acres in the Everglades, while simultaneously canceling most the outstanding legislative land grants. The railroads sued, of course, but either lost in court or, more often, settled for relatively small percentages of their original claims.

Ironically, rather than solving the state's problem, it created a new and potentially even more vexing situation. The argument Jennings had used most often, and most convincingly, to win the railroad lawsuits was that it was the duty of the state under federal and state law to drain the wetlands, and only then sell them. But the state had no money to implement a drainage program. So Jennings and his successor, Napoleon B. Broward, sold huge tracts of land to mail-order retailers such as Richard J. Bolles and E.C. Chambers for less than two dollars per acre. These sales were configured in "checkerboards" of alternative sections, or square miles. In theory, by selling the land in an interspersed pattern, these big sales would make the state's drainage program self-financing. The reclamation program would dry both the privately purchased sections and the state's adjacent parcels. When reclaimed, the state could sell these now-dry alternative sections at ten to twenty dollars an acre—enough to recoup the losses incurred in making the initial sales at heavily discounted prices. Meanwhile, Bolles, Chambers and the other big-block speculators were selling ten-acre plots to smallholders via mail-order for $250 per plot. Most of these involved some level of illegality, usually mail fraud resulting from the deceptive nature of the sales material they transmitted through the post office.

Since 1898 the U.S. Department of Agriculture had provided assistance to the states for planning drainage and irrigation systems through its Office of Experiment Stations (OES). In 1905 Charles G. Elliott, chief of the Drainage Investigation Division of OES, approached Governor Broward with an offer to assist the State of Florida with Everglades reclamation planning. Engaged in a bureaucratic turf war with the Department of the Interior's new Reclamation Service, the intention was to secure a special Congressional appropriation for the project—upwards of $100,000—that would prevent the Reclamation Service from swallowing up the irrigation and drainage investigation divisions of OES, a move Agriculture Secretary Wilson wasn't sure he really objected to. Broward enthusiastically embraced the offer of assistance, but the appropriation was twice rejected. Lacking an appropriation, Elliott tried to talk his supervisor, Elwood Mead, out of starting the survey, but Mead decided to proceed, taking funds out of the OES regular annual appropriation, spread out over a number of years. Eventually, $11,000 was spent.

Mead assigned the project to supervising engineer J.O. Wright. Wright made a brief trip to Florida in November 1906 and over the winter of 1906–07 he had two survey crews working under his direction for three months. The following winter of 1907–08, he extensively traveled across south Florida, mostly by small boat. During his trips he met often with Governor Broward and other state officials.

Elliott expected him to have his report completed by late 1908, when Elliott returned from an extended trip to Europe. He was disappointed to learn that little progress had been made. In February 1909, a lawyer named Henry Hall, who worked with several Everglades land sales firms, visited the offices of the drainage division. He reviewed the work Wright had completed so far. Somehow, Hall secured a missive from Secretary Wilson instructing Elliott to give Hall an extract from Wright's report. Afterwards, a copy was sent to the State of Florida, where it became the state's official drainage plan. This document became known as the "Wright Report extract."

The Wright Report itself was completed in May 1909. It was processed through the usual pre-production channels and assigned the serial number Bulletin 218. In August, a visitor named Henry Wheeler asked to review the manuscript. He pointed out what he thought were several glaring errors in calculations. Elliott was again out in the field, but supervising engineer Arthur Morgan, who reviewed the report with Wheeler, agreed that it was badly flawed. He secured permission from Elliott to delay printing. Elliott eventually took the job away from Wright and had a team of office engineers heavily revise the report. This "Elliott Report" was completed in late January 1910.

Because the Everglades report was taking so long, and there were so many requests for information, Elliott had a junior engineer prepare a one-page mimeographed flier providing basic meteorological, soil, and drainage information for those writing to the office inquiring about the topic. Many of the land sales firms were angered by this circular because its data contradicted their wildly over-inflated claims, such as the temperature never dropped below freezing, or that fertilizer was unnecessary for any type of crop. Secretary Wilson ordered the circular withdrawn, and all requests for information were referred to state authorities.

In February 1910 Wright was offered the position of Chief Drainage Engineer of the State of Florida, at a salary of $5,000, about $1,700 more than was usual for this type of work, and State of Florida salaries typically ran below average. Moreover, Wright's hiring was specified as a condition within a settlement agreement reached between the state and the large railroad landowners in early 1910. In it, the land companies withdrew their opposition to the levying of an acreage tax to support the creation of a new Everglades Drainage District. In return, the state agreed to use the tax money to drain land in ways favored by the railroad landowners. Generally, this meant adhering to the plan outlined in Wright's February 1909 extract for Henry Hall.

At this time, Secretary Wilson directed that the Elliott Report of January 1910 not be published. Ostensibly, this was done because of objections raised by Dr. Beverly Galloway, director of the Bureau of Soil Conservation. However, Joseph Arnold, chief editor and director of publications for the Department of Agriculture, later admitted that the report was actually cancelled because the entire topic of Everglades drainage had become too controversial.

In August 1910 Florida Senator Duncan Fletcher sought and received an appropriation to publish a compendium of acts, laws, reports and other documents related to the Everglades and their reclamation. A.D. Morehouse, Elliott's assistant, received a galley proof this document, *Senate Document No. 89*, as part of the normal review and comment process. He noticed that it contained the old Wright Report version originally prepared for Bulletin 218. He corrected his copy by replacing the Wright Report with the subsequent Elliott Report. He also inserted several background documents related to the Everglades survey of 1906–09, including administrative directives, progress reports, journal entries, and other material. Following Senator Fletcher's orders, these changes were deleted and the Wright Report was placed back in, using a copy of the galley proof for Bulletin 218 that an Everglades land salesman named Thomas Will had arranged to have stolen from the Government Printing Office.

In October 1911, two months before *Senate Document No. 89* was printed, the Washington *Times* published a series of articles, more or less correct, that accused Agriculture Secretary Wilson of suppressing the two reports, the Wright Report and the January 1910 mimeographed circular. A few points were muddled, but they were accurate enough to cause great consternation within the Department of Agriculture. USDA solicitor George McCabe ordered all documents related to the Everglades impounded. On November 17, Secretary Wilson ordered Elliott to prepare a report on the history of the Everglades project. This was delivered on November 21. Some 3,000 words long, it was well written, straightforward, and clear.

On December 15, 1911, a Jacksonville newspaper published a feature story on the "suppressed" documents and on Everglades land fraud in general. It was heavily based on Elliott's November 21 report. Someone had leaked it to the press. On February 3, Elliott and his deputy, A.D. Morehouse, were terminated, and others were suspended. The termination gave no reason, but Elliott was told that he had mismanaged departmental accounting procedures related to Congressional appropriations and submitted false accounting documents. Representatives Clark of Florida and Bathrick of Michigan filed complaints with the House Committee on Expenditures in the Department of Agriculture seeking an investigation.

The first month of the hearings focused mostly on the mimeographed circular and the various drafts of the Wright Report, and while it went into great detail, the only new information not previously available to the public was the news that the charges against Elliott and Morehouse originated from J.O. Wright. Wright had told the Agriculture Department's accountant, Mr. Zappone, that Elliott had asked a North Carolina landowner and businessman named John Wilkinson to cover a $120 monthly salary shortfall for a federal surveyor working in his county because the Office of Experiment Stations had run out of money for the fiscal year. He was repaid a month later. Asked why he did this, Wright said that Elliott had been interfering with his work and abusing him since he left for Florida 30 months before. Asked for details, he was vague. Asked why he waited two and a half years to report the malfeasance, he could not answer.

Approximately one month into the hearings, a man named John Seip from Chillicothe, Ohio, testified. Seip was young, under 40, and wealthy, the son of a large-scale beef, pork and mutton farmer and meatpacker. Seip met J.O. Wright in September 1908 at a drainage conference organized by Congressman J.N. Small at New Berne, North Carolina. As a result of this meeting, Seip had Congressman Small petition for a survey of the Moyock swamp, 26,000 acres within the larger Great Dismal Swamp near the Virginia border, for Seip's Provident Land Company, asking that Wright be assigned to the job. Seip testified that at the New Berne conference, Wright offered to negotiate the purchase of a dredge at no money down, arrange for the creation of a state drainage district to float bonds to pay for the Moyock dredging, and find buyers for the drained land in exchange for $7,500 in stock in Seip's company.

A month earlier, the State of North Carolina asked the Drainage Investigations

Division to perform a drainage survey at Lake Mattamuskeet, a 50,000 acre shallow, aquifer-fed lake that the state owned and had been trying to drain without success since colonial days. North Carolina was trying to sell it for $100,000, but without soil and drainage surveys, nobody wanted to buy it. Wright was also assigned this task. The state, glad to have the federal government pay the cost of the survey and provide technical assistance in getting the bond district approved, offered Wright a $5,000 commission if he could find a buyer for the lake. Wright tried to talk Seip into buying the lake and put him together with John Wilkinson.

Wright proposed that Seip and Wilkinson put up $100,000 to buy the lake. He would write an engineer's report that put the post-drainage value of the land at $1,400,000. The district would float the bonds and pay the cost of development, and Seip and Wilkinson would give him $40,000 in stock. Unknown to Wright, Seip traveled to Wilkinson's home in Belhaven, North Carolina. Hearing about Seip's proposed Moyock arrangement, Wilkinson told Seip that he and Wright had a similar arrangement about a year earlier with Wilkinson's Albemarle Development Company. Wilkinson gave Wright $5,000 in stock to set up a drainage district, sell bonds, and so on, but Wright didn't do "a damned thing." Seip, in turn, told Wilkinson about Wright's Moyock plan. Wilkinson pulled out of Mattamuskeet.

With Wilkinson no longer interested, Wright found a potential replacement: Assistant Secretary of Agriculture Willett Hays. After describing the lake over a casual lunch, Hays invited Wright to his office for a longer talk. Between April and September 1909 Hays tried to interest his former college president, Leigh Hunt, in the project. Ultimately, Hays was not successful and another, unrelated group of partners called Mason, Webb and Kerr bought the lake.

In the committee hearings, over the next six months, Willett Hays, Leigh Hunt and John Wilkinson all verified various parts of Seip's story under Congressman Moss's careful questioning. Wilkinson also verified that he had received a letter from Elliott explaining that the Office of Experiment Stations had a cash shortage for June 1909. Could he pay the full salary for the surveyor for June and then be compensated in July? About $120 was involved. Wright was in town for a visit and Wilkinson asked if this was on the "up and up." Wright said it was fine; it happened all the time. It would be a big help to the office.

Called back to the stand five months after his first testimony, Wright verified almost everything that Seip, Hays, and Wilkinson had said. Asked again more intensely why he thought it necessary to report Elliott to the Department's investigator for the Wilkinson transaction, Wright provided this explanation:

After Mason, Webb and Kerr had purchased Lake Mattamuskeet, they had retained him as a consulting engineer. In October 1910, Elliott wrote the Clerk of the Court of Hays County, where Lake Mattamuskeet was located, in response to a letter from the clerk notifying him about the formation of a drainage district. Elliott recommended that the clerk retain an independent engineer to check the existing plans. The clerk agreed, and the reviewer found several flaws, requiring $2,500 to redesign it.

In December, the chairman of the Lake Mattamuskeet Drainage District contacted Elliott, asking him to review these latest plans himself. Elliott did, and discovered that Wright had again modified them, apparently to lower costs. He again found them deficient. He met with Mason, Webb and Kerr and outlined his concerns. They agreed to most or all of his changes. A day or two later, Mason, Webb and Kerr met with Wright in Washington, D.C. Wright said the changes were a waste of money. The partners said they were going to go ahead and make the changes. Wright went from this meeting to the Department of Agriculture to press his allegations of financial mismanagement. The "harassment" that Wright alleged was, in fact, Elliott's continued attempts to correct Wright's bad engineering.

Perennially short of funds due to delinquent tax payments, the Everglades Drainage District limped along until the hurricanes of 1926 and 1928 wiped out the settlements on the rim of Lake Okeechobee. The state formed a separate flood control district with the same boundaries, but it too was largely insolvent. After the Great Flood of 1947, the two were joined in the Central and Southern Flood Control District, run by the Army Corps of Engineers. The State of Florida finally got the federal assistance it had sought for a century, but for flood control, not reclamation. The effect of the Moss Committee Report in North Carolina is harder to gauge, because unlike Florida, by 1912, drainage was decentralized into some 66 independent, bond-issuing drainage districts. Some succeeded, some failed, most muddled along somewhere in between. Several attempts to drain Lake Mattamuskeet were made. All failed, and the lake is now a national wildlife refuge.

II

In recent decades, a new appreciation has emerged for the interconnectedness of North America's wetlands as biological and ecological entities. Draining or damming the annual flood plains of the Ohio, Missouri, and Mississippi Rivers has irreversibly changed the character of the Louisiana bayou country and the Mississippi River delta hundreds of miles to the south. Draining the Limberlost Swamp of northern Indiana shifted the pattern of migratory bird flocks west, overloading the Cheyenne Bottoms of west-central Kansas.[4] As a consequence, the decision-making over, and implementation of, drainage and reclamation projects has increasingly been transferred from the local level to regional, state and even multi-state authorities through federal legislation such as the Reclamation Acts of 1902 and 1939, which unitized water control in thirteen western states under the Bureau of Reclamation, or through the creation of gigantic federal agencies such as the Tennessee Valley Authority.

But few appreciate how the *land* in wetlands has also become a national commodity, bought, sold, advertised, and brokered on a nationwide basis. The Wright Report Incident has a historical significance beyond the initial shock value of the blatant corruption it exposed and the breathtakingly casual, almost cynically indifferent belief by some participants that they were entitled to special government privilege, no matter how undeserved, unfair, or illicit. This significance is the window it opens into an emerging era in America: a time when land became a nationwide consumer good. It began with the Homestead Act of 1863, which granted a settler 160 acres of government-owned land for only a filing fee after five years of residence and use, or permitted him or her to purchase the land for $1.25 per acre for 160 acres, or $2.50 per acre for 80 acres or less, after six months of occupancy and use.[5]

But most smallholders were not able to afford $200 for 160 acres, or even $100 for 40 acres. Nor could they afford to fence off, plow or otherwise utilize a tract for the five years needed for complete preemption without having to raise working capital by selling off sub-parcels, which they could not do until the Government Land Office granted clear title at the end of five years. Many could not afford the local property taxes due on a parcel of land as large as 160 acres after title was transferred. Hence, many, if not most, homesteaders purchased smaller parcels from a railroad such as the Southern Pacific, Union Pacific or Great Northern, who had received massive land grants and had already gone through the process of surveying, subdividing and registering smallholdings with local authorities.[6]

By purchasing from a railroad or a railroad subsidiary, there was no need for the smallholder to file paperwork, secure a surveyor, or worry about preemptive claims or claim-jumpers. Mortgages and advice were often available. Lots could be swapped if there were problems with the original selection. And often, the railroad land cost little more than government land. The railroads were already in the vanguard when it came to the management, recordkeeping, and legal affairs attendant to the holding of huge expanses of right-of-way; the marginal costs of adding commercial reality portfolios were low. As Henry Flagler, president of the Florida East Coast Railroad often said, the object in managing ancillary lands was to make new freight customers out of farmers and small business owners, not to make a killing off land sales.[7]

But by 1912, a new breed of mail-order marketing men had overrun the old-blood railroad land barons. It is true that the Model Land Company, the real estate arm of the Florida East Coast Railroad, did publish a rather energetic magazine, *The Homeseeker*, but it still retained a reasonable semblance of the truth. More importantly, the MLC sold its lands through well established local realtors such as Frederick Morse and Pepper & Potter, both of Miami.[8] (The publicity magazine of the Southern Pacific Railroad, *Sunset*, was even more indirect. A high-class, heavily illustrated travel magazine along the lines of *Collier's*, *Harper's Monthly*, or *Look*, the magazine began publication in 1911 and continues, albeit under different ownership, to the present.[9]) The era of the land huckster began with the Oregon and Everglades mail-order sale operations of Richard J. Bolles in 1909, and reached its peak with the south Florida "Binder Boom" of the early 1920s. It died, very suddenly, with the hurricanes of 1926 and 1928.[10]

At one point in 1910, John Seip expressed concern to J.O. Wright that with all the virgin land in the Everglades that the State of Florida was trying to drain, there would be a surplus of reclaimed farm land on the national market and that Mattamuskeet farms would not sell.[11] Wright replied that he needn't worry, as the Everglades soils were too thin and too lacking in important nutrients to make viable agricultural land. At the time, the revelation of this letter was headline news because Wright was chief drainage engineer of the very entity that was trying to turn three million acres of this land into farms, but the point here is that a speculator in North Carolina was worried about developments in Florida affecting the supply and demand for his product, retail farm land. Similarly, Richard J. Bolles's assistant told former governor Broward that the Florida Fruit Lands Company had difficulty selling mail-order lots in their Everglades development until after their Oregon development, with 14,000 farm lots of ten acres each, sold out and the lottery to assign plots was held in the fall of 1909.[12]

By the first decade of the twentieth century, transportation and mass communications had made land a national commodity. This was land on a retail scale, 10 to 40 acres, and land intended for agricultural use, either for those who wanted to pursue agriculture as a full-time profession, or alternatively, as an avocation; an adjunct to a suburban blue collar job such as mechanic, construction worker, or sometimes even a white-collar office clerk. In North Carolina, Hugh MacRae, owner of the Tide Water Power and Transit Company in Wilmington, established five settler communities in the southeast portion of the state on cut-over lands for Germans, Poles, Italians and other immigrants. These were "farm villages" combining homes in town with relatively small farm plots (two to forty acres) for high-value, labor-intensive crops such as vegetables or tree crops. Farmers commuted a short distance from home out to their field, often renting an expensive implement, such as a mule and plow, from the town co-op along the way. All were successful to some degree, the most thriving, New Berne (Newberne) becoming a sizable industrial city that outgrew its farm village identity by World War I. The only part that never really caught on was the idea of living in town and commuting out to one's acreage.[13]

On the other hand, none of the farm villages of south Florida survived the sharp drop in commodity prices that accompanied the Great Depression. Most did not last as long as World War I. Thomas Will's Okeelanta, a privately financed farm village in Palm Beach County southeast of Lake Okeechobee, barely survived until 1922, when short-cycle climate change flooded it out almost continually for a decade. Okeechobee City, established by the Florida East Coast Railroad on the northernmost point of Lake Okeechobee in 1909, was sold to Buffalo steamship magnate William J. Conners in 1921. He intended for it to serve, New Berne fashion, as a farm village to support 30,000 acres of adjacent farmland he also bought from the railroad. A toll road he built to connect Okeechobee City and West Palm Beach ran between the shore of Lake Okeechobee and this farmland, known collectively as Connersville.[14]

But Taylor's Creek, which ran between Okeechobee City and Connersville, so often flooded that the project was abandoned by 1929 and the highway taken over by the state. Most of Connersville is now within the Dupuis Reserve State Park and the Corbett Wildlife Management Area. The only Everglades settlements to survive the depression and the hurricanes of the 1920s were corporate towns on the south rim of Lake Okeechobee dedicated to processing sugar cane and sugar cane byproducts such as bagasse for cellulose: Clewiston, Moore Haven, and Belle Glade. They sit behind a 35-foot tall earthen dike built and rebuilt by the Army Corps of Engineers almost continuously between 1930 and 1965, and that is once again being re-engineered.

Unlike North Carolina, the long-term determinant of land use in South Florida was suburban development, not rural or village-based agriculture. In 1978, the coastal wetlands of North Carolina measured 1.8 million acres. Of this, 567,000 acres were partially or completely drained, and a roughly equal amount was considered potentially drainable. Sixty-five percent of all lands were owned by timber or paper companies or other corporate farms. Protected and park lands amounted to only 23 percent. Urban areas were so insubstantial that they were aggregated within a general "other" category of 12 percent, most of which was made up of small private farms.[15]

The situation in South Florida was far different. Of the 3.2 million acres in the predrainage Everglades, 700,000 acres south and southeast of Lake Okeechobee became situated within an Everglades Agricultural Area (EAA) designated in the 1947–49 Central and Southern Flood Control Plan. Of this, 300,000 acres were used for sugar cane, 200,000 acres were used for vegetables or pastureland, and 200,000 acres were fallow or undisturbed. The latter category slowly increased after 1990 as the state and federal agencies bought land from sugar processors and returned them to wetlands to filter out phosphate runoffs.

Outside the EAA, 1.1 million acres were urbanized, and 1.4 million acres were parks, preserves, or government-owned water impoundment areas. Thus, active rural agricultural uses about 1990 accounted for about 16 percent of the predrainage Everglades (almost all of which are large corporate farms), while urban and suburban land uses more than doubled this at 35 percent.[16]

This suburban expansion came in two discreet bursts, the first during 1920–1926 and the second after World War II, with an extended period of almost complete inactivity between. Often, entire suburbs started but never developed during the mid–1920s boom became vast expanses of empty, abandoned, weed-strewn residential streets and sidewalks when developers walked away from subdivisions suddenly worth less than the taxes needed to keep them. Moreover, they stayed that way, frozen in time, for over 20 years. Then came a new generation of World War II veterans who had passed through one of the area's temporary military facilities and returned to seek homes and jobs in the sun, able to get readily available, low cost VA or FHA-insured mortgages.

By the 1960s affordable residential air-conditioning made south Florida an attractive year-round destination, and now many of the neighborhoods platted in the 1920s were actually built, but with ranch houses sprawling over two or three of the old 5,000 square-foot lots originally laid out for 1920s wintertime bungalows. Despite this, agricultural land in south Florida actually increased until the 1990s, but only because state law made such lands virtually exempt from county and local property taxes. The sight of a commercial lot on the corner of two busy arterial roads on the suburban fringe, empty save for a realtor's billboard and a few scraggly cows or a desultory palm tree farm, became a common sight. By 2010, most of these "tax ranches" were gone, swallowed up as the Miami-Ft. Lauderdale-West Palm Beach urbanized area, hemmed in between the Atlantic and a montage of Everglades parks, wilderness areas and water conservation basins, became, surprisingly, one of the densest urban areas in the nation.[17]

The vision of governors Jennings and Broward of turning the Everglades into a smallholder's paradise failed utterly. The land was too expensive to reclaim for agriculture, except for a heavily subsidized, politically strategic crop like sugar cane, farmed on an industrial scale. But urban growth made suburban yards of Bermuda grass the most valuable "crop" of all—except for, in the ultimate irony, water. The Everglades were not saved for their own benefit, but because they were needed to protect freshwater supplies for the South Florida metroplex. The synthetically created wetlands to the west of the urban development boundary drive fresh water down, into the shallow aquifer, providing pressure, or "head" that drives eastward, pushing back the underground westward migration of salt water from the shoreline. Without the urban boundaries and the conservation areas, the lower Atlantic seaboard cities would be afloat atop a layer of brackish saltwater.

On the other hand, the land that J.O. Wright surveyed so energetically before 1910 in North Carolina was essentially put to use in the form he envisioned. The biggest differences were that more of the agricultural land was turned to silvaculture then he predicted, and much more of the farmland was in the hands of corporate or large family-corporate farms. Although Lake Mattamuskeet itself was never successfully drained, almost all of the land surrounding it, except to the south, along the first colonial-era canal, was farmed. Similarly, the land surveyed by J.O. Wright for John Wilkinson's company, along the present Ablemarle Canal northeast of Belhaven, has been systematically crossed with feeder canals and is extensively farmed.[18]

But in the end, while the Albemarle-Pamlico Peninsula and the Everglades ushered in (sometimes rather rudely) a new era in American land consumerism, neither stayed in the historical vanguard. The Pocosin Wetlands became the domain of drained timber farms and corporate specialty crops; the Everglades ended up providing some reclaimed acreage for houses, and far more vitally, unreclaimed land in various states of alteration to quench the thirst of those neighborhoods.

III

Even in this age of digital information (and let me add that for the thorough researcher it is still a lot less digital than you might think) the historian is still dependent on the aid and comfort of others. Head of Special Collections Althea "Vicki" Silvera and associate Cesar Becerra at Florida International University did much to draw attention to my last Everglades book, *Roads Through the Everglades*, and Vicki gave me a good start on this project by finding several of the obscure Congressional hearing transcripts on the "Pinchot-Ballinger" and "Wiley-McCabe" affairs that preceded the Wright Report hearings, as well as the Florida Flood Control hearings of the 1920s and 1940s that came after. FIU was also the source of John T. Stewart's journal of the Drainage Investigation Division's 1907 expedition and survey.

As always, the librarians and archivists are the true stars of this project. Tab Lewis at NARA's Archives II facility in College Park was kind enough to fill out a pull slip and have it waiting in advance for the Solicitor's files from the 1912 Moss Committee hearings. Yailenis Diaz of the Public Records Office of the South Florida Water Management District was able to accurately locate both the hand-written and edited final minutes of the early years of the Everglades Drainage District. The reference staff of the New York Public Library's 42nd Street Branch located both their paper and electronic versions of Volume 2 (Parts 29 through 43) of the Moss Committee Hearing transcript. (Volume 1 of John Stewart's annotated copy of the transcript is available electronically through the main University of Florida catalog.) Michele Wilbanks, Terrence Phillips and Elizabeth Haven Hawley of the Department of Special and Area Studies of the University of Florida Libraries facilitated the downloading of the only known photographs of J.O. Wright, taken from a souvenir program for the opening of the New River Canal issued only a few weeks before he resigned (or was fired) over the growing scandal. Similarly, Scott Sanders of the Antioch College Archives was kind enough to facilitate the transmission of a high-resolution image of the only known photo of Charles G. Elliott. Vann Evans of the North Carolina State Archives assisted in the transfer of images from the H.H. Brimley and Hugh MacRae Trucking Development Company collections. Adam Watson likewise assisted with images from FloridaMemory, a part of the State Library and Archives of Florida. The staff of the Florida Collection of the Miami Public Library helped facilitate access to the microformed copies of several turn-of-the century Florida newspapers, including those in Miami, Ft. Lauderdale, Fort Myers, Tallahassee and Jacksonville.

As has been the case before, the Alvin Sherman (main) and Panza Maurer (law) libraries of Nova Southeastern University have been extraordinarily helpful in securing vital paper, electronic and interlibrary loan material. A special thanks goes to Nora, my involuntary officemate these last long weeks as we two "riskers" waited out the worst of the SARS-COVID pandemic. We have missed the virus so far and haven't driven each other crazy, and as an added perk we did make Electra the dog awfully happy.

1

Sort of a Plan of His Own

> There seems to have been in the minds of the Trustees, beginning with the first administration of Governor Bloxham [1881–85], when Legislative land grants were first recognized, the idea that the Fund belonged to the railroads ... the idea became so firmly affixed that one former trustee argued that drainage was being accomplished by the building of railroads, for it was necessary in constructing the roads, to dig ditches alongside the line of the road, and thus the original purpose of Congress would be complied with.
>
> —*Report of the Joint Commission to Investigate the Acts and Doings of the Trustees of the Florida Internal Improvement Fund*, 1909[1]

The Wright Report controversy originated with the 1905 attempt of Florida Governor Napoleon Bonaparte Broward to create a State Board of Drainage Commissioners and an Everglades Drainage District supported by an annual acreage tax. This effort, which was not fully implemented until 1913, after Broward's death, was itself tied up in the long and tortured history of Florida land politics.

Florida became a territory of the United States on July 10, 1821, two years after the signing of the Adams-Onís Treaty in which Spain ceded both East and West Florida to the United States. East Florida, garrisoned out of St. Augustine, and West Florida, based in Pensacola, had been colonies for 35 years, although neither were continuously occupied. Twenty-four years after gaining territorial status, on March 3, 1845, Florida became the 27th state of the United States. A slave state, Florida was paired with a free state, Iowa, for the purposes of admission.[2]

During the territorial period from 1821 to 1845, treaty obligations and Congressional mandates controlled the disposition of Florida's lands. Under the terms of the Adams-Onís Treaty, the United States agreed to honor valid Spanish land grants, and Congress created a board of commissioners that sat in Pensacola and St. Augustine to hear these claims. In particular, the Arredondo Grant claim of 300,000 acres in Alachua and the Forbes Purchase, a million acres along both banks of the Apalachicola River, took decades of legal action to resolve. In other cases, large grants were legitimized without controversy. Henry Sanford, for example, purchased a 20,000-acre land grant approved by the board on the south rim of Lake Monroe from its Spanish owners in 1870, founded the town of Sanford, and built the South Florida Railroad to Kissimmee.

In 1824, Congress passed the Donation Act, permitting settlers who occupied and improved lands within Florida between February 21, 1819, and July 17, 1821 (the day that territorial jurisdiction began), to acquire valid title to a maximum of 640 acres (one "section," or square mile) of eligible lands. Claims obtained through a Spanish or English land grant were exempted.[3] Land offices for the sale of surveyed public land were established in Tallahassee and St. Augustine in 1825 and 1826 respectively, and in Newmansville in 1842.[4]

The primary reason the Spanish Government had agreed to transfer Florida to the young republic was the cost in money and lives of the Seminole Wars, which flared in 1817–18 and 1835–42. In truth, these "wars" were the result of incursions by United States troops and irregulars into Spanish territory seeking to provoke and dislocate Seminole and Miccosukee peoples who had committed the twin offenses of occupying promising farmlands and sheltering escaped slaves.[5]

To encourage their further displacement and justify their forcible removal to the west (the Seminoles and Miccosukees were themselves relocation refugees, mostly Georgia and Alabama Creeks who had fled south to avoid forced removal), Congress passed the Armed Occupation Act in 1842. In exchange for establishing and defending a farm for five years, a homesteader would be given title to 160 acres of land. It had to be south of present-day Gainesville, not on lands reserved for native Americans, and not within a Spanish or English land grant, whether disputed or not.

About 1,200 permits were approved, granting title to 200,000 acres, mostly south of Gainesville and around Tampa Bay. However, 144 permits were filed in southeast Florida, extending from the Indian River valley near today's Vero Beach to the northern Keys. Sixty-six were disallowed (mostly for failure to settle) and 78 granted. Twenty-nine grants were located in Dade County (which then included today's Broward County). From the standpoint of the settlers, the most onerous requirements were that they had to personally appear before the federal General Land Office agent in St. Augustine, and each claim had to conform to section lines. The personal appearance requirement was relaxed at the insistence of Governor Yulee, changed to a system where the settler only had to appear in person before a local magistrate.[6]

The most problematic aspect of the law was that each quarter-section claim had to line up with established section and half-section lines. If a claim's boundary was not squarely north-south, or was shifted off its section lines, the land lying outside the quarter-section would be disallowed when the discrepancy was discovered. However, most of Dade and Palm Beach counties were not yet federally surveyed by the Geologic Survey. When government surveyor George McKay started laying out section lines in the area in 1845, the problem could usually be resolved by shifting property lines to match section lines, but sometimes this resulted in overlapping properties or, in one case, shifted a homesteader's gist mill outside his land.[7]

At the time of admission, Florida was granted 500,000 acres (781 sections) to promote internal improvements under an 1841 act approved by Congress for all newly admitted states.[8] Under legislation supplementing the act authorizing its statehood, Florida was also granted eight sections of land (5,120 acres) for a state capitol, which the territorial legislature had already decided should be at Tallahassee. More significantly, section sixteen, the center section of each township, was reserved for the support of the public schools of each county. This land could be used to locate facilities, or sold, rented, farmed or otherwise utilized for revenue. This totaled about 600,000 acres at the time of admittance.[9]

II

As early as 1845 the Florida Legislature appealed to the federal government for funds to survey the southern wetlands, already known as the Everglades.[10] In June 1847 U.S. Secretary of the Treasury R.J. Walker tasked Buckingham Smith with the job of visiting and preparing a report on Everglades drainage. He was not to perform a formal survey, but instead to gather as much existing information as available and verify it with his own eyes. This survey was undertaken in response to a proposal introduced by Florida Senator James D. Wescott, S.338, a bill "to authorize the draining of the Ever Glades, in the State of Florida," and to then transfer title in the drained lands, which were still in the possession of the federal government, to Florida.[11]

Smith was an unlikely choice. He was a lawyer, not an engineer. In 1839 he had been secretary to territorial governor Robert Reid, a member of the territorial legislature from 1841 to 1843, and speaker in 1843. Later, he joined the diplomatic service, was stationed in Spain and Mexico, and became an expert in antiquarian records related to the Spanish colonial administration of the new world in general, and Florida in particular. His primary qualifications appeared to be that he was honest, reliable, and already located in St. Augustine.[12]

Smith's 135-page report laid the groundwork upon which most subsequent engineering would be laid. It rested on three assumptions, all incorrect. One, draining the Everglades was a matter of lowering Lake Okeechobee: drop the surface level five feet, and everything south and east of the lake would dry out. Second, because the surface of the Lake was somewhere around 22 feet above sea level during the wet season, the lake could be lowered using gravity canals to the sea, without locks, dikes, or pumps. Hence, it would be cheap to build the necessary infrastructure. Third, because of the presence of all that water, it never froze in the Everglades, so any tropical agricultural crop was viable.

As would also be true with many later surveys and technical documents, those leaning on Smith's report to score rhetorical points felt free to claim that Smith said things he did not actually say. In this case, Senator Westcott and others said Smith calculated that a million acres of the Everglades could be drained for half a million dollars. In fact, Smith never asserted any such thing.[13] Smith did include as an appendix a letter from Lt. Colonel S.H. Long of the Topographical Engineers to Senator Wescott in which Colonel Long estimated that a million acres of the Everglades could ultimately be made usable for $300,000. The Secretary of the Treasury must have thought this was a bit optimistic, as in his letter transmitting Smith's report to the Senate, he bumped this figure up to $500,000. (Smith himself never actually stated *any* dollar figure.) Estimates of a million acres for a dollar an acre would become the Holy Grail driving Everglades reclamation efforts for the next 60 years.[14]

Two years later, Congress passed the Swamp and Overflowed Lands Act of 1850, a bill intended to patent (i.e., grant) all inundated, non-navigable waters in Arkansas to that state. It permitted the Arkansas legislature to either grant or sell lands patented to it, but in either case, the proceeds of such lands had to be applied exclusively to reclamation.[15] At the last minute a one-sentence paragraph was added conferring the same benefits to any other similarly situated state, and ultimately fifteen states took advantage of the legislation. Under this act 20,151,806 acres were eventually conveyed to Florida.[16]

The State of Florida, in turn, approved legislation in 1855 creating an Internal

Improvement Fund (IIF, or "the Fund") to take possession of, and manage, all patented lands. The Fund was supervised by a Board of Trustees comprised of the Governor as chair, and the attorney general, treasurer, comptroller and state register of public lands comprising the board. The Fund could hold, sell or grant homesteads of up to one acre to settlers, and sell larger blocks to enterprises (partnerships or corporations) contingent upon specified improvements being made to the land. The Fund started life with the 500,000 acres that the state had received at statehood in 1845, and any swampland patented under the 1850 federal legislation. Having already sold 142,793 acres through the State's Register of Lands, the first Board of Trustees reported a treasury balance of $116,319.[17]

The structure of the Fund contained two flaws: first, its enabling act did not require the trustees to invest its proceeds in reclamation efforts or other activities that would create salable lands, as required under the 1850 federal legislation. Proceeds could be invested in stocks, bonds, or almost any financial instrument. Second, the Fund did not have to sell land for cash—in exchange for making an improvement, it could offer an enterprise commensurate land grants. In fact, only two of the state act's 32 paragraphs addressed its ostensible function of taking title to overflowed lands, holding, improving and selling them to homesteaders, and utilizing the proceeds for further reclamation. The other 29 paragraphs concerned the issuance, management and retirement of railroad bonds and land grants to encourage new rail lines.

Railroads were given alternate sections of land ("checkerboards") extending six miles to either side of an approved grade, or 3,840 acres to the mile. The state legislation permitted the Fund to invest its financial reserves in railroad bonds by co-signing the bonds, in essence converting them from highly speculative commercial paper into government bonds backed by the State of Florida, which could be sold for a much higher price on financial markets, which was the same as selling them for a lower interest rate.[18]

The use of checkerboard land grants actually worked against the goal of reclamation, because it doubled the land area that any prospective private developer had to drain to create a salable asset. Projects that subdivided a holding into smaller areas, then used dikes and pumps to drain left half the land within the diked area in the hands of the Fund. From the perspective of the state, the whole reason the grantee received the land at little or no cost was to create drained land that the state could then sell at market rates, but private developers were loath to invest in reclamation projects that did not internalize the full benefits of their investment. Railroads, on the other hand, required no such sacrifice.

But the assets of the railroads, totaling about 400 miles of lines, were lost with the advent of the Civil War. As the war ended, David Levy Yulee, a former governor and director of the state's largest railroad, the Florida Railroad, devised an elaborate rescue plan for him and his fellow railroad owners, and with the imminent threat of a Republican reconstruction takeover, was able to pull it off. Between 1867 and 1869, the state seized the bankrupt lines (including Yulee's) for defaulting on their bonds and sold them. However, the sale was rigged and the former shareholders were able to reclaim them for a fraction of their worth. Moreover, the sale scrubbed them clean of their bonded indebtedness. As a result, the reorganized railroads emerged debt-free, but the Fund, as guarantor, was now saddled with the interest payments and accrued debt on the pre-war bonds.[19]

The Fund's largest creditor was a New York man named Francis Vose of the firm of Vose and Livingston, described colorfully in one legislative report as "a little, grasping, weazened-face fellow, with a heart no bigger than a mosquito's gizzard."[20] Before the war his firm had had taken $195,000 in bonds from several railroads to pay for steel rails, and by 1870 he claimed the debt, with accumulated interest, totaled around $656,000. The Fund extended a blanket offer to all bondholders to cash out for 20 cents on the dollar. Many smaller creditors accepted, but Vose refused and sued. The Vose suits, together with a freewheeling Republican carpetbagger administration, initiated a spate of ever wilder canal, drainage and construction project offers. For example, the Southern Inland Navigation & Improvement Company, a paper entity owned by former Lieutenant Governor William H. Gleason, was deeded 1,360,600 acres for a price of one dollar.[21]

A 1909 legislative investigation noted:

> The records show that from July 1, 1868, when Governor Harrison became president of the Board … to January, 1877, when Governor George F. Drew assumed the duties of the office, there seems to have been no fixed purpose during these [four] Republican administrations, except to loot the fund. the Auditor's report shows a balance of cash on hand December 10, 1868, of $139,200.20, and at the other end of this period, when the Fund was turned over to Governor Drew's administration, there was a balance of only $1,095.21 in the treasury.[22]

Vose finally stepped in, asking a Federal court in Pensacola for an injunction to prohibit wastage of the assets backing his bonds by blocking any transfer of land by the IIF except through a cash sale. This was granted in December 1871. The Fund's trustees partially ignored the order by continuing to accept bond coupons of the formerly bankrupt railroads as payment for land. (Turning in the coupons was the equivalent of canceling future interest payments owed by the Fund on that bond.) On May 16, 1872, Vose returned to the Pensacola court and asked the judge to put the Fund into receivership. The request was granted. The receiver ordered the return of lands granted for dubious projects, such as the 1.36 million acres granted Gleason's Southern Inland Navigation & Improvement Co.[23]

Vose subsequently offered to settle with the receiver for $560,000, then a couple of months later, lowered his offer to $400,000.[24] The trustees declined, explaining that they had less than $20,000 in the treasury and no offers for the land. They did have a sales agent in London, John Fry, but his job was frustrated when an attorney representing Vose, John Drew, arrived to spread the bad news of the receivership and its cash-sale requirement. (Drew may also have been working for William Gleason.) At one point Fry and Drew worked together to put together their own mega-deal. For $900,000, a group of European shadow investors (possibly Dutch) would purchase 3 million acres of land. Of this, $617,658 would go directly to Vose. The remainder, $282,342, would go to the Fund. The IIF would also return the 1.36 million acres clawed back from Gleason's Southern Inland Navigation Company, along with another million the receiver had ordered Gleason personally to return. Gleason and Southern Inland Navigation would construct a now somewhat better defined cross-state navigation canal and the European investors would drain the acreage. In short, the Fund would deed approximately 5.4 million acres for $900,000, slightly over sixteen and a half cents per acre. This was too far out for even the Fund trustees, who vetoed it in August 1877.[25]

The Internal Improvement Fund sat moribund. As one report explained: "the fund was being eaten up by compound interest, costs, receiver's allowances, and other expenses of litigation, and it was obvious that only by a sale of considerable quantity of lands at one time could it be saved."[26] But slowly, things were changing. The wild-eyed speculators. the Yulees, Gleasons, and Frys with their colored maps and frayed collars were giving way to a new wave of feet-on-the-ground businessmen: Henry Sanford, Henry Plant, Henry Flagler and others. Nine years after the Fund entered receivership Governor William Bloxham found his own four-square businessman in Hamilton Disston, whose father Henry had started the famous Philadelphia Keystone Saw and Tool Company, better known as the Disston Saw Works. Born in 1844, Hamilton took over the firm at 34 when his father died. He was an astute businessman and manager and Disston's thrived. But Hamilton wanted a project he could put his own imprint on.

Hamilton Disston, scion of the Keystone Saw Works in Philadelphia and the first large-scale Everglades developer. Had he lived a decade longer, the history of the Everglades could have been entirely different. This photograph was taken in 1889, seven years before his untimely death from a heart attack in 1896 at age 52. Photographer unknown [State Archives of Florida, No. RC02832].

The background of the deal is unknown. The most common story is that Disston was in Florida on a fishing trip, possibly as a guest of Henry Sanford, who owned 20,000 acres of land on the south shore of Lake Monroe in what is now suburban Orlando and a railroad between Sanford and Kissimmee.[27] Negotiations started around January 1881. What emerged was a gigantic plan. Disston and his associates proposed to drain all the wetlands in south Florida, everything south and east of today's Orlando except for the Atlantic shoreline, twelve million acres in all. For every two sections Disston drained, he would keep one and turn one over to the Fund, checkerboard-style.

The contract was executed on May 31, 1881, but the trustees soon learned that under the terms of the receivership, it was invalid. Vose himself was now dead, but with interest, his heirs were owed $900,000. Together with other creditors, the Vose heirs had filed a petition with the court to have it take control of all the Fund's holdings—around 14 million acres—for an immediate auction-block sale.[28]

Bloxham was running out of time. He traveled to Philadelphia to explain the problem to Disston, who agreed to an alternative scheme that was, if anything, even more audacious. As a down payment on the twelve-million-acre plan, Disston would outright purchase four million acres between Lake Okeechobee and Lake Kissimmee on the north, and Lake Okeechobee and Fort Myers on the west. He would drain this land by channeling the Kissimmee River from Lake Okeechobee north up to Lake Kissimmee; dredging the Caloosahatchee River, which ran from Fort Myers east to Lake Hicpochee, nine miles short of Lake Okeechobee; and digging a canal to connect Lake Hicpochee and Lake Okeechobee, thereby creating a navigable route from Fort Myers on the Gulf of Mexico to Lake Okeechobee, across the lake to the Kissimmee River, then north almost a hundred miles to Lake Kissimmee.

Disston's purchase was shaped like a backwards "L," starting at today's Orlando, running south to Lake Okeechobee, then west to the Gulf of Mexico at Fort Myers. Some questioned the price of 25 cents an acre, but the harping stopped when Bloxham delivered the check to the Vose court and lifted the receivership on July 8, 1881.[29] A year later, Disston sold half of his four million acres to Sir Edward Reed, of Kent, England for $500,000. The check went directly to the Fund, arriving just in time to make an installment payment due on Disston's original purchase, preventing a default. (Reed bailed out in 1887, selling his holding to two American investors.) Disston set up bases in Kissimmee and Fort Myers. In February 1883 he and a party of dignitaries were able to travel by steamboat from Fort Myers to Lake Okeechobee. Four months later a civil engineer retained by the Fund estimated that 535,285 acres had been drained.[30]

By the end of 1884, a giddy Internal Improvement Fund had deeded Disston 1,175,000 acres on the contingency portion of his drainage contract. Then things started to go sour. Governor Bloxham was succeeded by Edward Perry in January 1885, and unlike Bloxham, he could not take credit for saving the Internal Improvement Fund, but he was left paying the bill. Some of the squatters displaced by Disston's company were able to prove that they were legitimate homesteaders under the Armed Occupation Act of 1842. An investigatory committee assembled by the Governor in 1887 asserted that Disston had actually drained only 80,000 acres of wetlands—the rest was dry only because a lack of rain over the last two summers.[31]

Disston's superintendent, Rufus Rose, pointed to 40 miles of canal dug at a cost of $250,000 and claimed 2 million acres had been reclaimed. Disston and the state compromised. Disston's option lands eligibility would be cut from twelve to two million acres, provided he and Rose could prove to the state engineer that they were adequately reclaimed. None of the 1.175 million acres already deeded would be clawed back, but to receive anything above that and get to the maximum two million acres, Disston and Rose would have to do a better job of draining the land already received. The status of the purchased four million acres remained unchanged.

But the depression of 1893 crippled Disston's Okeechobee Land Company. By then, it had been deeded 1,652,000 acres of the available two million acres in option lands.[32] It had planted 2,000 acres of sugar cane, 1,000 acres of rice, and several hundred acres of vegetables. He had founded Tarpon Springs and Disston City (now Gulfport). He had dredged the St. Cloud canal to the north and the Ninemile canal from Lake Okeechobee to Lake Hicpochee to connect the Caloosahatchee River and the big lake. (The Caloosahatchee River did not originate from Lake Okeechobee, but at Lake Hicpochee, a few miles southwest. Lake Okeechobee fed Lake Hicpochee via surface flow and numerous shallow channels, which varied depending on the season.)

However, it's not known for sure how much land he was able to sell at retail. He mortgaged everything for $2 million and shut down most operations. There was a very real fear that the depression—the deepest economic downturn between 1871 and 1929—could ruin the Keystone Saw Works. He returned to Philadelphia to attend to the family business. On April 30, 1896—after the worst of the recession had passed—he died of an apparent heat attack in his bathtub. (A long-standing rumor that he shot himself has been disproven by careful scholarship by Joe Knetsch.[33]) His heirs unloaded what remained of

The Disston organization's sugar mill on the St. Cloud Canal, near Kissimmee, about 1887. Photographer unknown (State Archives of Florida, No. NO48558).

the Okeechobee Land Company for $70,000. Most of it became the United Land Company. The saw works survived.[34]

Having saved the Fund with the Disston sale, the state now appeared to go about systematically trying to destroy it again. A legislative investigation from 1909 noted that from the time William Bloxham took office in 1881, through three successor governors, and the return of Bloxham for a second term in 1897, the Fund's land holdings were almost depleted through railroad grants. The report marveled that "there seems to have been in the minds of the Trustees … the idea that the Fund belonged to the railroads."[35] The blame lay not with gubernatorial malfeasance, as was the case immediately after the Civil War, but with the legislature, specifically a legal instrument known as "legislative grants," direct awards of land for public or private works already accomplished or (more commonly) promised sometime in the future. These grants circumvented the orderly structure the state had created in the Internal Improvement Act of 1855.

Governor Drew had vetoed these direct legislative grants as early as 1855, but a provision in the Internal Improvement Act contained a loophole that allowed the legislature to circumvent a veto and make a grant anyway if it had set up a trust to funnel the lands through. Starting with the lifting of the Vose receivership, the legislature resurrected this pre-war mechanism. Knowing he had no means to fight beyond a veto, Bloxham elected not to antagonize the legislature and recommended against, but did not fight, the legislative grants.[36]

From 1879 to 1899, 92 such acts were approved by the legislature. Between 1881 and 1900 the Fund's trustees honored these grants by either issuing deeds or certificates.

Abandoned Disston harvesting mill, probably for sugar cane, left over from the 1890s, as it was found in 1907. Photographer unknown (State Archives of Florida, No. NO28667).

The abuse of legislative grants reached its peak after the end of Bloxham's first administration in 1881 and the start of his second in January 1897, when the legislature passed a series of railroad acts to augment the standard-formula award of 3,849 acres per linear mile of new construction with additional grants of 8,000 to 20,000 acres per mile. Unlike the formula grants, these were not within the twelve mile corridor—they could be anywhere.[37]

The railroads argued that in building their lines, they had to dig ditches to build up their grades, and these ditches were the means by which they drained the lands granted to them, so they met the reclamation requirement of the act. In fact, the ditches did nothing, and the railroads had every incentive not to drain their lands, because this would subject them to higher county property taxes. They were interested in either resource extraction (timber, turpentine, phosphate or shell mining); or selling land in large-block sales, not in homesteading.[38]

When the first Bloxham administration began, the Fund had 17,000,000 unencumbered acres. The Disston purchase immediately disposed of 4 million acres. The railroads received 8.3 million acres in standard-formula Fund grants. Canal and drainage companies received 2.7 million acres. Miscellaneous grants, including legislative grantees and the Disston bonus lands, totaled 9 to 12 million acres. According to Rufus Rose, former Disston drainage superintendent, now working for James Ingraham at the Model Land Company, at least some of these miscellaneous grants were out-and-out fraudulent.[39]

By 1889, the Fund under Governor Perry, knowing it had no lands to issue because they had not yet been patented to the state, handed out "certificates" to the railroads, entitling them to ill-defined land "whenever same shall have been patented to the State of Florida." These certificates could be read in two ways: the bearer was eligible to a certain amount of acreage *when* the land was patented; or the bearer was entitled to this acreage *if enough* land was patented.[40]

To make matters even more complex, the legislature had passed a number of acts that, intentionally or not, opened the lands patented in 1850 to homesteaders. Claims filed under the federal Armed Occupation Act of 1842 had seniority in time over land patented to the state under the 1850 Overflowed Lands Act, and the Fund's trustees were, more than once, required to return land or compensate settlers who had been evicted by the Disston operation and who subsequently established valid homestead deeds under the 1842 act. These evictions, usually undertaken after inadequate investigation by the Disston companies, were part of the reason the Disston plan became increasingly unpopular during the administration of Governor Perry.[41]

The state legislature enacted a new Pre-emption Act in 1881. It clarified a provision within the state constitution that guaranteed the concept of homesteader preemption, but did not specify a procedure or establish the amount of land a homesteader was entitled to. Under the 1881 act, a homesteader could lay claim to 160 acres if the land had been granted to a railroad or canal company, but the firm had defaulted on their deadline for installing infrastructure, reverting the land back to the state. (It was likely aimed at the Disston bonus lands.) The homesteader had to work the land for one year and send affidavits from two franchise-eligible citizens attesting to his efforts. The Internal Improvement Fund maintained circuit-riding inspectors to verify the legitimacy of these homesteads and establish a fair purchase price, usually two dollars per acre.[42]

The right to settle a homestead was given much more support by the Settlers' Act of 1883. It permitted a homesteader to work one acre or more of any unclaimed tract for one year, file an affidavit, and receive 80 acres of land for a price of 25 cents an acre. As originally written, it placed no limitations on the lands eligible for homesteading except proscribing the 500,000 acres originally conveyed at the time of statehood, so the lands conveyed in the 1850 federal Swamp and Overflowed Lands Act and subsequent overflowed lands patents were eligible. At the time, nobody worried much about the southern wetlands, but 30 years later it would prove to be an even bigger thorn in the side of the state than the Armed Occupation Act had been to the Disston operation.

After Governor William Jennings fought to have large open-ended commitments to railroads and canal companies scrubbed from the land patented to the state in 1903 through the creation of the Everglades Drainage District, he claimed that these railroad grants remained as residuum, and would spring back to life if the Everglades were not actually drained, a principle he called "reversion." Although the language of the court decisions and settlement agreements reached in the process of establishing the Everglades Drainage District strongly suggest that the land companies waived any future claims in exchange for specific, up-front deeds of 10 or 20 percent of their original claims, thus voiding any future encumbrances, the potential problem of conflicting deed filings of small homesteaders and the threat of reversionary claims of the railroads was always one that the trustees knew about, but didn't act on until it was too late. For example, it wasn't until 1912, after the trustees had actually been sued (and lost) to a frustrated potential homesteader that the Settlers' Act was amended to exclude the 1903 patent lands.[43]

III

In January 1901 William Jennings became governor. Up to this point he gave little indication that he would become one of the state's leading progressives. Born in Illinois, he earned his bachelor's degree at what is now Illinois State University and a law degree in 1885 at the Union College of Law, predecessor of the Northwestern University school of law. After graduating, he moved to Florida, opened a law office, and served as a county judge, then a state legislator for eight years before being elected governor, mostly on the strength of his family ties to cousin William Jennings Bryan, Progressive Party candidate for president. Once elected, he proved to be a tireless progressive, albeit one who was not shy about asking for compensation for his time and legal talents, which were very good.

Impressed by reclamation efforts he had seen on a trip to California, Jennings was determined to put the Internal Improvement District back on its feet. At the time, the federal government still owned almost three million acres of swamp and overflowed lands to Florida, but the railroads and their affiliated land companies claimed the state owed them eight million acres in legislative land grants.[44] Jennings and a research assistant spent five months going through the state archives and various offices, eventually coming up with about 1,000 pages of exhibits. Armed with this data, Jennings was ready to make his move.

First, he secured the federal patent, which had ostensibly been held up since 1897 over the details of native American tribal lands but was actually stalled to prevent the state legislature from immediately transferring title to the railroads. On March 21, 1903, the federal government patented 2,862,080 acres to the state, believed to be the last major federal holdings in Florida. Immediately prior to the transfer, the Fund's trustees formally adopted a policy of only selling lands for money. Soon after, it sold 103,000 acres of land in the panhandle to one Neil Wade for $223,000 in cash. The Fund followed this several months later with the sale of 100,000 inundated acres in Monroe County to Charles Scott for $30,000.[45] Both the railroads and their land-holding subsidiaries sued, claiming that their prior legislative grants and certificates should take precedence.

Jennings, together with the Fund's counsel, issued a legal opinion containing three main points: one, the trustees sitting during any one gubernatorial term had no power to bind future boards of trustees to any commitment or promise. (Because the state constitution then limited the governor to a single four-year term, the "term" of the Fund's board of trustees was also four years.) Thus, a fee simple absolute deed was the only instrument with a lifespan lasting beyond the term of any sitting board of trustees. Any certificate, option, contingent grant or other promise to convey land at some indeterminate future date, expired when the current gubernatorial term ended.

Second, the patent of land made by the federal government in March 1903 did not convey any retroactive property rights to the state. Therefore, no claim asserted against the Fund arising from a cause originating before that date could affect these lands. They were owned by the Fund free and clear and could not be encumbered by any act of the state prior to 1903. Finally, the Internal Improvement Fund was the only entity authorized by legislative act to take possession of land from the federal government. Because it never held title to any land, the legislature did not have the power to make land grants.[46]

The railroads and land companies sued, of course. In January 1905 Jennings stepped down at the start of the administration of Napoleon Broward, proud that "we trustees, from 1901 to 1905, did not deed a single acre of public lands to any railroad."[47] Governor

Broward appointed Jennings as counsel to the Internal Improvement Fund and vowed to carry on his policies. "I handled the litigation of 20 suits involving the entire fund," recalled Jennings. The Southern States Land and Timber Company and the Louisville and Nashville Railway had sought a court order blocking the sale or transfer of any lands by the Fund until the certificates and legislative grants were honored. They also demanded the proceeds from the Wade sale, asserting that the land sold to Wade lay within a larger area promised them through a legislative grant to their company. In May 1907, the federal court denied the order, and authorized the fund to sell land in blocks no greater than 100,000 acres. In December, the companies agreed to a settlement of $110,000 in cash and 374,831 acres of land (out of $265,000 and 1,477,000 acres claimed). The other so-called "railroad" claims were settled along similar lines.[48]

Jennings and Broward had scored a major victory, but it also saddled them with a tremendous burden: they had stood up to the railroads in the courts based partially on an argument that the land should be drained and sold to homesteaders. In fact, a month before he stepped down, Governor Jennings had testified to this in defending the Fund's refusal to honor certificates and the legislative grants in the Louisville and Nashville Railroad lawsuit. Less than a month after Broward took office in January 1905 Jennings wrote him that during the L&NRR trial he had been asked "if I, as a trustee, understood and acted upon the belief that that my first and chief duty in handling the swamp and overflowed lands was to have the lands drained and reclaimed, to which I answered in the affirmative." He was then asked if any money had actually been paid for reclamation. He answered no because "we found the fund in such a condition—so many claims by the railroads and other claims against the fund—that we had not been able to undertake the work of drainage."[49]

The need to free up the Fund to undertake the work for which it was intended—reclamation—became a factor the court took into account in making its decisions in the various certificate and legislative grant cases. The primary purpose of the Fund was to drain swamp and overflowed lands. A railroad executive admitted that they had no interest in draining these lands, and in some cases, actually believed it worked to their detriment by causing human settlement to occur on lands far from their existing rail lines. The Fund, on the other hand, wanted to begin reclamation, but could not because of the railroad policies of previous administrations. If Jennings, Broward, and the Fund trustees wanted to establish that Jennings's testimony was more than courtroom rhetoric, they needed a reclamation program.

The extent to which a failure to successfully drain the Everglades created a "reversionary right" by the railroad landowners has already been mentioned. The settlement agreements reached during 1907–10 usually included a waiver clause in which the railroads agreed to forego any claims that may accrue in the future, but the legal means the legislature used to circumvent the statutory control of the IIF trustees before the time of the second Bloxham administration was to funnel the land through trusts and just what any given trust agreement said, what conditions it set, and if Jennings's subsequent settlement agreement did, in fact, erase them, was very uncertain.

The means Broward sought to implement his broad-scale drainage program work was a new Everglades Drainage District, run by the same board of trustees as the Internal Improvement District. It was essentially an alter ego of the IIF, but where the Fund was financed through the sale of land, the Drainage District was to raise funds through a five-cent per acre annual tax levied on lands within its boundaries, roughly four million acres. Governor Broward initially hoped to create the district through an amendment to the state constitution. The legislature agreed to put it on the ballot, but the measure was soundly defeated at the May 1906 primary election.

The legislature had established an interim district through state statute on May 29, 1905, and Broward and Jennings were forced to rely on this for legal authority. It was immediately attacked by the railroads as unconstitutional, and in April 1907 a federal circuit court upheld the landowners, determining that the legislature could not delegate its taxing authority to the drainage district. One of the main points of contention had been that the drainage commissioners lacked the engineering expertise to determine which lands were capable of reclamation (and thus subject to taxation) and how they could drained. Broward and Jennings started to re-craft a new law.[50]

Rather than wait for engineering studies to be performed, Broward initially borrowed a set of 1896 plans left over from the Disston project. A report prepared by James Kreamer for the Disston companies suggested that a four-foot drop in the surface level of Lake Okeechobee would be sufficient to allow agricultural production to take place over most of the area east and south of the lake.[51] Kreamer recommended starting with a canal from Lake Okeechobee to the St. Lucie River, 24 miles northeast. His estimate was that this St. Lucie Canal could be done in 18 months and would cost $250,000.

In the fall of 1905, the Internal Improvement Fund had commissioned three of their own studies, one examining a canal directly east from the lake to the Atlantic Ocean, the second evaluating a canal running southeast to Lake Worth near Palm Beach, and the third, by engineer John Newman, mapping a 40-mile canal from the lake south-southeast to the New River at Ft. Lauderdale. As one visiting federal drainage expert observed: "He [Broward] has a sort of a plan of his own and is evidently the engineer as well as promoter and pusher of the whole drainage scheme … while the Governor is aided by the other members of the board, it is evident that he is carrying this matter forward in a very energetic, and possibly, arbitrary, manner."[52]

With no income flowing into the Everglades Drainage District due to the *Southern States Land and Timber Co. et, al.* lawsuit, Broward tapped into the $400,000 already in the Internal Improvement Fund's treasury and decided to start digging the first canal immediately. Politics as much as engineering decided the first job: the St. Lucie canal was the most promising from a technical standpoint, but Broward was not very popular in the Stuart-Fort Pierce area, so the Internal Improvement Fund's trustees decided to start with John Newman's route from the New River in Ft. Lauderdale, where Broward was wildly popular.[53]

Newman had been James Ingraham's engineer on his now-famous trek across the Everglades in April 1892 from Fort Myers to Miami. It was a grueling 22-day expedition. Had the weather turned worse, or if Newman hadn't recognized a hammock in the headwaters of the Miami River fourteen miles upriver from the mouth at time when morale and food were starting to run out, things easily could have turned out badly. Rufus Rose and Newman were the two most experienced drainage engineers in South Florida.[54]

Two dredges were ordered from Chicago, assembled over the winter of 1905–06 and on July 8, 1906, the *Everglades*, under the command of Newman, began cutting its way out of town along the north fork of the New River from what is today the Sailboat Bend neighborhood of Ft. Lauderdale. The *Okeechobee* followed along the south fork of the New River a few months later under the command of Hampton "Cap" Holloway, who, with his brother Scott, would make a lifelong career of dredging that would eventually take them as far as Pearl Harbor and Manila. The two dredges diverged as they progressed, the *Everglades* progressing northwest, the *Okeechobee*, after a short, two-mile swing southwest in the south fork to cut a boat channel, turned due west. As they moved west, they slowly diverged.

By assessing its tax on a flat per-acre basis (rather than on a per-value basis) Broward's second, 1907 Drainage District proposal was skewed in favor of smallholders. Nonresident landowners held 4,044,500 acres within the district; they were to pay $211,476 a year, or 5.2 cents per acre. Residents held only 185,020 acres, they would pay $9,250 per year, or 4.9 cents per acre.[55]

Meanwhile *Southern States Land and Timber Co. et. al. v N.B. Broward et. al.* ground on. Almost 1,000 pages of testimony and evidence were submitted. Broward and Jennings's modified law passed the legislature on May 29, 1907. More importantly, Jennings secured the voluntary agreement of the landowners by excluding certain lands that the railroads did not want to sell, but on the other hand did not want to develop, either. (For example, the Florida East Coast Railroad wanted to exclude 57,000 acres in Cape Sable that it intended to use as a fresh water supply for Key West.[56])

According to Jennings, an important reason the big landowners began to consider a settlement was that they realized it might actually be possible the drainage district could pull off the job of creating reclaimed land that could be sold at relatively high prices, and they did not want to be the ones responsible for killing off the effort. Out west of Ft. Lauderdale, engineer Newman was reporting that each linear mile of progress was draining 906 acres (1.4 sq. mi.) of land sufficiently to begin farming. Farmable land could be sold for 20 dollars, a mark-up of between 200 and 900 percent. A tentative settlement was reached in 1908, but final agreement was not reached until early 1910.[57]

What finally convinced the big railroad landowners was the advance release of an excerpt from a forthcoming report by the U.S. Department of Agriculture's Office of Drainage Investigations. The report, being prepared by James O. Wright, said many of the same things the Buckingham Smith report had in 1848. Draining the Everglades was dependent on lowering the surface level of Lake Okeechobee; this could be done with a series of seven surface canals; it would not be necessary to dike or pump; the whole thing could be done for less than two million dollars. After receiving the excerpt, Governor Gilchrist passed it on to the legislature, who reproduced it as a supplement to its daily *Journal* and endorsed its recommendations.[58] (This document later became widely known as the "Wright Report excerpt.") Between January and April 1910, the major landowners signed parts of the memorandum of understanding, paid their back taxes for 1907–09, and prepaid their taxes for the years 1910–12.[59]

Through the settlements with the L&N Railroad, Southern States Land Company, and the other major landowners, Broward and Jennings had managed to save about four million acres of land—provided that it could be drained. By the end of 1907, Newman could report that the two New River dredges had dug about four and a half miles of canal and drained about 12,000 acres, the maximum progress that could be made with the money available. The land sales weren't exactly rolling in. R.P. Davie bought 27,500 acres in the present Town of Davie for $2.00 an acre; his Davie Reality Company later bought 80,000 acres in what is now west Broward County for $100,000. The Tatum Brothers took 80,000 acres along the future route of the Miami Canal in the area of the present Dade/Broward line at $1.25 an acre. Then, in the waning days of his administration, Broward stuck his big deal.[60]

IV

Richard J. Bolles was born in 1843 in New York City, the son of a doctor. He was a natural-born (some say manic) salesman who purchased a seat on the New York Stock Market at 23. "Money will assuage almost every other grief," he once wrote in his unsparingly candid diary, "and the want of it, I really believe, is the only thing that, in my case, with my nature, gives me unbearable suffering."[61] He gave up stockbrokering to relocate to Colorado Springs and speculate in silver mines, mostly the Mollie Gibson. He made and lost several fortunes in quick succession, including one to a divorce. He cashed out the Mollie Gibson in 1901 for eight million dollars to start the Oregon Valley Land Company.[62]

The Oregon Valley Land Company was an unadulterated land scam, located in the parched foothills of eastern Oregon. Bolles bought about 1,000 square miles of unsurveyed, dry public land. He subdivided it, mostly sight unseen, into ten-acre farm tracts, with a handful of larger tracts of between 20 and 1,000 acres scattered about. He then sold each ten-acre "lot" on time payments for $200, with the promise of future irrigation ditches and roads. But he didn't actually sell defined parcels of land—he sold certificates conveying the right to participate in a giant "auction." But at the auction, only certificate holders could bid, and only parcels in the Bolles Tract were up for sale: 14,000 bidders, 14,000 plots.

In actuality, the "auction," held on September 9, 1909, was really a lottery; calling it an auction was a very small fig leaf intended to dodge state gambling laws. On the appointed day, your certificate number would be called, and a blue pellet would be drawn containing your allocated township, range, section, block and lot. You could be lucky and draw one of the big 1,000-, 320-. or 160-acre farms.[63] But probably not: the odds of drawing anything other than one of the standard ten-acre plots was about a thousand to one, and your chances for the big thousand-acre farm was 14,000 to one.

On the other hand, there was no guarantee that the ten-acre parcel you did draw had water, was flat enough to farm, or, for that matter, wasn't at the bottom of ravine. It didn't really matter, because you couldn't hope to find it. That's because Bolles hadn't laid survey monuments beyond one stake at the center of each section. That meant there was one stake for every 64 farmsteads. The plots were simply lines on a map. Nor did the participant get an actual deed: he or she received a trust certificate that contained a description of the lot, but actually conveyed only an undivided share in the entire 14,000 acre tract, with the right to claim the described parcel once it was surveyed to the satisfaction of the State of Oregon and local authorities. It does not appear that any of the land was ever surveyed down to the lot level or that any of the promised irrigation or road improvements were ever built.[64]

There are various stories about how Bolles and Broward connected. The most reliable starts with F.E. Bryant, one of the founders of the City of Lake Worth and a friend of both men. Bolles and Bryant were in New Mexico in the spring of 1908 scouting out land for another Oregon-type development. Spending the night at a sheep ranch, they met Harvey Duval, a democratic party fixer and occasional office holder from Jacksonville, who was recovering from either bronchitis or tuberculosis.[65] Duval told Bolles about the bountiful, cheap land in the Everglades, which Bryant was able to verify. When he returned home, Duval tipped off Broward about the meeting.

Broward and Jennings traveled to Denver later in the year for the 1908 Democratic National Convention along with Arthur Williams, head of land sales for the Southern

States Land and Timber Company. After the convention, Broward, Jennings and Williams went south to Colorado Springs where they met Bolles and R.P. Davie. Williams had primarily come west with Jennings and Broward to meet Davie, who had taken out an option on 109,000 acres of land along the south rim of Lake Okeechobee, which was the richest, best land in the Everglades.

While all the men were meeting at a hotel, a telegram arrived for Davie. He turned to Williams and told him that his people had closed on a much larger deal, and he would have to forfeit his option payment on the Lake Okeechobee land. Since Davie had already paid an option price of one dollar an acre, this would mean he would have to forfeit $109,000. Jennings and Broward took Williams aside and asked him if he would be willing to sell the land to Bolles for the unpaid balance of the sales price. Williams agreed, if Bolles paid cash. Jennings and Broward went to Bolles and asked him if he would buy the land for the unpaid balance remaining on the land, and pay $54,500 to Davie, thus reducing by half his forfeited deposit. As a commission, Jennings and Broward asked for half the land, that is, 27,000 acres each. The land was a high-risk investment; giving half of it away was worth much less than cash. Bolles agreed. Williams and Davie both thought it was an excellent plan.

Thus, Davie got half his down payment back, Bolles wrote a check for $54,500 less than Davie would have paid (although he did only get half as much land), Southern States sold their land for the original price, and Broward and Jennings each got 27,000 acres of land on the south rim of Lake Okeechobee. At this time, Broward was still governor, and Jennings was chief counsel for the Internal Improvement Fund. In 1909, Jennings told a state legislative committee that his law firm made $32,000 in income outside of his work as chief counsel to the Fund. Based on limited evidence in the William Jennings papers, as much as 10,000 of this was paid by Bolles's Florida Fruit Lands Company.[66]

A few days after the Colorado Springs sale, Bolles bought 500,000 acres of land from the Internal Improvement Fund for one million dollars. He got the land on five-year time payments, and of the $2.00 per acre he paid, the Fund agreed to forward $1.50 to the Everglades Drainage District to pay for reclamation. He then turned around and started selling it by mail for $240 per ten-acre lot using his by-now well-oiled Oregon system.[67]

Whether Bolles cheated the state depends on how you look at it. The land was sold in checkerboarded sections, lying south of the future route of the South New River Canal, ten miles west of where R.P. Davie was starting his experimental farm and town. (Today, this land is in west Broward County, south of I-75 [Alligator Alley] in uninhabited Water Conservation Area 3B.) When drained, the sections still in the hands of the Fund would sell for between 15 and 20 dollars an acre. The money Bolles paid would have mostly gone into reclamation costs anyway. It is true that Bolles stood to make a lot of money, but he was also taking the risk that the drainage project would not work and was, in essence, betting that the Everglades Drainage District engineers knew what they were doing. If the drainage plan did work, the Internal Improvement District would make a lot of money by selling land reclaimed with someone else's money.

On the other hand, what Broward and Jennings didn't realize (or more likely, were paid to overlook) was that by repeating his Oregon land-lottery system, Bolles was actually shifting the risk to those who answered the ads of his Kansas City–based land sales company. Buyers who made 24 payments of 10 dollars received a "clearance certificate" for one of the 12,000 "farms" and a town lot in the new city of "Progresso" near Ft. Lauderdale.

Unlike the Florida Fruit Lands farmsteads, Progresso was a real place. In November 1890, the Florida Coast Line Canal and Transportation Company sold 1,310 acres of land for $1.75 an acre on the Middle River west of Ft. Lauderdale to the Florida Fiber Company, a firm organized by Duncan Fletcher, Chairman of the Duval County School Board, and three others. The plan was to grow and harvest sisal plants for ropemaking. The sisal plants failed, but the Florida East Coast Railroad put their new Miami extension through one corner of the site. In exchange, the railroad's engineer platted a 1000-lot town site called "Progresso" for the Fiber Company. A few lots sold near the railroad station, but nothing spectacular happened.[68]

Fletcher, who by now had served terms as Jacksonville mayor and state representative, announced his candidacy for U.S. Senate in November 1907. A month later the incumbent, Stephen Mallory, suddenly died. Governor Broward appointed William James Bryan, a cousin of IIF counsel William Jennings. In March 1908, Bryan died of typhoid fever and Broward told friends in private he intended to run for the Senate the following month. He named a place-warmer, William Milton, to hold the seat.[69]

Fletcher decided to take on Broward. While the two traded accusations of railroad influence, the race was strangely quiet on the topic of the Everglades land companies. Broward won the first "all comers" primary but lost to Fletcher in the runoff by 3,000 votes. In early 1909, Richard Bolles took out an option on Progresso and the surrounding unplatted Florida Fiber Company land, and purchased it outright in February 1910 for 20 dollars an acre, a total of about $26,000.[70] By then, the company already had 2,878 customers making time payments and was predicting that the "auction" would take place around mid–1911, when all the certificates were sold off.[71]

The Bolles land sale was Broward's last act as governor. He was succeeded by Albert Gilchrist in January 1909. Gilchrist was a middle-of-the road Democrat who did not want to alienate the big land interests, but also wanted to move the Everglades Drainage District project forward.[72] As of January 1, 1909, the dredge *Okeechobee* had progressed 7.6 miles in 22 months at a cost of $52,700. The *Everglades* had gone 7.5 miles in 31 months at a cost of $61,800. Between July 1, 1909, and January 1, 1916, the Fund anticipated payments of slightly over one million dollars from the Bolles, Davie, Tatum Brothers and W.R. Comfort Company land sales. Of this, $500,000 was from the Bolles contract.

Of the 20.2 million acres of land patented to the state since 1850, 8.7 million acres had gone to the railroads, 2.8 million to the canal companies, 4.0 million to Disston, roughly 500,000 acres to other non-sale grantees, and 2.26 million acres had been conveyed through individual deeds, for a total of 18.673 million acres, leaving the fund with 1.531 million acres to convey, all of it in the Everglades.[73]

If Broward and Jennings's big bet on the two dredges slowly working their way west didn't pay off, the Fund's trustees would have no real chance of getting Davie, the Tatums, and especially Bolles to make their installment payments, no real chance of getting the big railroad landowners to continue making their five-cent-a-year property taxes to the drainage district, and no real chance of ever turning any of those last one and a half million acres of patented land into money. Broward's carefully built house of cards would all come crashing down.

2

This Country Is Not Good for Anything

> You asked what I thought of the country. With the exception of a few miles around Goodno's ranch at Thompson [near Fort Myers] and a few spots along the Caloosahatchee River, the country is not any good for anything but scrub palmetto or pine. Nothing will grow in sand and that is all there is. Most of the country is used for cattle range and the grass is so poor that three year olds won't bring as much as a two month's old Kansas calf.... If ever thoroughly drained so that it was dry, it would burn like so much tinder for thousands of square miles.[1]
>
> —Letter from Lawrence Brett, Fort Myers, to J.O. Wright, March 3, 1907

The federal government long had an established policy of assisting states in the reclamation of land and the creation of navigable waters through the Army Corps of Engineers, the Interior Department and the Treasury Department. The General Survey Act of 1824 authorized the army engineers to survey roads and improve navigation on major rivers. The U.S. Geological Survey of the Interior Department, created in 1879, surveyed and mapped public lands and interior waterways. The oldest of all was the Survey of the Coast, created as a bureau within the Treasury Department. In 1878 it adopted its present name, the Coast and Geodetic Survey. Its functions were much like those of the Geological Survey, but for shorelands and tributaries adjoining navigable waters.[2]

After the Civil War, states and localities sought to augment dry-land farming with irrigation networks, but lacked the expertise in agricultural engineering necessary to plan such systems, so the Congressional Appropriation Act of June 16, 1880, gave the Department of Agriculture a grant to collect irrigation data, and an Office of Irrigation Inquiry was established to collect this data and study artesian wells. This office was deleted from the annual budget and ceased operations in 1895.[3]

In 1887, Congress passed the Hatch Act providing for a $15,000 grant to each state to create agricultural research stations. To administer the program the act allocated $10,000 to create an Office of Experiment Stations within the Department of Agriculture. The department did very little research of its own until James Wilson was appointed secretary in 1897 by William McKinley. Wilson did not come into office intending to make research a priority, but found it necessary if he was to secure larger appropriations from Congress, which was one of his paramount concerns.[4]

Between 1897 and 1912, Wilson established seven new scientific bureaus, four in 1901 alone: Plant Industry, Forestry, Soils, and Chemistry. The Office of Experiment Stations was also expanded to include its own in-house research functions. The Nutrition Investigations division was established in 1894 and the Irrigation Investigations division in 1898. It was soon apparent that in many cases, irrigation issues were inextricably tied to the proper drainage of excess water from natural sources and artificial irrigation. This was especially true in the old Midwest, mid–Atlantic and south, where the terrain was flatter and the land marshier than in the high plains and far west. Thus, in 1902 a Drainage Investigations Division was added to give the Office of Experiment Stations the ability to prepare plans and provide expert advice about large drainage projects, and to assist in the preparation of area and sub-regional plans. Henceforth, the division was called the Irrigation and Drainage Investigations Division. These were split into a separate Irrigation Investigations Division and a Drainage Investigations Division in 1907. In 1915 both were combined again into one unit called the Rural Engineering Investigations Division.[5]

James Wilson, Secretary of Agriculture, 1897–1913. Wilson was not only the longest serving Agriculture Secretary, he has been the longest serving cabinet secretary in the history of the country, sixteen years, a record that will probably never be broken. A progressive when he took office in the McKinley administration, he had become an anachronism by 1912, focused mainly on the department's new headquarters building, which he hoped would be named after him. It was not completed until 1930. Photograph by Harris & Ewing, 1911 (Library of Congress No. LOT 6798 [item] [P&P]).

Much of the success of the irrigation and drainage divisions can be attributed to their first director, Elwood Mead. Mead was a true polymath, talented as an engineer, administrator, and teacher. Born in 1858 in Patriot, Indiana, the son of a farmer, he received a bachelor's degree in agriculture and science from Purdue in 1882. He joined the faculty of Colorado State College, where he taught several subjects, for two years. He resigned, moved east, and earned a degree in civil engineering from Iowa State College and a master's from Purdue. In 1885 he returned to Fort Collins and was jointly appointed professor of irrigation engineering and assistant state engineer.[6]

He moved to Cheyenne to become Wyoming's Territorial Engineer in 1887, where he stayed for ten years, changing title to State Engineer when Wyoming entered the Union in 1890. In 1897 his wife Florence died, leaving him with three small children. With no family to help raise them, he decided to return east at the same time that Agriculture Secretary Wilson was looking for someone to take over the then-new Irrigation Investigations Division of the Office of Experiment Stations.

However, the job Mead really wanted was director of the Hydrographic Division of the Geologic Survey in the Interior Department, a small unit dedicated mostly to developing stream gages and investigating better ways to measure flowing water. It was headed by Frederick Haynes Newell, an engineer with little experience, but many close

Dr. Elwood Mead, 1923. From 1899 to 1907, Mead was the director of the Irrigation and Drainage Investigations Division of the Department of Agriculture. For much of this time, he was also a visiting professor at the University of California at Berkeley. In 1907 he left the United States to accept a position with the State of New South Wales in Australia. Photograph by National Photo Co. (Library of Congress No. LC-DIG-npcc-10136).

contacts, including John Wesley Powell, Gilbert Pinchot, and future president Theodore Roosevelt. Hired in 1888 to undertake a large-scale irrigation survey of the west, Newell stayed with the Geological Survey even after Congress cut the project's funding in 1900 and transferred what little remained of the survey money to the Department of Agriculture. Mead wanted Newell's modest position for two reasons. First, everyone knew that President Roosevelt was working with Nevada Representative Francis Newlands to craft an act that would provide federal aid for irrigation projects within thirteen western states. This was passed four years later as the Newlands Reclamation Act, also called the Reclamation Act of 1902.[7]

Mead's job at the Agriculture Department was nothing to turn your nose up; after the drainage division was added to the irrigation division in 1902, Mead had over $100,000 a year in research funds at his disposal, but that was the problem: it was all *research* money. Mead wanted to undertake the type of irrigation engineering and construction he had already accomplished in Colorado and Wyoming but on a larger, regional scale.

Second, he loathed Fred Newell and was sure Newell would make a botch of it if the Geological Survey was named the lead agency for the 1902 Reclamation Act. Newell's only practical experience was in stream gauging. Mead and Newell had butted heads as far back as Mead's days with the State of Wyoming. Mead, along with Representative Newlands, believed that reclamation projects should be state based—indeed, they had to be, because the federal government could not, in their opinion, own interstate water flows. Newell and the president believed that the federal courts would back their assertion that interstate river water was federal property. (They were wrong.)[8]

Moreover, most of the western men believed that Newell not only was incompetent, but that he had an inherent bias against the west. But between his exigent family needs and Newell's contacts in high places, Mead's options were limited, and he accepted Secretary Wilson's offer in July 1898. (He did, however, retain his Wyoming position as a consultant for the better part of a year to hedge his bet.)[9]

But after three years of growing influence at the Office of Experiment Stations, Mead's star began to fade in the new century. In 1901, he attempted to expand his office into a "Bureau of Rural Engineering," with both research and implementation functions, including draining eastern and southeastern wetlands. He was turned down by Secretary

Wilson and his immediate supervisor, A.C. True. "I was given to understand that the program for the indefinite future would be restricted to an investigation of irrigation laws and such physical investigations as the Experimental Stations could undertake," rued Mead in a letter to a colleague after meeting with Wilson in 1901. Instead the Drainage Investigations Division was created.[10]

Mead believed that the reclamation functions of the Newlands Act should be placed in the Agriculture Department, but he ended up having little say in the final formulation of the Newlands Act. In May 1901, he was involved in a streetcar accident that required the removal of his right arm and forced him to relearn to write. In addition, he was struggling with an unhappy second marriage that soon resulted in the social stigma of a divorce. Representative Newlands himself was taken out of the picture for the last months of deliberation when his wife died, and he had to return to Nevada. Newell, Pinchot and Roosevelt prevailed; the Reclamation Act of 1902 assigned the job of western irrigation to the Geological Survey, soon renamed the U.S. Reclamation Service; Newell had emerged from the fray victorious.[11]

In 1904 Senator Henry Hansborough of North Dakota attempted to create a separate office of engineering within the Department of the Interior, making its chief effectively an assistant secretary over the Reclamation Service. It was intended as a gift for Mead and as a way to separate and organize what would today be called the geo-engineering functions of the Department from its land management activities; its was lobbied to death by Interior Secretary James R. Garfield.[12]

In 1899 Mead had undertaken an irrigation survey financed through funds raised by the California Water and Forest Association, with in-kind assistance

Frederick Hayes Newell, Director of the Bureau of Reclamation, Department of the Interior, about 1923. Newell and Elwood Mead were bitter rivals, and the decision to place the Bureau of Reclamation under Newell within the Department of Interior in 1902–03 rather than under Mead in the Department of Agriculture ultimately led to Mead's departure for Australia in 1907. Photograph by Harris and Ewing (Library of Congress No. LC-H261-3344 [P&P]).

A.C. True, about 1914. When Elwood Mead left for Australia in 1907, True, the Director of Experiment Stations, was given direct supervision of the irrigation and drainage sections. A man accustomed to accommodating the hundreds of state experiment stations, colleges and extension services funded under the Hatch Act, he permitted the Irrigation and Drainage Investigations Division to drift along virtually unmanaged until someone finally realized the money that could be made from insider trading on the lands being surveyed and investigated. Photograph by National Photo Co. (Library of Congress No. LC-F82-4907 [P&P]).

provided by Stanford and the University of California. Impressed by his work, University of California President Wheeler offered Mead a professorship in 1900. Mead agreed to accept a half-time appointment and by 1902 was regularly shuttling back-and-forth between Washington and Berkeley. In 1906, a newly remarried Mead was planning to move his family full-time to Berkeley, but the April San Francisco earthquake damaged the University of California campus and depleted the state's budget. Mead's full-time professorship had to be deferred. In mid–1907, despairing the loss of his California professorship and skeptical of the support that he could continue to expect from Secretary Wilson, he accepted an offer from the State of New South Wales in Australia to become its chief engineer. Although he returned to the United States for two visits, he remained in Australia until relocating to California in 1915.[13]

Throughout much of 1906 and 1907, the staff of Mead's division was called on to fill in for their increasingly absent chief, and the division lacked the managerial guidance it vitally needed. The Office of Experiment Stations had been allocated $10,000 for irrigation investigations in 1897 without any specific organizational structure to manage it. By 1904 the Irrigation Investigations Division was spending $74,200 a year and the budget when Mead left in 1907 for the two units together was $150,000. Upon his leaving, the division was ostensibly split into a separate irrigation division and a drainage division. However, this "reorganization" was a fiction, existing only within the internal bookkeeping of the Office of Experiment Stations. The Secretary's office continued to report a single line item for a Division of Irrigation and Drainage Investigations to the Treasury Department and Congress.[14] In reality, the Office of Experiment Stations had, upon Mead's leaving, eliminated his managerial role and split it between two subordinates, Charles Elliott (drainage) and Samuel Fortier (irrigation), without relieving them of any of their existing technical responsibilities. Fortier was recalled from his field position at the extension service office at the University of California, and Elliott didn't even get a raise to go with his promotion.[15]

A. C. True remained as Chief of the Office of Experiment Stations, but there was now no single administrator overseeing the extensive field work of the two divisions, nor was True's past experience of much relevance to the work that had been done by Mead's division. True primarily worked with states to advance cooperatively funded programs, such as extension services, state cooperative programs and agricultural programs in land-grant colleges and universities funded under the Hatch Act of 1881.

Prior to 1906, USDA pass-through funding for state extension services was only $15,000 per state per year. Many state officials and congressmen thought that the entire department should primarily be a distributor of funds to the states, with only incidental functions carried on in Washington. This friction was alleviated somewhat by the Adams Act of 1906, which doubled the per-state apportionment, but it never entirely went away. "The job of the Office of Experiment Stations must have been a most uncomfortable one at times," notes an agriculture department historian. "A. C. True, was, however, remarkably successful, in part due to his ability to assuage the suspicions of station leaders and to convince them that his ultimate loyalties lay not with the Department of Agriculture, but with the state stations."[16]

Clearly, this was a valuable skill for someone tasked with the distribution of pass-through funds to states and localities. However, it was not very helpful from the standpoint of a subordinate responsible for undertaking independent field research, and who sometimes had to be the bearer of bad news to state or local officials. Elliott and Fortier needed a strong superior like Mead committed to the independence and scientific objectivity of his bureau. After Mead left, the Office of Experiment Stations became a hodgepodge of functions, some of them mutually contradictory. True was on the side of the states (or at least sympathized with their woes); but the in-house investigation divisions had to constantly be on their guard to avoid being dragged into intramural state-level fights or unwittingly duped into advocating someone's commercial interest. True's testimony in the 1912 Moss hearings showed that he did not understand much about how his office operated outside of the experiment stations, nor what the policies and procedures of the Department of Agriculture were regarding directly funded field operations.[17]

Finally, although Mead was an excellent engineer and an outstanding administrator, he had one fault: a propensity to invest his own money in projects his agencies were involved with, and to make personal business decisions based on inside information collected through the work of his office. He invested in Wyoming irrigation projects while state engineer; at one time he owned 1,000 acres on Elkhorn Creek. After taking over the Irrigation and Drainage Investigations Division he subscribed to $5,000 in stock in a California land holding company. His personal belief was that he, as an investor, was taking an equal risk to that of any other investor, and was entitled to a fair profit. On the other hand, a conflict that created a loss or increased risk of loss to a settler or smallholder was patently unacceptable.[18] While Mead's somewhat loose definition of what constituted a conflict of interest was a reflection of his times, it was not a universal standard. Arthur Morgan, an engineer in the Irrigation and Drainage Investigations Division, recalled that Charles Elliott "was punctiliously honest, so much so that he carried two lead pencils, one for office and one for personal use."[19]

II

Charles G. Elliott was born in Lowell, Illinois, in 1850. He received a B.S. from the University of Illinois in 1877 and a graduate degree in civil engineering in 1893. He worked in Illinois, Iowa, Indiana and Wisconsin and managed the sewer systems in Indianapolis, Indiana (1884) and Peoria, Illinois (1887–89). He was employed by Illinois State College from 1890 to 1901 in the extension service, preparing both state and U.S. Department of Agriculture bulletins. He edited the *Drainage Journal*, based in Indianapolis, in 1901–02 before starting work at the Department of Agriculture as agent and expert in July 1902. In May 1905 he was promoted to Drainage Engineer and made Chief Drainage Engineer in June 1907. The following October, upon Mead's leaving, he was promoted to Chief of Drainage Investigations. He wrote two books: *Practical Farm Drainage* in 1882 (revised 1908) and *Engineering for Land Drainage* in 1903 (revised 1911 and 1919).[20]

The idea for federal technical assistance to the State of Florida resulted from a meeting between Elliott and Napoleon Broward in Tallahassee on January 3, 1905, when Elliott was apparently in town for Broward's inauguration as governor.[21] Elliott had been to the Everglades once before, in August 1904. Professor Rolfs, Director of Plant Pathology at the Agriculture Department's Bureau of Plant Industry in Miami, asked for help in selecting a parcel of land that could be drained at a reasonable cost to establish an experimental farm. Elliott inspected land from Boynton, 40 miles north of Miami, to Cutler, fifteen miles south of Miami, and between two and ten miles inland.

After meeting with Elliott, the new governor and his predecessor, William Jennings, now counsel to the trustees of the Internal Improvement Fund, made their own reconnaissance of the Everglades. It was mostly a trip through the former Disston holdings, and Rufus Rose, Disston's former chief engineer, went along. Starting from Fort Myers on February 1, the party went up the Caloosahatchee River to Lake Okeechobee, across the lake, down a dead-end canal that Rose had dredged from South Bay decades before to see what kind of shape it was in, then backtracked to the lake and headed for the north shore and the Kissimmee River, the object of so much of Rose's time and Disston's money. Although so weed-choked they had to pole much of the way, they were able to work their way up to Kissimmee, with Rose taking soundings every few hundred feet to see how badly the canal had silted in.

On the return trip, they barely squeezed their way back out west from Lake Okeechobee to Lake Hicpochee, the first link of the Caloosahatchee River to Fort Myers, which they reached on February 10. (Until it was widened and deepened years later, tourists and surveyors alike learned the hard way that, for reasons never fully explained, it was easier to ground a boat in Lake Hicpochee [or Ninemile] canal going downstream—towards Fort Myers—than upstream, to Lake Okeechobee. There are stories of captains getting stranded in Lake Okeechobee, for weeks, sometimes months, at a time.)[22]

Florida Governor Napoleon Broward (1857–1910; served 1905–09). Although often portrayed as the architect of Florida's Everglades drainage program, he was largely continuing the work of his predecessor, William S. Jennings (served 1901–05), a highly skilled lawyer who developed a strategy for invalidating land grants handed out, sometimes corruptly, almost always rashly, by the legislature during the period 1870–1890. Photograph by The Budget Company (Library of Congress No. LC-US262-117335).

After returning to Washington, Elliott prepared a brief synopsis for the *1904–05 Annual Report* of the Agriculture Department. It noted that none of the Everglades proper had been drained, although the Florida East Coast Railroad had, at great cost, successfully drained areas east of Lake Okeechobee by opening and widening already existing streambeds. The soils, being marl-based, generally required copious amounts of fertilizer, especially for citrus. The reliability of marl in dikes and levees was unknown. (Marl, unlike its chemical cousin, limestone, is "hydrophilic," that is, it returns to its plastic, clay-like state every time it is wetted.) Therefore, he recommended proceeding with small, experimental farms similar to those tried by the Bureau of Plant Industry, enclosed with marl dikes and ditched to lower the water level within the enclosure. "The success of this method of drainage will depend on whether a good dike can be made of the marl soil and whether the head of water back of the dike may not force water through the underlying porous tracts into the inclosed [sic] area."[23]

During the inaugural visit, Elliott was impressed by Napoleon Broward's can-do approach, but cautioned Mead about his "possibly arbitrary manner." Elliott believed that

Rear left: William Jennings, Florida Governor 1901–05. Rear right: Napoleon Broward, Florida Governor, 1905–1909. When Broward succeeded Jennings as governor in 1905, he appointed Jennings as counsel to the Trustees of the Internal Improvement Fund, allowing him to continue the reforms he had initiated in 1902 to block legislative land grants, mostly to railroad and canal companies. Photographer unknown, c. 1909 (State Archives of Florida, No. RC02832).

"we should be pleased to become identified with the matter and would render such assistance as far as we were able," but any help "would be dependent largely upon the appropriations the coming Congress would make."[24] That last sentence is key; it was probably the reason that Mead and Elliott approached Broward in the first place. An Everglades investigation would be a huge project, requiring a special Congressional appropriation, estimated later by Elliott at $150,000. Mead's turf was under threat from Newell and the Bureau of Reclamation, and from Wilson's apathy. But the Bureau of Reclamation didn't have jurisdiction over wetlands drainage, especially in the east. A $150,000, multi-year drainage investigation project would go a long way towards guaranteeing that the Irrigation and Drainage Investigations Division didn't get broken up, transferred, or both.

Elliott was honest enough to warn Broward "many of the popular press accounts of the achievement of drainage are overdrawn than is justified by the facts at hand … the drainage of any large area is a stupendous undertaking which should be considered most carefully from the beginning." The closest comparison Elliott could draw was the draining of the Sacramento River at San Francisco Bay near Richmond, which began in 1881 and was still underway. Ultimately, the project, centered on Sherman Island, required dikes and pumps with a capacity of 51,000 gallons per minute. "Seepage through the levees and soil is very considerable … these lands described have not been reclaimed without repeated destruction of banks and most discouraging losses to the owners of lands and promoters of work." Later accusations that Elliott talked Broward into a bill of goods when he offered to assist the state in a drainage investigation fail in the face of this March 24 letter, containing a nationwide litany of cost overruns, unrealized expectations and outright failures. Large-scale drainage projects were not a game for the faint of heart—or those with a tight purse.[25]

Throughout 1905 and early 1906, Elliott and Broward communicated back-and-forth, most often regarding the details of drainage district laws in other states. At one point, Broward admitted to Elliott that if the railroads continued to hold out in their lawsuits over the per-acre taxation of the Everglades Drainage District, he would proceed anyway under eminent domain and pay damages later, but still hoped he could get a constitutional amendment on the upcoming ballot to create a statewide drainage district.[26]

In January 1906, Broward took up Elliott on his offer to perform a drainage investigation of the Everglades area, writing Agriculture Secretary Wilson that he wished to have Elliott's division perform a survey to locate canals and levies. "I understand from Mr. Elliott that the appropriation made by Congress with which you make experiments and investigations is very limited," he wrote, "I will ask each of our Congressmen to write you or call on you."[27]

There lay the problem. Senator Taliafero, from Jacksonville was wholly indebted to the Florida East Coast Railroad for his 1905 campaign expenses.[28] The FEC was particularly opposed to any large-scale drainage program because of the holdings of its Okeechobee Land Company on the east side of the lake. It was one of the most fertile areas of the Everglades, and the railroad had already partially drained it, and hoped to sell plots to homestead near its model town, Okeechobee City, on the northernmost point of the lake. While there is no evidence that the other Senator, Stephen Mallory, or any of Florida's three representatives were equally compromised, the wishes of the railroad landowners could not be ignored.[29]

As Elliott had pointed out in January, Broward appreciated that a survey of the magnitude Elliott was describing could not be fitted within the normal annual operating budget of the Irrigation and Drainage Investigations Division. It would require a special congressional appropriation. Broward wrote to Florida Representative Stephen Sparkman, asking him to meet with Secretary Wilson to explore the possibility of a special appropriation for the project. Wilson dissembled, believing that the survey could be managed within the general annual appropriation for the division if spread out over the next two or three years.[30] In response, Elwood Mead wrote Representative Sparkman that he and Charles Elliott believed that given "the area to be reclaimed, 4,000 square miles, and the agricultural value of the land when reclaimed would seem to make its reclamation a matter of national interest … in order for us to render such assistance, however, it is necessary that we should reach some agreement with the State." In fact, Elliott estimated that the project would cost over twice the drainage division's entire annual budget of $70,000.[31]

Nevertheless, Mead and Elliott wrote a letter to Broward over the signature of Secretary Wilson in May, pledging Wilson to confer with members of Congress who may be interested in securing appropriations for an Everglades survey. They added that "I [Wilson] shall also be glad to detail the engineers of this department engaged in drainage investigations for a conference with yours from time to time for the purpose of determining the best plan and most practical methods." In May 1906 Congressman Sparkman followed this up with a meeting with Wilson to discuss an Everglades survey appropriation.[32]

In June 1906 Senator Steven Mallory introduced a joint resolution apportioning $10,000 for an Everglades survey, but it was objected to by New Jersey Senator John Kean (where extensive federal drainage investigation efforts were ongoing in the Hackensack Meadowlands) and the bill languished and died. No special appropriation for an Everglades survey was approved for many years.[33]

Secretary Wilson was under pressure from Governor Broward and the Florida Congressional delegation to get the survey started, so he decided to proceed using the general budget appropriations available to him. Elwood Mead set aside $11,000 over three years for the Everglades project. According to J.O. Wright, who at this time was holding a temporary commission as drainage expert under Elliott, Mead approached Elliott in July 1906 about undertaking the Everglades work. Elliott tried to dissuade him from starting the project, arguing that this budget was vastly inadequate for a project of this scope. Mead then turned to Wright, one of Elliott's full-time drainage engineers, and asked him if he wanted the job. Wright said yes but cautioned that the work should not start until winter.[34]

Elliott disputed this, and the record appears to bear him out. On July 11, 1906, Elliott wrote Wright in Oswego, Kansas, where Wright was working on a project surveying the Neosho River, updating him on the status of the Everglades proposal. "Governor Broward of Florida has called today and in company with Mr. Allen [acting Chief of Experiment Stations] we have talked over the Florida situation. It is now practically understood that we will take investigations substantially as you and I outlined them in our conversation before you left."[35] It appears that Wright was assigned the Florida investigation by Elliott, not Mead, and the reference to Allen indicates that Wright's selection was not made on the spur of the moment, but after deliberation between Allen, Elliott and probably Mead.

Wright had traveled to Kansas about July 7, and from there, he went straight to North and South Carolina, and then to Florida on November 17. Allen sat in on the meeting because Mead left for Berkeley sometime in May. No such meeting of the type Wright describes could have occurred. According to Elliott, Wright was given the project because he was available, because Governor Broward suggested him, and because most of his recent field work had been in the South.[36]

III

Wright was born in Jamestown, North Carolina, in what is now the Greensboro metro area, in 1850 (the same year as Elliott) and moved with his family about 1868 to Indiana. In 1879 he married Katherine E. "Kate" Espy, and after the death of one infant the couple had a son, George, in 1884. He started teaching in the district [elementary] schools of Indianapolis and was appointed principal of the 11th District School in 1877. Starting with the fall semester of 1878 he transferred to Indianapolis High School to teach math. He ran into trouble in February 1881 when he was fined by Esquire [i.e., magistrate] Woodward of the Marion County Court for assaulting one of his students, Charles B. Fawkner, in what appears to have been a case of inappropriate corporal punishment. By 1884 he had left the Indianapolis School District and was principal of the combined school at the small town of Centerville, Indiana.[37]

About this time he left teaching to work for a local drainage district near Lafayette, Indiana. In the *Proceedings of the Indiana Society of Civil Engineers and Surveyors for 1888*, he is listed as a drainage engineer based in Lafayette.[38] He worked as a dredging contractor in and around Lafayette and Indianapolis through the 1880s and early 1890s. Kate died in 1898 and two years later he married Katarine Vinnedge in Indianapolis. At the time, he was 50, she was 30. They had a daughter, Helen, about 1902. Between 1894 and 1902 he was general manager for the Western Dredging and Improvement Company, a contractor on the massive Chicago River Sanitary Canal project that reversed the flow of the Chicago River away from Lake Michigan.[39]

He caught the attention of the Chicago project's chief engineer, Isham Randolph, for a novel mobile long-reach conveyor he had developed for delivering spoil to the top of large banks.[40] He then moved to New Orleans and became a consulting engineer. He was recruited by Elwood Mead in 1905, who needed a local part-time field engineer in Louisiana for the drainage division. In May 1906 he moved to Washington and began working full-time. A year later, in May 1907, he passed the civil service examination, moved to Washington and was promoted to supervising engineer at the drainage division.[41]

Arthur Morgan, an engineer at the Drainage Investigations Division who would go on to head the Tennessee Valley Authority, had a low opinion of Wright's abilities:

> "Shortly after Mr. Wright was taken into the service it was found that he was a very good public speaker and for the greater part of the time that he was in the service he was employed as a public speaker, explaining the general benefits of drainage to the people in the parts of the country where drainage was not practiced. That was Mr. Wright's calling, to a large extent. For that reason Mr. Elliott had not had the opportunity to discover that Mr. Wright was completely incompetent as an engineer ... the subjects that he discussed were largely accounts of the benefits which drainage had brought to countries where drainage had been done, and that did not require the ability of an engineer."[42]

On the other hand, Morgan's admitted brilliance, lack of patience with those who could not keep up with him, and bad habit of dismissing those who disagreed with him as inept or dishonest, proved his undoing more than once, including his time at the TVA. Morgan was a generation younger than Wright and Elliott, born in 1878 in Cincinnati but raised in Minnesota. His father was a surveyor and engineer. Sickly as a child with meningitis, he worked in construction and other odd jobs in Colorado for three years and attended the University of Colorado for a time but returned to Minnesota after a semester or two.[43]

He went to work for the family surveying firm about 1898, teaching himself hydraulic engineering because it was a new field not dominated by one of the engineering societies. His first wife, Urania, an osteopathic physician, died shortly after giving birth to their first child, so he accepted a job with the Department of Agriculture in Washington in 1907, the same year he was accepted to the A.S.C.E. He continued working on a contract basis after he started his own firm, Morgan Engineering, in late 1910. In 1933 he was appointed to the chair of the TVA board, where he clashed with the even more intelligent and imperious (but politically astute) David Lilienthal, who also sat on the TVA board. He lost his battle with Lilienthal, was fired by Franklin Roosevelt, and retired to the presidency of Antioch College.[44]

Unlike Morgan, many congressmen and local elected officials found Wright invaluable. In 1907 he gave 37 lectures, most on congressional educational tours, in addition to performing drainage surveys in Kansas, New Jersey, North and South Carolina, and Florida.[45] Governor Broward requested him by name to help in Florida. Wright worked intensively with both elected officials and civil servants in North Carolina between 1907 and 1910 to create drainage districts in the Albemarle-Pamlico Peninsula, including authoring a model drainage district act modeled after ones in Illinois and Louisiana. It impressed State Geologist Joseph Hyde Pratt so much that he published a paper on it in the *Journal of the Elisha Mitchell Scientific Society*. The state's congressman, John Small, said, "no man has contributed so much to initiate this movement as Mr. J.O. Wright," and "we all owe him a debt of gratitude." But Morgan's assessment of Wright's technical abilities was also backed up by A.D. Morehouse, Elliott's assistant. "I had been impressed that he was a very ready talker," Morehouse later recalled, "but I had never been particularly impressed as to whether his talk could be backed up with real engineering knowledge."[46]

Morgan and Morehouse's weakness was that they were technocrats who saw everything through the lens of pure engineering talent. They—especially Morgan—could dismiss someone as a mere "public speaker," a mid-level officeholder of modest skills, while failing to appreciate how a man who was happy to shoulder the unpleasant and unpopular job of assisting elected officials with the "constituent service" job of circuit riding on a lecture tour, or of attending a state drainage convention, or sketching the layout of a simple drainage plan, could turn such drudgery into a path to access or influence; a way to gain a friendly ear or protective hand in the fierce political world of Washington. A pure technocrat may decry someone willing to pitch in and help with the basic spadework of the political process as a "public speaker," but an engineer who hid behind his drafting table and slide rule never built up any credits in the all-important favor bank, either.[47]

IV

Wright received his formal written assignment from A.C. True on November 17 and left for Florida the same day, returning to Washington on December 1. He went alone, first to Tallahassee to meet with Broward, who assigned him a couple of clerks for two days to undertake a records search through the state files. He gave an interview to a local reporter and whether he meant to or not, gave him the impression that the entire annual budget of the Irrigation and Drainage Investigation Division, $152,500, had been allocated to the Everglades survey.[48]

Just before Wright left to go south, Florida held its 1906 mid-term primary elections. Broward had hoped to circumvent the Everglades Drainage District lawsuits by creating a statewide drainage board through a constitutional amendment. He campaigned for it harder than most of the candidates stumped for their individual offices, but the amendment was defeated soundly, losing by 5,000 votes in 27 of 60 counties, including all the urban counties but Dade (which, until 1915, included today's Broward County).

To make things worse, Frank Clark, the federal prosecutor who had investigated and tried Broward in 1897 for running guns to Cuban revolutionaries in his tug *Three Friends*, was elected congressman.[49] Elliott, already concerned about trying to fit an Everglades survey into his division's normal working budget, grew even more skeptical: "I regret that the drainage amendment was not adopted in the late election," he wrote Wright. "I think it indicates quite clearly that the opposition to such work is quite strong. This feature of the case I think we should not forget in our cooperation with the State authorities."[50]

After leaving Tallahassee, Wright caught a steamer down the west coast to Fort Myers, on the mouth of the Caloosahatchee River, then traveled upriver to Lake Hicpochee, partially by steamer, partially by motor skiff. He backtracked to Fort Myers, then caught a steamer around Cape Sable to Ft. Lauderdale, where Broward met him and they traveled to the dredge *Everglade*s on the North New River, which was being captained by Gus Burr, a colleague of Wright's from the Chicago Sanitary Canal project. At this point the *Everglades* had been at work for about three months and its twin, the *Okeechobee*, was still being assembled at Sailboat Bend by the Featherstone Foundry and Machine Company of Chicago, with trials set to start just after New Year's.[51] After Thanksgiving dinner with Burr and his men, they proceeded west a few miles on a shallow-draft Glades boat. Backtracking to Ft. Lauderdale and a visit to the drydocked *Okeechobee*, he traveled south to Miami and was taken up the Miami River to the Miami Falls, about four miles upriver, returning in early December.[52]

Wright did not actually accompany the survey party on this winter's expedition, returning for a congressional speaking tour through Arkansas and Louisiana that lasted from mid–January through mid–February, when he traveled to Kansas to finish his Neosho Valley work.[53] A week after Wright returned, Lawrence Brett and John T. Stewart, both drainage engineers, arrived in Fort Myers.

There may have been some friction between Brett and Stewart before the expedition started, but there is little evidence one way or the other. John Stewart was born in Loda, Illinois, in 1868. He received his degree from the University of Illinois in 1893. He worked as a surveyor and civil engineer in and around Illinois from 1893 to 1897. He was hired as a field assistant at the U.S. Geological Survey in 1899 and went to work at the Department of Agriculture in 1904; he was probably recruited by Elwood Mead. Soon after participating in the Everglades survey he left to take a teaching post at the University of Minnesota, taking leave in 1909 to get a graduate degree in civil engineering at the University of Illinois. He returned to St. Paul as professor and head of the agricultural engineering department, a position he held until his death in 1928.[54]

Lawrence Brett was almost a generation younger. Born in Larned, Kansas, the son of a real estate salesman, Brett earned his bachelor's degree in civil and mining engineering at the University of Kansas in 1906 under Professor Frank Marvin, one of the pioneering engineering educators. His first job was with the Drainage and Irrigation Investigations Division, as local per-diem help on the multi-year Neosho Valley flood and drainage survey in southeast Kansas. It was there that he first met J.O. Wright, the project manager. In 1907 he transferred to Department of Agriculture headquarters in Washington, where he boarded with Wright and his family.[55]

Stewart and Wright, on the other hand, disliked each other intensely, if not before the expedition, then certainly by the time it finished. Elliott did not help matters by keeping the men he had selected for the trip in the dark until the absolute last minute, even after Wright had arrived in Florida. "I have made no arrangements for detailing men for the Florida field party," Elliott wrote Wright in Fort Myers. "I have not officially mentioned the Florida work to Mr. Stewart, thinking that under the circumstances it would be better to wait." This was two weeks before the job started.[56]

Brett, with assistants E.W. Chadwick, Paul Funderhide and H.A. Kipp, ran a line of levels from Fort Myers along the Caloosahatchee River to Lake Okeechobee, then south to a place called Brown's Store or Brown's Landing, about 30 miles south of the lake. Traditionally, Brown's Landing demarcated the place where the pineland trail known as Captain's Ker's Road ended and the Everglades started. From here, Brett's party crossed the Everglades to Pompano.[57]

Stewart, with the other party, hired a local guide named I.F. Singletary and performed a survey roughly following Captain Ker's Road southeast from Fort Myers, past Immokalee, more or less straight to Brown's Landing. Stewart recorded daily temperatures and rainfall, took samples, and interviewed long-time locals, especially farmers and cattlemen, which he recorded in great detail in a journal that has been published at least once in the twentieth century.[58]

Wright later savaged the work of Stewart. He claimed that while Brett and his men were slogging across the Everglades, Stewart was "going through the woods to Brown's Store, killing deer and turkey, fishing, and generally having a good time." Worse, Wright claimed that when Stewart arrived at Brown's store several days after Brett's party, he simply returned to Washington, insinuating that he avoided the hard work of running a chainline across the Everglades. "Stewart never got into the Everglades and he doesn't know anything about them," Wright later said.[59]

However, there is a paper trail, and it doesn't do a good job of supporting Wright's statements. According to Elliott, Stewart directed the entire expedition, with Brett and Chadwick as his assistants. In the journal he kept through the expedition, Stewart confirmed that two lines of levels were run, one by Brett along the Caloosahatchee from Fort Myers to Lake Okeechobee to Brown's Store, then through the Everglades to Pompano, and the other by him and Singletary across the dry pinelands to Brown's Store. Stewart ran his survey in interrupted segments, between which he shuttled men and supplies to Brown's Landing, then out to pre-arranged meeting points to support Brett's work.[60] In his report on the expedition to A.C. True, Elliott stated: "Mr. Stewart's journal contains much information relating to the Everglades which he collected from residents and those familiar with conditions in south Florida," although he acknowledged that the work of Brett's Everglades party was quite arduous.[61]

Brett, who wrote Wright several times during the expedition, did not express any criticism of Stewart, although he agreed that the survey work in the Everglades was very difficult. Stewart did miss one re-supply mission, forcing Brett to backtrack nine miles to Brown's Store and return to the survey crew. This may have been part the source of Wright's anger, although Brett himself attributed it to mere bad luck and the difficulty of arranging logistics in such harsh, featureless conditions.[62]

The claim that Stewart left Florida long before Brett and his crew is pure fabrication. Brett's party started from Brown's Store across the Everglades on March 3. Wright wrote Stewart (who was already on the Atlantic coast, sending in supply runs) on March 16 that when the party arrived, they were to start back west again running another line of levels. It was apparent that Wright was fixated on getting survey lines laid down to the exclusion of everything else. Stewart replied in no uncertain terms that he wasn't going to start out into the Everglades in April, and he wasn't sending anyone else out, either.[63]

The work ended on April 6. Brett and Chadwick had to be in Washington on April 17 to take a civil service examination. They left for Washington about April 9. Stewart traveled back across the state to Fort Myers for another week or ten days to settle accounts and arrange for the storage of the party's gear at Fort Myers and Brown's Store, leaving for Washington about April 19. The total expended on field work was $3,637.66. Later, as a professor at the University of Minnesota, Stewart told a reporter for a Minneapolis newspaper that "personally, he would not invest in land in the Everglades." Asked to answer J.O. Wright's attacks on his and Elliott's professional qualifications, he deferred to Arthur Morgan at the Morgan Engineering Company, who had recently written letters to *Engineering News* on the subject.[64]

On August 20, between this and the following winter's expeditions, Governor Broward and Wright met in Washington. Wright proposed that the survey focus on the area from Brown's Store to the Atlantic coast, and from the south shore of Lake Okeechobee as far south as he could go, hopefully Ft. Lauderdale. Brett had suggested that high water would be the best time to do this, so Wright recommended that Broward provide the party with a shallow-draft boat that they could work from. Broward agreed that the Internal Improvement Fund would provide a boat and crew.[65]

By now there was increasing friction between Elliott and Wright. Elwood Mead had left for Australia, and Elliott was directly supervising Wright and the other engineering staff. Elliott wanted to send Stewart down again; Wright wanted Brett. On November 8, about a month before the party left Washington for Florida, Wright met Major Dapray, Governor Broward's factotum in Washington. Dapray told Broward that Wright complained that he and his men should already be in Florida, but were being held back by Elliott, who was traveling through Louisiana, Mississippi, and Arkansas inspecting a drainage proposal being advanced by the Missouri Pacific Railroad.

Wright supposedly heard that the three states were seeking a $50,000 congressional appropriation to undertake a survey. He was afraid it would be approved, and he would be assigned to the project. Wright asked Dapray to pass on to Governor Broward his request that Broward try to persuade Agriculture Secretary Wilson to keep the Everglades survey alive, and more importantly, put Wright in sole command of the project. "It is better to leave in charge of the Federal part of the work in the Everglades a man who is in sympathy with the state plans, and is willing to work and cooperate with the Governor and his chosen agents" is the message Dapray was asked to pass along. Moreover, Dapray suggested that Wright be sent to Florida to lecture, ostensibly on soil conservation and crop production, then use his talks to promote drainage. "Congressman Hobson recently tried this plan in Alabama, and Congressman Small in N.C."[66]

Broward did write Secretary Wilson, but it was to congratulate him on the work Wright and Elliott had already done, and inform him that he would be in town in a couple weeks when the National Drainage Conference met in Baltimore on November 25–27. It appears that the reason Wright and his men were not sent to Florida until December and January was because of the conference, where both Elliott and Wright were to read papers. Broward was anxious to confer with Secretary Wilson, Elliott and Wright before the next season's work commenced, and the conference was an ideal chance to meet.[67]

Dapray had a habit of providing Broward with accounts that were somewhat voluble.

In Wright's later account of their meeting, he told Broward only that he and Dapray "had a very pleasant visit and he told me a great deal about your work." In addition, Wright already had commitments for part of the period Dapray thought he should have been in Florida. He was in Wilmington and Raleigh, North Carolina, between December 9 and 12 surveying the Angola Bay Swamp.[68]

Lawrence Brett arrived in West Palm Beach about December 11, 1907, along with Fugate and Kerin. Brett spent a month examining a possible route for a ship canal from

Left to right: Governor Albert Gilchrist (1909–13); Florida State Drainage Engineer J. O. Wright and former Hamilton Disston engineer and then-current State Chemist Rufus Rose, April 1912. From the brochure *Souvenir: Official Opening of the Gulf to Atlantic Waterway of the Everglades Drainage Canal, April 23–27, 1912* (Box 21, William Sherman Jennings Papers, P.K. Yonge Library of Florida History, Special and Area Studies Collections, George A. Smathers Libraries, University of Florida, Gainesville).

Lake Okeechobee to the Atlantic Ocean via the St. Lucie River. Wright arrived on January 26, 1908, and he and Broward were able to charter a shallow-draft cabin cruiser in Fort Lauderdale. Brett's men ran two lines of levels from the Florida East Coast Railroad track along the Atlantic coast west across the Everglades at Jupiter, on the north border of Palm Beach County, and at Hillsboro, on what is now the Broward-Palm Beach line. While Brett's crew was doing this, Wright, in the cabin cruiser, went north to Stuart, where the St. Lucie River enters the Atlantic and followed it upriver about half-way to Lake Okeechobee. They doubled back to the Atlantic and went north to Sebastian Inlet, then backtracked to Ft. Lauderdale and up the New River to John Newman's dredge on the South New River Canal. Again doubling back to the Atlantic, they ended at Miami, a total of about 17 or 18 days. During this time, Wright was accompanied by his wife.[69]

When Brett and his men finished their work, Wright had Brett take the boat around to Fort Myers while the Wrights went by train to Miami and Key West, then by packet steamer to Fort Myers. At Fort Myers, Wright and Brett used the cabin cruiser to travel up the Caloosahatchee River to Lake Okeechobee, a difficult voyage, as it was mid-winter, and the river was low. On April 8, they completed their survey of the lake, but by this time, the water level had dropped so much that the boat's owner and captain, Clyve Merchant, was not able to get it back down the river to Fort Myers. Wright and Merchant struck a deal: Wright would buy him a drum of gas, and the State would pay him half a day's charter rate ($5.00) until he could get back to Fort Lauderdale. He was stranded until September, blowing the state's $100 budget. A couple of the trustees groused that it would have been better to just buy Merchant's boat outright.[70]

On February 28, while the Wrights were in Miami on their way to Key West, Wright gave a speech at the invitation of the Miami Board of Trade. What he said is a matter of dispute. According to Wright, he merely reiterated what Governor Broward had said during his campaign: that Lake Okeechobee topped out at 22 feet during the wet season, so it was simple logic that it could be drained through gravity canals to the sea. But newspaper accounts of the talk make it sound like a sales pitch for the Everglades. "There are no engineering difficulties to overcome," Wright was quoted as saying, "it is a simple proposition and only requires the digging of sufficient ditches and canals." The land was exceeding fertile, and if drained, would not desiccate, but instead would "become more compact and within a year or two produce a variety of crops." He thought the Glades land would easily out-produce Louisiana in rice and sugar cane production.[71]

Joseph Parrott, vice-president of the Florida East Coast Railroad, sent a letter to Senator Taliaferro complaining about Wright's speech, and Taliaferro, in turn, sent a letter to Secretary Wright asking him to have his men lay low until the survey was finished. "Those who are opposed to drainage because of the incident increase in taxation and for other reasons, not unnaturally resent Mr. Wright's public expressions on the subject, and look upon them as a trespass beyond his designated duty."[72]

Notice that ambiguous phrase "and for other reasons." Wilson hadn't managed to survive as a cabinet secretary for fifteen years under three presidents by playing the fool, and he responded by informing Taliaferro that "if now you tell me that this matter is in politics and that it is not desirable that our people should further interfere with Florida drainage problems, it would be a very easy matter for us to withdraw our force from the state."[73]

A little crass perhaps, but a time-tested approach. It got the desired reaction from Taliafero:

> Pardon me please, but you appear to have entirely missed the purpose of my letter. I do not wish, of course, the Government's investigations into our drainage problems discontinued. It was not of these that my correspondents complained, but only of the public discussions of the question by your agent in advance of the completion of his work, of his report to you, and of such action and comment as you should deem proper.[74]

Wilson frequently claimed that the Department had a policy of never issuing interim reports or data, but the Department of Agriculture had so many policies and procedures, many of them trivial, self-contradictory or nonsensical that nobody really knew what the department stood for. You could travel to North Carolina with a congressman to extol the virtues of draining the Green Swamp or the Great Dismal Swamp and be hailed as a hero, but if you did the same for the Everglades, you were releasing unauthorized advance information. Small wonder that Wright initially shrugged it off. Back in May, Governor Broward had asked Wright for a copy of the maps and field notes from the first season's expedition. The Secretary's office approved the request in two days with a cover letter that didn't even bother getting Wilson's real signature; it used a rubber-stamped facsimile.[75]

However, while Wilson did respond to Taliafero's complaint with a modest bit of political gamesmanship, he also took it quite seriously within his own dominion. He wrote A.C. True that "Senator Taliaferro thinks that Mr. Wright's public utterances are unwise, and I am inclined to agree with him." He ordered True to get a report from Wright and to tell Wright not to make public appearances. Wright filed his report on March 30, and Elliott assured him, "I have no doubt that your letter will explain the situation to the satisfaction of the Secretary." By then, Wright was already in Fort Myers, relating to the office how, with Florida's high railroad freight rates and the spot market prices for fruits and vegetables set in far-off New York, he saw a farmer getting paid 46 cents for three crates of grapefruit. Elliott suggested that it might be a good time to wrap things up, and on April 12, Wright started home for Washington. Total expenses for this expedition had run $4,712, not counting the cabin cruiser the state had leased from Mr. Merchant.[76]

3

Simply Fundamental Hydraulics

Mr. McCabe: Didn't you discuss the arrangement of the report and the subject matter with Mr. Beal [the departmental editor] from March to April 1909?
Mr. Elliott: No sir, the report had not been presented to me yet.
Mr. McCabe: How do you explain the date on the manuscript, February 1909?
Mr. Elliott: I explain this way: Mr. Wright simply dated his report back to the date when the special extract was prepared.
Mr. McCabe: Then the committee is to understand that Maj. Wright is mistaken in his testimony before the committee where he testified that he completed his report in February, that the excerpt for Mr. Hall was taken bodily from that report, the introduction written, and sent out.
Mr. Elliott: He was incorrect in his testimony. I will not venture to guess why.[1]

—"Testimony of Charles Elliott," Moss Committee, Day 17 (March 17, 1912)

Upon Wright's return, Elliott directed him to begin work on the report and left for a field trip to Europe until September. When he returned, Elliott found the report in essentially the same condition it was when he left, and he recalled being "disappointed that no more progress had been made." He asked Wright why he had not worked on it, Wright replied that he had been in North Carolina most of the time, "and besides, the administration had changed in Florida, and he did not think there would be much call for a report."[2] This was partially true. Napoleon Broward would be term-limited out of office on January 2, 1909, and by mid–1908 Albert Gilchrist had already won the two-stage Democratic primary, guaranteeing that he would be Broward's successor. However, there was no reason to believe that Gilchrist was any less enthusiastic about the Everglades survey than his predecessor, and he wasn't.

But it was also true that Wright had been called away to North Carolina. On August 17, Congressman John Small of North Carolina wrote to Secretary Wilson, asking that he dispatch Wright to Hyde County to perform a drainage survey of Lake Mattamuskeet. A year earlier, in August and October 1907, Wright had traveled with Congressman Small on two lecture circuits across the state. Wright had been enthusiastic about the potential for agriculture development in the Albemarle-Pamlico lowlands if they were properly drained, and Small had been impressed by Wright's interest and knowledge. For the first two weeks of August 1908 he had again accompanied Small on a lecture tour, and Small's August 17 letter was, in essence, a request that the Department of Agriculture waive its limit on the amount of time that one investigator or engineer could spend in a congressional district. Elliott may have been disappointed at the progress Wright had made on the Everglades report, but Representative Small's request was approved, and immediately after Elliott's return, Wright left to spend another month, from September 9 to October 2, in North Carolina. In late September, North Carolina Representative Albert Douglas wrote Secretary Wilson and asked Wright to make a survey of a drainage district proposed by the Carolina Land and Lumber Company near Moyock. Assistant Secretary Hays authorized surveys at both Lake Mattamuskeet and Moyock and Wright spent part of November and December at both, although most of the actual field work was undertaken by S.H. McCrory at Mattamuskeet and H.M. Lynde at Moyock.[3]

Wright later stated that he completed the manuscript of the Everglades report on February 25, 1909. However, Elliott disputed this, and according to multiple sources in the drainage investigations division and departmental timesheets, Wright did not turn in the first draft of his report until late May 1909, and nothing resembling a completed version of the report exists in the files before then.[4]

Wright and Elliott do agree that in February 1909 a lawyer named Henry C. Hall, from Colorado Springs, came to the drainage division office and asked to read a copy of the report. From this point on their accounts differ. Wright said he was allowed to read the draft report, but his request for a copy was denied, as it was the policy of the Department not to publish or release copies of draft documents. A couple of days later Hall returned with another lawyer, John Rankin, and some kind of instructions from the Secretary directing Elliott to let Hall have a copy of its technical section on drainage, covering the proposed canals and their configurations. (Wilson later claimed he never wrote any such letter. Elliott said his instructions were verbal, from True. True said he didn't recall giving Elliott any such instructions, verbally or in writing. Hall equivocated when asked about it. No letter was found in the files.[5])

Wright then extracted one section from the report and had a stenographer type a copy of the section and had the graphics shop prepare a hand-drawn copy of the map. Rankin was in a great hurry, telephoning almost every day until the typescript was ready.[6]

But according to Elliott, there was no report for Hall to read. It hadn't been written yet. He did, however, look over the draft map and review Wright's field notes, Stewart's journal, and what little of the draft report had been prepared so far. Hall asked for a transcription of the notes. Elliott said that could not be done. A few days later, A.C. True said that the Secretary had instructed him to have Elliott prepare a report of some type for Hall. (Wilson denied this. True said he had no recollection of it.) Elliott asked Wright how long it would take to prepare a report containing the data Hall had been asking about. Wright replied about two weeks. Wright prepared the report and put a cover date of February 25, 1909, on it. Elliott agrees that Rankin pestered just about everyone in the office until Wright had finished writing his report, which ran to about 14–16 pages, about twenty percent of the first draft of his full report. Wright, however, denied that he had written a document especially for Hall and Rankin in advance of the main report. He maintained that the document he prepared for Hall was an extract lifted out of the first draft, which he had just finished. Elliott was just as certain that the first draft was not completed until May.[7]

Henry C. Hall was a lawyer from Colorado Springs. R.J. Bolles said at the time that he thought Hall was working for Harvey Duval, a Jacksonville lawyer who was probably representing the Hamilton Disston heirs, and who may have been trying to dig up dirt on the Bolles purchase because it contained land the Disston heirs were trying to assert a claim to under a railroad grant dating back to 1838.[8] On the other hand, any of the big railroad land owners could have hired him. On January 31, 1909, the railroad landowners had entered into a settlement agreement resolving their dispute over the constitutionality of the Everglades Drainage District and its per-acre annual tax. The agreement was not satisfactory to either side, mostly because of the unclear drainage plan the District intended to follow. When Henry Hall discovered that Wright was creating a new plan, even if it was, at this stage, only a map, he found the sword that could cut through cut through the Gordon knot tying up the litigation: the agreement could simply specify the plan contained in Wright's document, if Wright could just get it transmitted to the state. It didn't need to be extensive: it was the map that mattered, and as Napoleon Broward noted: "Mr. Wright had a fine map."[9]

Later, Congressman Higgins asked Wright if anyone else besides Hall had stopped by the Drainage Investigations Division to review the forthcoming report. Wright kept trying to evade the question by misinterpreting it as an inquiry about mailed-in requests for information, of which there were hundreds. Higgins would not let him go and Wright finally had to admit that "I was told that a man by the name of Bullis called there in my absence and occupied my desk for three or four days and read my report." Asked who he was, Wright answered "New York or Boston, and Bullis finally bought a large area of land in the Everglades." By this time, Wright had been the drainage engineer for the state for two years, knew R.J. Bollis well, and could probably quote off the top of his head the number of taxable acres he held within the Everglades Drainage District. One has to wonder whether he got away with one or was given a free pass. In any event, it appears that the prime mover behind the Florida Fruit Lands Company himself came in to review Wright's work.[10]

Once Hall had gotten his copy, both Wright and Morgan suggested that it would be a good idea to send a copy to Florida Governor Gilchrist, and on March 6 Elliott gave a draft transmittal letter to True to forward to the Secretary; essentially a request for permission to send the copy to Florida. Wilson agreed and a copy was sent under a cover letter from Wilson. A week later, Gilchrist replied to Secretary Wilson seeking permission to publish it. Wilson agreed on March 27.[11] In May, a joint committee of the Florida legislature endorsed the plan and urged the Fund to "push with all possible dispatch the work on the Glades, and if possible, let several of these canals on contract to reliable, responsible bidders."[12]

Wright's assertion that the first draft of the entire report was completed as early as February 25 is improbable. His itinerary log indicates that he was either in North Carolina or in the office working on North Carolina drainage plans from November 17, 1908, to March 12, 1909, with the exception of February 1 to 21, 1909, when he was in the office working on three reports, including the Everglades report. His timesheets agree with this. They show that he spent no personnel hours between August 1908 and January 1909 on the Everglades report, and only 27 percent of his time during the month of February 1909. But in March 1909 he spent 64 percent of his time; and in April, 79 percent. The records appear to indicate that he *started* work on the report in February 1909, not that he *finished* it.[13]

Also, Wright's version leaves four months unaccounted for *after* the manuscript was completed. Joseph Arnold, Chief Editor and Chief of the Publications Division of the Department of Agriculture said that his division received the manuscript for first examination on July 7. While there was an in-house review procedure within the publications department of the Office of Experimental Stations, headed up by Walter Beal, it typically required only two weeks.[14]

Elliott recalls that Wright gave him the finished manuscript of the report in late May. It contained the material sent to Hall and the State of Florida, and much other material. Elliott forwarded it to Mr. Beal for what amounted to an in-house review. According to Elliott, Beal found many stylistic shortcomings: the arrangement of the sections was unsatisfactory; it contained too many unsubstantiated opinions; it was verbose in places. Beal remembered reviewing the manuscript, and while he recalled making the same general comments Elliott attributed to him, he noted, "I do not recall that there were any important changes to the manuscript." As far as Beal was concerned, it was a routine request for a revision.[15]

Wright, on the other hand, claims that Beal had the manuscript from February to June, and that he, Beal and Elliott had several meetings, but he could later recall only those changes that Elliott requested. Elliott stated that after receiving his and Beal's comments, Wright refused to revise the report "on the grounds that he had done his best with it, and if anything better was needed some one else would have to prepare it." Elliott then made "some quite radical changes," and resubmitted it to Beal, who approved it and sent it on to Joseph Arnold.[16]

Arnold received it on July 7, assigned it serial number "Bulletin No. 218," noted its publication run of 5,000 copies on its job order card, ordered galley proofs, and noted on the job card that the Bureau of Entomology was to receive a copy of the galley proofs for review, all standard protocol. The galley proofs were returned to Arnold's office on July 30. They were proofread and sent back to the printer. The Bureau of Entomology had no comments. The page proofs were ready August 4 and sent to the Office of Experiment Stations for final review. On August 16, the page proofs were sent to the government printing office for publication. The scheduled printing date was set for September 1 or 2.[17]

Then everything fell apart.

II

While the galley and page proofs of Bulletin No. 218 were being prepared, both Elliott and Wright were away. Elliott was on the Pacific Coast and Wright was in North Carolina. A.D. Morehouse was acting chief and Arthur Morgan was the senior engineer working in the Washington office. A man named Harold Wheeler came by the Drainage Investigations Division in mid–August and asked to read the manuscript of the report. Wheeler was a lawyer from San Francisco who was at times associated with the New York firm of Bryne & Cutcheon, who represented several Everglades land interests.

He had a copy of the excerpt that Wright had prepared on February 25 for Henry Hall and the State of Florida. He asked Morgan several questions that Morgan thought were quite perceptive. Wheeler thought the estimated costs per cubic yard of canal excavation were extraordinarily low, especially for blasted stone. Morgan agreed. He thought the estimates of canal excavation did not properly take into account slumping of the sand banks back into the canal. Morgan also agreed.[18]

Wright's basic plan originated with James Kreamer's plan for of the Disston Land Company in the 1880s.[19] It was expanded upon by a survey for the Miami River canal done by Rufus Rose for the Florida East Coast Sugar and Drainage Company in 1898, plus the three studies done by the Internal Improvement Fund in 1905, most notably the South

New River plan prepared by John Newman. These, in turn, formed the basis for the map and plan given to Henry Hall and Governor Gilchrist.

It proposed nine canals in total. Five were either finished or under construction by 1909: the Miami Canal; South New River Canal; North New River Canal, Caloosahatchee Canal (completed), and Ninemile Canal from Lake Okeechobee to Lake Hicpochee (completed). Four were new or proposed: Middle New River Canal; Hillsboro Canal; North Canal to Lake Worth; and a west, or Shark River, canal running due south from Lake Okeechobee to Brown's Store.[20]

Wright's plan was based on the presumption that Lake Okeechobee would fall during the dry season from evaporation and outflow to a low of around 16 feet. During the wet season it would start to fill again, mostly from the Kissimmee River basin to the north, Fisheating Creek to the northwest, and Taylor's Creek at Okeechobee City. During the peak of the wet season, Wright assumed the basin and the lake proper would receive 24 inches of rain over a 62-day period. Part of this would soak into the ground. Part would evaporate. Part would drain into the lake. Some would have fallen as rain

Left to right: Bryan Jennings (son of William and May Mann Jennings), William Jennings Bryan, Richard J. Bolles, May Mann Jennings (wife of William Jennings), William Jennings, standing beside the uncompleted New River Canal, 1911. Photographer unknown (State Archives of Florida, No. NO27123).

Dredge "Okeechobee" working its way north up the South New River Canal, about 1907. The man in the left foreground is Capt. Hampton Holloway of the Holloway Brothers Contracting Company, who would later go on to dredge Pearl Harbor and Manila Bay. Photographer unknown (State Archives of Florida, No. RC07786).

directly into the lake. The canals had to be big enough to carry away the water that fell or drained into the lake over this 62-day peak period before the surface rose to 19 feet. But given Wright's figures for average rainfall, evaporation, and surface permeability, the lake would, over the course of two years of average wet and dry seasons, dry up and stay dry.

Wheeler maintained that this was because Wright grossly overestimated the daily evaporation from both the Kissimmee River basin and the lake itself. In other words, his canals were way too small because they were based on an assumption that much of the lake would evaporate away every year. In addition, the elevations Wright gave for the surface levels of Lake Okeechobee and Everglades standing water at various stages (high water, low water, Everglades surface at Brown's Landing, etc.) didn't match his profile charts. It wasn't enough that Lake Okeechobee was higher than sea level. If a canal ran at, for example, a 9-inch to the mile downhill grade for the first 20 miles, then flattened out to a six-inch to the mile grade, then returned to nine inches, the water would slow down at the lower, flatter segment in the middle, acting as a dam that would block the flow from the upstream segment. The canal would have to be widened almost continually from source to mouth to compensate for this. He subsequently detailed his concerns in two letters he sent to Wright in North Carolina.[21]

After Wheeler left, Morgan went through the galley proof of the forthcoming Bulletin 218 with a more careful eye. He found additional errors beyond those that Wheeler found. For example, Wright did not take into account the fact that the canals would have less capacity at the south rim of the lake at the start of the wet season, when the surface level was down to 16 feet, then in September, when it was over 19 feet. He consulted with Morehouse and the two men decided to contact Elliott to ask his permission to hold up the publication of the report. Elliott wired back that he had reviewed the draft and thought there was no reason to hold it up.[22]

A day or two later, Morgan and Morehouse, communicating through Mrs. Elliott (who acted as her husband's unpaid executive secretary) sent a second cable reiterating their request to hold up the publication of the report, and Mrs. Elliott may have sent her own cable. Elliott replied with instructions to contact Walter Beal, the editor for the Office of Experimental Stations, with a request that he ask Mr. Arnold, the editor for the Agriculture Department, to delay printing. Beal spoke with Arnold on September 1, just as the plates were about to be set in the press. The plates were temporarily shelved at the printing office and the page proofs held. Elliott returned on October 13.

Upon his return, Elliott performed his own calculations, discovered errors even greater than Wheeler and Morgan and directed Wright, who by now had returned to the Washington office, to recalculate the drainage figures. "He [Wright] had computed these ditches on a wrong principle, the error of which would not appear until the figures were tested, and I spoke somewhat sharply about the ignorance he had shown, as it was simply fundamental hydraulics," Elliott recalled.[23]

Part of Elliott's irritation was that these figures were already out in the world, as part of the February 25 extract sent to Henry Hall and the State of Florida. There was no way that Elliott could add new canals. All he could do was either widen or deepen them, and possibly, add control structures. With the help of an assistant, Wright revised his calculations and re-submitted them in January 1910.[24]

According to Wright, Elliott's revisions "did not change nor increase the size of the canals, but provided the same discharge capacity from Lake Okeechobee."[25] This is true. Wright estimated that to handle the load from the two-month peak period, the canals required a discharge capacity at the lake of 3,993 cubic feet per second (cfs). Elliott estimated 2,572 was needed for a 68-day peak period. What Wright didn't say was that in his calculations he did not consider downstream drainage as an integral part of his plan. Wright estimated that the Everglades drained at a rate of 2.5 cfs per square mile, and that his canals drained about 2061 square miles of land. They would therefore need to be widened to carry a cumulative 9145 cfs at their outlets. Elliott estimated that the Everglades drained at a rate of 6.75 cfs per square mile, but that the canals would only drain one mile to each side of the canal. This equaled about 548 square miles and would create a flow of 6,271 cfs at the canal mouths, including the input from the lake.[26]

The main problem was not so much that Wright's numbers were wrong, but that they calculated a meaningless scenario. That is, Wright calculated the canal capacity needed to drain Lake Okeechobee while assuming away all the water in the Everglades to the south through which the canals ran. A later report prepared by Mead, Hazen and Metcalf for the Everglades Land Sales Company of Chicago made an attempt to replicate both the Wright and Elliott methodologies for lowering Lake Okeechobee, then performed its own more detailed estimates. It reached a peak load about 25 percent higher than Wright's estimate, 4,925 cubic feet per second over 60 days. But when it came to the canal capacity actually needed to drain the lake *plus the whole Everglades* at the same time, Mead, Hazen and Metcalf reached an estimate that was an order of magnitude higher, 43,750 cubic feet per second. But keep in mind, as Elliott noted, Wright's plan

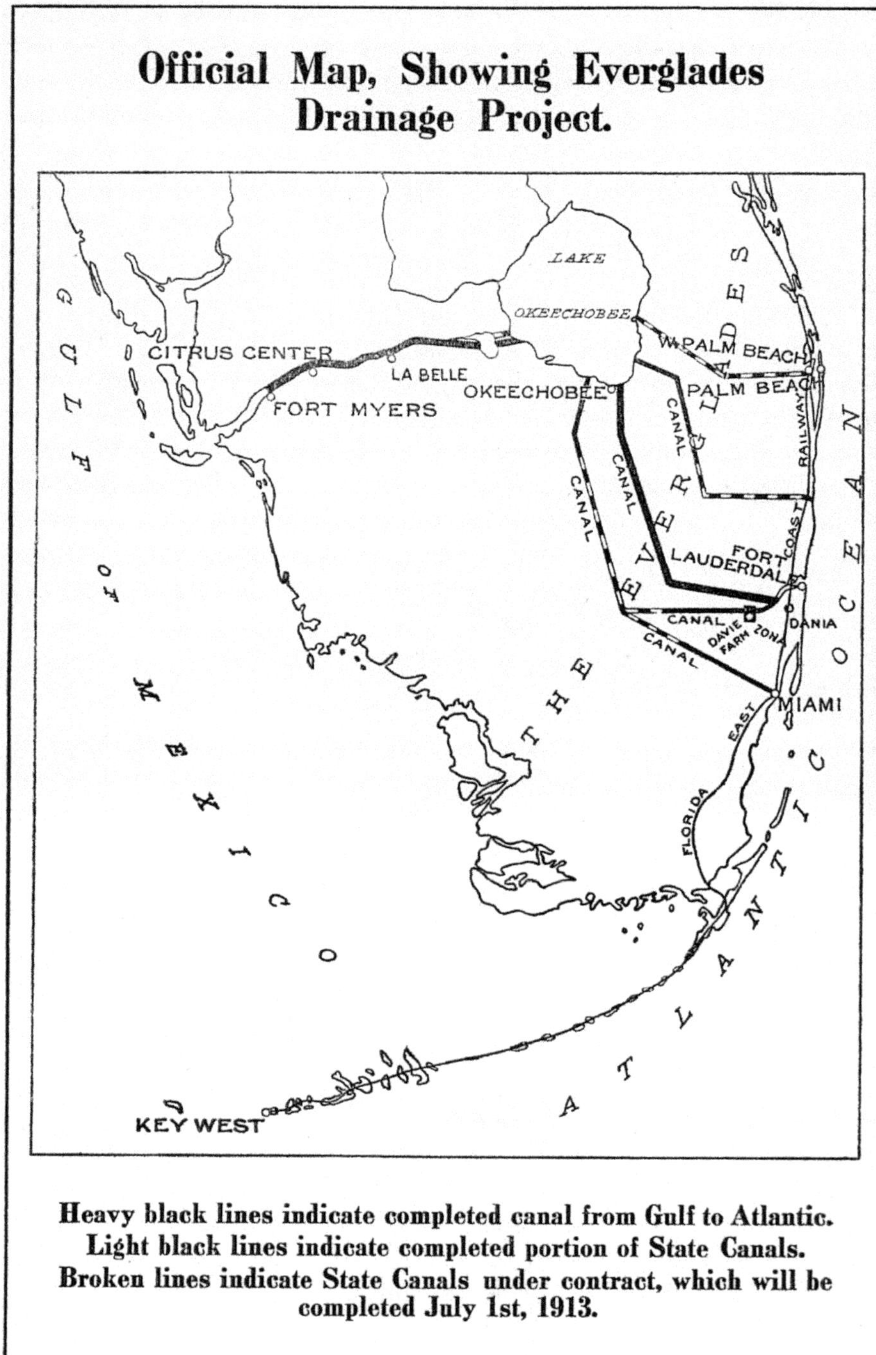

Map of the 1909 Wright Plan, with progress as of April 1912. The mid-1913 target date for completion would not be met for several decades. "Citrus Center" was a fanciful name for Fort Thompson that never caught on. From the brochure *Souvenir: Official Opening of the Gulf to Atlantic Waterway of the Everglades Drainage Canal, April 23–27, 1912* (Box 21, William Sherman Jennings Papers, P.K. Yonge Library of Florida History, Special and Area Studies Collections, George A. Smathers Libraries, University of Florida, Gainesville).

would *not* drain the whole Everglades without thousands of miles of lateral canals also being dug. At most, Wright's eight canals would drain 548 square miles lying adjacent to the canals, about 12 percent of the total Everglades.[27]

"At the time this final report was being prepared, I suggested to Mr. Elliott it might be desirable not to publish any report at all with the meager data which was at hand," recalled Morgan. "He replied that the difficulty about that was that all the excerpts had all been made public and were being used in the advertising literature of the land companies."[28] In response "Wright presented discussions in an attempt to support his deductions and conclusions, but they were not convincing, and, in the estimation of the engineers engaged on the report, did not establish his claims." He did, along with an assistant engineer, recalculate some of his tables, but did no further work. (To his credit, he was also working on the Neosho Valley report at the same time.) As a result, the Everglades report languished. Elliott himself was finally forced to complete the work, which required the next four months.[29]

In the meantime, the Department of Agriculture was receiving a large number of inquiries from around the country about soil, drainage and weather conditions in south Florida. Some of these were people who had seen Bulletin 218 listed as a "forthcoming

Looking northwest up the recently dredged Miami Canal towards Lake Okeechobee. The original channel of the smaller south branch of the Miami River is at left. The road in the foreground is the present NW 12 Avenue. The photograph is taken from the viewing tower at Musa Isle, a popular wintertime tourist attraction at the original confluence of the south and north branches of the Miami River. Photograph taken 1915 by the Detroit Publishing Company (Library of Congress No. LC-D4-72404).

publication" on the back page of other Department of Agriculture reports.[30] Others were from people who had seen the ads or flyers from Richard Bolles's Florida Fruit Lands Company or one of the other sales firms, such as the Everglades Land Sales Company. Bolles alone sold 12,000 "clearance certificates," entitling the buyer to participate in his April 1911 land lottery, and Bolles was only one of a half-dozen or more major mail-order land companies. Ultimately, over 1,500 requests for information were received by one or the other offices within the department.[31]

The State of Florida was extremely anxious to have Bulletin 218 released. After Governor Broward's 1905 statute creating an Everglades Drainage District was defeated in the courts and the 1906 constitutional amendment to create a statewide board of drainage commissioners lost in the polls, he and William Jennings re-crafted the 1905 statute in 1907 in an attempt to remove its fatal errors. The L&N Railroad and the Southern States Land and Timber Company, among others, again sued and again received an injunction blocking the imposition of the land tax, but they and Jennings kept negotiating while the suit rumbled through the courts.

By late 1909, with two dredges at work and two more almost assembled, the railroads were amenable to dropping their injunction if several conditions were met. The tax was to be reduced to five cents per acre. Several large swaths of land never intended for future development or agriculture should be omitted. The railroads wanted control over the selection of the new district's chief engineer and prime contractor. And of course, a specific plan had to be presented first. As soon as he had gotten the Wright Report extract in March 1909, Governor Gilchrist had sent it to the legislature, who had incorporated it into a joint committee report prepared pursuant to a concurrent resolution and published it in May 1909.[32] That at least gave both sides a specific map to work with, but a full-scale plan was really needed. By December 1909 the sides were trading draft settlement agreements back-and-forth, but the lack of a full report was starting to slow down the process.[33]

A second issue was William Jennings's long-running campaign for a full federal survey of the Everglades, not just a cursory drainage investigation. Back in 1848, Florida Senator Westcott had introduced a federal bill (S.338) that would have, unlike the later Swamp and Overflowed Lands Act of 1850, paid for the drainage of the Everglades, *then* turned over the swamplands to the State of Florida. To support this bill, Westcott submitted a lengthy technical report called "Senate Report Committee No. 242 of August 1848," of which the Buckingham Smith report was the centerpiece. The bill did not pass, but the Report was printed and widely circulated.[34] Jennings, for one, believed that Florida had not received all that was rightfully due it under legislation preceding the 1850 Swamp and Overflowed Lands Act, and the federal government really should, if it wasn't going to pay for the reclamation itself, at least foot the bill for a comprehensive survey.

In November 1909 Jennings asked Florida Senator James Taliaferro to sponsor a bill that he had written authorizing federal funds to drain and survey the Everglades. Taliaferro, who represented the railroads, was a willing, but not enthusiastic, sponsor of the bill. He put off Jennings with the excuse that he had inadequate documentary support to take it to the floor of the Senate. Taliaferro wrote Jennings that he needed some solid facts and evidence to back him up, something more than the brief Wright Report excerpt. In the end, Taliaferro did put Jennings's bill in the clerk's basket, but it did not pass, primarily because the land was not reclaimed, a requirement imposed by the federal Swamp and Overflowed Act of 1850, but also because Taliaferro was not willing to stick his neck out over the legislation without something comprehensive like the Buckingham Smith report to back him up.[35]

Jennings scaled his objective back to getting funding for a federal survey of the Everglades and renewed his lobbying after Taliaferro was defeated and Duncan Fletcher took his seat in the U.S. Senate. Fletcher agreed to offer a bill in the spring of 1910, but like Taliaferro, he believed he needed more documentation than the Wright Report extract. He wanted the full Bulletin 218 and wanted to know why it hadn't been released.[36]

The final reason the state was anxious to get a full version of the Wright Report was Broward and Jennings's still-lingering fears about a return of the 1902–07 legislative land grants and land certificates, a doctrine called "reversion." J.O. Wright later explained to a congressional committee what this somewhat obscure legal principle was about:

> *Rep. Floyd*: What do you mean by claiming a reversionary interest in the Everglades?
>
> *Mr. Wright*: As I understand it, certain State officers under the governor are designated as the trustees of the Internal Improvement Fund. That Fund arises from the sale of public lands, for certain purposes, and they are the trustees in charge of the Fund. In accepting the Everglade land from the Federal Government, it was stipulated that it was ceded to the State for the purpose of drainage and the revenue therefrom was to be used for the purpose of reclaiming these lands. It is my understanding that there is a claim made that the land must be sold and the money expended for reclamation purposes. And when there is enough land sold to thoroughly reclaim the Everglades, if there is a residue left, then that would be applied to satisfy the claims of companies claiming land from Florida....
>
> *Rep. Moss*: According to your best information, is there going to be very much of this reversionary interest?
>
> *Mr. Wright*: I think if the Everglades are thoroughly drained, there will not.
>
> *Mr. McCabe*: And if they are not thoroughly drained?
>
> *Mr. Wright*: If they stop now, it would all be left.
>
> *Rep. Moss*: But if they were all drained, you think that interest would disappear?
>
> *Mr. Wright*: Yes.[37]

In fact, it is open to debate whether any part of Jennings's "reversionary interest" theory was an accurate interpretation of the law, but the important thing is that it was an accurate rendition of what William Jennings *thought* the law was, along with most of the railroad lawyers he had dealt with on the original legislative grant cases going back to 1902.[38] Drain the land, and only the Internal Improvement Fund can dispose of it. Fall down on the drainage plan, and all those old certificates and legislative land grants from the 1870s and 1880s spring back to life, with a total acreage that exceeds the stock of land still held by the Fund.[39]

III

By 1909 the Fund's treasury was starting to run thin. The proceeds from the big land sales to Bolles, Davie and the Tatum Brothers only went so far. Only four dredges were at work. The *Everglades* and the *Okeechobee* worked the North and South New River Canals. By mid–1909 each had dug about eight miles in a little less than three years. John Newman had learned the hard way that you couldn't dredge through rock—you had to remove the overlying muck, back off the dredge, blast the underwater rock to bits, switch the shovel's head from a sand bucket to a smaller rock bucket, and dig up the rubble. (According to Hampton "Cap" Holloway, rock buckets lasted two weeks.) The *Caloosahatchee* had just started working its way east from Fort Myers, two months after the

Miami had begun digging northwest along the Miami River.[40] Any expansion of the work depended on the five-cent per acre tax of the Everglades Drainage District, and the district depended on an agreement with the railroads, and that depended on an upbeat plan from the Department of Agriculture, which wasn't forthcoming.

Given the delay while Wright, Morehouse, Morgan and the other engineers in the Drainage Investigations Division worked out their differences (or failed to), Elliott instructed R.D. Marsden, an assistant engineer, to prepare a simple, one-page front-and-back quick-information sheet with basic information from the Soils Division and the Weather Bureau on south Florida that could be run off on a multigraph (mimeograph) machine. It contained no signature, because Elliott anticipated that most of the letters being forwarded to him from the Secretary's office would require that they be accompanied by at least a short personal letter from someone on the staff. Elliott ran it past Walter Beal, who said it looked good. It was ready about January 28 and by early February about 170 had already been sent out. Elliott doubted if they would need a second printing, because on January 28 the much worked-over Everglades report was finally sent on its way to Mr. Beal at the editorial office. A.C. True, Elliott's boss, later said he did not know about the circular, but if he had, he would not have objected to it, didn't think there was anything wrong with it, and could think of no rule against it.[41]

After Elliott and A.C. True requested the recall of Bulletin 218 from the printing office, Elliott reworked it with the help of several engineers in his office and re-submitted it to Mr. Beal, on January 28, 1910. Beal reviewed it and passed it on to Joseph Arnold, Beal's counterpart for the entire Department of Agriculture, on January 31. Arnold, seeing how extensively the report had been revised, took the draft with him to a meeting with Secretary Wilson on February 7.[42] Arnold later gave two conflicting versions of what happened next.

Arnold's first version is that, after reviewing it, Secretary Wilson determined that the report should be held "for further careful investigation." Arnold sent a draft to Beverly Galloway, Chief of the Bureau of Plant Industry, who passed it on one of his junior scientists, Dr. C.L. Goodrich. Goodrich recommended that large sections of it, almost all pertaining to the drainage plan, be deleted. Goodrich was out in the field when Arnold initially sent him the review request, so Goodrich could not review it until late May and did not mail in his review until June 13. On June 15, Arnold send a letter to the Government Printing Office informing them that no replacement for the recalled bulletin would be submitted, as the department had decided to cancel it.[43]

There are some problems with this story. First, Arnold later admitted that he actually hadn't received Goodrich's memo by the time he sent his letter to the printing office canceling publication of the bulletin. In addition, Goodrich's boss, Beverly Galloway, said that he had never seen Goodrich's memo, let alone had a chance to approve it, before it went to Arnold, and admitted that this was inconsistent with office protocol, which required that he, the bureau chief, to approve all reviews of other bureaus' draft publications. Galloway's deputy, Mr. Powell, recalled that the Bureau of Plant Industry was being pressed by Agriculture Secretary Wilson's office for Goodrich's memo, and Galloway admitted that he did authorize Powell to send the memo sight unseen.

While Galloway had no official comment on the proposed report at that time, he did unofficially tell the Secretary's office that he thought it was overoptimistic as to the agricultural productivity of reclaimed Everglades land. "The land speculators would have taken advantages of it," he later recounted. On the other hand, "I had no point to make regarding the drainage matter," mostly because he was a plant biologist, not an engineer. However, it was the "drainage matter," not the plant industry section that was the subject of Goodrich's memo.[44]

This leads to the greatest unexplained gap in Arnold's first version of the story. Dr. Goodrich, like Galloway, was a research botanist. He admitted that there was no special reason the report should have been given to him for review, as he knew almost nothing about either the Everglades or drainage engineering, and that he had never before recommended changes to a draft report on topics outside of plant industry. Yet Dr. Goodrich's memo recommended taking the report's section on drainage, comprised of nine subsections, 4,500 words, and 7 tables, and to reduce it to roughly 175 words:

> Examinations of this great area have not been made in sufficient detail to secure the facts that are necessary to secure an intelligent design of a drainage plan for the Everglades. Little is known regarding the amount of rock that will be encountered in excavating the canals. It should be understood that the estimates of the amount of excavation and the cost of work are based upon extremely meager information concerning the material that will be encountered and the contingencies which may arise during the execution of the work. No estimate is made of the cost of controlling gates at the lake end of the ditches, locks for navigation, nor weirs for regulating the water in the ditches during dry seasons. These structures will be required in the complete drainage and development of the Everglades. The plans and estimates herein are only suggestive.[45]

This would have thrown away every word Wright wrote, keeping only a few scattered sentences, mostly qualifiers and cautionary statements inserted by Elliott between September 1909 and January 1910, now strung together into a single paragraph.

Arnold's second explanation was more straightforward: he did recommend that the July 1909 version be published, and then, five months later, recommended that the January 1910 version be killed and the July 1909 version not be resurrected, not because of anything within the two documents, but simply because the whole topic of Everglades land sales had become too controversial during the interim.

"I recommended that it be suppressed because of irreconcilable differences within the Department, and on account of differences that had arisen outside the Department," Arnold recalled. By mid–1910, it was widely known "for several weeks" that the Agriculture Department was publishing Bulletin 218: "how it got out, I don't know." Seemingly everybody had an interest, political or financial, in the contents "and they were anxious to know what the report contained. I had frequent inquiries. Some urged that if the report was a boom for the Everglades, it ought not to be printed. Others claimed that if it was an unfavorable report on the Everglades, it ought not to be printed."[46]

This is supported by the cover letter that Dr. Goodrich, the plant specialist, sent his boss, Dr. Galloway, on June 4, a week after Arnold received his report. In it, he cites no technical grounds for his recommended edits, instead commenting that "the Everglades proposition is being fostered by politicians and land promoters, therefore all matter of a speculative nature should be omitted, lest it may be so used as to mislead prospective investors in Florida lands." Also, the transmittal letter from Mr. Powell, Dr. Galloway's assistant, to Mr. Arnold, is dated June 6, not June 15, as Arnold claimed, in advance of Arnold's June 7 meeting with Secretary Wilson.[47]

One of the individuals who seemed to know the most about what was contained in the still-unreleased draft Wright Report was a magazine editor named Thomas Will. Thomas Elmer Will is impossible to figure out. An arch progressive frequently referred to by his correspondents as "comrade," a follower of the famous conservationist Gifford

Pinchot, he seems to have spent an inordinate amount of his later life working land scams that he may actually have believed in. Born in a log cabin in 1861 in Illinois, he taught elementary school at age seventeen for a year or two, then attended the State Normal School at Normal, Illinois (now Illinois State University), graduating in 1885. After working again as a teacher and principal for three years, he enrolled at the University of Michigan, transferring in 1889 to Harvard, receiving a bachelor's degree, and, in 1891 a masters.[48]

He taught for two years at Lawrence University in Appleton, Wisconsin, moved to Boston for a year, apparently writing, then accepted a faculty position at the Kansas State Agricultural College, now Kansas State University, in 1894. He was well regarded but tended to become involved in nationwide political issues such as bimetallism and public ownership of utilities (admittedly, both of concern and benefit to farmers), that drew the ire of legislators and was fired. This was followed by stints at Ruskin College in Trenton, Illinois, and Fairmont College (now Wichita State University). He moved to Washington in 1905 to work for the Bureau of the Census, then accepted a temporary position with Gifford Pinchot's Forest Service, touring the Chautauqua circuit lecturing on forest conservation. In September 1906 he accepted the editorship of *Conservation*, the magazine of the American Forestry Association, located in Washington, doubling as the Association's secretary.

In the summer of 1909, Will received an article submittal from John Clayton Gifford, a cofounder of the magazine. Gifford was an acknowledged authority on conservation. He was the first to earn a doctorate in forestry, at Cornell. But besides being an academic, he was also a bank president, a land speculator and home builder. Richard J. Bolles, E.C. Chambers, and R.P. Davie all were all his clients or customers. Will published Gifford's article, which again repeated the claim that the Everglades could be drained for a dollar an acre, in August 1909. Intrigued, Will wrote to Governor Broward in July 1910, who recommended Richard Bolles's Florida Fruit Lands Company, who paid Broward generously to make just such references.[49] Will himself traveled to Florida in January 1910 and upon his return resigned from the American Forestry Association to set up the Washington office of the Chicago-based Everglades Land Sales Company.[50]

The Everglades Land Sales Co. was a cooperative sales office for the Everglades Land Co., the Everglades Sugar and Land Co., the Miami Everglade Land Co. and the R.P. Davie Reality Co. It was incorporated in Florida, with major offices in Chicago and Miami. Its president was Vance Helm. At the time Will started, the general agent for the Washington office was E.C. Howe, who had formerly worked for the Interstate Commerce Commission as a stenographer. Will would later explain that "the most charitable explanation of Mr. Howe's conduct is that he is in a measure deranged." It appears that Will may have been hired by Vance Helm to replace Howe, but Howe apparently had some partnership share in the firm and would not go away quietly. Eventually he left to go sell land along the Panama Canal.[51]

Sometime in early February (Will thinks it was the 6th or 7th, but the 6th was a Sunday), Howe came by the offices of *Conservation*. Will had tendered his resignation and was in the process of closing out his last issue before moving over to the Everglades Land Sales Co. offices. Bulletin 218 was still not released, but Howe was upset about some flyer or circular on the Everglades that the Drainage Investigations Division was sending out and wanted Will to accompany him. Will agreed.

They first met with J.O. Wright, who said he had nothing to do with it. They then met with Elliott. Howe's main complaints were that the circular indicated that the range of temperatures measured at the Kissimmee weather station included a low of 28 degrees in February 1908 and that it stated that certain crops, citrus in particular, would likely need copious quantities of fertilizer on drained soils. Elliott was unsympathetic, asking only if Howe thought the statements were false. Howe replied that was not the point. Elliott waived him away, referring him to A.C. True, who gave him a similar response. Howe and Will then attempted to get an audience with Secretary Wilson and may have spoken with him briefly.[52] Will later gave this account to a colleague:

> As to [the newspaper reports]: Howe and I did see Elliott and True in February 1910, at which time, Howe, with his usual prudence and judgment, and greatly to my disgust, did exactly the thing the papers stated. I discountenanced the proceeding then and there in his presence, and afterward apologized for him in his absence and made it clear that I had no use for such methods.[53]

Elliott and Morehouse verify this, although they portray Will as perhaps more passive, simply fading into the woodwork. Although Dr. Will was a man who enjoyed the sound of his own voice, he also, from sometimes painful experience, knew the tactical value of silence. This was especially true in this case. Unknown to either Howe or the staff at the Office of Experiment Stations, Will had already read a copy of the full Wright Report. In late January, while an editor at *Conservation*, he had arranged for Samuel Copper, a foreman at the Government Printing Office, to steal a galley proof of Bulletin 218 for him. After reviewing it for a day or two, he gave it back to Copper, who replaced it in the Printing Office's files.[54]

It is obvious that Howe was upset that the information contained in the one-page, double-sided information sheet contradicted some of the wilder claims that Everglades Land Sales Co. was distributing in its brochures, such as that it never froze in the Everglades, or that the soils were, as one brochure put it, "deep uniform, and black; absolutely richer than the than the valley of the Nile." (It was actually a vegetative peat, lacking in potassium, nitrates and several trace minerals, and like any other peat, if dried out, desiccated into a light, fibrous, highly flammable substance barely resembling soil.) The brochure of one company, the Florida Everglades Sugar Land Company, was so over the top that the Miami post office issued a fraud order and informed the Miami *Metropolis*, the second largest newspaper in the city, that they would not transmit copies of their paper by second-class mail if it contained ads by the firm.[55]

In any event, Will and Howe's trip was superfluous. A few days earlier, on Friday, February 4, Florida Senator Fletcher, after receiving a telegram from Governor Broward expressing concern about some publication Fletcher wasn't really sure about, visited Agriculture Secretary Wilson. Before his visit, Fletcher, trying to find out what Broward was referring to, asked around and had been given a copy of the mimeographed circular and brought it with him. Wilson had not seen it. He summoned Joseph Arnold and a couple of department heads to find out about it. After a few minutes of investigation, they verified that it was genuine, and about 175 copies had been distributed. Wilson instructed A.C. True to stop sending it out and to prepare another containing a brief, boilerplate response directing all inquiries to Florida state authorities. According to Elliott, by March 1910 the Secretary's office simply stopped forwarding Everglades inquiries to the drainage division. The Office of the Secretary, on the other hand, sent out about 1,500 of Wilson's boilerplate responses by early 1912. It was either at or immediately after this February 4 meeting that Joseph Arnold showed Secretary Wilson the heavily revised January 28 version of the Everglades report for the first time.[56]

Years later, at a congressional committee hearing, Will was asked if he had anything to say at the February meeting between him, Howe and Elliott about the circular. Will recalled that the only thing he said was to ask J.O. Wright whether he intended to accept the offer to become the chief drainage officer for the State of Florida and the Everglades Drainage District. Taken aback, the committee chairman immediately jumped in to ask if they were still talking about this same meeting, February 6 or 7. Will said yes. The chairman asked him how he learned of this job offer before anyone else. Will replied that he didn't; it was all over Florida; everyone knew it. It was on the record; it was in the newspapers in south Florida.

Part of the settlement agreement that William Jennings had worked out with the Southern States Land and Timber Company and the railroads agreeing to form the Everglades Drainage District said that the state would hire J.O. Wright, by name, to be the chief engineer at $5,000 per year. It was right there, in the settlement agreement, in Paragraph 5: "The Drainage Commissioners and Trustees shall employ J.O. Wright, Esq., now supervising Drainage Engineer of the United States, as Drainage Engineer."[57]

The chairman was momentarily speechless. Somebody jumped in to change the subject.[58]

4

Land Richer Than the Valley of the Nile

> Bolles and his associates were held in the highest esteem by the locals. In many northern cities, however, the reverse was true. Their operations had, in fact, created a nationwide scandal. Bolles himself was indicted and others were charged and some convictions gained. Bolles remained steadfastly in Florida where the courts held that he had acted in good faith.... Local people had always liked the small, dapper Bolles, who was gentle and courteous at all times. Many felt that that he was being persecuted unduly, and that he had fulfilled his obligations, but the state had failed to uphold its part.
>
> —Philip Weidling and August Burghard, 1974[1]

Shortly after Secretary Wilson ordered A.C. True and Elliott to stop sending out their one-page flier in early February 1910, a group of Florida businessmen called upon Representative Frank Clark to ask when the Everglades report would be issued. Clark and a couple of the Floridians went to the Department of Agriculture, first calling on Joseph Arnold. Arnold told them the same thing he had told Thomas Will, that he thought the report would be out within a month, and that it would be about 60 pages long. Clark then called on the Secretary, who was decidedly less optimistic. "The Secretary said in effect that he was tired of that Everglades business; that he didn't propose to do anything until our people could all get together and agree on something."[2]

Wilson was in an awkward situation with southern Democratic legislators. He got along with most of them, and behind closed doors sympathized with their biggest grievance, that Republican administrations wanted to allocate too much of his department's budget to Republican strongholds in the upper Midwest and west, shortchanging Democratic southern states like Florida. He tried to steer a middle ground, but it was not easy, and to come against such internecine conflict in a deep south state on top of everything else was little short of maddening. Thomas Will also visited the Secretary about this time, and was told almost exactly the same thing: that until the Florida legislative delegation, and its federal and state representatives achieved some consensus on the Everglades, he was not going to stick his neck out.[3]

Things did not get better. In May, Napoleon Broward and James Taliaferro survived the all-comers primary for senator and moved on to the Democratic primary runoff in two months. Taliaferro, who apparently did not have the overt backing of the Florida East Coast Railroad and the Consolidated Land Company this time, lost in the two-man runoff to Broward by 2,500 out of 50,000 votes cast. With only the formality of the general election in November, Broward and his family took a New England vacation lasting until September. He returned ill, suffering from what appeared to be a gallstone attack. He died on the operating table on the night of October 1. According to William Jennings's brother Douglas, a physician who attended the autopsy at the request of the family, Broward died of an occluded bile duct, resulting in jaundice. The occlusion, in Dr. Jennings's opinion, was caused by a cancerous tumor on the surface of the liver. Nathan P. Bryan, brother of William James Bryan, a U.S. Senator from Florida who died suddenly after serving 40 days in office in 1908, was appointed to his seat.[4]

The heretofore smooth-running land sales machine of R.J. Bolles's Florida Fruit Lands Company started to make some rattling noises in March 1911. The requisite 12,000 "Clearance Receipts" having been sold, the land lottery was scheduled for March 15 on the town site of Progresso, at the northern edge of Fort Lauderdale. By the appointed day, about 5,000 purchasers had assembled, most living in tents or wagons. The "auction" was actually a lottery, as all the farm sites had been pre-sold; the purpose was to allot a farm plot to each clearance receipt holder, plus a house lot in Progresso. As previously noted, two lucky buyers would receive a 640-acre parcel; two others, a 320-acre parcel, and so on down to four 20-acre sites. There were 14 bonus plots in all. Thus, the odds of winning one of the bonus sites were slightly over 1 in 1000. The lottery would take about ten days. On March 20, trustees would be appointed to deal with the paperwork.[5]

Those buyers who had traveled to attend the lottery tended to make haste to one of two places after their blue pellet had been called: east, to the Ft. Lauderdale post office or

Swamp buggy developed by the Florida Fruit Lands Company to survey their holdings in what is now far west Broward County. Richard J. Bolles stands second from left. Photographer unknown, taken 1911–12. Library of Congress No. LC-D4-63406.

west to the Bolles tact. If they went to the post office, that usually meant they were trying to flip their parcel or had already made a deal with someone. A reporter who tried to mail a dispatch on March 20 found a 90-minute line at the post office. Those who headed west to the Bolles Tract could only roughly locate their plot. Bolles's surveyors had accomplished less than in Oregon: only the corners of each township, a block of 36 sections, were staked. It hardly mattered; the South New River Canal would not be finished for another year, and was actually dammed to maintain a high enough water level to float dredges, flooding the land worse than it would be in its natural condition. One purchaser from Iowa exclaimed: "I have bought land by the acre, and I have bought land by the foot, but by God, I have never bought land by the gallon."[6]

As the lottery came to an end, company officials named the three trustees who would execute the transfer of the clearance receipts. Problems immediately arose. The original mail-order contracts said that trustees would be appointed but didn't specify by whom. There were between 1,500 and 5,000 purchasers milling around (depending on who was doing the counting), and an increasing number of them started to voice the opinion that they were the ones who had the legal power to make the selection. Bolles prudently decided it might be a good idea to let the assembled throng vote for their choice of trustees.

The three trustees then discovered they had no real power. Their only legal duty under the bylaws of the firm was to accept clearance receipts, look up the farm lot and town lot awarded to that receipt number in the lottery, and then award a trust deed that gave the individual an undivided ownership share in the entire Bolles Tract and the Progresso subdivision, with the promise that a deed of conveyance for each parcel would be issued when an official survey took place. However, the state would not survey the land until Bolles finished paying for it, in 1916, as it was both overflowed and under lien to the Internal Improvement Fund. The trustees did the only thing they could: they sued the Florida Fruit Lands Company.[7]

V.W. Helm, perhaps somewhat put out that Bolles had refused to participate in the advertising co-op that the Everglades Land Sales Company had assembled, wrote Thomas Will upon learning of the suit: "confidentially, I hope the trustees will win, for the reason that it would be nothing short of crime to deliver all of that land without some kind of secondaries, or laterals, or both."[8]

But all the land sales firms, including Helm's, sold their plots using the Bolles model, through the mail. Some firms did organize boat trips up the partially-finished canals to look at their blocks of land, others took buses to show off the Department of Agriculture's subtropical experimental farm south of Miami (now the Fairchild Tropical Gardens), much to the frustration of the facility's staff, who knew it was located on high and dry ground atop the coastal ridge some ten or twelve feet above the level of the Everglades, with completely different soil and agricultural characteristics than the overflowed lands the firms were selling. None of them improved their land with roads or lateral canals.[9]

The vast majority of the farm sites were bought sight unseen, except for elaborate brochures and booklets. There was one catch to this method: selling through the mails made the land companies subject to postal investigations and possible criminal liability for postal fraud. On the evening of July 13, 1911, Thomas Will was attending a Washington, D.C. meeting of the Everglades Home Builders' Association, a booster or "homeseeker's" club organized by Will as a marketing front for his Everglade Land Sales Company. A reporter from the Associated Press announced that a Fraud Order had been issued against the Florida Everglades Land Company of Chicago, which does not appear to be one of the landowners Will's firm represented, but which was a co-sponsor of the Home Builder's organization. The meeting immediately broke up.[10]

By this time over 50 firms in Chicago alone were speculating on tracts of various sizes in the Everglades usually purchased from the railroads or one of the new big-block buyers, because their land was cheaper than land bought from the state. They would either set up a marketing front or hire one such as Will's Everglades Land Sales Company. When the hypothetical farm sites were sold out, they closed shop or moved on to another tract. Congressman William P. Borland of Missouri, representing the district where Bolles's Florida Fruit Lands Company had its mailing address, and Representative Frank Clark of Florida had, as early as 1909, started urging the Department of Justice to investigate Everglades land sales. But the U.S. Attorney for the Western District of Missouri, Leslie J. Lyons, was simultaneously lawyer for the Florida Fruit Lands Company. Borland went to U.S. Attorney General George Wikersham, who had a special agent prepare a report on Lyon's activities. The agent turned in his report to Wikersham, who put it in his office safe and refused to let anyone read it, including members of Congress.

Similarly, former Florida governor William Jennings, general counsel for the

Cartoon by James M. Carson (1887–1950) appearing in a Back to Broward League pamphlet, 1913. The League was an advocacy organization of smallholders who had purchased Everglades land, usually from one of the large promoters, to lobby the state to complete the job of draining the Everglades and to make the necessary surveys to allow them to occupy their designated homesteads (State Archives of Florida, No. DG1858).

Internal Improvement District, was also Bolles's Florida lawyer. Any time a matter concerning one of his interests was heard before the trustees, Jennings moved to the other side of the table, and the Fund's outside counsel, General William Ellis, would be called in to take his seat. This was considered adequate protection against conflicts of interest, at least until 1912 when General Ellis became the fund's full-time lawyer. (Later, testifying under oath, Ellis admitted that he, too, had been on the Bolles payroll, although he never clarified when.)[11] Neither the post office or the Department of Justice took action until Republican Woodrow Wilson assumed the presidency in early 1913. The State of Florida never prosecuted anyone for abuses related to Everglades land sales.[12]

However, unknown to the Department of Justice or the state, the Post Office's Inspector General had continued its investigation, notwithstanding the obstructionism of Attorney General Wikersham. On October 1, 1910, Postal Inspector H.N. Graham requested that Agriculture Secretary Wilson send him information pertaining to the department's investigation into soil conditions and plant industry in the Everglades area. Interestingly, Graham specifically requested the raw data collected by John T. Stewart in early 1907. This was the data that Wright had disparaged at the time in order to convince Elliott to send Lawrence Brett, not Stewart, on the second field expedition to south Florida during the winter of 1908. Secretary Wilson instructed Elliott to comply, and Elliott sent Graham both the Elliott Report and the field journals and report that Stewart prepared in May 1907 after his return to Washington.[13]

The prevailing wisdom (especially in the newspapers) was that the railroad land companies were on one side, while the state and the new retail land speculators, such as R.J. Bolles's Florida Fruit Lands Company, were on the other. This was more a perception than a reality. It is true that with the exception of the Florida East Coast Railroad's Model Land Company, the railroads rarely sold land on a retail basis.[14] But after the lawsuits over the Everglades Drainage District were settled in 1910, they had a substantial interest in selling big blocks of land—anywhere from 22,400 to 134,400 acres—to land speculators like Bolles who subdivided it into parcels and marketed it to smallholders.

What Governor Gilchrist and the Trustees of the Internal Improvement Fund did openly acknowledge was that the Everglades drainage project was entirely leveraged. The new participants such as Bolles, Davie and Tatum and, later, E.C. Chambers, had bought land from the Fund (and to a lesser extent, the railroads) on five-year time payments, were dividing them into smallholdings, and selling them retail on short-term installment plans, typically two years.

From out of these retail sales, the land speculators were making their time payments to the Fund and paying their five-cent-an-acre annual drainage tax to the Everglades Drainage District. That money paid for a ramping up of the state's drainage efforts from two dredges in 1907 to nine dredges in 1911. As soon as the dredges finished their job, the land would dry and could be settled, and the state could then start selling the land in its own checkerboarded sections to smallholders for 20 to 50 dollars an acre.

Tax revenues in 1911 were very small; about $200,000.[15] The whole financial juggernaut would roll along only so long as people continued to make retail land purchases to the land companies, in advance of drainage. If sales collapsed, the hundreds of thousands of dollars in sunk costs expended so far would be lost. As one drainage engineer put it: "every undertaking of every character whatsoever in the drainage district is dependent upon the drainage enterprise.... Drainage is the entire foundation upon which the whole fabric of development and life of the district exists."[16] Thomas Will's boss, V.W. Helm, put it more bluntly: "this project depends largely on public confidence in its wisdom and ultimate success, such confidence being essential to the sale of the lands."[17] And now, the state was counting on its chief drainage engineer, J.O. Wright, for that "ultimate success."

II

On October 8, 1911, the Washington *Times* printed a story by a reporter named Judson Welliver. It was fairly brief, but fundamentally accurate: a report intended to be published by the Department of Agriculture in January 1910 had been suppressed at the request of Governor Broward and Senator Fletcher because it concluded that much more would be required to drain the Everglades than had been estimated in the February 1909 Henry Hall excerpt released to the State of Florida. The excerpt had been published by the state as its official drainage plan two months later, but now there were serious reservations among the Department of Agriculture experts about whether it would work.

The Welliver story's one weakness was that it conflated the Wright Report and the one-page flier from January 1910 in a couple of places, especially when it came to the story of Fletcher and Secretary Wilson's meeting of February 7, followed by Wilson's order to discontinue publication. This account was true for the flier, but not for Elliott's revision of the Wright Report.[18]

At almost exactly the same time, the full Wright Report *was* being published, but in its original July 1909 version, as part of a compendium report sponsored by Duncan Fletcher entitled *Everglades of Florida: Acts, Reports and Other Papers, State and National, Relating to the Everglades of the State of Florida and Their Reclamation*, the title itself explaining why everyone referred to it simply as *Senate Document No. 89*. It is typically believed that the Welliver article started the "Report Wars," but the die was cast months earlier when the decision was made to assemble *Senate Document No. 89*, and its origins actually go back decades.

In 1848, Florida Senator Westcott introduced a federal bill (S.338) that would have, unlike the later Swamp and Overflowed Lands Act of 1850, paid for the drainage of the Everglades, *then* turned over the swamplands to the State of Florida. To support this bill, Westcott submitted a lengthy technical report called "Senate Report Committee No. 242 of August 1848," which featured the Buckingham Smith report. The bill did not pass, but the report was printed and widely circulated.[19]

In 1909, William Jennings, then counsel for the Internal Improvement Fund, had asked Florida Senator James Taliaferro to sponsor a bill that Jennings had written authorizing federal funds to drain and survey the Everglades. It died without a vote, partially due to a lack of current data.[20] Jennings scaled his goal back to merely getting funding for a federal survey of the Everglades and shifted his target to Duncan Fletcher when Taliaferro was voted out of office after falling out of favor with the Florida East Coast railroad and the Consolidated Land and Timber Company. Fletcher agreed to put a bill in the clerk's basket as S.7305 on March 22, 1910. It used the Wright Report excerpt as the basis for its assertion that the Everglades were ready for surveying and sought an appropriation of $10,000 for the job. It was allowed to die in April 1910.[21] Fletcher told Jennings that he was going to have to come up with his own version of *Senate Report No. 242* if any kind of appropriation was going to have a chance.

Thomas Will offered a slightly different version of the report's origins. In March 1911 the Everglades Land Sales Company published a book. John C. Gifford's *The Everglades and Other Essays Relating to Southern Florida*, mostly a compilation of essays he had previously published in *Conservation* magazine. It was intended to be a form of high-brow propaganda for the Everglades, with statistics replacing blatant tub-thumping, and at least a modest grounding in reality maintained in its facts and conclusions. Ironically, Vance Helm wrote Will that Gifford had complained to him that his book was being misquoted by salesmen from other land companies to make wild claims that Gifford never stated. More specifically, they maintained that Gifford had written that every species of subtropical fruit and tree discussed in his book would thrive in the Everglades, which was nonsense.[22]

Will had heard similar stories, and with Wright's Bulletin 218 apparently cancelled, he wrote out a proposal for a government report that would compile historical and scientific works on the Everglades that could be used as the definitive source of information by the land sales companies, submitting it to Senator Fletcher in early May 1911. Coming on top of Jennings's request for a survey appropriation, Will's proposal fell on fertile ground.

In June, Fletcher asked Thomas Will to start assembling material for a compendium report on Everglades reclamation.[23] Former Governor Jennings was the other compiler-editor. Jennings had an almost encyclopedic knowledge of the historic documentation about the Everglades. Jennings himself had ordered reports written and assembled in support of his 1903 move to have all remaining federal lands patented to Florida. In one letter to Senator Taliaferro, he had rattled off almost 50 reports, studies and government documents relating to the Everglades that pre-existed the Wright Report.

However, when Senator Fletcher himself was asked about the origins of *Senate Document No. 89* he seemed to place an inordinate emphasis on disseminating the Wright Report in the form that Wright himself had written it in the spring of 1909, before Harold Wheeler, then Arthur Morgan and A.D. Morehouse, had questioned the competency of the report:

> I conceived the idea then [in the spring 1911] of preparing a Senate document that would give the records, acts, National and State papers, reports, and other papers relating to the Everglades and their reclamation, and the Wright report which was not published.... I was able to get this, what appeared to me to be a full, authentic copy of the page proofs of this, and being the only Wright report available to me, at least I thought it ought to be published for the benefit not only of the State and those directly interested in the Everglades, but those who might be interested and those who were inquiring about them from all over the country.[24]

Will and Fletcher's secretary went to various libraries and offices to collect the historical documents throughout June and July. Instead of going to the Department of Agriculture for a copy of the Wright Report, he asked Thomas Will for one, who provided him with a copy of the Bulletin 218 version. He did not ask Will how he came into possession of an unpublished report. Asked later if he was ever aware that a newer version (the Elliott Report) existed, Fletcher said no, but that he "had heard of the Wright report for something like a year and was looking for it to come out, wanting it to come out, and hearing it talked about here and there." Will was never asked how he came into possession of this copy of the report. It was never clear whether this was the same copy he got in February 1910, or managed to copy it, or whether he got someone to steal it for him again. (Twenty years later, when he admitted to it and named his co-conspirator, he only spoke of only one theft.)[25]

As if this was not confusing enough, both Fletcher and Will also gave a second story about how the Congressional printing office came into a copy of the Wright Report. On July 26, Will wrote his boss, Vance Helm: "you will be interested to know that my part of the document work is practically done and the matter was referred to Senator Fletcher." On September 13, Will wrote: "Document was held up by Mr. Elliott of Agriculture Department getting hold of it and attempting largely to make it over.... The matter has been gone over at this end and sent to Senator Fletcher who is daily expected to return it." On October 4, Will again wrote, noting: "I had, this morning, a letter from Senator Fletcher stating that he will be here next Monday with the document. The Elliott suggestions have evidently made him a lot of work."[26]

The background to these somewhat cryptic references is this: on August 7, 1911, Senator Fletcher's resolution appropriating funds for *Senate Document No. 89* was approved. About August 25, Walter Beal, editor for the Office of Experiment Stations, received either a manuscript or an early proof of *Senate Document No. 89* from B.D. Stallings, Joseph Arnold's deputy at the office of editing and publications at the Agriculture Department. Reviewing it, Elliott and A.D. Morehouse identified the earlier Wright Report as being among the 60 or so documents it contained. It was a straight galley proof of Bulletin 218, down to the serial number on the cover page. Having prepared a heavily revised version in January (the Elliott Report) that Secretary Wilson had ordered shelved in June, they of course believed that *Senate Document No. 89* should contain the later version.[27]

Being a compendium document, it also, in their opinion, lacked several important documents from the 1906–10 period, such as Elliott's original 1904 research report evaluating potential sites for a subtropical station near Miami; progress reports from the 1907 and 1908 Stewart-Brett field investigations; excerpts from John Stewart's 1907 field journal; and other material. Morehouse prepared a series of insertions, lettered A-I, with letter "F" being the new drainage plan that Elliott's engineers had used to replace the one prepared by Wright. Morehouse gave these to Walter Beal and Beal transmitted these to Arnold, via his deputy, Stallings, on August 30, 1911.[28]

Arnold then gave this material to George Carter, the head of the Joint Committee on Printing, the editorial office for Congress. Given the concern in the Secretary's office over the supposed suppression of the Everglades report, Arnold contacted Carter at the Joint Committee to warn him not to confuse the two different versions of the report, the proposed Bulletin No. 218, now obsolete, and the Elliott revision. To his surprise, Carter was aware of the two versions and told him that "the committee intended to include in the document, the one for which Senator Fletcher's resolution had been introduced, the Bulletin.... I told Mr. Carter that I thought it was unfair for them to print a bulletin to which the department had not given its assent. I did tell him that. He advised that he thought the [Senate] committee had a perfect right to use that if it so desired." Arnold admitted this was true but insisted that the bulletin number had to be omitted from the front. Carter said he would check, but he thought that was a reasonable request.[29]

On August 23, Congress recessed, and Senator Fletcher arrived home to Jacksonville on the 25th.[30] A few days later, J.O. Wright was in Jacksonville and William Jennings met him and told him that Fletcher wanted him. Wright could not meet just then, as he was on his way to Tallahassee for a meeting of the Internal Improvement Fund. A conference was arranged at Jennings's law office the following Monday. Fletcher said that he had received a call from George Carter in Washington, and it was necessary for Wright to review the Everglades drainage report. He was shown into an empty office and was handed what appeared to be a galley proof, greatly marked up with deletions and lengthy insertions marked by letters: "Insert A," "Insert B" and so on. This was apparently a printer's dummy of *Senate Document No. 89*, with Morehouse's A-I insertions and edits, the same document that Morehouse prepared and gave to Walter Beal.

Wright was asked to sift through the new material and identify his work. The editing took about six hours. Fletcher left immediately afterwards, but Jennings worked the entire time in an adjacent office on the older legal and historical documents that would go into the front of *Senate Document No. 89*. It appears from comments that Will made afterwards that Wright did more then simply edit the "Elliott Report," he removed all of the material that Morehouse submitted. "Nothing, either from Elliott or anyone else, is going into that document," he wrote Vance Helm on October 14. This would have been a significant effort, as Morehouse had submitted about 110 pages of material, including the text of the Elliott Report.[31]

On August 29, the secretary of the Trustees of the Internal Improvement Fund received separate letters from Thomas Will and Senator Fletcher informing them of the impending release of *Senate Document No. 89* and offering them bulk pricing on quantities over 250 copies. The Trustees immediately ordered 10,000 copies.[32]

In late September, Mr. Stallings called Elliott and said that Mr. Carter wanted to meet at the office of the Joint Committee on Printing. At the meeting, Elliott repeated the explanation that Arnold had made earlier about the two versions of the report. Carter stopped him and said "this copy I have here was prepared and arranged by Dr. Will and is the copy, as I understand it, that is that is to be printed as a Senate document." Elliott noted that except for deleting "Bulletin No. 218," the same title page had been retained, down to the July 25, 1909, date, and it was the same text. None of the material Morehouse had added or substituted had been included. "Mr. Carter seemed quite hostile to any suggestions I might make or did make … when I saw these changes I understood the position of Mr. Carter. I recognized what I now believe to be a fact, that the people interested in the sale of Everglades lands undrained were attempting to dominate the publication of every report which had been sent out of my office upon the Everglades."[33]

Carter later confirmed most of this narrative, including the involvement of Dr. Will as editorial coordinator. However, he asserted that he did not know that Will worked for any Everglades land interests, and he emphatically denied that anyone at the Department of Agriculture was ever asked to make editorial contributions to *Senate Document No. 89*. If a galley proof was sent to the Office of Experiment Stations, or the Drainage Investigations Division, it was unauthorized or a mistake. It was Senator Fletcher's document, and nobody was authorized to make editorial contributions except through him.[34]

What is implied by this second version is that Senator Fletcher, Wright and Jennings, working for six hours in Jennings's law office with only a copy of Wright's May 1909 typewritten manuscript to guide them, were able to take the cut-up, marked-up, printer's dummy prepared by Morehouse and Elliott and revert it back into a perfect, word-for-word rendition of the galley proof of Bulletin 218.[35] This is absurd. The only explanation is that Fletcher did not want to admit that he had resorted to using a bootleg copy of the page proofs. The story originated from Mr. Carter, head of the Congressional Joint Printing Committee, in a newspaper article published very early in the controversy, and when Will admitted that he was the source of the Wright Report used in *Senate Document No. 89*, it was necessary to keep up the pretense to avoid admitting the lie.[36] The only other possible explanation is that the "manuscript" Wright referred to was not his manuscript of May 1909, but a typewritten copy of the February 1910 copy that Thomas Will had arranged to have had stolen for him and that he alleges he kept for only a few days.

Senate Document No. 89 was issued on December 1, 1911. "Just received a copy of Senate Document," wrote V.W. Helm to Thomas Will. "It is a peach!" The Everglades Land Sales Company promptly ordered 1,000 copies. "I am inclined to believe that *Senate Document No. 89* in the hands of our agents will answer all the knocks of the malicious and ignorant ones."[37]

Some Everglades historians, especially A.J. and K.A. Hanna, have asserted that *Senate Document No. 89* was a mere a pretext to print the Wright Report in its earlier version.[38] This is probably an exaggeration. The much shorter Wright excerpt had already been printed in the *Journal of the Florida Senate* in May 1909, and by the Internal Improvement District as a pamphlet in 1910. As will be discussed later, the trustees of the Internal Improvement District believed the Wright Report extract (especially its map) was time-sensitive, because it helped bolster their case in a lawsuit, *Trustees v. Root,* that was working its way through the appeals process.[39] There was less urgency when it came to the full report. There was at least as much interest in the Buckingham Smith Report and other historical material contained in the new Senate document as in the Wright Report.

However, the purely historical reportage in the Senate document was carefully selected and edited to portray Everglades drainage in the best light possible, much of its data was obsolete, and no attempt was made to point out which measurements, surveys, statistics or analyses were no longer current or had been supplanted. In the end, it was presented as a compendium of historical documents, of which the Wright Report was simply one of the most recent. But on the other hand, most of the material in Morehouse's inserts, not counting the Elliott Report, was at least as valuable as some of the older accounts of scientific and survey expeditions, and the fact that this matter was rejected out of hand is suspicious. Even if there were page limits, as Fletcher later asserted, some of Morehouse's material was more valuable than other material that was included, some of which was little more than filler material.

III

On August 27, the Washington *Times* ran the first in a series of letters and articles on "The Florida Land Swindle." The Everglades Land Sales Company had gone beyond being merely a marketing office and had purchased several thousand acres of its own land to sell. To be on the safe side, Will pulled the abstract of title out of the safe deposit box and reviewed it. "An examination of the abstract of title ... shows that this abstract has not been certified, and that the Company's lands apparently bear an incumberance [sic] of some $66,000," Will advised Vance Helm. He urged either the Chicago or Miami office to get a lawyer to work cleaning up the title.[40] Judson Welliver's first article appeared on October 8. It is a measure of how out of touch that Thomas Will and the other land salesmen had grown that he assured Vance Helm on October 14 that he had a good meeting with Welliver and that the next article would be "wholly different in character from the first." Welliver probably thought it was, in his own way, a very productive interview as well.[41]

The second article, which appeared on October 15, was a blockbuster. Three thousand words long, it was mostly accurate, but like the first article was a little muddled in places. For example, it confused the two versions of the Everglades report, Wright's October 1909 version and Elliott's January 1910 version, and conflated the Wright Report and the one-page circular once or twice.

But what it got right was enough to send off alarm bells from Tallahassee to Colorado Springs. Wright produced a report. Elliott found it patently unacceptable, but only after Henry Hall had tricked Secretary Wilson into releasing an excerpt. Wright was rewarded with a high-paying job at the State of Florida. Elliott had his men fix the report, but Wilson refused to publish it because he was too embarrassed to admit his department had approved such a flawed document in the first place. Senator Fletcher did an end-around the Agriculture Department by publishing Wright's version in *Senate Document No. 89*, possibly with a stolen copy of the report. The Post Office and the Attorney General were both investigating the Everglades land sales companies for fraud and misuse of the mails. Some of these firms may have given thousands of acres of land to current and former state officials, or put them on the payroll, or both, to secure their cooperation. All very ugly, all very true. And in an assertion that may have had the most long-lasting impact, Welliver wrote that if Wright had not quit to take the job in Florida, Elliott would have fired him. Finally, Welliver claimed that Florida Representative Frank Clark was among those who tried to have the one-page flier and the Wright Report suppressed.[42]

That was wrong, and it made Clark exceedingly angry, especially since the most likely source for this was either Senator Fletcher or Governor Gilchrist, which meant Welliver had been fed deliberate disinformation to blindside Clark. Clark had been the federal prosecutor who had prosecuted Napoleon Broward in 1895 for running guns and guerrillas to the Cuban revolutionaries in his tug *Three Friends* in violation of the U.S. neutrality laws. Since then, everyone assumed that he was against the drainage project because he was an enemy of Broward. In fact, he and Broward had buried the hatchet after the start of the Spanish-American War in 1898, largely because Broward, unlike many Broward associates such as J.M. Barrs, refused to taunt Clark as a drunkard (he was a recovered alcoholic), even when they were working on opposing sides of an issue. Thus, while they may not have been good friends, they could, and

Frank Clark, U.S. Representative for Florida, 1905–25. As a federal attorney, Clark prosecuted Napoleon Broward in the 1890s for running guns and contraband to the nationalist revolutionaries in Cuba. Broward was convicted, but the conviction was mooted by the Spanish-American War of 1898. Photograph taken about 1912 by Clinedinst of Washington, D.C. (Library of Congress No. LC-USZ62-111670).

did, work together when they had mutual interests. Their relationship was based on pragmatism. In fact, Clark helped campaign for Broward's drainage district constitutional amendment in 1906.

Clark was even more incensed by Welliver's assertion that Duncan Fletcher was the hero who had fought to get the information out by compiling *Senate Document No. 89*, which was scheduled to be released any day. Clark did not know the full story yet, but he knew that Wright, Will and Jennings had edited the version of Wright's report that appeared in the Senate document, and he doubted that anything good could come out of that.[43]

Clark took his anger out on Secretary Wilson. Clark wrote Wilson on October 20, reminding him that he and four landowners had called on Wilson in spring 1910 about the one-page flier. According to Clark, at this meeting Wilson had said that the flier had already been recalled, and that Bulletin 218 would be out in about ten days. (Clark did not mention the rumor alleging that Wilson said at this meeting that he wasn't in the business of protecting people too stupid to buy land without looking at it first.)

Clark asked when the original report would now be published. Wilson replied with an opaque answer that could be interpreted to mean that the "original" report would be published in a few days as part of *Senate Document No. 89* or that the Department had the one and only copy of the "original" Wright Report and that with the imminent publication of *Senate Document No. 89*, they saw no reason to do anything with it. (This may have been a reference to the Elliott version, of which there was in fact only one copy in existence, in Elliott's desk since early 1910.)[44]

Clark wrote back complaining that was just the problem: the version of the Wright Report had been edited by Jennings, Wright, and that salesman, Will, so nobody could know what was supposed to be in it. Wilson wrote to Clark, in more detail this time, and said he had talked with Elliott, who told him that the original report was not satisfactory, and that he, Elliott, was the person who ordered the first version cancelled. He would look into it further and get back to Clark with more details.[45]

The confusion could have been within the Department of Agriculture. When Clark demanded to known the status of the "original" copy of the Wright Report, the secretary's office told Elliott's division to retrieve all their "original" copies. Elliott's office thought this meant the extract given to Henry Hall and the State of Florida, which was simply a 16-page manuscript of which one original and a few carbon copies had been made. Elliott dutifully transmitted the original and honestly told Wilson there were no copies, and this is what Wilson informed Clark. During this period, it is difficult to discern to what extent the parties were cross-talking because they were genuinely confused about what each other meant by "original," and to what degree they were being disingenuous or deceptive. (There was one copy of the Elliott version. It was in Elliott's desk in October 1911. There were three typewritten copies of Wright's May 1909 manuscript which nobody knew about until they were found in a storeroom in February 1912. It is unknown how many copies of the galley proof of Bulletin 218 there were; a handful at most.)[46]

So things kept snowballing. Wright wrote A.C. True on October 27 to complain that Elliott was either misquoted or lying when he said that Wright had been fired and demanded a recommendation letter. True replied with an accommodating letter: Wright had discontinued employment on February 15, 1910, through voluntary resignation to accept a position with greater pay and responsibilities with the State of Florida.[47]

Actually, this was as much a shading of the truth as was Welliver's article. Wright had incurred the disfavor of Elliott and True starting in late 1909 due to his involvement in some drainage districts in North Carolina, which appear to have encroached over the line into becoming matters of personal interest, to the extent of pulling strings with congressmen and Assistant Secretary Hays to get permission to travel there beyond the Department's guidelines against expending a disproportionate share of the division's budget in any one congressional district.[48]

Elliott and True were seriously discussing whether to transfer Wright to another field office or fire him when Wright announced that he was leaving for Florida. "That seemed to be a solution to a rather acute question in our office, and we were glad to let the matter pass," Elliott recalled. Wright asked for a furlough, which would have let him take up temporary contract work from the Department in the future. This was customary for resigning professional-level employees in good standing. Elliott did not consider Wright to be in good standing, and a furlough was refused, although technically, he did resign.[49]

On October 30, W.R. Hardee, one of the men who claimed to have accompanied Frank Clark to Secretary Wilson's office when Clark went to find out why the Wright Report had not been issued, wrote a letter to the Jacksonville *Metropolis*. Seeking to rebut the charges that Clark was one of the legislators trying to suppress the report, Hardee recounted the meeting, which he claimed happened as far back as December 1909. This would have been helpful to Clark as far as it went, but Hardee went on to claim that Wilson said at the meeting that the "report" (probably referring to the one-page circular) "had been suppressed at the request of those interested in the sale of Everglades lands," and that "I [Wilson] am not running this office for the protection of fools who do not know any better than to buy something that they did not see and do not know anything about."[50] (Clark himself claimed only that Wilson had said that the Department would not issue anything so long as the state's legislative delegation was in such discord. Will recalled Wilson saying almost exactly the same thing when they spoke a few days later.[51]) Wilson flatly denied the substance of Hardee's letter.[52]

Panic was slowly growing at the offices of the Everglades Land Sales Company. "I am enclosing another article, this appearing in yesterday's Chicago *Examiner*," wrote V.W. Helm to Will on December 7, "It might be well also for you to see our friend Frank Plummer." Plummer was an Everglades Land Sales Company vice president in Jacksonville. Representative Clark, a real estate broker, had a few years earlier tried to arrange a sale of land involving Plummer and Helm along the St. Johns River near Jacksonville. Earlier, he had sponsored an appropriation bill to construct a drainage canal for the region. Helm was suggesting that Will try to blackmail Clark.[53]

The next day Judson Welliver published his next installment. This time he correctly identified the one-page flier and the Wright Report and gave an accurate timeline of each. Much of the article was concerned with the lawsuit by the trustees of the Florida Fruit Lands Company against R.J. Bolles, and suggested that a congressional investigation was imminent, possibly involving the land sales company, possibly concerning the suppression of the Elliott version of the Everglades report.[54]

Elliott was out on a field survey for five weeks until November 12. When he returned there were two demands waiting for him. First, Representative Clark wanted a complete timeline for the Everglades report. Second, Attorney General Wikersham had written that the report had been subpoenaed and requested a copy immediately. With the only copy of the Elliott version in his desk, he ordered it duplicated and sent to Wikersham. Wikersham's clerk sent it back, saying that was not what he wanted—he wanted the "real" report, the one J.O. Wright had written. Elliott responded that there was no such Department of Agriculture bulletin, and they should consult with Mr. Wright or Senator Fletcher for further details about any reports prepared by Mr. Wright, possibly those appearing in *Senate Document No. 89*, which was not a Department publication.[55]

That crisis temporarily out of the way, Elliott prepared a lengthy chronology for the Secretary on November 21.[56] Anyone reading this report would have the pertinent information of the story so far, and most importantly, would be aware of the different versions of the Everglades report. Moreover, one would know that the term "original" when it came to the Everglades report was meaningless; it would be necessary to specify what document, at which stage of the production process one was referring to. Elliott also presented some frank opinions about what had gone wrong. In essence, a very large, very expensive survey had been attempted on the cheap. The result was inadequate data, bad data, borrowed data, or sheer guesswork, all thrown together. Second, the project was led by an engineer who did not know his limitations or, for reasons known only to himself, did not care.

Unknown to Elliott, the Secretary's office had also solicited a narrative statement from Wright a few days after Elliott's report. He essentially gave his side of the story, but it is clear he was specifically asked if he had seen or heard of any requests for the suppression of his report. He said he had not. He believed the one-page circular had been stopped by the Secretary in February 1910 because it was incorrect, which he agreed with. He believed it was intentionally misleading and designed to discourage Everglades land sales. Wright verified the meeting in Jacksonville in September 1911 in which he, Jennings and Fletcher edited the printer's dummy submitted by Morehouse so that it would "conform to the manuscript secured from your department." (He did not explain why they needed to edit the dummy "to conform" to the Wright Report if they had already "secured" a copy of it.) He concluded that "Although the report has not been published, the drainage work is going forward.... Every fact stated in the report by me has been absolutely verified, so far as the work has advanced. It matters little now to the state or the country at large whether this report is published or not. The reclamation of the Everglades is an assured fact."[57]

He may have told Wilson that it didn't matter to him but did. He took the text of his statement, expanded it significantly, and published it as a brochure entitled "Why Was Wright's Report Suppressed?" Actually, the Internal Improvement Fund published it, paying for 3000 copies of it. In it, Wright did address the rumor that he had been offered the job of chief engineer in Florida in exchange for a favorable report. According to Wright, he received a telegram from the plaintiffs in the Everglades Drainage District litigation asking him if he would consider the job, and if so, how much he would want for the job. What he didn't say was that this salary, $5,000 was more than double his salary at the Agriculture Department ($2,250).[58]

Three weeks later, on December 15, somebody leaked a copy of Elliott's memo to the Jacksonville *Metropolis*, the hometown paper of William Jennings and Duncan Fletcher.[59] At about this time, Elliott was called into a meeting in the Secretary's office with the Department's Solicitor, George McCabe, Mr. Ashley, McCabe's investigator, and Secretary Wilson. Wilson said there was going to be a congressional investigation, and that they needed to start gathering up all the correspondence and files relating to the Everglades survey and everything else related to their Everglades and Florida work. At a follow-up meeting with Ashley and McCabe, Elliott turned over the three copies of

Wright's manuscript that had been found in a storeroom. McCabe told Elliott to begin preparing a three-column document: No.1 would be the May 1909 manuscript; No. 2 would be the Bulletin 218 galley proof in the version it was in when Elliott ordered the printing stopped on October 1, 1909; No. 3 would be the Elliott version. Ashley said he would have three carbons prepared, one each for McCabe, Ashley and Elliott. By using three stenographers, Elliott finished this on December 28.[60]

Immediately after the New Year's holiday, Elliott went to McCabe's office to get his copy. McCabe told him that he could not have a copy of the 3-in-1, nor could he have any of the materials used to prepare it back. Asked why, McCabe said that he was protecting the Secretary's business. A.C. True sent a memo to Elliott the next day saying he had violated office policy by giving all the copies of the material to McCabe and Ashley. Elliott replied that he could hardly refuse an order of the Solicitor of the Department of Agriculture, especially when he chose to lie to his fellow employees. True simply repeated his order that Elliott secure a copy of all the documents he gave McCabe. Elliott began to suspect that he was getting sandbagged, especially when McCabe explained that he thought the biggest problem he saw in reviewing the reports was Elliott's attitude, insinuating that he had not done enough to protect the Secretary's interests. He went looking for a lawyer.[61]

Wright later gave a muddled account of his actions in the fall of 1911 and early 1912. He said that in September, he met with Elliott and Morehouse on good terms in Washington. When the Welliver articles came out, he wrote the letter to A.C. True, asking for the recommendation letter. He never did explain why he didn't write Elliott directly, and he later said that he never knew if Elliott ever read the letter he sent to True. Wright claimed the Jacksonville *Metropolis* article of December 15 was the reason for his subsequent actions, but admitted "the article was garbled," which was true. "It said that if I would make a favorable report I would be taken on down there at an advance in salary." It did not, nor did Elliott's November 21 report make any reference to this issue, although Judson Welliver's article on October 15 did allude to it.[62]

On January 20, Wright was in Washington on other business and met with Thomas Will in Washington in the morning, then with Mr. A. Zappone, head auditor for the Department of Agriculture. From his office in Tallahassee, Wright wrote V.W. Helm: "I have bottled up Elliott while I was in Washington, so there will be no further criticism from him." Confused, Helm wrote Will to ask him what Wright was talking about. Will, recounting his morning meeting with Wright, said that Wright "charged that a number of gross irregularities, for which Mr. Elliott is directly responsible, have occurred in his division. It was Wright's belief that 'Elliott has been hushed up at the department.'"[63]

Wright's effort to "bottle up" the controversy spun out of control. On February 3, Secretary Wilson fired Elliott and his assistant A.D. Morehouse, and suspended the accountant of the office of experimental stations, F.E. Singleton, for misuse of funds.[64] Clark released to the press the 3,000-word report that Elliott had sent to Wilson on November 21, the document that Frank Huffaker based his Jacksonville *Metropolis* story on. Overnight, the national press turned the narrative from a "suppressed report" story into a whistleblower's saga. On February 8, the *New York Times* reported that the "misuse of funds" involved the year-end shifting of $900 in funds between the drainage division and the irrigations division. Neither division had a separate appropriation; the only Congressional line item was for the entire Office of Experiment Stations. It then developed that Elliott's division actually ran a surplus; it was the irrigation division that needed to make up a shortfall. It was unexplained how or why Elliott had broken any rules.[65]

Two days later it was reported that J.O. Wright, chief drainage engineer of the State of Florida, was the one who had brought the charges against Elliott and Morehouse. Arthur Morgan, now in private practice, wrote to Representative Moss that Wright had made the charges at the behest of Secretary Wilson in order "to cover up his embarrassing position" regarding the Everglades report. Morgan wrote: "Mr. Elliott rather unwisely talked to a friend and told him he understood the report was held up because the Florida people did not want it published, which was the statement the Secretary made to him. This brought out the Florida Congressman [Clark] at once with denials, and Mr. Elliott is attacked from the two sides and obliged to shield the Secretary and keep still."[66]

But now there was this new accusation, that the Everglades drainage investigation report had been sanitized in William Jennings's law office before appearing in *Senate Document No. 89*. Indeed, it could be possible that *Senate Document No. 89* was produced only in order to get an expunged version of Elliott's report out and stifle the version that drainage investigations intended to release.[67]

Agriculture Department solicitor McCabe denied any wrongdoing or cover up. Clark claimed that McCabe *was* covering up. Representative Ralph Moss of Indiana, chairman of the Committee on Expenditures in the Department of Agriculture, announced that hearings were needed, and scheduled the first session for Saturday, February 13. Thomas Will guessed the hearings would take about three weeks.

They required 42 sessions and did not conclude until August.

5

It Looks Peculiar to Me

> That Solicitor McCabe was determined to get rid of Dr. Wiley was perfectly plain, but what was surprising was that the Secretary of Agriculture should have allowed him to, in effect, manage someone else's department.... It seems probable that the President can reach only one conclusion: that Secretary Wilson, being 78 years of age, has outlived his usefulness and his place should be taken by someone who will attend to business and not relegate it to subordinates; and that Mr. McCabe, evidently too big a man for the place he occupies and having no respect for the courts, for his fellow workers in the Department, or for Congress, should give way to a better and safer man.
>
> —Dr. Henry T. Brooks, September 1911[1]

The House Committee on Agriculture was not a neutral ground. It was used to controversy. In fact, the scheduling of the Everglades hearings had to wait until February so work could be completed on the final report for what had proven to be an equally scandalous matter, the so-called "Wiley-McCabe Affair."

The mutual mistrust between the Department of Agriculture and the House Agriculture Committee went back before this, all the way to 1905. That year, C. Hart Merriam of the Biological Survey of the Interior Department and Gilbert Pinchot convinced President Theodore Roosevelt to transfer thousands of acres of timberland out of the Interior Department's General Land Office (predecessor of the Bureau of Land Management) into a newly created Forestry Service of the Department of Agriculture, headed by Pinchot. The legislation provided that the Forestry Service receive no annual appropriation, but instead had the power to retain all funds earned from timber sales and other fees in a "special fund" that was carried over from one fiscal year to the next without need for congressional authorization. In other words, Pinchot had almost complete financial autonomy.

Wilson himself had mixed feelings about his huge new bureau. "He [Pinchot] is a fine fellow himself," Wilson wrote Roosevelt in July 1905, "but he has some eight hundred people under him now, and we have quietly let out a good number of them who were transferred from the Interior Department, because they were not the kind of people we feel like carrying."[2] The act never went through the Agriculture Committee, and as Colorado Congressman Henry Moore Teller explained, "I have never doubted that the Government of the United States could take any measures necessary to protect its property by Congressional act, but I do deny that an executive officer of the Government has the right to legislate as to how lands shall be preserved." Pinchot overplayed his hand when he began levying road fees, canal fees, and other user charges to timber companies and other lessees that were not envisioned in the 1905 transfer legislation. The 1907 federal appropriations bill eliminated the Forest Service's "special fund" and curtailed most of its extended rule-making authority.[3]

President Taft was inaugurated in March 1909 and a month later began ordering the return of timberlands from various categories of reserved and protected lands back to

Theodore Roosevelt and Gifford Pinchot onboard the presidential yacht *Mayflower*, 1907. Pinchot was one of Roosevelt's closest and most trusted advisors. Photographer unknown. (Library of Congress No. LC-US26-55630).

the General Land Office (GLO). In addition, he named as Interior Secretary Richard A. Ballinger, who had been GLO Commissioner from January 1907 until March 1908, when he returned to private life as a land and timber lawyer in Seattle. In mid–1909 GLO agent L.R. Glavis uncovered evidence that Ballinger, during the interim between his resignation from the GLO and his appointment as Interior Secretary, had doctored a series of 33 questionable coal-bearing land claims in Alaska originally applied for in 1904 by a prospector named Clarence Cunningham, who subsequently optioned them to a Guggenheim-backed investment pool operating out of Seattle for a hundred times what he paid for them. After being appointed Interior Secretary, Ballinger then allegedly tried to get these claims perfected without the necessary review. Because the land in question was within the Chugach National Forest, Glavis informed Forest Service agents O.W. Price and A.C. Shaw, who joined his investigation. Glavis met with Shaw and Pinchot in August 1909 and they assisted him in preparing a brief against Ballinger, which Glavis presented to President Taft on August 17, 1909. Glavis was subsequently reassigned, then discharged on Taft's orders.[4]

Richard Ballinger, Head of Government Land Office; later Secretary of the Interior. The accusation—backed up by Gifford Pinchot—that Ballinger had manipulated the sale of Alaskan coal leases to a strawman fronting for wealthy New York investors led to a joint House/Senate investigation committee and the effective end of his career. Theodore Roosevelt was so enraged that he decided to run against his hand-picked successor, William H. Taft, guaranteeing the end of 16 years of Republican rule in the White House. Photograph c. 1909 (Library of Congress No. LC-USZ62-97993).

Taft issued a directive prohibiting government employees from communicating with Congress or the press, but after Glavis was fired, Price and Shaw took their evidence to *Collier's* magazine, which published it. They were fired by Wilson for violating the presidential directive against public communications. In January 1910 Senator Dolliver, Chairman of the Senate Agriculture Committee, sent a letter to Pinchot requesting information about the Cunningham claims and the firing of Glavis. Pinchot prepared a letter in response defending Glavis's investigation and the work of Price and Shaw. Wilson ordered him not to reply to Dolliver. Pinchot sent the letter anyway, which Dolliver read on the floor of the Senate. Taft then fired Pinchot. The letter, and Pinchot's firing, enraged Roosevelt, who was hunting in Africa at the time. Upon returning, he announced that he would unseat Taft as the Republican nominee for president at the upcoming Republican convention in 1912, opening two years of internecine warfare within the Republican party.[5]

A joint congressional investigation into the "Pinchot-Ballinger Affair" was authorized in March. In the process of forming this committee, House Republicans revolted against their own speaker, Joseph Cannon, when he used his traditional power of committee assignment to select Republican congressmen loyal to Taft and unsympathetic to the more conservation-minded Roosevelt without consulting his membership. House Republicans, led by George Norris of Nebraska, rose up in the "St. Patrick's Day Revolt," joining Democrats in passing a rules resolution that stripped the speaker of the power to make committee assignments. The Republican congressmen then caucused among themselves and voted on who they wanted to fill the three House Republican seats on the twelve-man bipartisan house/senate joint investigation panel.[6]

Publisher Robert Collier had been warned prior to the start of the hearing that Ballinger would try to sue the magazine for libel, and that the government attorneys would concentrate on gathering testimony that could be used in such a lawsuit. Collier hired Louis Brandeis, a superb courtroom examiner, to act as counsel for Glavis. It was an inspired choice. Ballinger was an anti-Semite who couldn't—or wouldn't—hide his repugnance at being interrogated by a Jew.

A contemporary report summarized the hearing this way: "A vast amount of testimony was taken.... The accusers of Mr. Ballinger were unable to bring convincing proof of actual misconduct in office, while Mr. Ballinger's attitude on the stand showed personal resentment and feeling to such a degree as to prejudice many against him." One of the revelations that came out during the hearings was that Attorney General George Wickersham had backdated his investigatory report into the Glavis case to make it appear that he had prepared it before Glavis's dismissal, the false implication being that Taft had made his decision based on Wickersham's information.[7]

In December 1910 a Republican majority and Democratic minority report were issued. The majority determined that the charges against Ballinger were not adequately substantiated and recommended no action as to Pinchot and the other three men. The minority report agreed that there was no definitive proof of wrongdoing, but recommended that Ballinger resign, as he had lost the confidence of the public.[8] The extent to which the Roosevelt—Taft rift was splitting the Republican party was exemplified by a concurrence to the minority report submitted by Republican Congressman Edwin Madison of Wisconsin, who crossed over to the Democrats' side to such an extent as to go beyond their recommendations:

> Conservation means elimination of waste in dealing with our natural resources. It should not prohibit present-day use where the use is required, but it is a crime, not alone against the present but future generations, to permit the waste of our minerals, our lands and our forests.... I regret that I am compelled to arrive at a conclusion different from that which was arrived at by the President ... in that the charges by L.R. Glavis against Secretary Ballinger should be sustained ... the charges made by Mr. Pinchot should be sustained; that Mr. Ballinger's course in the administration of the General Land Office and the and in the Department of the Interior has been characterized by a lack of fidelity to the public interest ... and he should not be retained in office.[9]

A month after the final report was issued, in the 1910 mid-term elections, the Democrats gained a majority in the House of Representatives, partially due to the Pinchot-Ballinger scandal, much more to the Republican party disarray resulting from the Roosevelt–Taft feud that the scandal first exposed. President Taft's brother, congressman Charles Taft, had been pressing his brother to get rid of Ballinger since the start of the hearings, and on March 12, 1911, he resigned. Secretary of Agriculture James Wilson had all of three months to catch his breath before the next, even bigger scandal broke, this one in his own front yard.

II

Harvey Washington Wiley was the Agriculture Department's Chief of the Bureau of Chemistry. The acknowledged expert on the adulteration of foods, he was the man President Roosevelt turned to when the muckraking reportage of Sinclair Lewis and Ida Tarbell on filthy packinghouses and quack medicines appalled and disgusted a nation. Wiley drew up much of the Pure Food and Drugs Act and lobbied Congress for its approval in 1906. After the law became effective at the start of 1907, Wiley took charge of its administration. Or rather, tried to take charge.

He immediately came into conflict with the Department's Solicitor, George McCabe. McCabe, and the position of Solicitor itself, were new to the Department. The office of the solicitor had been created in 1905, and McCabe was its first incumbent.[10] The solicitor's office reflected the increased complexity of a Department that had grown from 925 professional-level employees when Wilson was appointed by President McKinley in 1897 to 3,750 in 1911. Many questioned whether Wilson, now 78 years old, a man with less than a year at Grinnell College, and who had never been anything other than a farmer before entering politics, had become an anachronism in an increasingly modernized, scientific world. A native of Utah, McCabe was young, admitted to the District of Columbia bar only in October 1902. He believed his office should administrate the Pure Food and Drug Act, which he saw as primarily a legal and administrative matter, and only secondarily an issue of laboratory expertise.[11]

But others believed McCabe was acting more as a one-man praetorian guard for Secretary Wilson. Before McCabe, that role had fallen to Wilson's son and private secretary, Jasper Wilson. Federal attorney Henry Martyn described the younger Wilson to Solicitor General William Moody in a letter written when he, the solicitor and Secretary Wilson were all investigating an allegation made in 1905 that someone in the USDA was leaking cotton production statistics to commodity traders, who were using them to rig cotton prices on the commodity exchanges:

> There has been a great deal of rumor about the Secretary's son and private secretary, Jasper Wilson … the general theory is that he is somewhat sinister and tough, and they go on to intimate that the pending lines of inquiry will finally run towards him … it is observable that young Mr. Wilson surrounds his father at all times and keeps undeviating watch and ward between him and the public. This is natural enough in order to protect and serve a father; but this scrupulous surveillance is somewhat noticeable just now … it would be well for Mr. Jasper Wilson to take a leave of thirty days at this juncture.[12]

Attorney Hoyt went on to say that he was less concerned about any possible involvement of Jasper Wilson in the sale of insider information than he was worried about spoliation of any evidence that young Wilson may come across that would be embarrassing to his father or would contradict any of his public statements, regardless of whether they were relevant to the current investigation. Hiring McCabe allowed Secretary Wilson to pull Jasper out of the public spotlight, although he did keep him on as private secretary until he retired in 1913. However, many felt that McCabe was just a better educated,

Harvey Washington Wiley, 1910. Given charge of enforcing the Pure Food and Drug Act of 1906 by President Roosevelt, the Agriculture Department's Chief Chemist was shunted aside by Agriculture Secretary Wilson and Solicitor George McCabe at the direction of Roosevelt's successor, William Howard Taft. McCabe and Wilson's attempt to fire and criminally prosecute Wiley for a trivial violation of an obscure department rule backfired when a congressional committee found flagrant mismanagement and abuse of power in the office of the Secretary and caught the Solicitor lying in his testimony. Photography by Harris and Ewing (Library of Congress No. LC-DIG-ds-13408 [P&P]).

slightly more polished version of the thuggish Jasper.

Both Wilson and McCabe clearly believed that McCabe's primary function was to protect Wilson and the Office of the Secretary. However, Wiley was a self-confident, outgoing if not flamboyant man who tended to see all problems through the lens of scientific expertise, and who often dismissed issues of procedure, public relations, and politics as distractions or outright interference. If the science called for some action to be taken, there was nothing else to discuss as far as he was concerned, and he was the man who knew and controlled the science.

In 1907, as the Department was putting together the apparatus to enforce the new law, Wilson hired as Assistant Chief Chemist Dr. F.L. Dunlap, an adjunct professor at the University of Michigan. Although his title and his location on the Department's organizational chart placed him as Wiley's assistant, he did not report to Wiley, nor did he work in the chemistry lab. He reported to Secretary Wilson through McCabe and his job was to oversee the processing of Pure Food and Drug enforcement actions. Wiley, Dunlap and McCabe made up an administrative board organized by McCabe called the "Board of Food and Drug Inspection."[13]

In theory, Wiley's laboratory would uncover an adulteration or a harmful substance and would pass it to the Board of Food and Drug Inspection. It, in turn, would process the necessary paperwork and if action was appropriate, forward it on to the Department of Justice. More often, it would defer or kill the recommendation on a 2–1 vote, with Wiley on the losing side. In 1909 McCabe added a further layer of protection with the Remsen Referee Board. Technically it was called the Remsen Board of Consulting Chemists, after chairman Ira Remsen, president of Johns Hopkins University. Although all were part-time advisory employees, they received salaries of $2,000 to $4,000, compared to Wiley's $5,000 a year.[14]

If an enforcement action had originated in Wiley's lab, gone through the Board of Food and Drug Inspection, been forwarded to the Department of Justice and resulted in a citation or lawsuit, the adversely affected firm could appeal the action to the Remsen Board. Three years after it was set up, Ira Remsen testified that he had never consulted Dr. Wiley, or even met him, although the Remsen Board had met several times with Secretary Wilson.[15]

Halting or postponing the processing of an enforcement action was called "abeyance." One of the more frequently used grounds for moving an action into permanent abeyance status was the so-called "Three-Month Rule." To prevent the inadvertent prosecution of a firm that had already self-corrected a non-conforming product as a result of the Pure Food and Drug Act, Wiley recommended that any laboratory finding of an impure, unsafe or ineffective substance be pulled out of the enforcement process if it had not been forwarded to the food and drug board within fifteen months. McCabe took Wiley's proposal and changed it to three months and made the statute of limitations dependent on when the food and drug board reported out its findings to the Department of Justice. Thus, McCabe and Dunlap could nullify the work of Wiley just by sitting on his recommendation for action for a few weeks.

Dr. Ira Remsen. Distinguished chemist and president of the Johns Hopkins University, he likely did not understand the extent to which Agriculture Secretary Wilson and Solicitor George McCabe were using his name to foil the enforcement provisions of the Pure Food and Drug Act, although he was unusually well compensated considering the time he was putting in as the head of department's Board of Consulting Chemists. Photograph 1909 by Pach Bros (Library of Congress No. LC-BZ-795-10 [P&P]).

Although few citations were reversed, the process for issuing new citations effectively ground to a halt. McCabe asserted that from January 1, 1907, the effective date of the act, through July 1911, his office had sent 2,765 cases to the Department of Justice for prosecution. Of these, 1,992 were criminal cases against shippers of adulterated and misbranded products, and 772 were seizures. About 1,400 were prosecuted and a decision in favor of the government was secured by the Justice Department.[16] But in 1910, after the abeyance procedure was put into place, 2,326 of 3,521 recommendations from Wiley's lab had been held in abeyance, and only about 520 of those passed on to the Justice Department had resulted in the issuance of a sanction that survived a Remsen Board appeal. Dr. Wiley estimated that by the end of 1911, more than 6,200 referrals had been moved into abeyance, 1,300 under the three-month rule alone.[17]

Some of reversals handed down were egregious. The whisky industry had been cited for "juicing" cheap, quickly manufactured product with grain alcohol and caramel coloring to reduce (or eliminate entirely) the need for barrel aging. The Remsen Board ruled that such product could continue to be called "whiskey," but if only pure ethanol and natural colorings were used—no wood alcohol, which could kill you. This reversed a customs house tradition in place since before the founding of the country that only grains and malts aged in charcoal-lined barrels could go into a product called "whiskey."[18]

But Wiley also stumbled. His most embarrassing failure was an enforcement action against the Coca-Cola Company for failing to list caffeine as one of its ingredients. The Department's own chemists could not agree whether the drink's (admittedly high—much higher than today) caffeine content came entirely from two of its main listed ingredients, kola nut extract and coca leaves, or whether unlisted caffeine citrate was added. At the end of the government's case, the court ordered a directed verdict in favor of Coca-Cola without the need for the firm to present a defense.[19]

A personality clash was inevitable. By 1910, Wiley and McCabe were spending more time fighting each other than enforcing the Pure Food and Drug Act. McCabe had a good mastery of legislative and administrative process and procedure, but he had a poor courtroom (or, more often, hearing-room) demeanor. He was an impatient, petulant questioner, was not quick on his feet and easily frustrated, and tended to personalize what were essentially workaday legal or administrative conflicts. Wiley had been recognized for many years as a leading scientist and could not take being treated like a piece of laboratory equipment, which is fundamentally how Wilson and McCabe saw him.

Wiley owned an apple orchard in his home state of Indiana. Each fall, after Washington's traditional summer break, he would return with a bushel of his newest hybrids. McCabe plucked a couple of moldy orphans out of the bottom of one basket, sent them to the lab, and cited McCabe for the interstate transportation of spoiled food products. Less trivial was the Heinz food matter. A.P. Heinz of Pittsburgh ran his pickle and sauce business as an experiment in corporate paternalism. Heavily dependent on female labor, he imported factory and management techniques from Europe to maintain a stable, healthy workforce. Unlike most of his fellow food industrialists, he was an early supporter of Wiley's research into safe food preservation and pickling techniques. Because of his support, Heinz became a target for harassment by McCabe, who filed a Pure Food and Drug Act enforcement action again him, alleging "Heinz India Relish" was deceptively labeled because it was not made in India.[20]

The so-called Wiley-McCabe affair began in the spring of 1911. Henry Rusby was a chemist and instructor at the New York College of Pharmacy. He had been one of Wiley's witnesses at the ill-fated Coca-Cola trial, and was a part-time Department of Agriculture employee, assaying drugs brought through the Port of New York. He was paid 20 dollars a day, but that was cut to nine dollars, the most permitted by the Department's pay schedule for by-the-day help. The Department's payroll schedule was ludicrous; devised in an era when the Agriculture Department hired field hands, not engineers and chemists, it had not been updated since before Wilson became Secretary. Over the years a number of workarounds had been devised by supervisors and division chiefs. Wiley used one of the more common, putting Rusby on an annual salary of $1,600 with the proviso that he would work for 80 days per year.

McCabe discovered the arrangement. The rules said salaried personnel could only work on a full-time basis. He turned the case over to Attorney General Wikersham, who issued an opinion agreeing that the arrangement was illegal but held that the violation was so *de minimus* that it did not warrant action by the Department of Justice. Wilson clearly intended to dismiss Wiley, but Congressman Ralph Moss, chair of the House Committee on Agriculture, and a Democrat from Wiley's home state of Indiana, intervened and convened a series of hearings starting in mid–1911.[21]

The hearings uncovered correspondence revealing the extent to which McCabe and Wilson wanted to get rid of Wiley; McCabe's efforts to harass Wiley and his personal and professional associates; the extent to which the hourly and salaried pay schedules within the Department were a shambles and laughingly ignored by middle management along with a host of other unworkable rules; and probably most of all, the desperate efforts of Wilson, old, tired and sick of Washington, to get everyone to be quiet, keep their heads down, and get along until the new administration (which, if Theodore Roosevelt made good on his promise to run as a third-party candidate, would almost certainly be Democratic, probably Woodrow Wilson) was inaugurated in March 1913 and he could go home to Iowa.

Not only did Congressman Moss feed Wiley each day's information, witness list and documents, he helped him secure the services of two veteran Washington defense lawyers, Henry Davis and former congressman William Hepburn. Moss made it clear that the hearings were less about Wiley and Rusby than the honesty and efficiency of the Department's enforcement of the Pure Food and Drug Act. As *The Literary Digest* put it: "When the Moss committee started out to find who wants Dr. Wiley fired and why, it was predicted that there would be some interesting disclosures. Now the newspapers are almost with one accord in agreeing that if anyone is to be fired, it is not Wiley, but Mr. George P. McCabe, Solicitor of the Department of Agriculture."[22]

Wiley told the Moss committee that McCabe's office maintained a "Permanent Abeyance Register" of referrals from his office that had been effectively killed. Moss asked McCabe if such a thing existed. McCabe replied, "Not that I know of." Unconvinced, Moss sent a letter to Secretary Wilson asking the same thing. Two days later, Wilson replied that he had the register in his office, but that it was incomplete and would have to be updated. "I am not willing to send an incomplete list, which would only give the committee an incomplete view of the situation." The implication was this "updating" would take an extensive amount of time, possibly several months. Moss replied that he would subpoena the log, and Wilson could update it after the committee received it. Wilson produced it. Only about 24 updates were subsequently transmitted. As Wiley asserted, the log ran into the thousands.[23]

A decided chill descend over the relationship between Representative Moss and Solicitor McCabe. But while Moss did a thorough job of raking Wilson and McCabe over the coals, in the end he chose not to go for the kill. In his final report, he found mismanagement everywhere, but it was hard to argue that on his own, Wiley had assembled an effective enforcement bureaucracy, or that McCabe, Dunlap, Remsen or even Wilson had knowingly acted to shield wrongdoers. To achieve some degree of consensus between the Republicans and Democrats on the committee, the report, when it appeared, was surprisingly bland, the hard decision-making kicked down the road to the 1912 budget authorization hearings for the Department of Agriculture, which would occur too late to affect the 1912 elections. On March 15, 1912, Wiley resigned. A few weeks later, President Taft wrote him a letter exonerating him and commending him for his years of service to the government.

With the Wiley-McCabe Affair out of the way, Ralph Moss scheduled the Everglades matter, technically assigned to a subcommittee, the Committee on Expenditures Within the Department of Agriculture, but with almost the same personnel as the earlier hearings. After the final report was issued on January 22, McCabe requested a delay in order to get his office prepared for the upcoming hearings. Moss said he could have until February 3.

III

The committee convened briefly on Saturday so Representative Bathrick of Ohio (D), could make a formal request for an investigation, along with a brief statement of his grounds for the request, largely based on the suppression of the Everglades report, then adjourned.[24] On Tuesday, the committee's work began in earnest. Frank Clark (D) of Florida, who, along with Bathrick had requested the inquiry, presented his reasons for petitioning the committee. However, he concluded not with a discussion of the Everglades report, but with a foreshadowing of what one newspaper called "yet another Wiley-McCabe affair":

> It looks peculiar to me; I do not understand it. I am not taking any part in the quarrels of the Department of Agriculture; they have enough troubles of their own over there. But this man, J.O. Wilson, in Florida now, in this proposition, shows up here in Washington on the 19th of January, the very day I left to go to Florida.... What is the result? Last Saturday, Mr. Elliott, the chief of the bureau, who has stood out against these flaming reports of Mr. Wright, and Mr. Morehouse, his lieutenant, are notified that their services are no longer needed at the Department; they are fired. This Mr. Wright seems to be a very powerful gentleman.[25]

He could only have received this information from Chairman Moss, who had been informed of Wright's visit to the Department of Agriculture by Wright himself on the evening of January 24, five days after his visit, but a week before Solicitor McCabe and Secretary Wilson decided to use his information to fire Elliott and Morehouse. Even before the first gavel fell on the hearings, Moss was already holding more cards in his hands than anyone else and was dispensing them strategically.[26]

The real start of the hearings was the opening statement of Solicitor McCabe. There had been confusion in the press between the Wright Report and the double-sided, mimeographed circular with basic meteorological, soil and drainage information about the Everglades that Elliott's office had circulated in January 1910 when the Wright Report (Bulletin 218) was held up.

After explaining this, McCabe had three points to make. First, the one-page circular was an unauthorized publication of the Department, and the Secretary ordered it discontinued because the Wright Report excerpt had already been printed by the Florida legislature, and because the publication of Bulletin 218 was believed to be imminent. Second, Elliott himself ordered that Bulletin 218 be delayed in September 1909. When his revised January 1910 version appeared, parts of it were so heavily criticized by Dr. Goodrich of the Bureau of Plant Industry that a decision was made not to publish it. Third, the dismissal of Elliott and Morehouse concerned financial irregularities in dealing with budget shortfalls in the Division of Irrigation Investigations, and not with anything related to any controversy over the Everglades report.

Immediately, McCabe was besieged with questions. Wasn't it Wright who preferred charges against Elliott and Morehouse? No, but he provided the information. Why did he wait two and a half years? It made him look just as guilty. McCabe didn't know. How much was at stake? One hundred and twenty dollars. Did the money go to Elliott? No, a plantation owner in North Carolina named Wilkinson covered a payroll shortage at the end of fiscal year 1909 and was reimbursed the first month of fiscal year 1910. Is it true that Wright's appointment as chief drainage engineer for the State of Florida was influenced by the content of his report? McCabe had no information about that. And finally, from Frank Clark: "Are you the same Mr. McCabe who figured in the Dr. Wiley case?" Yes.[27]

Mr. Zappone, the chief accountant for the Department of Agriculture was the first witness, called to answer two questions. First, the cost of preparing the Everglades report, including field work, writing, editing and cartography, but not printing, was $11,017, spread over fiscal years 1907–10.

It was harder to explain the alleged improprieties. From the standpoint of the Congressional budget, the Division of Drainage Investigations and the Division of Irrigation Investigations did not exist. There was only a single line-item for both within the Office of Experiment Stations. The Office then made its own in-house administrative sub-allocations, which were not legally binding. Elliott's Division of Drainage Investigations ran a surplus of roughly $400 for the fiscal year ending on June 30, 1909. However, the Division of Irrigation Investigations was $800 in the red. Thus, it appears that when the books were closed on 1909, the Office of Experiment Stations as a whole was short approximately $428. As this was a Congressional line item, it could not be shifted to another section or bureau.

It was hard to budget for the Office of Experiment Stations, because it relied heavily on matching funds from the states to run co-operative stations and college programs, and many states had different fiscal years. Why Elliott's division was expected to help make up for the shortfall when it did not run a deficit was unknown to Zappone—probably because it was assumed that both divisions would go to the same state-level "cooperators" for one-month partial payroll advances to tide everyone over to the start of the next federal fiscal year. Instead, Elliott went to Wilkinson, a wealthy landowner, farmer, and chairman of a drainage district in North Carolina who was already a small-scale federal contractor, for the $120. Zappone did not know why. It was clear that nobody, either inside or outside the Department, realized any personal gain from these fund shifts.[28]

Wright was on the stand for two weeks. Initially, there was little that wasn't already known. He described the Florida investigation in detail. He thought the work of Lawrence Brett was exemplary the first winter of 1907 and that of John Stewart, who was nominally the head of the expedition, of little use, intended mostly to please Dr. Elliott. He did not volunteer the information that Brett roomed with him and his wife. Wright and Elliott had disagreed about who should accompany Wright the second winter and eventually Elliott acquiesced to Wright's wishes that Brett should go along. The writing of the report was delayed because Wright had been assigned to assist Representative Small of North Carolina in drawing up a state drainage law and putting it into place.

He described his involvement in *Senate Document No. 89*.[29] In September 1911, he had been asked by William Jennings to meet with him and Senator Fletcher at Jennings's law office. This was after he had started work for the State of Florida. He could not go that day, but went the next week. Fletcher gave him a galley proof of about 80 pages that he said he had been sent by Mr. Carter of the Joint Committee on Printing, the congressional printing office. It was not a galley proof, but apparently a page proof of the never-issued Bulletin 218 covered with numerous blue-pencil marks, cut-outs and paste-ins, a so-called "printers dummy." Wright said he had a copy of his original manuscript from early 1909, and with the aid of this he was able to revert the dummy back to the Bulletin 218 configuration.[30]

On February 16, four days before Wright's testimony, the Agriculture Department printed the 3-in-1 document that McCabe and Mr. Ashley had prepared in late December as "Exhibit B of No. 5."[31] It was a three-column comparison of Wright's original manuscript, dated (actually, misdated) February 25, 1909, which he completed in late May. This was referred to throughout the hearings as version "No. 1." The middle column was the text of Bulletin 218, dated June 25, 1909, and referred to as the "No. 2" version. In the right-hand column was "No. 3," which was the Elliott Report of January 28, 1910. No printed copy of the Elliott Report was ever prepared prior to this exhibit. When, in 1912, a team of drainage consultants preparing a private report for a Florida land company wanted to incorporate data from the Elliott Report into its document, it had to turn to "No. 3" of "Exhibit B of No. 5," because it was the only published version in existence.[32]

A close reading verifies that the Wright Report included in *Senate Document No. 89* and "No. 2" are, with the exception of a few one-sentence transitions made necessary by its shift from a Department of Agriculture bulletin to a section within a Senate report, identical. The differences between "No. 1," the original Wright manuscript, and "No. 2" are substantial, but primarily editorial. Sections were transposed, excess verbiage was removed, tables rearranged. It is clear that Elliott re-worked it significantly even before Harold Wheeler and Arthur Morgan caught its calculation errors.

This leads to one of the great unsolved mysteries of the hearings. Why would William Jennings and Senator Fletcher have Wright spend six hours in Jennings's law office re-converting a printers dummy of the "No. 3" Elliott Report back to the "No. 2" Wright Report, using a copy of the "No. 1" manuscript, only to end up incorporating a word-for-word reprint of "No. 2" (Bulletin 218), which Fletcher later admitted he had a copy of? Wright himself admitted that the version of the report that appeared in the senate document was his original report as modified by Mr. Beal and Elliott and set up in the print shop for Bulletin 218.[33]

The only other real surprise was Wright's steadfast insistence that he completed the first draft of his report in February 1909 and that the so-called Wright Report excerpt prepared for Henry C. Hall was lifted out of this manuscript. In other words, he maintained in the face of all other evidence and testimony to the contrary, that he had a full, complete manuscript of his report ready as early as February 1909. Nonetheless, he agreed with Elliott that the manuscript did not go to Mr. Beal at the editorial desk of the Office of Experiment Stations until June. Wright also agreed that he was told in the fall of 1909 that the report had been pulled out of the print shop for editorial reasons. He verified the abusive visit of Thomas Will and E.C. Howe to the Division of Drainage Investigations in early February 1910 concerning the mimeographed circular but maintained that several of their arguments were legitimate.

Chairman Moss specifically asked him about the provision in Paragraph 5 of the settlement agreement between the railroad land companies and the Trustees of the Internal Improvement District specifying that he should be hired as chief engineer of the Everglades Drainage District at $5,000 per year. He admitted that it was a condition of the agreement, but said that he did not know about it until he received a telegram from

Tallahassee asking him if he would be interested in the job and how much he would want to be paid. He received a second telegram two days later with a job offer. He was never asked directly if this job offer was conditioned on the contents or conclusions of his Everglades report.[34]

He also testified that his Everglades drainage plan would not drain most of the land in the Everglades Drainage District without private lateral canals, and verified that the land that R.J. Bollis was selling for $240 per ten-acre parcel had cost him fifteen dollars per parcel, and would not be drained even after the first canals were completed in 1916.[35] He believed the agricultural future of the Everglades was sugar cane: "there are a great many crops that can be grown there, but the conclusion I have reached is that the settlement and salvation of the Everglades is sugar cane."[36]

Wright's initial cross-examination by Solicitor McCabe was lengthy and technical, dealing with the alleged drainage calculation errors that Arthur Morgan, Harold Wheeler, Elliott and others had found in Wright's "No. 1" draft. In summary, Elliott's revised figures were not, in terms of volume, that much different from Wright's, but assumed that the state's drainage canals would be much less comprehensive in reclaiming the Everglades. Wright reached a figure of three to five dollars an acre that he believed would definitely reclaim the land south of Lake Okeechobee; Elliott estimated five dollars per acre for a system that would lower Lake Okeechobee, but it was impossible for him state the extent to which lowering Lake Okeechobee would actually reclaim the lands to the south and east, or what agricultural uses they could be put to, without further study.

Like Dr. Wiley, Elliott and Morehouse had hired Henry Davis as their defense attorney. At the close of committee questioning on Friday, Chairman Moss indicated that Davis could begin his cross-examination of Wright Monday morning. After recessing, McCabe went to the Department of Justice and, in what was obviously a pre-arranged move, conferred charges against Elliott and Morehouse with Attorney General Wickersham, asking him to convene a grand jury. Simultaneously, Representative Higgins of the committee, a Republican from Connecticut, filed a motion to suspend the Moss hearings until after the grand jury had returned its report. It was both a stalling tactic and a way to keep the committee from subpoenaing additional documents, probably those that either McCabe had not yet produced, or that he had not yet been able to secure. Moss denied the motion and continued the hearings for Monday morning, February 19, as scheduled.[37]

Davis's cross examination of Wright started with the Wright Report excerpt. Try as hard as he could, Davis could not shake Wright from his story that he finished the entire manuscript on February 25, 1909, and that the so-called Henry Hall excerpt or Wright Report excerpt was lifted out of a finished manuscript. According to Wright, it was not true that the Henry Hall document was a separate, specially prepared 16-page document prepared well in advance of the report's manuscript, which was not finished until late May. Elliott contradicted this story. Beal contradicted this. Morgan contradicted this. Morehouse contradicted this. Still, Wright stuck to his story.[38]

To make the tale even more curious, Secretary Wilson said he never wrote a letter to the drainage division instructing them to prepare (or extract) a report for Henry Hall or anyone else, although he did recall being asked permission to allow the State of Florida to make the extract public after they received it, and he assented to this. Elliott could not clearly recall whether he was given a letter by A.C. True, or verbally instructed by him to have Wright prepare the brief report. True couldn't remember anything. No copy of any letter could be found. Asked about the incident, Henry Hall refused to answer, responding only that he had secured the extract "legally."[39]

The time logs, however, do not support Wright. They indicate that after returning from Florida on April 22, 1908, until February 25, 1909, he was away from the office on field trips, mostly to North Carolina, almost 100 days. He allocated 100 percent of his personnel hours to the Everglades project from January to June 1908, but only 53 percent in July 1908, followed by zero hours each month until February 1909, when he allocated 27 percent to the report. In March and April, after he claimed to have finished the report, he put in 64 percent of March 1909 and 79 percent of April 1909. In other words, after working full time on the project throughout the winter and spring of 1908, he dropped the project completely starting in July 1908 for almost six months, not resuming work on it until (probably) late February 1909, at which time he again worked on it a little over half-time during March–May 1909.[40]

The urgency for the Wright Report appears to have been triggered by a small farmer in what is now Broward County named Charles Root. In June 1907 he homesteaded a parcel of land near Davie Farms by cultivating at least one acre and erecting a home, shed, fences and other improvements. In February 1908 he filed an affidavit with the Florida Commissioner of Agriculture attesting that he was the head of a household, over 21 years old, a citizen of Florida, and had made these improvements for his own use and not with the intention of selling the land. He also paid 20 dollars. Under the provisions of the 1883 Settlers' Act,[41] the Fund should have transferred a deed to 80 acres to him, as it was still owned by the state and otherwise unencumbered.

The trustees refused to do so. Instead, they sold the land to a man named James Cordner without responding to Root. The trustees admitted that at the time they sold the land to Cordner, they knew of Root's pending application. (It appears they didn't tell Cordner, either.[42]) On February 1, 1910, the Florida supreme court issued its first decision in the case. In a brief opinion, they noted that the land Root sought was not "needed" or "vested" to carry out any of the purposes for which the Internal Improvement Fund existed. It was therefore available for homesteading under the Settlers' Act. It was ordered to turn over the land to Root.[43]

The Fund then appealed the case back to the Florida supreme court, which re-heard it two years later. This time, the trustees asserted that under their enabling act of 1855, they were prohibited from selling lands "appropriated or applied" to the task of draining wetlands. Nobody argued with this. But the trustees further argued that under the 1906 enabling legislation creating the Everglades Drainage District, "all of said lands, including the eighty acres in controversy, were necessary for the execution of the work undertaken and begun," because the revenue from big-block sales was needed to finance the project.[44]

A plain reading of the Settlers' Act suggested that while Root could not stake a claim to land designated for canals, the trustees argued that every square foot of the drainage district fell within this same category. In other words, Root argued that "appropriated or applied" defined public *uses* (roads, canals, dikes); the trustees argued that "appropriated or applied" applied to public *uses* and public *purposes* (any land needed to advance a legitimate public interest, even if the public didn't have direct access to it).

The court held in favor of the public *use* definition, not because it was inherently superior, but because it allowed the court to apply the textbook solution to a conflict of laws problem: if two laws potentially conflicted, and one of them can be interpreted in two ways, then it shall be interpreted in the way that allows both laws to peacefully co-exist. The Settler's Act said Root should have the land, the Swamp and Overflowed Lands Act said that all land "necessary" for drainage had to be retained, so "necessary" should be defined as public use, because that meant the laws did not conflict with each other. It also meant that Root should get his 80 acres.[45]

Root argued that it didn't make any difference if the court applied the public use or the public purpose definition, because there was no defined public utilization in either sense, because there had been no drainage plan in 1907 when he homesteaded the land. Since nothing had been designated, how could the state claim it was "appropriated or applied" if there was no plan, no map? It therefore became very important for the State of Florida to get an adopted drainage plan as soon as possible. Thus, the hasty scramble in February 1909 to get a map and some kind of report to back it up. While getting the Wright Report extract and adopting it as Florida's official drainage plan the following month may have prevented any future Roots from homesteading atop a canal right-of-way, the argument that the entire Everglades Drainage District was "appropriated" was always a thin one not cured until the Settler's Act was later amended later in 1909.[46] Ironically, the Florida supreme court issued its second and final ruling in the *Root* case half-way through the Moss Hearings, on April 9, 1912.

After finishing with the Wright report extract. Davis then asked a series of seemingly innocent questions that appeared to knock Wright off his stride. After finishing his field work in Florida in January 1908, did he come straight back to Washington from Jacksonville? No. Where did he go? Did he not remember? Possibly North Carolina? Yes. How about Asheville? Maybe. The question is straightforward enough. Yes. Who did you meet? Several people. You say you were delayed in finishing the report—from February to May in fact. A heavy work load? Yes. In the field? Yes. Where? Around. North Carolina? Mostly. You seem to have spent a lot of time in 1908 and 1909 in North Carolina. How much? A few days? A week? More? A month? Yes, about a month, in 1909. On behalf of Congressman Small? Yes, mostly. Between June 25, 1909, and February 15, 1910, when you left the employment of the federal government to become chief drainage engineer of the State of Florida, were you in Washington? A few weeks. Where were you the rest of the time? Out on trips. Where? Various locations. North Carolina? Sometimes. When Harold Wheeler came by the office of Drainage Investigations and told Mr. Morgan that he thought your calculations for canal estimates were in error, did you talk to him? No. Why not? You were out in the field. Where? North Carolina. I see.[47]

Davis closed his cross-examination by asking Wright why he waited two and half years to bring Elliott's alleged financial improprieties to the attention of Mr. Zappone. Wright said that he had read Judson Welliver's newspaper article in the Washington *Times* on October 15 in which Elliott was allegedly quoted as saying that Wright had been fired. Wright wrote to A.C. True, Elliott's boss, to object and demand that Elliott correct the record. True then provided the letter that verified that his resignation had been voluntary. Wright did not know if that letter was shown to Elliott, nor did he attempt to contact Elliott directly. He admitted to Davis that reporters in Washington often misquoted sources and did not know if Elliott was misquoted or was trying to cast aspirations on him.[48]

Under Davis's questioning Wright defended his actions by citing the other article appearing in the Jacksonville *Metropolis* on December 12. This was the article by Frank

Huffaker that was apparently based on a leaked report that Elliott had prepared for Secretary Wilson on November 21 containing a descriptive chronology of the Everglades project. Wright testified that when this article appeared the trustees of the Internal Improvement District were quite upset and told him "Wright, you can't ignore this any longer. It is up to you to make an explanation of this matter. It is injuring you and it is injuring the State."[49]

Wright admitted that the newspaper coverage of Paragraph Five of the settlement agreement of January 28 did raise a lot of eyebrows in Tallahassee. The trustees of the Internal Improvement District were so concerned by appearances that they printed several thousand copies of a one-page flyer denying any impropriety, in addition to the 3,000 copies of Wright's own brochure, "Why Was Wright's Report Suppressed."[50] Davis asked Wright if it was retaliation for this newspaper article that drove him to report Elliott to Zappone and Ashley at the Agriculture Department.

"I did not do it as a matter of retaliation, but as a matter of defense … a man has a right to defend his person, his property, and his reputation…."

"In other words," Davis said, "cutting him off, your tactics were to whiten yourself by blackening Elliott."

Attorney Davis's cross examination was followed by cross-examination from the committee members. Wright did not know there was an internal investigation in progress within the Department of Agriculture when he went in to talk to Zappone and Ashley on January 20. Mr. Ashley told him this during the meeting. He made only one visit, on January 20. They gave him no details, nor told him what was going to happen.

He did not know who Mr. Harold Wheeler was, and had never met him.

IV

Chairman Moss intentionally put the blunt and self-confident Arthur Morgan on the stand before the shy and retiring Charles Elliott. Privately, Morgan had been one of the first to defend Elliott by condemning the quality of the work in the original Wright Report in a lengthy letter to Secretary Wilson on January 29. "The inaccuracy of the engineering reasoning in that report [Wright's version] is extreme," he stated. "To have it published it would have been a very serious reflection upon the character of service performed by the Department of Agriculture."[51]

Morgan had become the leader of Elliott's public defense. He was probably the author of an unsigned editorial that appeared in *Engineering News* on February 22. It concluded:

> When an engineer is unjustly assailed, and especially when the attack involves, to a greater or lesser extent, the general reputation of the profession as well as his own, has the profession at large any responsibility in the matter? … If the engineering societies can act to expel the member who has been proven dishonorable and unworthy, why can they not also act to defend their member whose reputation is unjustly attached?[52]

This was raising the stakes way over the McCabe-Wiley affair. In the earlier case, there had been individual expressions of indignation over McCabe's treatment of Dr. Wiley, but the *Engineering News* editorial elevated the matter to a class war: this was not an attack on a man, it was assault on the profession of engineering by a pseudo-professional, a lawyer acting on behalf of an utter non-professional, an unschooled farmer. It was followed on March 28 by a signed article by Morgan in which he, almost table-by-table, laid out the errors in Wright's version of the report. An accompanying unsigned editorial, probably also written by Morgan, demanded that "what the State of Florida should do is to stop all work now in progress and submit Mr. Wright's plans for the Everglades drainage to a commission of competent engineers. That, of course, should have been done in the first place."[53]

No less eminence than Isham Randolph, probably America's foremost active civil engineer, personally wrote Secretary Wilson censoring him for a "cruel wrong" to bring

Arthur Morgan testifying before Congress, 1930s. After leaving the drainage investigations division in 1910, Morgan became a consulting engineer, President of Antioch College, and Chairman of the Tennessee Valley Authority. He was highly critical of later State of Florida drainage plans that tried to salvage the Wright Report recommendations. He believed the Everglades could only be reclaimed in small sections, each contained within secure dikes and continuously drained by pumps. This photograph was taken during the 1930s while he was Chairman of the TVA. Photo by Harris & Ewing. (Library of Congress No. LC-H22-D-5115 [P&P]).

"ruin and dishonor" upon one for a mere "technical violation." "The memory of the Wiley episode is too fresh with our people to be patient under a repetition of the same tactics," Randolph wrote. "This case stirs me to the depths."

When Morgan and McCabe sat down across from each other on the morning of February 26, each man knew he was facing an adversary that sought to end to the career of the other, and each had the talent and willpower to pull it off. McCabe was ready. Under his pile of papers was a 12-page, legal length brief containing every rumor, half truth, innuendo, and personal and professional misstep that Morgan had made in his career, and he intended to use it as soon as he got the chance.[54]

Morgan opened with a brief biography. He had gone to work for the Office of Experimental Stations in 1907 because "I knew Mr. Elliott, who is the foremost drainage engineer in the United States, and a man of international reputation."[55] Morgan verified that it was Harold C. Wheeler, a lawyer from California, who came by the offices of the Drainage Investigations Division on August 16, 1909. This was the same day that the proofs of the Wright Report were sent to the Government Printing Office. Wheeler asked to read the manuscript of Wright's report. Wright was not in the office, so after reading it he asked to speak with Morgan. Wheeler expressed some reservations about the report that he believed were quite glaring errors. He though that the projected costs of excavation, at four cents a yard for earth and eight cents a yard for rock, far too low. Morgan agreed. Wheeler believed that the failure to allow for slumping (the tendency of the banks of a newly-dug canal to partially back-fill to the bottom of the canal) was improper for a canal dug through sand. Morgan agreed. He thought Wright's estimates for evaporation from the surface of Lake Okeechobee were wildly optimistic. Morgan again agreed.

After closely reading the report for the first time, Morgan concluded that it was little more than a series of estimates piled on top of estimates. Asked how much he thought it would take to do a proper plan, Morgan replied that a comprehensive reclamation plan would require at least another two years and a $100,000.[56]

Concerned over what he had discovered, he went to A.D. Morehouse, and the two men telegraphed Elliott requesting permission to pull the report back from the printing office. Elliott telegraphed back with instructions that he had reviewed the report and thought it was all right. The two men went to Elliott's home and talked to Mrs. Elliott, who served as Dr. Elliott's personal secretary, explained the problem to her, and on September 1, Dr. Elliott sent a request to Dr. Beal, editor of the Office of Experimental Stations, asking him to go to the printing office and revoke the printing of the bulletin. Beal found the plates being loaded into the presses, but no printing had yet been done. The plates were shelved.

Much of Morgan's testimony was taken up with the minutiae of the different estimates reached by Wright and Elliott. Morgan testified that Elliott felt constrained by the prior release of the Wright report extract. Many of its details were fixed and couldn't just be erased and re-written. The best he could do was clean up the tables of canal capacity and alter the configuration of the canals to improve their flow while keeping the aggregate amount of spoil generated about the same.[57]

Elliott's figures for the amount of drainage needed to meet Wright's goal of draining three feet of lake level during a 62-day wet season were about the same. In fact, Elliott's capacity was smaller—2572 cubic feet per second as opposed to Wright's 3938. The main difference is that Wright assumed his canals could handle inflows from projected future laterals sufficient to drain the Everglades, because the Everglades drained at the rate of

90 cubic feet per township, or 2.5 cubic feet per square mile. Elliott admitted that nobody knew how much the Everglades drained, but based on sparse data and comparison with other wetlands, he estimated 6.75 cubic feet per square mile. (That was still low. Fourteen to 40 later proved to be a more accurate range.)[58]

Elliott narrowed and deepened six of the eight canals to compensate for subsidence of peat-based soils and prevent overflow given their extremely flat slopes from source to ocean. Elliott would have changed the course of the canals but "the map showing the ditches, made to accompany the report had already been engraved and could not be well changed. Hence, the relative widths and depths of the canals were adjusted."[59]

Elliott also had his men recalculate "fall per mile," "depth of flow," and "discharge" for each canal because Wright calculated these when the lake was at its highest level, and thus there was the greatest pressure ("head") pushing the water out of the lake down the canals. Instead, a mean velocity or mean head was substituted. Finally, Elliott directed Morgan to add that "each of the canals ... carry the surplus flow from the lake and drainage from a strip of land one mile wide on either side when the canals are in good condition." The canals were eight miles apart, so there would be a six-mile zone between them that would go unaffected. In Wright's plan these six miles would be filled in with private laterals and feeder canals. But Morgan and Elliott warned that "Any number of branch canals would accomplish no good because the main canals would not have capacity to receive the water."[60] If built as envisioned by Wright, the canals would lower the level of Lake Okeechobee and nothing more.

Chairman Moss asked two obvious questions. First, how do you know your figures for dredging are correct and Wright's are incorrect? Morgan replied: look at the reports issued by the trustees of the Everglades Drainage District. They are running 8 cents per cubic yard for sand, not 4 cents; and 20 cents for rock, not 8 cents. That's why they are scaling back their work from 38 million cubic yards to 17 million cubic yards.

Second, the chairman asked, how did the report get as far as it did before Harold Wheeler caught the errors? Morgan replied that the Office of Experimental Stations issued several bulletins and scores of shorter publications each year, and Dr. Elliott did not have time to review the calculations in each in detail, especially after Elwood Mead left to go to Australia in 1907. He had relied on the competence of Mr. Wright. He had been wrong. "I regard Mr. Wright as absolutely and completely incompetent for any engineering work," he stated.[61]

Under questioning, Morgan said that he did not believe the Everglades could be drained for one dollar per acre or reclaimed to a condition where the vast majority of land was suitable for agriculture for five dollars an acre. He was uncertain how much it would cost. His best guess was ten to 30 dollars an acre, depending on whether irrigation costs were included.[62] He had no opinion as to whether the report as a whole should be published, as he considered that a policy question.

McCabe's cross examination was, as Morgan later recalled, "like a police court lawyer trying to break down a criminal witness ... he assailed, accused, bulldozed and browbeat." Still, it was largely ineffectual, because Moss held his courtroom theatrics in check. He had seen McCabe in action through four months of the Wiley-McCabe hearings, he did not like what he had seen, he did not hide the fact that he did not like what he had seen, and he kept McCabe on a short leash.[63]

When Morgan and Morehouse first contacted Elliott, McCabe asked, didn't Elliott originally order them to go ahead and have the document printed? Yes. So he and

Morehouse were guilty of insubordination? Oh, probably. But within a few minutes of reviewing the report upon his return, Elliott agreed it could not be printed, so how insubordinate is protecting the credibility of a superior?[64]

Isn't it true that Mr. Elliott gave him an extra week's pay when he quit the department? No, because he never quit the department. On February 19, 1910, he transferred from annual salary status to per-diem status when he started his own firm. He was owed train fare back to his base, his home at St. Cloud, Minnesota. He had two and a half day's leave accrued. He was provided the rest of the week in lieu of travel costs. Was this within the rules of the department? Morgan did not know, although it was common. Who approved this? Dr. True, the man who recommended that Mr. Elliott be fired for not following the rules. Wasn't in fact his new firm located in St. Cloud? No, it was located in Memphis.[65]

And finally:

Mr. McCabe: Would Mr. Wright's plan drain the Everglades in your judgment?
Mr. Morgan: No.
Mr. McCabe: Would Mr. Elliott's plan have drained them?
Mr. Morgan: He does not say it would.
Mr. McCabe: I am asking you know.
Mr. Morgan: I do not know.
Mr. McCabe: What is your opinion?
Mr. Morgan: I doubt it would have fully drained the Everglades. With the addition of lateral canals he described, it would have gone far.
Mr. McCabe: You think Mr. Wright's plan would not have drained them at all?
Mr. Morgan: I think it would have been a decided failure.
Mr. McCabe: If I understand you then, in your opinion, Mr. Wright's plan would not have drained the Everglades?
Mr. Morgan: That is my answer.
Mr. McCabe: And Mr. Elliott's plan would?
Mr. Morgan: As to Mr. Elliott's plan, I do not express an opinion.
Mr. McCabe: I am not asking your opinion. You testified yesterday that you had examined this data, and this committee is entitled to the benefit of your opinion.
Mr. Morgan: I will give the committee my opinion directly and it is this: we frequently refuse to give an opinion on the feasibility of work until we get the necessary data, and in this case we have not got the data to give an opinion that is final on this matter, or to give an opinion that I would want to enter into testimony.
Mr. McCabe: You have enough data in order to give a report that Wright's plan will not drain it.
Mr. Morgan: Yes.
Mr. McCabe: Why won't the same data enable you to give an opinion as to whether Mr. Elliott's plan would?
Mr. Morgan: It would take very much less data to say that some plan is unfeasible than it would to say that some other plan is feasible.
Rep. Sloan: You mean to say, Mr. Morgan, you have not enough data now to determine the feasibility or nonfeasability of this drainage system?
Mr. Morgan: Yes, that is exactly what I mean.
The Chair: Thank you Mr. Sloan. Anything else, Solicitor?[66]

Senator Fletcher was given the privilege of ending Morgan's session. He had one main question: why are you so opposed to Everglades reclamation? Morgan's answer was emphatic: he wasn't. "I do not want to go on record here as saying that the reclamation of the Everglades is undesirable, and I do not want to go on record as saying those efforts ought to cease."

> ...but such development will be a commercially slow process and will take a considerable number of years. There are a good many questions that have not been worked out, and to put a great many small landowners on 10 or 20 acre tracts without knowledge of the conditions, and the different conditions worked out, will mean a loss of investment to those landowners ... it ought to be better advised than it has been, and it is doubtful wisdom to provide for selling to a great many small landowners land which is difficult to subdivide and requires special ability in handling it and of which very little is known.[67]

The Senator, knowing when to quit, thanked Mr. Morgan.

6

Adventures in Draining the Great Dismal Swamp

> I warned Mr. Tarault that he should be cautious in selling that land to Mr. Seip in exchange for notes, as I had been told that Mr. Seip had been less than forthright in the past in honoring his notes. Mr. Tarault turned to me and asked, "what honest man would want this land?"
>
> —Mr. Wiley, Mr. Tarault's neighbor,
> Moyock, North Carolina, 1912[1]

Everyone was expecting either Elliott or his assistant, A.D. Morehouse to be the next witness when the proceedings resumed on Monday. Instead, a man nobody had ever heard of, John Seip of Chillicothe, Ohio, took the stand on the afternoon of February 28. Rumors said that Chairman Moss had come into possession of a bundle of letters sent to Seip that were so explosive that Moss had federal marshals deliver a subpoena to him on Friday. Some said the letters had been written by Wright, others said they had come from the office of the Assistant Secretary, Willett Hays, still others from the Secretary himself.

Great Dismal Swamp, near Lake Drummond on the Virginia–North Carolina Border, about 1890. Photographer unknown (State Archives of Florida, No. MSC5681).

One newspaper printed what they claimed was a letter written by a high official within the Agriculture Department to Wright referring to a "great opportunity to make some money" in a drainage project being evaluated by Wright's division when he was at the federal government. Others claimed the so-called "letters" didn't exist or were forgeries.[2]

It was quickly apparent that Mr. Seip was a truly oleaginous character. Asked his profession, he replied, "I count myself as a farmer more than anything." In fact, he was a land speculator with a rich father and an aversion to paying his bills and honoring contracts. His story would not have been believable had it not been subsequently verified, not the least by Wright himself. The story is convoluted, and each of the witnesses involved had only a portion of the full picture to tell, so it is related here mostly in its entirety, but except for Seip, whose testimony was considered blockbuster news, the full story spun itself out over the course of two or three weeks.

J.O. Wright accompanied Representative John Small on a series of educational meetings across Small's congressional district in North Carolina in August 1907. Over nine days, Small, Wright, and two or three other experts from the Department of Agriculture gave presentations in eight towns or cities on best practices in drainage, crop rotation, fertilization, and other topics. The following year, Small asked A.C. True to again lend him Wright for another six-city speaking tour during October.[3] One of the locals Wright met was a prosperous farmer and contractor named John Wilkinson.

John Aaron Wilkinson lived in Belhaven, where the Pantego and Pungo Creeks joined to form the Pungo River, a small bay on the north side of Pamlico Sound. Born in rural Beauford County in 1864, he left his parents' farm to go to work as a yard man for a lumber company in Virginia. After a few years he was promoted to the manager of a sawmill at Edenton, North Carolina. Then, in 1891 he moved to Belhaven and built a new sawmill. There are two versions of this story. One is that he was hired as an independent contractor by the giant John L. Roper Lumber Company to build the Belhaven mill and dock; the other is that he built them through his own company and the Roper firm then bought him out a year or so later. In either case, he did become a vice-president of the Roper lumber company, he did buy several thousand acres of cut-over land from Roper adjacent to the village of Pantego, about eight miles from Belhaven, that he planned to drain and turn into farms, and Roper did expand the mill into a sizable factory and wharf that became the economic heart of Belhaven.[4]

The Roper company went back to 1865. That year, Francis R. Baird and John L. Roper began a lumber and sawmilling partnership near Norfolk, Virginia. Roper was a former Union soldier with an eye for timberlands. Familiar with the cut-over, second-growth forests of his native Pennsylvania, he was overwhelmed by the thousands of acres of old growth pines and hardwoods he saw in Virginia and North Carolina.[5] When Baird died in 1876 Roper reorganized the firm as a corporation and in 1885 renamed it the John L. Roper Lumber Co., with offices at Norfolk.

But in 1873, while it was still Baird and Roper, the firm changed the course of North Carolina land law. The case, *Eastern Land, Lumber and Mfg. Co. v. State Board of Education* (1887) is a little complicated, but the basic facts are these: in March 1873, John Gray Blount sold Baird and Roper 90,000 acres of swamp timber land in Dare County, on the west shore of Pamlico Sound, across from Roanoke. Baird and Roper registered the deed, started paying taxes and began timbering. John Gray Blount's great-great-grandfather received the grant from the legislature in 1795. It described the land only generally, as was the custom of the era, using natural landmarks such as rivers, streams, and so forth.

As far as anyone recalled, nobody had been on it, nor had paid its taxes, until Baird and Roper looked it up and bought it.

In 1887, after Baird and Roper had been working the Blount Tract for 14 years, the Board of Education, which owned all unclaimed wetlands in the state, asserted ownership, based on records that showed that in October 1807 the Sheriff of Tyrrell County (the land was in Tyrrell County at that time) filed a deed against one Thomas Fitts, seizing a parcel of land matching the description of the Blount Tract for non-payment of taxes, transferring it to the governor. However, no deed conveying the land from Blount to Fitts was ever recorded.[6]

The court ruled that the Sheriff's deed was not, by itself, valid proof that Blount conveyed his land to Fitts prior to October 1807. But the heart of the court's argument was that the state statute that permitted the Board of Education to retrieve property on the grounds of non-payment of taxes was invalid, because the Board of Education could only seize land through judicial foreclosure in open court; the same procedure a mortgage lender would use to recover his collateral from a defaulting lender. In other words, North Carolina could not undertake the type of wholesale vacuuming of old land grants or forgotten land titles that William Jennings did when he was Florida governor in 1902. The revocation of every certificate or the cancellation of every legislative grant would require a court order of foreclosure, even if the specific location of the parcel in question was only partially defined. This effectively made the type of statewide drainage program that Florida had undertaken impossible. North Carolina could never recover lands conveyed in ancient and subsequently forgotten land conveyances by simply filing a document attesting that they had been abandoned, or that taxes had not been paid.

John L. Roper. Roper was co-founder of the largest lumber and shingle-making company in the south during the years between the Civil War and World War I. Reportedly, the Roper company once owned or controlled over a million acres of first-growth timberlands. Photo by C. M. Bell Studios of Washington, D.C., 1875 (Library of Congress No. LC-B5-24588 [P&P]).

After 1885, John L. Roper expanded deeper west and south into North Carolina, building mills in several locations, including two on the Albemarle-Pamlico Peninsula: Roper (1885), a few miles from Albemarle Sound, then Belhaven (1891), on Pamlico Sound to the south. By this time, the Roper Company had become one of the largest lumber companies in the mid–Atlantic south with some 400,000 acres of owned land and 150,000 acres of leased timberlands.[7]

This was a revolutionary time in southern forestry. Previously, high-grade timber—mostly cypress or longleaf pine—had to be hauled or rafted long distances to water-powered sawmills. Semi-mobile steam engines powering circle and band

John Roper Company sawmill, Moore County, North Carolina, about 1895. Photo by Herbert H. Brimley (Brimley Collection, North Carolina State Archives, No. PhC-42-Bx13-Forest and Forest Industries-F1).

saws replaced water-powered pit saws, and by 1909 steam was being replaced with more moveable large, slow-turning Brayton internal combustion engines. The new dry kiln turned loblolly pine, previously used only to burn in steam engines, into usable dimension lumber. All this allowed sawmills—especially the highly specialized mills for making cedar roof shingles in demand in Europe—to be made smaller and distributed closer to timber stands, rail heads or navigable waterways. Between 1880 and 1920, North Carolina generated 10.2 million acres of cutover timberlands, most of it pine, most of it in the eastern lowlands.[8]

To transport raw timber or processed lumber out of the Albemarle-Pamlico Peninsula by water the company used its own wharf at Mackey's Ferry on Albemarle Sound, about six miles from Roper. Raw timber went straight to the dock; processed lumber and shingles were cut at Roper, then sent on to Mackey's Ferry. Wilkinson's new sawmill and wharf at Belhaven gave the company the option of hauling to the south. But still, the only way to move raw timber out of the company's land either north or south was by oxcart over corduroy roads. So in 1887 the Roper firm chartered the Albemarle and Pantego Railroad, a 29-mile single-track line running between Belhaven and Mackey's Ferry via Roper. The railroad was completed in 1890 or 1891.

In 1891 the Roper lumber company, its 500,000 acres of timberland and the Albemarle and Pantego Railroad were purchased by the Norfolk and Southern Railroad. The railroad and lumber company together were acquired for about five million dollars and were purchased through a complex series of stock and bond swaps with a Norfolk and

Interior of a steam-powered sawmill, North Carolina, about 1900. Lumbering and sawmilling was one of the most dangerous occupations during the steam era, rivaled only by mining. Photo by Herbert H. Brimley (Brimley Collection, North Carolina State Archives, No. Ph C42-Bx13-Forests and Forest Industries-F4).

Southern subsidiary, the Virginia and Carolina Coast Railroad. The Norfolk and Southern went bankrupt in 1910 and was reorganized, intact, as the Norfolk Southern Railroad. After the reorganization the John L. Roper company continued as a wholly-owned subsidiary of the Norfolk Southern, but the Albemarle and Pantego, and the Virginia and Carolina Coast railroads both disappeared into the Norfolk Southern system.[9]

In 1905 John Roper retired. His sons were already heavily involved with the Newport Shipbuilding and Drydock Corporation (not to be confused with the Newport *News* Shipbuilding Company) and became less active in the affairs of the lumber company. Wilkinson was briefly an officer in the Albemarle and Pantego Railroad and remained a vice president of the Roper lumber company through and after the bankruptcy reorganization of 1910. He also remained a stockholder in the Norfolk Southern and had several of his own enterprises, including the Belhaven Lumber Company. In 1907, he and his brother Samuel started a 10,000 acre development called Terra Ceia near Pantego on the Albemarle and Pantego Railroad line using the cutover land he had bought from the Roper company in the 1890s. Part of this work was completed before the state passed its new drainage district law in early 1909; about half was completed using a district formed pursuant to the law. By 1912 three canals drained as much as 20,000 acres.[10]

Belhaven, North Carolina, 1938. North is to the top. The area shown is slightly more than one mile by one mile. The by-now former John Roper sawmill and wharf is the large pier in Pantego Creek to the northeast of the downtown docks. John Wilkinson's mansion is at the farthest southern tip of town. The Terra Ceia development is just out of the photograph along the highway leading north away from the town (USDA aerial photograph 1938-ABP-26-77).

Shortly before one of his lecture tours in August 1908, Representative Small wrote both Secretary Wilson and Assistant Secretary Hays to request a drainage survey at Lake Mattamuskeet, in Hyde County, about 20 miles southeast of Belhaven. This land was unimproved and owned by the State Board of Education. Small asked specifically for Wright to be assigned to do the preliminary investigation, noting that "he is a well equipped and valuable man." His request was referred to Elliott, who allocated $2,500 for the job and assigned Wright to the project.[11]

Hyde County is the oldest county in North Carolina and is one of the oldest continuously operating political jurisdictions in North America. The first recorded account of Lake Mattamuskeet by Europeans was by a group of English settlers from Ocracoke in 1585 on a mission to eradicate or dislocate indigenous peoples from the area. Lake Mattamuskeet was a smaller version of Lake Okeechobee, a depression in the underlying rock strata of the Albemarle-Pamlico Peninsula that reached down to about sea level, deep enough to create a shallow bowl. It was originally seven miles wide by 20 miles long and drained slowly southeast into Wysocking Bay. After a widespread crop-damaging flood in 1836 its owner, the State Literary Board (later, the State Board of Education) excavated a seven-mile canal from the lake to Wysocking Bay using slave labor. This drained the lake from 120,000 acres to 50,000 acres, the size it was at the time Wright first visited it August or September 1908.[12]

In September 1908 requests were received at the Office of Experimental Stations from U.S. Rep. Albert Douglas of Ohio and U.S. Rep. P.J. McCumber of North Dakota on behalf of an unnamed constituent asking for a drainage survey of yet another site, "a large body of swamp land" at Moyock, in far northeast North Carolina adjacent to the Great Dismal Swamp of Virginia about 130 miles from Mattamuskeet. In 1764, George Washington, nine partners and 138 limited partners obtained a charter from the State of Virginia for a new company "Adventurers for Draining the Great Dismal Swamp." Starting at Lake Drummond in Virginia, about eight miles northwest of Moyock, the "Adventurers" proposed to dig a canal to the edge of the swamp and harvest 40,000 acres of timber. Housed at a compound called "Dismal Town," a hundred rented slaves dug a canal five miles long and twelve feet wide, finishing about 1768.

Although the Adventurers proposed to settle the land and raise cotton, rice and tobacco, the firm, like so many that came after, went no farther than timbering. By the time the Revolutionary War temporarily shut down operations, eight million cedar shingles a year were being exported to the old country. Washington, in debt after eight years of virtually unpaid presidential service, sold his interest in 1795 to pay for the upkeep of his Mount Vernon estate, but the company continued into the nineteenth century. The canal is still there, widened and diked. It is believed to be the oldest continuously operated canal in the nation.[13]

Secretary Wilson replied to Representative Douglas suggesting that his constituent directly contact Elliott with a request for a survey. In early October John Seip wrote to the Office of Experimental Stations. He said he was secretary of a firm called the Carolina Land and Timber Company. He indicated that he was the party that Douglas had been referring to, and requested that J.O. Wright, by name, undertake a survey.[14]

Elliott was reluctant to take on the Moyock project, as he had been told by Wright, who had been over the site in the fall of 1907 and was somewhat familiar with the area, that it was a fairly large proposal with many different landowners. Also, when Wright had been there, the Carolina Land and Timber Company had their own engineer working on the project, and Elliott suspected that Seip was asking for federal assistance for a project that only benefited a single corporate landowner, which, while not outside department rules, was frowned upon as an unwise use of scarce government resources.[15] However, Representative Small lobbied Secretary Wilson for the survey, and Assistant Secretary Hays approved it on November 11, 1908. Although Elliott wrote to caution that his office had already started the Mattamuskeet survey, and thus there could be a delay before the Moyock survey could start, work begin within a month.[16]

Elliott would have been even more reluctant to take on the project if he knew Seip's history. John Seip was born in 1858, the son of Charles Seip, a butcher and farmer who produced his own beef, hogs and mutton at five farms he owned at the time of his death in 1902. After graduating high school, John Seip started Culter and Seip, a wholesale boot and shoe distributor. Despite his business success, he was considered by locals in Chillicothe to be something of an eccentric. He talked his father into building the biggest house in Chillicothe in 1899 in an eclectic mash of Queen Anne and Italianate styles.

(Local legend says he changed plans half-way through in an attempt to convince an Italian heiress he met on vacation to move to America and marry him.) He was an enthusiastic archaeological collector with a taste for Spanish-American and American Indian antiquities, many apparently rustled. His first big land venture was the Virginia Land and Lumber Company. He purchased 10,900 acres of swampland near Norfolk for next to nothing, sold it to a company he created for $50,000, and left it to his local partners to figure out how keep it going under the debt load. The firm went under in 1905.[17]

Seip had purchased a parcel of land near Moyock called the Tarault Tract in July 1906 from Joseph Tarault and Richard Norton. It measured 9,192 acres and Seip purchased it for $70,000, most of it in notes. He then sold it to the Carolina Land and Timber Company, comprised of himself, H.C. Hosier, A.B. Lukens (both locals) and E.S. Skilder of Norfolk. Later discovering a minor error in the description of the parcel, Seip refused to make good on a $10,000 note made out to Tarault. It took six years and several appeals, but Tarault eventually won his case in 1912 and was awarded $17,925, the additional $7,925 representing damages for wrongful dispossession and interest that had accrued on the unpaid note.[18]

Wright was also assigned this project, although like Lake Mattamuskeet, he did not actually do the field work. At Lake Mattamuskeet, S.H. McCrory undertook the survey, and at Moyock, H.M. Lynde did the field work. Wright did, however, prepare the final report for Mattamuskeet. The drainage plan was completed in April 1909. Lynde prepared the plan for Moyock, which was finished in February 1909.[19]

Wright spent much of his time in 1908 and 1909 in North Carolina when he was not in south Florida. He was in North Carolina almost continuously from August 1908 through the end of the year, and he made six field trips there between January 1 and the end of May 1909. When he was not overseeing the work of McCrory and Lynde, he was assisting Representative Small with the drafting of a statewide drainage district law. Much of the final work was done at a drainage conference held in New Berne (then called Newberne) in September 1908. He later helped Small lobby for it in the North Carolina legislature, where it was passed in March 1909.[20]

In outline, the legislation permitted either the majority of owners in a defined area or the owners representing 60 percent of the land in that area to petition for the formation of a drainage district. If the petition requirement was met, the county clerk was required to appoint a competent civil engineer, or to secure the services of a competent engineer from the state or the U.S. Department of Agriculture, to make a preliminary survey. If the reviewing engineer found that the district lands met certain criteria laid out in the law, the engineer's report and the petition went to the state circuit court. If no injunctions against it were filed, the district was approved and could float bonds, levy per-acreage taxes and enter into drainage contracts.[21]

Each acre was taxed on a sliding scale, as determined by the reviewing engineer, based on how much that acre would cost to be drained, and how much its value would increase once improved. It was not uncommon for a drainage district, after unwilling or unqualified landowners dropped out, to include the land of only one or two large landowners, but the district was separate entity, with its own legal rights and responsibilities. The system relied upon an honest, objective engineer to first, determine that the aggregate benefits of a district would exceed the value of the bonds its projectors proposed to issue, and second, to fairly and accurately assess the increase in market value (the "increment") each plot of land would realize, so it would pay a fair share of the tax burden. If approved, the district could float bonds totaling no more than the aggregate increment (not the total land value, the total increment) for a total of thirteen years, with the first annual repayment to begin in the third year and extend for ten annual payments.[22]

John Seip said he first met J.O. Wright on September 9, 1908, at the New Bern conference. Wright, on the other hand, believed they met a year earlier, in the fall of 1907, at one of Representative Small's lecture circuit stops. According to Seip, he learned of Wright from one of his North Carolina business partners, A.B. Lukens, who told Seip that Wright had been helping Wilkinson with a drainage project being undertaken by Wilkinson called the Albemarle Development Company, apparently another name for the Terra Ceia project. Wright was, of course, working for the Agriculture Department, but he told Seip that he soon planned to leave government service. Seip said, "My negotiations with Mr. Wright were all based largely on his statement that he did not expect to stay with the government long," but his actions suggest the opposite: his only real interest in Wright was the fact that he had access to government resources and government influence.[23]

Seip, at first through the Carolina Land & Lumber Company, then through a new company called the Provident Land Company, planned to drain and subdivide 26,000 acres of the Great Dismal Swamp near Moyock once the new law was passed. Seip said that he agreed to give Wright $7,500 in stock in the yet-to-be formed corporation. In return, Wright was to sell bonds of the district and convince the American Steel Dredge Company to take bonds in lieu of cash for the purchase of a new dredge. He was also to "furnish suitable buyers for the land in small tracts at prices that were satisfactory to us," and to secure a drainage (i.e., dredging) contract at a reasonable price. "I said to him that in connection with our development work down there that I thought I saw various channels in which he could be useful to us. He said 'I know a great many people.'"[24]

Representative Floyd of the Moss Committee wanted to know just what Seip expected Wright to do, especially after Seip admitted that one member of the Moyock Drainage Commission was already (secretly) a partner in Carolina Land and Timber:

> *Rep. Floyd*: What particular influence did he have in North Carolina with the other members of the [drainage] commission? You did not anticipate having any difficulty in getting the member of your company who was on the board to give you the [dredging] contract, did you?
>
> *Mr. Seip*: No, but the member of our company would not have permitted the contract to come to us had it not been the lowest bid.
>
> *Rep. Floyd*: Oh, I understand. They would have had to conform to the law. I understand that perfectly.
>
> *Mr. Seip*: And they would have had competition.[25]

Seip implied that the yet-to-be formed corporation intended to do its own dredging because it owned almost all the land in the district and because "we had decided to increase the yardage over and above that specified by the department fully per cent [sic], and we did not want to be in a position where somebody else would have that contract and come in and do the work and hold us up on the additional work."[26] In other words, Seip planned to pad the bills sent to the drainage district, so he wanted a dredging company of his own to do the work.

When H.M. Lynde finished the Moyock survey on February 6, Wright sent the official copy to Seip in Ohio, not to the clerk of the Currituck County court as required in the soon-to-be approved drainage law. He also put Lynde's name on the plat as the official engineer so his would not appear on the filed documents. Once the survey had been completed at Moyock, the attention of both men temporarily refocused on the even larger project at Lake Mattamuskeet until the legislature had a chance to pass the new state law and the survey and other paperwork could be filed and processed by the county court for the formation of the new drainage district.[27]

The Board of Education had originally planned to drain and develop Mattamuskeet itself, but with the passage of the new drainage district law, the governor, who was concerned about graft, decided it was best to just sell it for cash and reap the immediate benefits for the school fund.[28] In March 1909 Wright wrote to Seip, suggesting that he buy the lake, drain it, and develop it. The Board of Education was asking $100,000 for the land under the lake. Wright wrote that he believed "I think I can indirectly control the matter," in other words, he thought he could help Seip get a better price. As a result of his government survey work, Wright had been hired by the Board of Education as their sales agent. If he sold the lake for $100,000, he would earn a $5,000 commission. He did not tell this to Seip.[29]

In an attempt to put a syndicate together, Wright introduced Seip to John Wilkinson. Wilkinson said he could be interested in the Mattamuskeet proposition. Seip, without informing Wright, traveled to Wilkinson's mansion in Belhaven to look over the lay of the land and meet his prospective partner.[30] Seip described the Moyock proposition, still in its early stages. Wilkinson told Seip that about a year earlier, in August 1907, Wright had made him a nearly identical proposition for the Albemarle Development Company. Wilkinson gave Wright $5,000 in stock; Wright was to arrange for the necessary government surveys and would buy a dredge using stock in lieu of cash and would raise money through the sale of stock and land. Wilkinson told Seip that Wright took his stock and did nothing.[31]

As Wilkinson later recalled:

> After Mr. Wright got my stock he had no more interest in my work [Terra Ceia] and he went from that to Wilson and he went into a drainage proposition there [Lion Swamp], and from Wilson he went to Moyock and went into a deal there where he was to have $7,500 out of that, and from that he went to Mattamuskeet, where he got his $5,000, but he took no further interest about the development of my property at all after he got my $5,000.[32]

This may not have been completely true. It appears that Wright did help Wilkinson with his Terra Ceia development, but under a series of different names. In April 1909, based solely on a verbal request made by Wilkinson in Wright's office at the Agriculture Department, Wright was able to get approval for a survey of the Pantego Drainage District, a 16,000 acre tract that included at least part of Terra Ceia. Although comprised of several landowners, over 90 percent of the land was owned by two companies: the John L. Roper Lumber Company and the Norfolk Southern Railway. The Roper company was, at this time, wholly owned by the Norfolk Southern. It appears that the portion not held in the name of the Roper company was owned by the railroad because at least part of it was being used for right-of-way.[33] From the Office of Experimental Stations, Omer Fairey and J.V. Phillips were assigned the field work under the supervision of J.O. Wright. The fieldwork on Pantego was completed in July 1909. The report, however, was not prepared by Wright until January 22, 1910, three weeks before he left to work for the State of Florida.

But at the time Seip was visiting Wilkinson at his home in Belhaven, in February 1909, it is true that Wright had done nothing to advance the interests of the Albemarle Development Company or Terra Ceia. Whether Wright was motivated to undertake the

Pantego Drainage District study to mollify Wilkinson, or as an incentive to get him to invest in the Mattamuskeet project with John Seip cannot be determined.[34]

As Wilkinson stated, Wright went from Terra Ceia to Wilson to evaluate bids on a drainage excavation contract called the Lion Swamp project. Wright evaluated the proposals, but the bidders all dropped out or were unsuitable. So Wright put the local authorities in contact with the Lawrence Brett Contracting Company, which did not yet exist. Brett had been Wright's lieutenant on the 1906–07 and 1907–08 field expeditions to south Florida. Brett also roomed with Wright and his wife and daughter in Washington, D.C, and they were, in Wright's words, "like brothers."

Wright was able to get a $10,000 dredge from American Steel Dredge Company for only $1,000 down because of all the North Carolina business he had been steering to them. He gave Brett another $1,500 to get the company up and running and Brett moved to Wilson in April or May 1909. The Lawrence Brett Contracting Company won the bid and did the Wilson job well, finishing about December 1909. The firm also expanded into civil engineering and continued in this line of work until the 1950s, increasingly specializing in roadwork, at least until the Great Depression. Charles Elliott granted Brett furlough status through early 1910 until it became clear that Brett's business would be successful, at which time Brett thanked Elliott for his help and resigned. In 1912, Wright sold his share of the business to Brett for a profit of $3,100 plus the cost of the dredge.[35]

However, the company later came in useful for another purpose. On Wright's instructions, Brett deliberately overbid on the Moyock project so that Seip's shadow firm would be guaranteed to get the job. Seip's shell game worked like this: the new Moyock drainage district issued a request for bids for dredging work that specified that the dredging contractor would be paid in drainage district bonds, not money. This was not in itself unusual, although under such an arrangement the district typically had to discount the bonds fairly deeply.

There were three bids: Wilkinson's dredging company, Lawrence Brett's company and the American Steel Dredge Company. American Steel manufactured dredges, but it was not a dredging contractor. Brett and Wilkinson deliberately bid high and American Steel won the contract. American Steel then subcontracted the work to the Provident Land Co., a Seip shadow company. Provident paid American Steel $11,000 in cash for a new dredge. As it completed the job, the district paid Provident in bonds. Thus, one of Seip's companies (Carolina Land & Timber) paid taxes on its land to retire the bonds held by another of his firms (Provident Land Co.), which, in turn, was making a profit draining land that Carolina Land and Timber would then sell for about ten times the price it paid as swampland. It does not appear that Brett knew about this; he simply put in the conservatively high bid that Wright advised him to submit.[36]

Wright first floated the Mattamuskeet proposition in March 1909, as the legislature was approving the drainage district bill. As Seip explained:

> I was to buy the lake bed. First, we were to organize a company with $500,000 capital. I was to buy the lake bed and receive stock in the company to the extent of the actual purchase price, the actual amount paid for the lake bed. Then we were to dispose of $250,000 of stock and pay for the actual cost of the work. That would leave $150,000 of stock in the treasury. Out of that stock Mr. Wright wanted 50 per cent, to which I objected. We finally settled on $40,000. The other $110,000 was to be left in the treasury and sold in the event that the actual cost of the work more than Wright estimated it would be.[37]

In return, Wright would act as chief engineer and general manager of the project.

He would also guarantee that that the Division of Drainage Investigations did the survey work, saving the landowners thousands of dollars. The asking price of the Board of Education was $100,000. Wright assumed that Seip didn't have that much money on his own, so he thought of Wilkinson. He sent Wilkinson a telegram on March 17 asking him to meet Seip and himself in the state capitol, Raleigh, on March 20.[38]

Seip believed that they could get a better price if a local bid on the land, so within a couple of days of the meeting, Wilkinson bid $60,000 on behalf of him and Seip for the lake. However, buyer's remorse quickly set in; according to Wilkinson, there were far too many unknowns: the drainage survey was preliminary; nobody knew what lay on the lakebed; no due diligence had been done on the land titles. "So I called the governor up and told him that I thought I had gone a little fast in the offer I made on the lake and that I thought I would like to withdraw it until an investigation could be made as to the fertility of the lake and I could learn a little more about Mr. Seip," Wilkinson later recalled. "'Well,' he said, 'if that is the way you feel about it, all right.'" The governor waived the bid. He also told Wilkinson that Wright was acting as sales agent for the School Board and would get five percent of the sales price. "$5,000 for selling it? I could readily see why Mr. Wright was so much interested in getting Mr. Seip and myself into the lake deal," recounted Wilkinson, "I dropped it, made no further offers."[39]

Wright arranged for the Bureau of Soils to conduct a soil survey of the lakebed, which was generally positive, although the lake was shallower than popularly believed, never more than six feet deep. On April 8, Wright found a new partner for Seip: Assistant Agriculture Secretary Willett Hays. During a casual lunchroom conversation, Wright started talking about Mattamuskeet "and he became much interested and invited me to come to his office.... He thinks there is a great opportunity to make some money and frankly said he would like to become interested in a company to purchase the lake and develop the land."[40]

Willett M. Hays was an unlikely senior administrator. He was born on a farm near Eldora, Iowa, in 1860. He attended Oskaloosa College, Drake University, and got his doctorate at the cutting-edge agriculture school of its day, Iowa State College in Ames. He was appointed assistant professor of agriculture at the University of Minnesota in St. Paul in 1890, where he help found (some say he founded) the discipline of modern plant genetics, with a specialty in grains. He was appointed assistant secretary in January 1905. In 1908 he took a year's sabbatical to teach plant genetics in Argentina.

He was not close to Wilson and was unknown to either Taft or Roosevelt. In fact, shortly before he was hired, Wilson wrote President Roosevelt that "I have made such inquiry as I could into the qualifications of candidates for Assistant Secretary, and find that none are particularly prominent along the lines of work done here." Failing a strong candidate, Roosevelt suggested G. Howard Davison, a gentleman sheep breeder, simply because he was from New York, or Gilbert Pinchot. The National Grange objected to Davison because he was "not a real farmer," and Pinchot preferred to stay, for the time being, at the Interior Department. That left Hays as the best of the rest. Given this background, some of Hays's more outré claims about being motivated primarily by the possibility of starting a model agricultural community at Lake Mattamuskeet sound a lot less incredible.[41]

In fact, Hays became quite insistent on being allowed to participate. Hays sought to interest Leigh Hunt of Bethesda, Maryland. Hunt was born in 1855. His undergraduate and law degrees were attained via correspondence courses. He taught school in Indiana and became a school superintendent at Mt. Pleasant and East Des Moines, Iowa. He was appointed president of the Iowa State College in 1885. However, his inexperience and abrasiveness led to his resignation after only one year. It was at Iowa State that Willett Hays, a student there, first met him

Hunt moved to Seattle and bought the Seattle *Post-Intelligencer* in 1886 and became a partner in a local bank. Initially very successful in the booming city, the bank went under in the panic of 1893 and he was forced to sell the *Post-Intelligencer* at a steep loss. He drifted to Shanghai, possibly to find new business opportunities, maybe to escape creditors. There, he met James Morse of the American Trading Company of Yokohama. Morse was looking for investors for a gold mine in Unsan, Korea owned by King Kojong. Hunt had no money, but convinced a former student, New York State Senator J. Sloat Fassett, to assemble a group of investors to put up a $100,000 line of credit. In 1897 Hunt and Fassett bought out Morse for $70,000. Two years later they bought out the King for $250,000 and a percentage of profits, receiving in exchange an exclusive 40-year concession. Hunt and Fassett made about $2 million each before the Russians seized the mine in 1904 during the Russo-Japanese War.[42]

By then he was living in Cairo, where he was involved in growing and processing Nile Valley cotton textiles in Egypt and Sudan. Just how he happened to be in Bethesda, Maryland, when Representative Moss's subpoena appeared at his door is somewhat unclear; he said in his testimony that he was still managing his cotton interests in the Nile Valley, and biographers state that he did not move back to the United States until about 1921.[43]

Hunt wrote Hays in July: "I am planning to organize a company of twenty millions capital to do in a large in general way what the enclosed prospectus would indicate to you," but he never gave any indication to Hays that he was interested specifically in the Mattamuskeet project. Wright, on the other hand, was ecstatic, writing Seip: "I want Asst. Sec. Hays and his friends, as I think it would be to our interest in selling the lands." Hays continued to be very interested even after Hunt failed to secure a third partner, asking Wright for a status report on August 13.[44]

In mid–1909, Wright prepared a prospectus for Hays that showed the project had a profit potential of a million dollars[45] (The following is the format he used):

50,000 acres of land at $20 per acre	$1,000,000
Drainage bonds, 6 percent interest	$400,000
Amount Invested	*$1,400,000*
Money expended on development	$260,000
Interest and sundry expenses	$60,000
Amount Spent	*$320,000*
Net Profit	*$1,080,000*

This is financial gibberish, as several members of the Moss Committee pointed out. The line "Amount Invested" is actually "Gross Income," and treats the $400,000 in bond revenue as income but shows no corresponding liability for repayment other than about three years' interest, $60,000 ("Interest and Sundry Expenses"). In other words, the bond issue is treated as a loan that never has to be repaid. A 13-year bond (the longest specified in the North Carolina law) for $400,000 at five percent would require a lump sum payoff of $718,000 at maturity or amortized payments totaling about $553,600, but the latter assumes the developers could start making annual repayments of $42,600 one year after the bond was issued; an unlikely scenario. Development costs of $260,000 were wildly low; the mammoth steam-powered pumping station at New Holland alone required $200,000 and the dredging another $300,000, not including dikes or roads.[46] However, for simplicity, we will take out the spurious interest payment ($60,000) and use development costs of $500,000.

Hence:

Land sales + bond revenue	$1,000,000 + $400,000 = $1.4 million
Development costs	$500,000
Bond repayment (lump, 1923)	($718,000)
Total costs	($500,000) + ($718,000) = ($1,218,000)
Net profit/loss	$1,400,000—($1,218,000) = $182,000 profit

This is a 15 percent rate of return on investment risked over a 13-year period, which is roughly 1.18 percent per year, compounded. This was less than the return on a 10-year U.S. Treasury note of the era (about 2 percent per year, paid annually). While this is a highly simplified estimate that does not take into account such things as interest income earned from the $718,000 gradually accruing in the bank until the bonds are paid in 1923, nor does it include operating costs for thirteen years, it does demonstrate that with $400,000 in debt, 50,000 acres of land, and an assumed land sale price of 20 dollars an acre, achieving profitability would be a real challenge, as subsequent landowners were to discover.

On September 17–18, Hays actually traveled to Mattamuskeet, along with Wright and a photographer from the Department of Agriculture, Mr. Williams. They stayed at John Wilkinson's mansion in Belhaven. Wilkinson was especially impressed with Mr. Williams. "He was a very efficient man. I think he makes some of the best photographs I have seen ... he took several photographs of my property, of crops and various things." He sent Wilkinson an album of photographs of his land to thank him for his hospitality, which Wilkinson appreciated very much.[47] All this, of course, was at the expense of the Agriculture Department, although Mr. Williams thought he was merely doing his job.

On September 19, the day after this meeting, Hays sent a telegram to Wright in North Carolina, asking him to secure a 20 percent interest in the Mattamuskeet development for him and his partners. On the 22nd, Wright replied that he had done so. However, this was untrue; by this time another partnership had taken out an option on the lake.[48]

Sometime in July, Seip had consulted a lawyer, who advised him that Wright's participation as both a sales agent for the state Board of Education and as a partner in the firm buying the land was a conflict of interest that would render the sale void. (Wright had admitted to Seip that he was making a commission on the sale in May, but Seip had already learned of it from Wilkinson in March.)[49]

Wright argued:

> you were not to compensate me for securing the lake from the state; but it was the understanding that when the lake was purchased by you that a company would be formed which would require capital and

> engineering talent to develop the land, and in consideration of my knowledge of the project and ability to interest capital, that I would be given a certain interest in the company. This the attorneys assure me is perfectly honorable and legitimate in every way.[50]

Perhaps, but as John Wilkinson said, it was still a discomforting thing to find out *after* one had promised to pay $60,000. At this point Seip pulled out of Mattamuskeet. A partnership named Mason, Webb and Kerr (later called the Southern Land Reclamation Company, but best known as the New Holland Company) purchased the lake and Wright received a $1,250 commission from the State Board of Education in 1911.[51]

Wright remained active in Moyock and Pantego. In December, he traveled to Currituck County to address a meeting of landowners in the Moyock Drainage District, telling them that once a petition had been filed and the process of valuation begun by the court, nobody could withdraw their land from the district. This may have kept the process from falling apart, but it was also a misrepresentation of the North Carolina law, intended to benefit John Seip and his company.[52]

In December, Wilkinson wrote Elliott on behalf of his own firm, the Belhaven Lumber Company, asking him to send Wright to mediate a dispute in the formation of the Pantego Drainage District. Elliott was skeptical, replying to Wilkinson that the Drainage Division hadn't turned in a survey report on the proposed district yet (even though a great deal of that year's budget had been expended on field work in the area, for which he was not pleased), and that from Wilkinson's description, the problems sounded like they needed a lawyer to iron out, not an engineer. Representative Small wrote Elliott to explain the problem.

The John L. Roper Lumber Company owned 6,500 acres of the 14,000 acres that sat more or less in the center of the proposed district. The remaining 8,000 acres formed a doughnut around the Roper land. About half of this was owned by farmers and half by the Norfolk Southern. The Roper company was objecting to the method by which its proportion of the tax assessment was being calculated. What Representative Small did not say was that the Roper company and the Norfolk Southern were the same, and that Small was a lawyer for the railroad.[53]

Wright did meet with Small, Wilkinson, and Mr. Lamb, general manager of the railroad on January 21. Lamb stated that the Roper company would not participate in the drainage district, and of course Small backed him up. Apparently, Wright said that a "doughnut without the hole" drainage district was technically feasible. Elliott wrote to Small saying that he disagreed with Wright; a drainage district that merely drained the doughnut of the railroad's right of way and the adjacent farmers without also draining the hole of Roper's land was implausible. He suggested that it was a pretext for the Roper company to reap the benefits of drainage without paying the bill. It was around this time that Elliott and True concluded that Wright was taking a commercial interest in the projects he was working on, and Elliott recommended that he should be transferred to a different region or fired. But he resigned in February "and that took care of the problem."[54]

While all this was happening, there was also trouble at Moyock. Seip and his local partners, Lukens and Bagley, were concerned by the flood of cheap Everglades land appearing on the market. Seip knew Wright had spent the last two winters working on an Everglades survey for the government, and during a ferry ride on January 22, 1910, asked him about it. Wright reassured him that the Everglades posed no real competition:

> He said that the Everglades did not have any great amount of agricultural value. He said it was under water and the land was underlaid with a strata of rock, and the land was barren of potash, which was an expensive mineral element, and he said at the same time that the Government should step in and do something to stop the sale of land to innocent purchasers. He said, too that the parties selling that land had actually invaded the agriculture building in Washington, offering the land to clerks.[55]

Also in January, the Board of Education wrote Elliott asking him to send Wright to a court "viewing" (valuation review) of the Mattamuskeet Drainage District petition on January 5. "As I understand, the viewers and engineer are required to become conversant with the general features of the district and make recommendations regarding the proper boundary of same, and whether or not the proposed work will be for the public good.... I do not see the propriety of Mr. Wright being present at the meeting," Elliott replied. This time Elliott won; on January 5, Wright was in Washington, ironically, working on Elliott's update of the Everglades report. He resigned a few weeks later.[56]

II

In addition to the projects Wright worked on, there was one that he did not, a smaller project called the Pungo River Drainage District, which was primarily intended to straighten and deepen the Pungo River running past Belhaven wharf and John Wilkinson's mansion, which overlooked a marina. In June 1909, Wright was in Belhaven looking it over. Wilkinson and Wright were driving through Wilkinson's land when Wilkinson turned to Wright and said, "Hey, I am going to be a government man now, too." Wright asked him what he meant. Wilkinson said that there had been a problem in getting out the month's payroll and Elliott had written him to ask if he would pay the government's half of one month's salary, $104, for an Agriculture Department surveyor, a Mr. Phillips, who was working in the area. Normally, the Department of Agriculture paid half of Phillips's salary and the local drainage district (which Wilkinson supervised) paid half. Wilkinson asked him if he thought there was anything strange about this. Wright said no, it was okay.

Then Wilkinson had an idea. A few months earlier, he had supplied four pairs of hip boots to Omer Fairley of the drainage division for his crew while they were working on the Pantego survey. Wilkinson had earlier complained that he had not yet been reimbursed the $24 he was owed for them. Did he think he could get paid back at the same time he got reimbursed for Mr. Phillips's salary? Wright said it made sense to him; he would speak to Mr. True about it when he got back to Washington. Wilkinson remembered being repaid, but could not remember if he received one check or two.[57]

Years later, in early 1912, a Mr. Ashley, who said he was from the Forestry Department, and never identified himself as an investigator, came down to ask about Wilkinson advancing the salary to Mr. Phillips back in 1909. Ashley said that Mr. Wright and Mr. Elliott were slurring each other, and he wanted to find out about this. The object of his visit was to hush them up. Ashley said his bosses wanted to stop them from attacking each other, and that was why he was looking into the case. Wilkinson said he barely remembered it. A few weeks later, Wilkinson was contacted by Mr. Wright, who asked him about the incident and asked if anyone from Washington had been around inquiring about it. Wilkinson thought it was kind of strange, all this over for a hundred and four dollars from three years before. He didn't even remember if he did get paid for the boots.[58]

III

Wright continued to contact Seip even after he started work as Chief Engineer for the State of Florida. He informed Seip that he had an attractive job offer in New York for $7,200 that would prevent him from taking up the Moyock work. Seip replied that he thought it was a good offer and Wright should accept it. Wright wanted Seip to hire the Brett Contracting Company to do dredging work for Moyock. Seip said that was up to his partners; he did not get involved in operations. Finally, Wright wrote: "I would like to know definitely whether or not it is still your intention to organize a development company at Moyock," presumably so he could collect the $7,500 he believed he was owed. Seip stopped answering him. Wright turned his attention to Seip's partner, Mr. Lukens, who suggested he come up to Ohio for a conference. Wright replied he didn't have that kind of time. Finally, he sent a demand letter to the Carolina Land and Lumber stating that if he did not get his $7,500, he would "take such action as I deem expedient to protect my interests."[59]

Seip had an answer for that, too. He had his correspondence with Wright and Assistant Secretary Hays copied, and in late 1911 bundled it off to Representative Moss in Washington. He claimed he did it "because he felt Mr. Elliott had been treated unfairly," but admitted that he didn't consider it until Wright wrote his company threatening legal action. Annoyed, his partners indicated that this was his, Seip's, problem, not the company's, and requested that he deal with it appropriately.[60] He did, in his own way. Wright tried to blackmail Elliott into silence, and he had tried to blackmail Wright into silence. Very simple.

After Chairman Moss finished his examination, everyone sat back, initially too stunned to say anything. George McCabe came weakly to the defense of Hays, pointing out that the Assistant Secretary did not actually invest anything in the Mattamuskeet proposition. He was met with a thundering silence.

Eventually, Representative Floyd asked Seip the question that most of the committee must have been wondering:

> *Rep. Floyd*: Let me see if I fully understand what was done in regard to the Moyock proposition. You entered into negotiations with Mr. Wright, who was in the Government service in 1909, to do certain things to further this project along, and in consideration you were to give him stock in the amount of $7,500 in the company to be formed?
> *Mr. Seip*: Yes, sir.
> *Mr. Floyd*: Your company then applied, upon his suggestion, for a survey of these lands.
> *Mr. Seip*: I believe so.
> *Mr. Floyd*: So that a survey was done at the expense of the United States Government?
> *Mr. Seip*: Yes, sir.
> *Mr. Floyd*: In order to carry out the project other than at your own expense, and to put the burden on the people of North Carolina, in part at least, it was necessary to get an act passed; a drainage act?
> *Mr. Seip*: Yes, sir.
> *Mr. Floyd*: You understand that Mr. Wright prepared that bill?
> *Mr. Seip*: I understood so, yes.
> *Mr. Floyd*: And it did pass?
> *Mr. Seip*: Yes, sir.
> *Mr. Floyd*: And under this law $55,000 in bonds were to be issued to pay for dredging in Moyock?
> *Mr. Seip*: $11,000 to pay for the dredge, $44,000 for the work.
> *Mr. Floyd*: And your company owned the dredging company that did the work?

Mr. Seip: Yes sir.
Mr. Floyd: And your company owned the land benefited by the drainage?
Mr. Seip: Most, but not all the land.
Rep. Floyd: Do you think Mr. Wright or anybody else could arrange a matter more satisfactorily to your interests than they were arranged, whereby the Government stands the expense of the original survey, and the State of North Carolina bears a considerable portion of the expense, and you get the contract and get paid for draining your own lands, or largely your own land?
Mr. Seip: It was arranged, it is well arranged, the work would not have been done today had [there] not been that kind of an arrangement.
Rep. Floyd: Then why did you refuse to pay Wright?
Mr. Seip: I don't know that Mr. Wright was just absolutely instrumental in making that arrangement.[61]

Chairman Moss thanked him for staying over an extra day to answer all their questions, and even the most hardened of machine politicians watched with awe, disgust or a combination of the two, as Mr. John Seip of Chillicothe, Ohio, slid out the door, untouched and unmoved by it all.

7

A Damned Lying Statement

> Thomas Will was the John the Baptist of the Everglades. He was sneered at, scoffed at, cursed and threatened, but he kept right on trying to build his city in the grass.
>
> —Alfred and Kathryn Hanna, 1947[1]

> As to Thomas Will, Mr. Elliott mentioned him, but I did not come into any real personal contract with him and have no memory of him. I don't know how much there is to remember.
>
> —Arthur Morgan, 1946[2]

In private, Chairman Moss had instructed all the participants that any discussion of *Senate Document No. 89* was out of bounds. It was a publication of the Senate; it had been paid for out of a Senate appropriation. But it was almost impossible to exclude everything, and once in a while something would break through the surface, such as J.O. Wright's description of editing the printer's dummy in William Jennings's law office in Jacksonville.

But on March 11, Charles Elliott hurriedly wrote Arthur Morgan:

> A new factor was introduced in the inquiry today. The committee had previously agreed that Senate Doc. #89 should not be taken up, and when anything came up that pointed that way it was stopped at once. Congressional courtesy, you know. Sen. Fletcher, however, wants to preserve the "integrity of Doc. 89," and some shadows had been cast over it in formal hearings. He asked to testify today and make a statement regarding the document. Moss warned him that the committee did not propose to take up that subject, but he did not refuse to hear the statement of the Senator, but warned it would oblige him to admit other testimony on that subject.[3]

Senate Document No. 89 was a compilation of about 65 documents relating to the reclamation of the Everglades, mostly excerpts of reports and legislative material from before 1900. Its significance was that it contained both the text of the Wright report extract and the text of the Wright Report, which the Agriculture Department had not published. Representative Clark asserted, loudly and publicly, that its sole purpose was to leak the Wright Report, and that the version that appeared in the senate document was not only an error-filled preliminary draft, but had been further selectively edited by William Jennings, Duncan Fletcher and Thomas Will to make it appear even more favorable to Everglades drainage than Wright's original version.[4]

However, Fletcher spent most of the early morning testifying about the mimeographed flyer that one of Elliott's junior engineers prepared in January 1910 and that Will and Howe came by to complain about. Objectively, it was of little importance, but it had become the focus of an ugly newspaper spat between Governor Gilchrist and Senator

Fletcher on one side, and Representative Clark on the other.[5] George McCabe, in his opening statement back in February, maintained that Wilson revoked the circular on his own initiative on February 9, 1910. Clark variously asserted that Wilson told him he suppressed the circular because he was getting hammered from both sides—Everglades boosters and detractors—within the Florida legislative delegation; at other times Clark claimed Wilson told him he did it because Senator Fletcher asked him to; on still another occasion he said that Wilson told him he did it to satisfy the big Everglades land sales companies.[6]

Duncan Fletcher, U.S. Senator from Florida, 1909–25, on his way to testify in the Moss Committee hearings, 1912. Photo by Harris and Ewing of Washington, D.C. (Library of Congress No. LC-DIG-hec-02713).

Solicitor McCabe maneuvered the spat into a debate about whether Elliott broke department rules in releasing the circular in the first place. In keeping with the department's Byzantine regulations, nobody could agree if it violated department policy, because nobody could agree on what the department's policy was, or whether it even had one. Elliott typically informed inquirers that it was the general rule of the Office of Experiment Stations to permit the review of work-in-progress in the office, but it could not send out drafts or preliminary reports without the permission of the secretary.[7]

A.D. Morehouse explained that the circular wasn't really a report. It replaced a system that existed before he arrived, whereby letters containing common inquiries would be marked by a member of the staff with a series of numbers. The numbers indicated pre-written paragraphs kept in a binder that the stenographers would use to type out semi-stock replies. There usually would be a personalized paragraph or two at the end of each letter. About January 1910, so many Everglades inquiries began to be received

A.D. Morehouse, Charles Elliott's assistant at the Drainage Investigations Division in 1911, was reinstated after the Moss Committee issued its final report, but moved to the Bureau of the Census, where he became an expert on business statistics. Photo c. 1914, by Harris & Ewing (Library of Congress No. LC-H261-767).

that Elliott had a junior engineer, Anson Marsden, prepare the flier. It was intended to be used as an attachment to regular letters. Elliott cleared it with Mr. Beal, the editor of the Office of Experiment Stations, which was standard procedure. Elliott, on the other hand, said it was Marsden's idea, but he approved it as "an excellent idea." Marsden did submit it to Mr. Beal for review, but Elliott said Morehouse was incorrect in his belief that it was submitted to Beal because Beal was editor; Dr. True was on leave and Beal was acting chief of experiment stations.[8]

Dr. True denied knowing about the circular before it went out, but had no objection to it, nor did he think it was a violation of any policy of the Agriculture Department or the Office of Experiment Stations. He could not cite any regulation either permitting or prohibiting it. Walter Beal acknowledged that he reviewed and approved it. He did not consider it an official publication, but merely a means of facilitating correspondence, and as such it did not occur to him to submit it to the Department's publication office or the Secretary's office.[9]

Joseph Arnold said that circular should "unquestionably" have been submitted to him at the publications office for review because it was "regarding a forthcoming publication." To justify his argument he pointed to a sentence in the flier that stated "further information regarding the conditions in southern Florida will be issued later by the Office of Experiment Stations."[10] Pressed for more detail, he asserted that the only acceptable reply, given that it contained information in, or about, a forthcoming bulletin would be to answer that there was no published material available on the subject. He claimed that there were written orders against sending out matter without the approval of the secretary, but was unable to come up anything except two intra-office memos, one for the Forestry Service and the other for the Bureau of Plant Industry. Both concerned anticipated actions affecting the acquisition or use of land, such as timbering or the planting of experimental plots or farms, where leaks could affect adjacent land values.[11]

Back in May 1907, Secretary Wilson, writing to Governor Broward, noted, "it is not usual for the Department to give out information about work at this stage, but since your State is already engaged in work with reference to draining Lake Okeechobee, and you desire this information in order to assist you in making the most effective use of public funds for this purpose, I shall make no objection to giving you a summary of this work." This could be interpreted as blanket permission for the Office of Experiment Stations to share work-in-progress information relating to Florida surveys, but Elliott did not interpret it that liberally, which is why he told Henry C. Hall to get the permission of the Secretary if he wanted a copy of the Wright excerpt in February 1909.[12]

Actually, the policy of the Agriculture Department was not wholly irrational. Back in 1903, a USDA statistician named Edwin Holmes prepared a white paper projecting that year's cotton production and damage from boll weevil infestation, which was a particular problem that year. The information leaked out and was used to manipulate cotton futures prices in several regional markets. President Roosevelt was extremely angry, and Secretary Wilson initiated an investigation that conclusively identified Holmes as the source. He apparently sold the information to pay off gambling debts. He was fired in late 1904.[13] However, while Wilson addressed the immediate problem, he failed to implement written polices, procedures or systematic checks to ensure that another occurrence did not happen. While he was vigorous and responsive in running day-to-day operations, the concept of a modern multi-divisional administrative structure eluded him, perhaps because of the rapid expansion of his department or the inordinate demands placed on his time and attention by the decade-long struggle to get a replacement USDA headquarters building sited and built on the Mall.

The Secretary had the final word on the subject. The circular, while "it was on paper, and it had come out of Washington, and was from the Department of Agriculture, really was not a publication at all." Regardless, it "was a clear defiance of orders," because "nobody has the authority to print and publish without our [office] knowing about it."[14] So there you have it: the flier was not a publication, but Elliott violated Department policy for sending out a publication without permission. Only one who has spent much of their career in the hallowed halls of government could be expected to grasp the celestial subtleties behind such an edict.

II

Eventually, the questioning of Fletcher turned to the more substantial topic of the Wright Report. He acknowledged visiting Secretary Wilson on February 4 after Governor Broward telegraphed him the day before. But that telegram complained about a forthcoming *bulletin* regarding the Everglades:

> *Jacksonville, Fla. Feb 3, 1910*
> Received a telegram "Bulletin coming out from Agriculture Department knocking Everglades." I earnestly ask that you investigate and prevent any such action if you can. I understand that Dr. H.W. Wiley, chief chemist, agriculture department, is opposed to having his name used by companies selling Everglades land.
> /s/ N.B. Broward[15]

Fletcher was visited that same morning by a Mr. Bowen, a partner of Thomas Will's at the Everglades Land Sales Company, who, when shown the telegram, explained that Broward must have been referring to the mimeographed flier. Bowen had a copy, and gave it to him.[16] As Fletcher later explained, it never occurred to him that Broward could have been referring to the Wright Report, because Broward, like everyone else involved with Everglades land, was chomping at the bit to get it released, so a complaint would have made no sense. In addition, Marsden's circular itself made reference to "further information ... that will be issued later."[17]

Thus armed with a copy of the circular, Fletcher went to Secretary Wilson's office.

Wilson knew nothing about it. Summoning Joseph Arnold, the Department's chief editor, Wilson asked him if it was genuine. After a brief investigation, Arnold verified that it was. Wilson ordered it recalled.[18] Arnold testified that:

> About 10 o'clock in the morning of the day I was called into the Secretary's office, and in the presence of Senator Fletcher, I was shown a copy of a typewritten unsigned letter relating to the Everglades and the bulletin in press on that subject, and I was asked by the Secretary if I was sending out that circular. He stated he had never seen it. I told him that I was not sending it out; that it had never been submitted to my office for the Secretary's approval. He then directed me to ascertain who had sent it out and to see that no further copies were distributed.[19]

Note that Arnold says he was shown *both* a copy of the circular *and the forthcoming bulletin then in press* (i.e., the Wright Report). Fletcher said that at this same meeting "He [Wilson] was quite emphatic about directing Mr. Arnold to have that thing stopped." Fletcher then said "Mr. Secretary, I understand that a report on the Everglades, as a result of the investigations made down there, has already been prepared, already completed, and has been ready for printing something like a year; and I am wondering why that it is not being gotten out. I mentioned that it was known as the Wright Report. … He said, 'I will send for it and look it up right away.'"[20]

This would imply that, contrary to Arnold's account, there was no copy of the bulletin at this meeting. Fletcher was asked directly at the hearings if he had been shown, or had seen, a copy of the Wright Report at this February 4 meeting. He answered "no."[21]

Finally, Thomas Will was in the Secretary's office several times during this period, and gave this account:

> When people were calling upon him in February, 1910 in connection with the Elliott two-page [circular], he seemed to grow exasperated over the fact that the Florida delegation in Congress was divided on the Everglades question … he brought his fist down on the desk and declared with emphasis, "I told them fellars that I wouldn't do a d—ned thing fer 'em til they quit fighting among themselves!" I think that shows his attitude pretty well. Now we know Senator Fletcher was trying to get the Wright Report published at that time, and Secretary Wilson had already promised him that he would publish anything Wright prepared.[22]

The decision not to print Elliott's heavily revised version of the Everglades report ("No. 3") was made in June 1910. In September 1911, a manuscript or early proof of *Senate Document No. 89* was circulated to the Office of Experiment Stations. It contained the July 1909 version of the Wright report. A.D. Morehouse testified about what happened next:

> In looking the galley proof over, I immediately saw that it contained the so-called Wright Report…. I took it that they were desirous of obtaining all the information on the Everglades that could be obtained…. I gathered together the majority of the reports which we had in our office files…. I immediately took the galley proof and these reports which I had gathered together and went over to see Mr. Stallings [Mr. Arnold's deputy], and he substantiated Mr. Beal's statement about having had a communications from the Printing Committee stating the committee would be glad to receive these suggestions…. I prepared what we call a "dummy," entitled "Inserts for Document 89" … the word came to me one morning that it was desired that I accompany Mr. Stallings to an interview with Mr. Carter, of the Printing Committee. I was preparing to accompany Mr. Stallings when Mr. Elliott came into the office [from out of town] so he went instead.[23]

These inserts were:

Insert (A):	Excerpts from Bulletin 158 (1904 Annual Report for the bureau).
Insert (B):	Outline of proposed Everglades survey, by C.G. Elliott, January 17, 1907.
Insert (C):	Progress report on Everglades survey, by C.G. Elliott, June, 1907.

Insert (D):	Report of preliminary drainage investigation, Florida Everglades, by C.G. Elliott, August, 1907.
Insert (E):	Instructions to 1907–08 field party, Everglades survey, by C.G. Elliott, October 24, 1907.
Insert (F):	Revised table of contents, Bulletin 218.
Insert (G):	Replacement section: "The Drainage Problem"
Insert (H):	Text of House Resolution 694, instructing Secretary of Agriculture to provide information pertaining to draining of Everglades
Insert (I):	Department of Agriculture's report in response to H.R. 694, May 20, 1910, with attachments.

It needs to be emphasized that what Morehouse received was a manuscript of the entire *Senate Document No. 89*, not just the Wright Report. Also, it was sent in the belief that comments and updates were being actively sought by the Congressional Joint Committee on Printing. Morehouse and Elliott took advantage of this invitation to alter "No. 2" to "No. 3," by excising a ten-page section containing most of the drainage engineering and cost estimates and replacing it with two new sections, "Insert F" and "Insert G." But in addition to this, several other reports and documents that were independent of the Wright Report, but were related to the history of the Everglades investigation, were also prepared for inclusion.

Elliott later verified that Morehouse did not give the Joint Committee on Printing a clean copy of his January 28, 1910, version (the so-called "Elliott Report"), because there was only one copy in existence, in Elliott's desk, where it had been since being returned from Mr. Arnold's office in June 1910, after Secretary Wilson decided to cancel its printing. However, if inserts E, F and G were inserted into the Wright version and a couple of introductory sentences changed, the Wright Report would become the Elliott Report.[24]

Returning to Arnold's account:

> I think that following Senator Fletcher's visit to which I have referred—perhaps the same day or the next day–I reported to him that I had the page proof back with the numerous alterations and changes in it, and I think he asked me to leave it with him. At any rate, that day or the next he instructed me to make a careful reading of it for him. On the 7th I took the proof to him and talked to him as a result of the reading.... It was evident to me from the many changes and much new matter submitted that there was a disagreement in the Office of Experiment Stations with regard to the matter herein, and that it was a time when extreme precautions should be exercised in the printing of the document.[25]

At the Moss Committee hearings, everybody assumed that the document Arnold was referring to was the printer's dummy that Morehouse prepared for *Senate Document No. 89*. But it was not. This follow-up meeting took place on February 7, 1910, *sixteen months before the draft of the Senate document was circulated.* Thus, there are two different "draft" documents: the first is the manuscript of the report Elliott prepared in January 1910, which is what Arnold gave to Secretary Wilson in the February 4 meeting and reviewed with him three days later. The second is the proposed Morehouse insertions to the initial draft of *Senate Document No. 89* that was prepared in July 1911. It is clear that Secretary Wilson knew on February 4, 1910, that an "Elliott Report" existed. But did Fletcher? Joseph Arnold says he showed it to him at the same time he showed it to Wilson at the February 4 meeting. Fletcher says he never saw it, all the way up to March 1912.[26]

But the crucial issue is not whether there was a copy of Elliott's proposed revision at the February 4, 1910, meeting between Senator Fletcher, Secretary Wilson and Joseph Arnold; the critical issue is whether Fletcher knew at this meeting that Governor Broward was referring to it when he stated in his telegram "Received a telegram 'Bulletin coming out from Agriculture Department knocking Everglades.' I earnestly ask that you investigate and prevent any such action if you can," because if Broward, who had been pressing for almost a year for the Wright Report's release, was now suddenly concerned about its publication, this would imply that knowledge about its transformation into the new, less favorable Elliott version had already gotten back to Tallahassee. It is quite a coincidence that the very day that Fletcher showed up at Secretary Wilson's office asking about some vaguely defined Everglades report that concerned Governor Broward was also the day Joseph Arnold showed Secretary Wilson the newer, decidedly less favorable Elliott version.[27]

At the time of the Moss Committee hearings, nobody put the pieces of this jigsaw puzzle together, but the evidence was in the files of Solicitor McCabe. His office put together a timeline accounting for the travel voucher and timecard allocations of J.O. Wright between February 1, 1906, and his resignation on February 15, 1910.[28] Between December 10, 1909, and January 20, 1910, he was in the office, and spent at least 50 percent of his hours working on "rewriting report on the Everglades of Florida." In other words, he spent six weeks working on the Elliott Report. He would have known everything that was in it, and it explains why Elliott was so insistent that he had the one and only copy of the manuscript from January 28, 1910, when it came back from the publications office, until November 12, 1911, when he turned it over to solicitor McCabe: there was always a question of who, if anyone, leaked it.[29] Wright not only knew what was in his report, he knew what was in Elliott's Report, and probably told Broward.

III

But lacking all the pieces of the puzzle, the questioning plodded along through a couple of hours of polite testimony and cross-examination on general topics before Moss asked, "now, then Senator, are there any other further statements you care to make in the matter?" The Senator replied that he wished to make some observations regarding *Senate Document No. 89*. As Elliott wrote to Arthur Morgan, Chairman Moss cautioned him about venturing into this topic. The Senator acknowledged his warning and waived his immunity. Henry G. Davis, lawyer for Elliott and Morehouse, said that being the case, he would reserve his cross-examination until the Senator had completed his statement. Everyone sat back and waited.

According to Fletcher He started compiling material in late June or early July 1911. The resolution approving the expenditure for *Senate Document No. 89* was offered by Senator Reed Smoot of Utah on July 16 and approved on August 7, 1911. The Senate recessed on August 23 and Fletcher went home to Jacksonville about September 1.

At about this time, the Senator was able to secure a copy of "what appeared to me to be a full, authentic copy, page proof of … Bulletin No. 218." This page proof of the "No. 2" version of the Wright report was apparently used to provide the material for the version that appeared in *Senate Document No. 89*.[30]

On September 8, Mr. Carter of the Joint Committee on Printing forwarded the proofs of various documents that were to go into *Senate Document No. 89* from Washington to Jacksonville. One of these was a marked-up, pasted-in printer's dummy that matches the description of the material put together by Morehouse and given to Joseph Arnold. Former governor Jennings was already at work helping Fletcher edit the material. He asked Jennings to arrange a meeting between him, Jennings and Wright at Jennings's office. Fletcher brought the printer's dummy. Wright brought a manuscript of his original February 1909 report. Between them they edited out all of the changes, Fletcher claimed, mostly because they lengthened the document, and Fletcher was on a page budget with the Joint Committee on Printing. When they were finished, the result was forwarded to Mr. Carter for insertion in *Senate Document No. 89*. Fletcher said very little about the participation of Thomas Will.[31]

George H. Carter, head of the Congressional Joint Committee on Publications. He arranged, along with Senator Duncan Fletcher, to keep Charles Elliott's and A.D. Moorhouse's corrections to the original draft of the Wright Report out of the version finally published in *Senate Document No. 89*. Photo c. 1915, by Harris & Ewing (Library of Congress No. LC-DIG-hec-18250).

If this account appears self-contradictory, it is. Almost at the start of his statement, Fletcher said that he received a copy of the page proofs of Bulletin 218 ("No. 2"; the Wright Report) and used it. Then, at the end of his account, he gave a long, four page explanation of how he was sent Morehouse's printer's dummy containing Elliott's "Insert G" and at least five additional reports, and (placing himself in the editing room), he, Wright and Jennings, using only a manuscript of Wright's February 1909 "No. 1" version, produced a perfect, word-for-word rendition of the "No. 2" version.[32]

This testimony was almost an exact recitation of the testimony J.O. Wright had given a month earlier, on February 19:

Mr. Davis: Tell me exactly what you did in reference to the preparation of this Senate Document No. 89. First, what was submitted to you in the material for your consideration at that time?

Mr. Wright: There was a bunch of galley proof, probably 60, 70, 80 pages, submitted to me to look through.... I laid aside the first 40 or 45 pages, and was then asked by Senator Fletcher to go over the remaining portion of that galley proof, which had been set up and printed and then had been marked over with a pencil and had attached to it by means of clips numerous exhibits or inserts to take the place of certain paragraphs. He asked me to go through that galley proof and point out to him, as best I could, just what part of that matter contained in that report had been agreed to by Mr. Elliott, Mr. Beal and myself, and transmitted to the Secretary on June 25, 1909, to adjust the text or matter contained in that proof that had been set up by the Department of Agriculture and run off into page proof.... I read them through and pointed out such points as I could distinguish as having been injected into the report. That is all the connection I had with it.

Mr. Davis: The galley proof of which you speak was not merely a galley proof of your report, but was a galley proof of what was afterwards became *Senate Document No. 89*?

Mr. Wright: Yes, sir.

Mr. Davis: These inserts of which you speak were all identified and, as you say, attached by means of clips to the galley proof?

Henry G. Davis, 1911. Davis was U.S. Senator from West Virginia 1871–83, then in private practice as a lawyer. As counsel for Dr. Harvey Wiley in the 1911 "Wiley-McCabe" hearings he exposed the perfidy of President Taft and Secretary Wilson and the perjury of Agricultural Department Solicitor McCabe. He was subsequently retained by C. G. Elliott and A. D. Morehouse for the Moss Committee hearings in 1912, when he effectively destroyed the careers of Elliott accusers McCabe and J. O. Wright. Photograph by Harris & Ewing (Library of Congress No. LC-H261-219 [219]).

Mr. Wright: Yes, sir.
Mr. Davis: As intended for substitution or submission?
Mr. Wright: Yes, sir.
Mr. Davis: And those you rejected?
Mr. Wright: Yes, sir.
Mr. Davis: Did you know at that time you rejected them that they were matter from the Office of Drainage Investigations, taken from the final report as submitted on January 28, 1910?
Mr. Wright: No, sir. I did not know at that time that a final report had ever been prepared. I was simply asked to point out matter which was not contained in the report which was submitted on June 25, 1909.[33]

It makes no sense. If everybody associated with the Senate document was sure they wanted the earlier "No. 2" version to go in and the later "No. 3" to stay out, why didn't everybody just admit it? You could easily verify this by doing a side-by-side comparison of pages 140–181 of *Senate Document No. 89* and the text of "No. 2" published in the so-called "3-in-1" document, that is, "Exhibit B of No. 5." In fact, Carter and Arnold discussed how the "No. 2" title page should be changed to drop its Bulletin 218 references and replaced with others appropriate to the senate document, and Fletcher corroborated this:

> After the first order was made—the resolution made to print the document—the first thing I heard from Mr. Carter regarding it was he saw me and said the Department of Agriculture wanted to strike out the number of the bulletin [on the title page] because the number had been given to another bulletin, and I said "why of course, strike that out."[34]

The answer started to come clear when the chairman asked Fletcher where he got the page proof of Bulletin 218. He answered that he got it from Thomas Will. Chairman Moss asked Fletcher, point blank, "why was it you declined to use Insert G," referring to the revised Everglades drainage plan in the Elliott Report. "Was it excluded because Maj. Wright would not stand for it?"

Sen. Fletcher: I do not remember anything specific about that. It was embodied in the other matter, mixed in with and attached to a lot of other surplusage, it was only a portion of the whole report, and it was what Maj. Wright would not stand for.
Mr. Moss: Then it was excluded because you felt it was included in the other matter, or because Maj. Wright would not stand for it?
Sen. Fletcher: Both. In other words, it was material that had been suggested by Mr. Elliott after the report had first been agreed up and without his [Wright's] concurrence, and as far as I know, after he had left the department.
Mr. Moss: Is it not a fact that you did reject Insert G and did publish the matter you received from Mr. Will?
Sen. Fletcher: I rejected the whole of that insert as it appears from page 558 to 590.
Mr. Moss: Did you ever ask the Department of Agriculture to submit you anything?
Sen. Fletcher: I did not.
Mr. Moss: Now, as a matter of fact, was not *Senate Document No. 89* gotten up without any cooperation from the Department of Agriculture?
Sen. Fletcher: It was gotten up and printed without any request of the Department of Agriculture.
Mr. Moss: You did, however, publish a matter that was handed you by Mr. Will, a person not connected in any way with the public service.[35]

Thomas Will did verify that, at one point, Fletcher and Jennings were using the marked-up dummy version of *Senate Document No. 89* that Morehouse and Elliott had created, and this was a source of vexation to them. On September 13, 1911, Will wrote his boss, Vance Helm that:

I am enclosing first publicity paper on Sen. Doc. 89. Document was held up by Mr. Elliott of Agriculture department getting hold of it and attempting largely to make it over. Among other things he arranged that the Wright report should be an Elliott report. The matter has been gone over at this end and sent to Senator Fletcher who is daily expected to return it.[36]

Three weeks later, on October 4, Will wrote again, and noted, "I had this morning a letter from Senator Fletcher stating that he will be here next Monday with the document. The Elliott suggestions have evidently made him a lot of work."[37] Then, a few days later, on October 14, he wrote: "Nothing, either from Elliott or anyone else is going into the document, as it now stands."[38]

There is one interpretation that fits these disparate facts. Initially, Jennings and Fletcher did start out with the printer's dummy that was given them by Mr. Carter, who, in turn, had received the inserts from Morehouse. These were a cause of consternation to Jennings and Fletcher, who attempted to have Wright reverse-engineer the "Elliott Report" back into the "Wright Report."[39] As noted earlier, if Wright was truthful in saying that all he had to work with was a copy of his manuscript (which the "3-in-1" document indicates was significantly different than the second, Bulletin 218 version) this would have been an all but impossible task. Hence, Thomas Will went to someone, probably Samuel Copper, a foreman at the Government Printing Office, and secured a clean copy of the Bulletin 218 page proofs sometime after October 9, 1911. These were then used to prepare *Senate Document No. 89*.[40] This is the reason that Carter did not want to give the printer's dummy back to Elliott: it was proof that there was another, later version of the Everglades drainage report in existence, which the preparers of the Senate document wanted to hide. This would have been Elliott's manuscript version of "No. 3" which stayed in his desk drawer until he turned it over to Solicitor McCabe on January 4, 1912.[41]

Elliott verified that he had, in fact, sent a letter to the Secretary in May 1910 stating that the "No. 2" report was not published in September 1909 "owing to a difference of opinion among Members of Congress and State authorities," and he still stood by that statement.[42] Elliott stated emphatically that Wright had prepared nothing beyond field notes by February 1909, and that the "Wright report extract" was not, in fact an extract; it was a brief report written by Wright only after Henry C. Hall received a note from the Secretary instructing A.C. True to accommodate Hall. There was no manuscript of a "Wright Report" until about May 20, 1909. Asked to account for the February 1909 cover date, Elliott stated that "Mr. Wright simply dated his report back to the date on which that special extract was prepared."[43]

Asked if the differences among the Florida congressional and state officials had resulted in an incomplete report being released, Elliott replied "no." Given the budget the project was allocated, the report had no hope of being complete; the most that could be hoped for was that its hopelessly inadequate data was correct; but this turned out not to be the case. Asked by Representative Mays what a complete investigation would entail, Elliott replied at least two years and $150,000.[44]

The most illuminating testimony concerned the inserts that A.D. Morehouse had prepared in September 1911 for *Senate Document No. 89*. George Carter of the Joint Committee had asked Morehouse and Mr. Stallings to come by, but at the last minute Elliott returned to town and he alone went over:

Mr. Carter had received from our office, through Mr. Stallings, copies of reports, manuscript copies of reports upon the Everglades and he wanted to ask some questions about them.... I explained to him that the report preceding had been withdrawn ... and I wanted him to understand that this final report was the only one which our office stood for and we wanted that printed. Mr. Carter seemed quite hostile to any suggestions I might make.... He said "I don't understand it as you do. This bunch of copy which I have here was prepared and arranged by Dr. Will and is the copy, as I understand it, that is to be printed as a Senate document." I said, "Then Mr. Carter, I am mistaken, I have not comprehended the situation. I will withdraw all these reports and all this matter we have submitted." But he declined to let me take it away.... I recognized what I now believed to be a fact, that the people interested in the sale of Everglades lands undrained were attempting to dominate the publication of every report which had been sent out of my office on the Everglades.[45]

(In rebuttal testimony, George Carter went on record as saying Elliott's statement "was absolutely false." According to the newspapers, what he actually said is that it "was a damned lying statement" and challenged the elderly Elliott to fight him in the hallway. Moss ordered him to calm down and instructed the recorder to strike most of his comments from the record.[46])

If there was convincing evidence that a concerted effort was made to bury the Wright Report, it came out in the testimony of Dr. Beverly Galloway, Chief of the Bureau of Plant Industry, and Dr. C.L. Goodrich, a junior plant scientist in his bureau. The "No. 2" version of the Wright Report had been circulated to the bureau in July 1909 and returned in a few days without comment. A manuscript version of "No. 3" (apparently Elliott's manuscript), was sent to Dr. Galloway, supposedly at his request. Dr. Galloway kept it for about a week and returned it to Arnold, because he wanted to have a relatively low-level scientist, Prof. Charles L. Goodrich, review it, and he was away until May. Dr. Galloway said that he did not prepare a review, but after reading it,

...it did strike me as being a publication that might be considered as controversial and might be considered, in some particulars at least, problematical, and for these reasons and other reasons, if I had been asked, which I was not, I probably would have given my opinion as to the fact that the publication should not be published.[47]

Although he initially testified that he was not asked, he later stated that he "could not say" if he had advised the Secretary, then later corrected himself, recalling, "I think the greater probability is that I advised the Secretary not to publish it."[48]

In May, Arnold again sent it to Prof. Goodrich. Prof. Goodrich replied with a memo on June 4, 1910, stating, "I think the subject matter of the bulletin would be received with interest by the public," but that "the Everglades proposition is being fostered by politicians and land promoters; therefore all the material of a speculative nature should be omitted, lest it may be used as to mislead prospective investors in Florida lands."[49] In fact, Prof. Goodrich did not red pencil any particular "speculative matter"; instead, he excised the entire drainage plan, about 7,500 words.

Prof. Goodrich admitted he was not a civil engineer. This was the first time he had ever commented on another bureau's report on any subject other than plant industry. Prof. Goodrich did not report to Dr. Galloway; he lacked seniority. He reported to his superintendent, Mr. Brodie, who reported to the Chief of the Office of Farm Management, Prof. Spillman, who reported to Dr. Galloway. Dr. Galloway stated that he never saw Prof. Goodrich's report. It went from Prof. Goodrich to Dr. Galloway's assistant, Mr. Powell, then directly to the Secretary's office. This was not normal practice; typically, anything going to the Secretary's office would be personally reviewed by Dr. Galloway first. The normal procedure was not followed at the request of the Secretary's office.[50]

It defies belief that a junior scientist reviewed those portions of an extensive report in which he had no experience or competence, recommended that an entire section be redacted, failed to process his review using proper procedure, and then no one at the Department of Agriculture questioned it. Prof. Goodrich's report was, in all probability, written long after a decision not to proceed with the publication of "No. 3," most likely after Representative Clark started investigating the fate of the circular and bulletin in October 1911, and was written either by Dr. Galloway or, more likely, George McCabe. It was so patently absurd, so clumsy, that it has the fingerprints of the solicitor's office all over it.

IV

Joseph Arnold testified that Mr. Carter told him that the copy of Bulletin 218 that the Joint Committee on Printing had come from the Government Printing Office, but he had no way to verify this.[51] Many years later, in 1935, Will wrote that he had gotten the copy he gave to Senator Fletcher "through the Government Printing Office largely by my own efforts, helped by Saml. E. Copper, foreman there, and Okeelanta pioneer."[52]

In this letter, Will clearly is referring to the theft he arranged in 1911 for *Senate Document No. 89*. It is an unsolved mystery whether this is the same copy he purloined in January 1910, when he was an editor at *Conservation* magazine. He was extensively questioned by Chairman Moss about the earlier theft. He claimed that in that incident he kept it only about two days. He did not copy or print any of it. He did not show it or share it with anyone. He did not pay or provide consideration of any type to his source. It was definitely the "No. 2" Wright Report. He did not know in February 1910 of the existence of a later "No. 3" Elliott Report. He knew that his source did return it. The only question he would not answer was the name of his source, although he admitted it was a government employee who became interested in Everglades land at one of his sales presentations, and later purchased some.[53]

Samuel Copper would have met both these criteria. The simplest explanation is that he stole a copy of the page proofs twice, the first time in January 1910, the second time in August or September 1911. The second most likely explanation is that Will received the August/September 1911 copy from Joseph Arnold, upon the request of Mr. Carter of the Joint Printing Committee. In either case, the idea of a civilian arranging for the theft of a government document for the purpose of giving it to a United States Senator so he can give it to a committee that had the authority to request it in the first place is faintly preposterous, but given the specific circumstances, entirely possible.

The version appearing in *Senate Document No. 89* was taken from a proof copy run off in mid–1909.[54] It is likely that Wright did sit down in Jennings's office and edit the printer's dummy prepared by A.D. Morehouse using his original "No. 1" manuscript. But if he did so, it was never used. It may have been a case of the right hand not knowing what the left hand was doing. Many hands were working on Senate Document No. 89 and Thomas Will's correspondence indicates that he and his cohorts were pressed for time. Will and Jennings were largely working independently of each other, with Jennings working on the older, legal material, and Will working on the twentieth century documents.[55]

In the end, *Senate Document No. 89*, like *Senate Report No. 338* of 1848, proved to be more a historical document than an effective piece of political propaganda. Although several of its older legal documents were edited down, the fact that so many copies of each anthology was published—at least 30,000 copies in the case of *Senate Document*

No. 89—means that these were often the only versions available, especially in the pre-internet era. In other cases, important documents were preserved *because* they became identified as significant due to their inclusion in *Senate Document No. 89*. It is entirely possible that we might not have a full text of the Buckingham Smith report today without it. While it failed in its intended purpose, it has become an invaluable historical record and is one reason why there is such a rich literature of Everglades history as compared to, say the Albemarle-Pamlico Peninsula of North Carolina, the Okefenokee Swap of Georgia, the Great Dismal Swamp of Virginia, the Hackensack Meadows of New Jersey or the Mississippi, Yukon, and Sacramento river deltas.

The irony, of course, is that the purpose of the Moss Committee hearings was to investigate the alleged "suppression" of the mimeographed circular and the Wright report. By the time the hearings were half over, no later than mid–March, it was apparent that these had become non-issues. The circular had been discontinued because Secretary Wilson was in a no-win situation, caught between the fractious Florida legislative and state delegations. He was used to the give-and-take of federal and local officials from one state seeking an advantage over another and was appalled when Florida officials appeared more interested in fighting each other than gaining any benefit for their state.

Despite the Solicitor's rather transparent attempt to provide a technical justification for rejecting the Elliott Report through a clearly fabricated negative review from the Bureau of Plant Industry, the Wright-Elliott Report had been pulled out of production first, because of glaring technical errors, then, when these had been at least somewhat addressed, because Secretary Wilson did not want to anger one or the other faction within the Florida delegations.

The original issues had become irrelevant. As the committee progressed through its second month and its twentieth session, it grew less about suppressed circulars and cancelled reports and more about the fundamental question of whether Secretary Wilson and Solicitor McCabe were running a department of the United States Government, an insane asylum, or a Persian Bazaar of greed, abuse and corruption

8

The Best Photographs I Have Ever Seen

Rep. Moss: You really feel it would have been proper for Mr. Elliott and Mr. Morehouse to have passed the hat among their friends to take up this question of a deficiency?
Dr. True: Under the circumstances, I think they would have been justified.
Rep. Moss: Do you really believe that is the only proper method by which the bills of a government agency can be settled?
Dr. True: I do not see any other way.[1]

—Moss Committee Hearings, Day 40 (July 31, 1912)

The last week in April was a very long one for Assistant Secretary Willett Hays. After the topic of *Senate Document No. 89* had run its course, Chairman Moss returned to the business of the North Carolina land dealings, starting with Professor Hays. To review, Representative John Small wrote to Secretary Wilson in August 1908 asking for assistance in making a drainage survey of Lake Mattamuskeet. Wilson was out on leave, and Hays forwarded the request to Charles Elliott. The work was urged on the drainage division by Representative Small of North Carolina and approved by A.C. True. The preliminary survey was made in October by S.H. McCrory under Wright's supervision.[2]

Willet M. Hays, Assistant Secretary of Agriculture, 1909–12. Photographer unknown, Bain News Service (Library of Congress No. LC-B2-2625-8 [P&P]).

John Seip originally contacted the Office of Experiment Stations in October, asking for assistance in surveying land belonging to his Carolina Land and Timber Company at Moyock. Elliott was initially skeptical about undertaking the project, as the chances of forming a drainage district were low under existing North Carolina law, but Representative Small insisted that it could be done under the proposed new 1909 law that would go before the legislature in the spring, so Elliott scheduled the work.[3]

While updating Seip in February 1909 on the Moyock survey, Wright mentioned that he thought the Mattamuskeet project presented a profitable opportunity. In March, he strongly recommended it to Seip, "as I think I can indirectly control the matter." It was about this time that the owner of the lake, the State Board of Education, told Wright that if he could sell it for $100,000, they would pay him a $5,000 commission.[4]

About March 17, Wright convinced Seip and a local businessman named John Wilkinson to go in together and bid $60,000 on the lakebed. However, Wilkinson had reservations about the quality of the soil under the lake and asked the governor, a friend, to release their bid, and the governor agreed. During this conversation, the governor told Wilkinson of the sales commission agreement between the state and Wright. Wilkinson passed this information on to Seip. Upset over Wright's lack of candor, Wilkinson declined to participate further in the Mattamuskeet sale. Seip, who was not himself a man accustom to straightforward dealing, did likewise, but did not tell Wright for many months that he had no intention of taking him on as a partner, as he wanted to use him as a means of securing additional government services and favors for his Carolina Land and Timber Company project at Moyock. Wright did not realize this until after he started with the State of Florida in February 1910.[5]

The files of Assistant Secretary Hays contained a considerable amount of correspondence regarding the North Carolina drainage projects, all of it routine, until April 8, 1909, about one month after the Seip/Wilkinson bid collapsed. Wright wrote Seip that he had lunch with Hays, and during a casual conversation, mentioned the Mattamuskeet project. Hays became quite excited and asked Wright back to his office for a longer talk. On April 23, Hays wrote to his former college president, Leigh Hunt, seeking to interest him in the project. Correspondence between Hays, Hunt and Wright continued until September 16, when Hays, Wright and a Department of Agriculture photographer named L.S. Williams visited John Wilkinson's home at Bellhaven, just north of Mattamuskeet. Williams took many pictures of Mattamuskeet and the Wilkinson farm.[6]

There were questions at the time concerning the propriety of the frequency and purpose of the trips that Wright was taking to North Carolina, and whether these trips, and that of L.S. Williams, had been approved through proper channels or whether the process had been circumvented through Assistant Secretary Hays's office. At the time, it was suspected that these were being approved to benefit the political ambitions of Representative Small of North Carolina. Outright self-dealing by employees at the Department of Agriculture was not suspected until Seip testified to this in February.

II

Professor Willett Hays joined the Department of Agriculture as Assistant Secretary in January 1905. An expert in plant cross-breading, he supervised many of the department's scientific and botany-based programs. In addition, he ran the committee that supervised the Agriculture Department's personnel and employment matters. It was surprising, then that he claimed to be unaware of any regulation that prohibited officers or employees from exploiting or receiving benefit from their office.

Chairman Moss read Rule 30 of the *Fiscal Regulations of the Department of Agriculture*, specifically prohibiting officers or employees "who are engaged upon investigations of special industries" from being "connected with or interested in any firm, company, or corporation whose scope of business includes the industry which the officer or employee is investigating for the department." In other words, not only was participation in a specific firm in which a conflict of interest existed prohibited, but participation in the whole industry was proscribed. Rule 30 also prohibited any employee from allowing "his name, his work, or his connection with the department to be used in promoting, or exploiting, or selling stock in any firm, company, or corporation, the scope of whose business includes the special industry which such officer or employee is investigating for the department."[7]

Hayes did not deny his was aware of Rule 30 but tried to argue that its criteria didn't apply to him because he really wasn't interested in Mattamuskeet as a business proposition. Chairman Moss then read a paragraph from an April 8, 1909, letter from J.O. Wright to John Seip:

> At the noon hour I was speaking to Mr. Hayes.... He thinks there is a great opportunity to make some money and frankly said he would like to become interested in a company to purchase the Lake and develop the land, says he can secure the capital needed and was confident he could sell the land at from $40.00 to $60.00 per acre.[8]

Hays's reply was "I became interested, but not as a matter of buying any land. I have long been interested in the matter of drainage.... I have never been a money maker."

Rep. Floyd: Let me ask you this. The letter quotes: "he frankly said he would like to become interested in a company to purchase the lake and develop the land." Did you say that?
Mr. Hays: I do not recall saying that.
Rep. Floyd: Did you take it up the way that you wanted to become one of the interested parties in the purchase?
Mr. Hays: Presuming the State was going to sell it, or had sold it, I may have said something of the sort.
Rep. Floyd: Well, do you think that it would be proper for an officer of the Agriculture Department to participate in the authorization of projects of these kinds, and to make surveys at public expense to test the soils, and after all this work had been done at the public expense, to have these same officers be interested in the project?
Mr. Hays: I would not think so, unless it were very remote. But I had no knowledge in signing this authorization, I had no knowledge at that time—
Rep. Floyd: Do you not think that the use of your name as Assistant Secretary in connection with any of these projects of that kind would greatly facilitate the promoters in getting parties interested in it?
Mr. Hays: It might somewhat.[9]

Hays then shifted his argument, claiming that it was not a conflict of interest, because it was the state that was selling the land. This proved to be merely going from the frying pan to the fire.

Rep. Higgins: The department of drainage were making investigations of some lands owned by the State of North Carolina, were they not?
Mr. Hays: Yes, sir.
Rep. Higgins: The result of this investigation would determine the policy somewhat of the State of North Carolina as to the sale of those lands, would it not?
Mr. Hays: Yes, sir.
Rep. Higgins: Would you regard it as within the official proprieties to be interested in the development of the land, even though the State had sold it, when you had information, official information, before the sale was consummated?
Mr. Hays: But I would not have thought of becoming a purchaser of land, for instance, from the State.
Rep. Higgins: Do you think that changes the propriety in the slightest degree?

Mr. Hays: I think it changes the propriety as to whether the State had already sold the land, and it had become private property.

Rep. Floyd: Then if title had passed from the State, to privately owned, and the drainage project originated through the Department of Agriculture to drain the lands, then you think there would be no impropriety in a member of the Agriculture Department investing in those lands?

Mr. Hays: There might be some impropriety, but it would not be in the same category as if it was public lands.

Rep. Higgins: So when an investigation is being made by the Department of Agriculture in privately owned lands regarding the feasibility of drainage, you regard it as within official propriety for a member of the Department of Agriculture to become interested in that as a commercial proposition.

Mr. Hays: I hardly know how to answer that.

Rep. Floyd: Now Professor, about this ownership of the land. At the time you were holding this conversation with Mr. Wright, were you aware that the State of North Carolina owned the land?

Mr. Hays: I knew that North Carolina had owned it, but I don't remember if Mr. Seip had bought it yet.

Rep. Moss: Mr. Seip never did own the land.[10]

After two days of this, Hays gave up or, more likely, just wore down and started answering the Committee's questions in the shortest, most straightforward way possible. The soil survey of the lakebed was initiated through a letter written by Senator F.M. Simmons to the Bureau of Soils on January 20, 1909. Soil Specialist W.E. Hearn was dispatched through several counties in North and South Carolina and Virginia in early 1909. Hyde County was not included, but at the request of Senator Simmons, Assistant Secretary Hyde gave Hearn written permission to add Hyde County to his itinerary, and Hearn performed a preliminary soil survey in February and March at an expense of $380, in addition to the $2,881 expended by the Office of Experimental Stations to perform the drainage survey at Mattamuskeet.[11]

Wright estimated that the purchase price would be S100,000 and that it would take three or four times that to develop the lakebed, which is why he urged Hays to recruit additional partners such as Leigh Hunt. Hays did not question Wright's *pro forma*, which estimated gross profits of a million dollars, although as we have seen, that document was nonsensical. Hays claimed he did not know of the commission arrangement between Wright and the State Board of Education whereby Wright would receive $5,000 for finding a buyer for the lake.

What Hays couldn't evade was the matter of Mr. Williams, the Agriculture Department photographer. On April 29, Hays wrote Leigh Hunt that he hoped to meet Hunt and John Seip for a reconnaissance of the lake, but Secretary Wilson needed him for a matter that would necessitate his remaining in town for several weeks. Hays was not able to arrange for a visit until September, at which time he was able to meet only Wright and Wilkinson. The party stayed two nights at Wilkinson's home at Bellhaven. They were accompanied by L.S. Williams, a staff photographer. Wilkinson was impressed by him "I think he makes some of the best photographs I have ever seen." Williams mostly took photos of the lake, but also of Wilkinson's farms. To thank Wilkinson for his hospitality, Williams gave him a small album of views of his holdings.[12]

Wright was in North Carolina at the time on a speaking tour. Initially, Elliott had refused his travel voucher because Wright's time in Representative Small's district exceeded the limits for Agriculture Department personnel to spend on educational tours in any one congressional district. Small appealed to Hays, who approved the voucher.

Hays claimed that it was Wright's idea to have Williams meet him and Hays at Mattamuskeet. Williams, who had no idea what was going on, cost the department $33.73 in reimbursable expenses. Hays did not charge the government his costs down to Mattamuskeet, but he did voucher his return costs, $15.75.[13]

Mr. Moss: Do you know whether or not this matter came to the attention of Mr. Elliott?
Mr. Hays: No, sir.
Mr. Moss: You don't know, or you know it did not?
Mr. Hays: I don't think it did.
Mr. Moss: As a matter of fact, you and Mr. Wright arranged to have Mr. Williams go down there?
Mr. Hays: As a matter of fact, Mr. Williams presented the matter to me, and I agreed to it.
Mr. Moss: You say Mr. Williams. Do you mean Mr. Williams or Mr. Wright?
Mr. Hays: I mean Mr. Wright.[14]

When Representative Sloan asked him, point-blank, "State whether or not you had any intention of profiting by reason of any information you had as an officer of the department in relation to this project," Hays could only answer "I formed no definite intent in the matter."[15] Months later, Hays still claimed that he had no intention of investing any

Exhibit of farm products in window of Tidewater Power Co., Wilmington, N.C. Photographer unknown (Hugh MacRae Trucking Development Co. Collection, N.C. State Archives, No. PhC 150-101).

money in the lake, nor of recruiting anyone else to invest in the lake. His only interest was to organize a model "country life community of racially efficient people on scientifically designed family farms."[16]

This claim sounds absurd on its face but may not have been. He may have been referring to the so-called "MacRae Villages" near Wilmington, North Carolina. Hugh MacRae was the son of Donald MacRae, one of Wilmington's wealthiest citizens. Hugh graduated from MIT in 1885 with a degree in mining engineering. When the elder MacRae died in 1894, Hugh inherited Wilmington's power plant, streetcar company, gas utility, and several dams and lakes, which he consolidated into the Tidewater Power and Transit Company.[17]

Starting in 1905, a new firm MacRae started, the Carolina Trucking Development Company, developed five demonstration farming communities on reclaimed, cut-over wetlands in the far southeastern part of the state near Wilmington: Castle Hayne; New Berlin; Marathon; St. Helena; and Artesia. All used the same model. Each community was populated by an immigrant community of Italians, Greeks, Poles, and Germans. Many, if not most, immigrants came from an urban background and had little experience in farming. Each village had a population of between 200 and 300 and was comprised of farms of between 2 and 20 acres. Typically, the owners of the smallest plots lived in the village and commuted out to their field. It was normal for landowners to "trade up" to larger farms as they gained agricultural proficiency. The land was sold on long-term, low-interest mortgages, with a first right of refusal in the event of resale reserved to the firm. The production of cotton and tobacco was prohibited; only truck crops and other specialty products that could return a profit on small plots were permitted. In each, the farmers were paid cash wages to work on common improvements, such as clearing canals, installing tile drains and building roads. An agricultural expert was provided for each community.[18]

Rail special to sell land at MacRae immigrant villages, 1909. Photographer unknown (Hugh MacRae Trucking Development Co. Collection, North Carolina State Archives, No. PhC 150-099).

Italian Brass Band, St. Helena immigrant colony, 1909. Photographer unknown (Hugh MacRae Trucking Development Co. Collection, North Carolina State Archives, No. PhC 150-105).

By 1912 the MacRae communities were being regularly written up in *Manufacturer's Record*, the *North American Review*, and *Collier's*. They inspired Elwood Mead to develop two model agricultural villages, Durham and Delhi, in 1917 for the California Land Settlement Board.[19] In this context, it is easy to see how Willett Hays, a plant biologist from a somewhat sheltered, academic background could be deeply attracted to the idea of trying to start a model community on the drained bed of Lake Mattamuskeet. This is, in fact, fairly close to what actually happened, although the short-lived town of New Holland was more of a traditional American subdivision than a planned model community. However, it appears that while Leigh Hunt was generally attracted by the idea, he never took the idea of scaling up a MacRae community at Lake Mattmuskeet seriously. It was too big; it was too expensive; too many landowners were absentees or investors, and MacRae had demonstrated that local ownership, finance and supervision were crucial elements.

However, it should be added that by the start of World War I, Hugh MacRae himself believed he had reached the limits of what could be accomplished through small, privately planned and financed model farming villages, and in 1921 begin working towards a much grander goal of the "Farm City," a vision that would pull him within the orbit of Elwood Mead, who by then had achieved his dream of displacing Frederick Newell as director of the Bureau of Reclamation.

III

J.O. Wright was called back to the stand in early June, not quite five months after his last appearance. "The committee will continue the North Carolina investigation [next week] and will call Wright back to the stand," Elliott wrote Morgan on April 25: "Moss is anxious to find some commercialism mixed up in our investigations in that state. Wright can't give much testimony of any type without involving himself in some crooked deals, and the office records are pretty full regarding his undertaking in that state."[20]

When called up to the stand, Wright began with a prepared statement. When he started at the drainage division, one of the first areas brought to his attention was the Albemarle-Pamlico Peninsula. Its potential was almost limitless, but "every one of the people there were asleep." It was he who approached Representative Small. It was he who made some fifty talks throughout the state. It was he who, after two years of work, organized the 1908 drainage conference at New Bern. It was he, Small and Joseph Pratt Hyde who authored the North Carolina drainage law that was passed in March 1909. As of June 1912, more than 60 districts had been formed. The unspoken conclusion: everything that he gained from this work, he deserved.[21]

Chairman Moss wasted little time. Did Wright know of Department Rule No. 30? "No." Who brought up the matter of the financial irregularities of 1909 with Chief Accountant Zappone and Inspector Ashley? He did. Why?

> I will tell you what I had told him [Ashley]. I told him I had submitted to this thing for two years after I had resigned my position and been a thousand miles away, and had no communications with the office, and had never been back there until the October preceding and that since that time they had been constantly knocking me and knocking my work that I was connected with, and I told them that it had to be stopped, and that I could tell them how I was going to stop it. Well, he says, how are you going to stop it? I told him that I came over there to request that it be stopped, and if they did not stop it I was going to file some charges.[22]

This is the same complaint Wright made back in February before the committee.[23] At that time, he told Chairman Moss he was incensed by Judson Welliver's Washington *Times* newspaper article of October 15, and Frank Huffaker's article in the December 15 Jacksonville *Metropolis*. But this time around, he didn't even mention the Welliver and Huffaker articles.

> *Mr. Wright*: After I resigned and left the office there, I was retained as a consulting engineer in this Mattamuskeet proposition.
>
> *Rep. Moss*: That may come up when we bring up the Mattamuskeet proposition
>
> *Mr. Wright*: This is one phase that might come up now. Mr. Elliott knew of this fact, and he had been trying his very best to dislodge me and my connection with it, and he had been criticizing my work down there and the report was made. He tried to put me down, and he tried very hard to put me in a bad light with the people developing that project; and when it came down to getting the money and the money proposition came up, and we wanted to sell bonds down there, I understand a bond house refused to take the money.[24]

During his testimony, Elliott had briefly touched on this matter. He stated that in January 1910, Wright had incurred the disfavor of him and his boss, A.C. True. He gave few details, other than it involved a matter of insubordination and was related to the Lake Mattamuskeet project. Elliott testified that he and True were discussing what action to take when Wright announced that he was leaving for Florida. "That seemed to be a solution to a rather acute question in our office, and we were glad to let the matter pass," Elliott testified.[25]

Chairman Moss returned to the Mattamuskeet issue the following day:

> *Rep. Moss*: You mentioned yesterday in your testimony that Mr. Elliott had been trying to oust you as the consulting engineer in the Mattamuskeet proposition?
>
> *Mr. Wright*: Yes, I think I did.
>
> *Rep. Moss*: In what way was it you understood he was trying to do that, to oust you?

Mr. Wright: Well, he wrote a letter to Congressman Small claiming that matter there should not be allowed to go forward without calling in a consulting engineer; stopped the proceedings down there and blocked the game and necessitated the calling in of a consulting engineer at a cost of $2,500 to pay him, and he made a report which was considered of no value at all. He simply confirmed the feasibility of the plan.

Rep. Moss: Is it not a fact, Major, that the Department of Agriculture was asked by the [drainage] commissioners there to go over these plans and do that work?

Mr. Wright: Yes, that is true.

Rep. Moss: Can you call to mind a single request to go down to that district and make those lectures; can you recall a single request for your services in connection with any proposition down there while you were connected with the department that was not acceded to by the department?

Mr. Wright: No, I think it was usually acceded to.

Mr. Moss: So every request along these lines which the department regarded as valid were granted?

Mr. Wright: Yes.

Rep. Moss: Is not the fact that the Department consented to go over these plans as a referee rather extraordinary?

Mr. Wright: No. I have known them to go over plans from other places, you know.

Rep. Moss: You say you know of such practice?

Mr. Wright: Yes.

Rep. Moss: So in this instance, the Department, examining those plans in an official way at the request of the men who purchased them and the North Carolina authorities was not an exceptional one?

Mr. Wright: If the Department had simply kept that letter out, there never would have been any question raised. The Department afterwards made a report in writing, repeating the report made, and saying that it should be submitted to a consulting engineer and that the plan was not what it should be; that it would not drain the land. There never had been any question raised at all; the people down there were perfectly able to take care of the proposition.[26]

Neither Elliott nor Wright's involvement with Lake Mattamuskeet ended in September 1909 when the partnership of Mason, Webb and Kerr purchased the lakebed, nor even when Wright left federal employment. In the summer of 1910, the Lawrence Brett Engineering and Contracting Company was awarded the contract to prepare the plans for the Mattamuskeet drainage project. It appears that Wright's continuing connection with the project was through the Brett Engineering firm.

On August 29, George Boyd, an engineer for the Lawrence Brett Engineering company, contacted Elliott and notified him that the revised plans for Lake Mattamuskeet should be completed about September 15. Boyd asked Elliott for the field notebooks from S.H. McCrory's survey, as the plans prepared at the time showed only a part of the area to be included in the final project.[27] On October 11, 1910, Elliott wrote to the Clerk of the Court for Hyde County. His Drainage Division had prepared the initial surveys and the Bureau of Soils examined the soil under the lakebed and reported on its probable fertility and usefulness, he informed the clerk. Due to the magnitude of the proposed Mattamuskeet project, its unique climate and topography:

> I suggest that before the plans proposed by the viewers and now on file in your office be adopted and the district established by the court, the report, plans and estimates be critically and carefully examined by a board of expert engineers so that in case modifications are found necessary they may receive due consideration by the court. As to the number and qualifications of the board, I suggest that three engineers be employed by the district: the first to be a mechanical engineer well versed in the design, cost and operation of large pumping plants; the second a drainage engineer who is well informed in the design of drains for large areas of land, particularly those requiring pumping; and the third a hydraulic engineer.[28]

On October 26, 1911, the Clerk of the Court wrote Elliott thanking him and agreeing with his suggestion that a board of review be hired by the local drainage district, and asked for recommendations for engineers who would do a good job for a reasonable sum.[29] There is no record of Elliott's reply, but this appears to be the letter Wright referred to in his testimony when he claimed that Elliott wrote a letter to Representative Small "stopping the proceedings" until the district brought in a consulting engineer. Obviously, the letter is not to Representative Small, it does not demand anything, although the clerk proved amenable to his suggestion, and Elliott recommended that a team of engineers, not just a consultant, perform a comprehensive review, both of the drainage plans, and of the construction plans for the pumping station. Regardless, Elliott's October 11 letter is apparently the one that so greatly incensed Wright.

Lake Mattamuskeet was turning into a monster project. Some 120 miles of canals, radiating out like a fan, fed a pump house containing four 850-horsepower engines, each driving a 49-inch centrifugal pump with a capacity of 250,000 cubic feet per hour that lifted the water four feet into an outlet canal to Pamlico Sound. The pump house measured 100-by-37 feet, not counting the adjacent powerhouse. It was the biggest steam-powered pump station in the word, and the second biggest of any type in the United States, bested only by the New Orleans municipal pumping station.[30]

However, by mid–1911 Mason, Webb and Kerr (now, the Southern Land Reclamation Company) was having trouble settling on a workable plan. The original 1909 Wright-McCrory plan had been replaced by the 1910 Brett proposal, which, in turn, was replaced by one prepared by J.F. Coleman of New Orleans, who had originally been

Lake Mattamuskeet drained, 1927. The lake stayed dry for less than five years before the pumps gave out and the lake re-flooded. It was never successfully drained and today is a National Wildlife Refuge. Photo by Herbert H. Brimley (Brimley Collection, North Carolina State Archives, Neg. No. PhC-42-Bx17-LakeMattamuskeet-F11).

brought in merely to review the Brett plan. Lawrence Brett revamped his earlier 1910 plan, and a mix of the second Brett plan and the Coleman plan appeared to be what the drainage district had settled on as it prepared to let construction contracts. In June and July 1911, A.D. Morehouse declined at least two requests for copies of the McCrory 1908–09 plan and report, explaining that they were now so obsolete that it was not worth the Drainage Division's time and money to prepare reproductions, and it was inadvisable to release such inaccurate data to the public. If one really wanted that data, Morehouse wrote, one should contact Wright in Florida, as he was the project's consulting engineer.[31]

On December 20, 1911, J.S. Mann, Chairman of the Mattamuskeet Drainage Commissioners, wrote Elliott to request that the Drainage Division "thoroughly examine the plans provided for the canals to be used in this District, and make us a written report therein, giving your views as to their efficiency." If the Drainage Division found them inadequate, "we would like for you to suggest such changes alterations as will, in your judgment make them [acceptable]." Mann explained that the proposed size of the project had changed from 120,000 acres in 1908 to the current 100,000 acres. The budget, however, remained at $400,000. Current estimates put the cost of work at $379,000, leaving little room for error. Hence, the district was anxious to get another expert opinion. Elliott agreed.[32] Coming more than a year after Elliott's letter to the Clerk of the Court, this is clearly a reference to a plan or plans different from those that Elliott had recommended be reviewed by a team of engineers in October 1910. On January 3, 1912, Representative Small wrote John P. Kerr:

> Further replying to your letter of the 20th in which you stated that you had forwarded to Mr. C.G. Elliott, Chief of the Office of Drainage Investigations, plans which you had adopted for the drainage canals in the District, and had asked him to examine the same.... I have today seen Mr. Elliott and through him, Mr. A.C. True, the Chief of the Office of Experimental Stations, and as a result Mr. Elliott has agreed to take up these plans and give them a careful examination.... This action is very courteous on the part of Mr. Elliott.[33]

This directly contradicts Wright assertion of "a letter to Congressman Small claiming that the matter ... should not be allowed to go forward without calling in a consulting engineer." This time, it was the chairman of the drainage district who was seeking the review, certainly with the concurrence of Representative Small, and with the approval of the Southern Land Reclamation Company. (In fact, J.P. Kerr of the Southern Land Reclamation Company met with Elliott in Washington on January 13 to review the documents and add others that the District did not have.[34])

It was apparent that the promoters, the court and the viewers (supervisors) of the local drainage district were worried about the tight budget, and readily agreed to a referees' review, as Wright admitted during his testimony. Although the focus of Wright's recollection was the October 11, 1910, letter, his real problems started a year later with J.S. Mann's December 1911 request to Elliott for a review of the latest in a long series of revised and modified plans. The fact that Elliott strongly suggested that the October 1910 plans be reviewed (apparently by the New Orleans firm of J.F. and E.H. Coleman instead of Elliott's recommended three-engineer team) is indicative of the trouble the project was in. It was experiencing a cascade of engineering dissention, with a series of experts disagreeing with each other's recommendations, and eventually, with each other's qualifications, about a project that, in the end, never could be made to work.

During the course of Elliott's review, it came to the attention of one of the Mattamuskeet partners, Charles Webb, that a Chicago bond dealer had received a tip that someone in the government had been casting aspirations on the Mattamuskeet proposition. Webb wrote Elliott, asking him to investigate. Elliott wrote that he would look into the matter and report back and Webb replied, thanking Elliott for his assistance. Two days later, Elliott replied to Webb, stating, "I have enquired at the office and am quite sure that this story did not emanate from this department." Elliott believed that the rumor started because of Morehouse's refusal to release the McCrory-era plans, instead referring inquirers to J.O. Wright in Florida. This apparently had been misinterpreted as official antipathy to the project.[35]

Elliott agreed to verbally brief Webb, Kerr and Douglas Graves before preparing a written report of his review. Unlike Wright's testimony before the Moss committee, there does not appear to be much reason to believe that Elliott was the source of any serious derogatory information, and the exchange of correspondence indicates no animosity between Elliott and the Southern Land Reclamation partners.[36]

In his review, Elliott noted that the original plan called for 14 canals. The original estimated cost was $462,744, over the allowed $400,000 budget. Thus, several canals were omitted in the supplemental report.[37] With fewer remaining canals, Elliott commented that their capacity would have to be expanded. (In fact, by 1917 the number of canals had be roughly doubled over those proposed in the original plan.) Wright, questioned by Elliott's lawyer, Mr. Bright, described what happened next:

Mr. Bright: Do you remember the day of the month you saw Mr. Zappone?
Mr. Wright: I guess about the 19th day of January.
Mr. Bright: What brought you to Washington at that time?
Mr. Wright: I came here for a conference with Mr. Webb, Mr. Kerr and Graves [Douglas Graves, president of Southern Land Reclamation Co.]
Mr. Bright: And did they report to you any findings of the drainage division on the plans that were submitted?
Mr. Wright: Yes, sir.
Mr. Bright: Did they point out to you certain errors which had been pointed out to them by the drainage division?
Mr. Wright: Yes sir, alleged errors.
Mr. Bright: You subsequently admitted those were errors?
Mr. Wright: No, I did not. I subsequently admitted they could deepen the drainage if they wanted to. I thought it was wasting money to do it, but they could do it if they wanted to.
Mr. Bright: Were the plans changed in that regard?
Mr. Wright: They were.
Mr. Bright: The finding of what the drainage division considered to be errors in your plans then was mostly the cause of your going to Mr. Zappone, was it not?
Mr. Wright: No, sir.
Mr. Bright: What was?
Mr. Wright: The attacks that had been made on me and my character by Mr. Elliott through the press and by different individuals.
Mr. Bright: Where did you go after your meeting with Mr. Webb, Mr. Kerr and Mr. Graves?
Mr. Wright: I called on Mr. Zappone.[38]

The Everglades were a sideshow; in the end it all came down to North Carolina. Wright met with Thomas Will on the morning of January 20 and told him what he was about to do or had just done. (Will and Wright met early on the 20th; it appears Wright may have met with Zappone on the afternoon of January 20, not the 19th as he recalled before the committee.) Wright insinuated to Will that he was doing it in order to protect the interests of the Everglades land sales companies; Will, of course encouraged him to do anything he could to end the interference of Representative Clark and of Elliott. Will probably did not even fully grasp what Wright was planning, as Wright told him a few days later that he met with, and discussed the Elliott accusations with, Representative Moss, not Zappone and Ashley. In addition, he told Will that his complaints against Elliott concerned only the Everglades report; he never mentioned Mattamuskeet. It can never be known if he shaded his account to Will, or if he paid two visits, one to Representative Moss and another to Zappone and Ashley at the Department of Agriculture, an unlikely possibility.[39]

The conclusion of Wright's testimony all but brought to a close the main body of the committee's work. After a recess of a few days, Moss convened a rump session of the committee to hear testimony narrowly focused on the subject of the claims of financial impropriety leveled against Elliott and Morehouse. He had promised Elliott he would do this in April, but only as a separate set of hearings to be held at the end when the matter of the supposedly suppressed reports was concluded. He could not promise Elliott that the subject would be addressed in the final report.[40]

Solicitor McCabe implored the Chairman not to explore this topic for fear of interfering with the grand jury investigation and inadvertently throwing immunity over those individuals who had been indicted and also appeared as witnessed before the committee. Chairman Moss told McCabe that he had raised the issue of the alleged illegalities in his opening statement, thus bringing the matter within the jurisdiction of the committee, and therefore it would proceed with the understanding that it was acting independently and without the active cooperation of the Department of Agriculture.[41]

Most of the testimony was technical and arcane. Accountant Zappone provided the hard data. The Office of Experiment Stations was budgeted for $150,000 in fiscal year 1909. After ten pages of accounting minutiae, Chairman Moss asked if his impression was correct that the bottom line was that "there seems to have been more work done in 1909 than there was money to actually pay for it." Zappone agreed.[42]

The next question was how much? Many more pages of technical detail. Bills often came in after the end of the year. Hence, Federal statute required that the books on any given fiscal year shall close three years after the last day of that year. On June 30, 1911, the Office of Experiment Stations as a whole had a positive balance of $411.68 on a budget of $150,000 for fiscal year 1909. This was turned back into the treasury. In other words, from the standpoint of the Department as a whole, there was no shortage. Any shortages internal to the Office of Experiment Stations, or any shifting of bills due or funds available from one budget year to another below the line-item level would require an audit at the level of the Office of Experiment Stations.

A.C. True, Chief of the Office of Experimental Stations, who had, on paper at least, recommended the dismissal of Elliott and Morehouse, was, from the standpoint of credibility, his own worst enemy. Anything he didn't know, he didn't remember. He never gave a straight answer when he could equivocate, generalize, or dissemble. He was either genuinely out of touch with his own office or simply stupid. He shamelessly looked to Solicitor McCabe for prompts. He came across as a weak, frightened, toadying bureaucrat scurrying for his life.

After presenting his office's audit report, he had to admit that its bookkeeping procedures were so bad that he couldn't tell the committee exactly how much the irrigation division had gone over budget. It was clear that the drainage division did not go over budget. The irrigation division did. Taken together, the two had created a budget shortfall. It could have been as small as $441 or as large as $1,970; the different audits varied. True's bookkeeper rejected $1,710 in year-end vouchers, so that is the figure the office was working with. Nobody could answer why an overage created in the irrigation division was split between both the drainage division and the irrigation division.

True's Byzantine answers reached the height of absurdity when Chairman Moss asked the natural question: if rolling over bills for a month to the start of the next fiscal year was wrong; wrong to the point of dismissing career men, what was the correct option?

> *Rep. Moss*: As you have indicated, the accountant was justified in putting these [vouchers] back so they could be settled by some other method, but what kind of method would have been proper for the account to select?
>
> *Dr. True*: If they could have secured outside funds from the cooperators, these bills would have been all right.
>
> *Rep. Moss*: Do you mean if they could have gone out and secured some one to donate the funds?
>
> *Dr. True*: Yes, sir.
>
> *Rep. Moss*: You feel it would have been proper for Mr. Elliott and Mr. Morehouse to have passed the hat among friends and taken up this question of a deficiency, that would have been a proper way of paying these bills?
>
> *Dr. True*: Under the circumstances I think they would have been justified in presenting the matter to the cooperators in such a way that they would have given them help.
>
> *Rep. Moss*: Do you believe that is the only proper method by which these bills could have been settled?
>
> *Dr. True*: I do not see any other way.
>
> *Rep. Moss*: You feel that the only remedy that Mr. Morehouse and Mr. Elliott had was to pass the hat among their friends and ask them to make good the overdraft?
>
> *Dr. True*: We were working with the experiment stations of different States that had state funds, with private parties, and with associations in other States [i.e., state extension services and agricultural colleges]. Those funds were not subject to the same limitations as Federal funds as regards the fiscal year, and they might be called upon to furnish more than they actually agreed to, and that would be a matter of negotiation.
>
> *Rep. Moss*: When you are cooperating, aren't those cooperators under agreements as to exact costs or terms?
>
> *Dr. True*: We have agreements.
>
> *Rep. Moss*: And do not those parties, having complied with their terms, have a right to expect the Government to comply with its terms?
>
> *Dr. True*: Only from a strictly legal standpoint.[43]

One can almost hear Solicitor McCabe slowly sliding under the table, melting away in Washington's July heat. (The correct answer, by the way, would have been to go to Congress for a budget amendment, as Moss pointed out the next day.) The committee kept True on the stand, mostly to torment him for another week until the accountant for the Office of Experiment Stations could prepare a single, coherent number. The final result: True's Office of Experiment Stations overspent its 1909 Congressional budget apportionment by $566.91. With that, Chairman Moss gaveled the hearings to an end.[44]

9

Vacillating and Deficient

> The drainage of the Everglades was no new project.... The Department of Agriculture entered upon this very responsible work of reclamation of its own initiative, but does not seem to have had a proper conception of the vast interests involved in the project. The work was undertaken without serious consideration, was not prosecuted vigorously or successfully, and was abandoned by the department ... the vacillating course of the department in its treatment of this important project ... was most unfortunate and subjected the Department of Agriculture to much suspicion and criticism.
>
> —Rep. Ralph Moss, 1912[1]

The final report was released on August 19.[2] It explained that the initial warrant of the committee had been to investigate charges filed by Representatives Clark of Florida and Bathrick of Michigan that public funds had been expended on a survey of the Everglades, but that the resulting report had allegedly been censored for inappropriate reasons.

There were majority and minority reports, split down party lines. The Majority Report was written by the committee Democrats: Ralph Moss, J.C. Floyd and R.L. Doughton.

(1) The Everglades survey, initiated in 1907, was undertaken without adequate consideration given for the budget or resources needed. It was essentially abandoned in 1909 after $11,017 had been spent. The report was delayed because the engineer in charge was overloaded with work in other states, most of it congressional constituent service visits of a low priority that should have been delegated to employees of a lesser grade. The release of the so-called "Henry Hall extract" or "Wright report extract" in February 1910 was unacceptable, given the preliminary state of work, the lack of technical review up to that point, and the misuse to which it was subsequently put. Responsibility for this misjudgment could not be determined. A final version of the report was prepared in September 1909 but was recalled by C.G. Elliott of the drainage division due to technical errors. A revised version was prepared in January 1910. Publication was refused by Secretary Wilson. The actions of both Mr. Elliott and Secretary Wilson were within their authority. The failure of this project resulted primarily from differences of opinion among the members of Congress and State of Florida officials. A contributing cause was irreconcilable differences among the engineers of the drainage division.

(2) The circular letter was created without the knowledge of Secretary Wilson. It was cancelled on the orders of Secretary Wilson on or about February 4, 1910. It was within his power to order its cancellation and/or replacement. No definite departmental rule or regulation prohibiting its creation or distribution could be found.

During the course of the committee's investigation other serious matters not initially anticipated arose, especially the financial involvement of Assistant Secretary Hays and former drainage engineer J.O. Wright in projects they were associated with as Government employees.

(3) The conduct of Mr. J.O. Wright was in contravention of the department's fiscal regulations and was incompatible with proper standards of official integrity. He accepted $5,000 in stock from the Albemarle Development Company (also known as Terra Ceia) while engaged in making surveys on its land. He accepted a fee of $5,000 to find a purchaser for Lake Mattamuskeet at the same time he was organizing a company to purchase it in which he expected to be given $40,000 in stock. While this was in process, he was also performing the government surveys and reports necessary to form a state drainage district and issue state-backed bonds to drain its lands. If he were still in federal service the committee would unhesitatingly recommend his dismissal.

(4) Assistant Secretary Hays sought to become financially involved in one of the projects, at Lake Mattamuskeet, in concert with Mr. Wright. His activities in this regard began on or about April 8, 1909 and extended until sometime after September 1909. That Mr. Hays did not ultimately become involved in the proposition was only due to circumstances beyond his control. Mr. Hays traveled to Lake Mattamuskeet on September 16, 1909 at Government expense and approved the travel costs of a departmental photographer to meet him and Mr. Wright at the lake for private purposes. The photographer was not aware of the improper use to which his services were being put.

(5) A deficit was created in the Division of Drainage Investigations only because of an outmoded and ineffective accounting system. This created a situation where an overage of $1,710 in the irrigations division was turned into an overage of $941 in the drainage division and $799 in the irrigation division with instructions to the respective division heads to solve the problem without resorting to a budget amendment. It was the determination of the committee that responsibility for the overage, and its partial allocation to the drainage division, which never did run a deficit, rested with the accounting office of the Office of Experiment Stations. Given these circumstances, the committee concluded that the termination of Mr. Elliott and Mr. Morehouse was an excessively harsh disciplinary action.

The Minority Report,[3] written by the committee's Republicans (Sloan, Higgins and Madden), concluded that:

(1) The so-called Wright Report was delayed, and ultimately cancelled, due to an apparently irreconcilable difference between the engineers in the Office of Experimental Stations.

(2) The Secretary had complete discretion over such publications as brochures and circulars, and he chose to exercise his authority in ordering the drainage division to discontinue sending out the January 1910 circular. There was conflicting evidence as to whether the management of the Office of Experiment Stations exceeded their authority in preparing and distributing the circular without the review and approval of the Secretary's office, but there was no question that he acted within his appropriate authority in revoking it.

(3) No action by the committee was warranted in either the case of Mr. Wright or Mr. Hays. No conclusive evidence was placed on the record that Mr. Hays received financial benefit from the North Carolina drainage projects. [The minority report was silent as to Mr. Wright.] It is not appropriate for the legislative branch to pass judgment on the day-to-day functions an executive branch department, including personnel policies and decisions.

(4) Nothing placed before the committee could lead to a conclusion that the dismissal of Mr. Elliott or Mr. Morehouse was done on the basis of malfeasance. Lacking such a finding, the committee lacked the jurisdiction to pass judgment on the personnel decisions of the Secretary of Agriculture.

In one of the first extensive histories of the Everglades, written in 1947, Alfred and Kathryn Hanna give a surprisingly good overview of the 1912 hearings, especially considering that the National Archives did not sort and process the Agriculture Department's files on the Everglades investigation until 1989. In their book, the Hannas claimed that a "confidential report," which they found in the records, contained "intimidations that he [Wright] had also profited in Florida."[4]

I found nothing to verify this. I did find a document that matched their description, a draft version of the Final Report prominently stamped "Confidential: Committee Print," at the top.[5] However, it varies from the published version in only a few small details, none substantive. Otherwise, I found no "report" linking Wright's actions to Florida land dealings. It should be noted that the majority report contains a veritable horror show of Wright's official corruption: the $5,000 in stock he received from the Albemarle Development Company, the $5,000 commission from the North Carolina Board of Education; the $40,000 in stock from Seip's Carolina Land and Timber Company, another $7,500 in stock promised from Seip's Moyock's-based Provident Land Co., and $2,200 from Seip's dredging bill overrun scam.

Almost certainly, Wright's "reward" from Florida was not land, but his salary as Chief Drainage Engineer. Keep in mind that his $5,000 annual pay was little short of extraordinary. Assistant Secretary Willett Hays and Solicitor George McCabe were each paid $5,000 a year by the Department of Agriculture. Except for the Secretary himself ($12,000), the only employee in the Agriculture Department who made more than $5,000 was Willis Moore, Chief of the Weather Bureau ($6,000). When Wright left the State of Florida in 1913, his successor as chief drainage engineer, Fred C. Elliott (no relation to Charles Elliott) received a salary of only $3,000.[6]

There is nothing in the original handwritten minute book of the Everglades Drainage District that sheds any light on the insertion of "Paragraph 5" into the January 31, 1910, final version of the *Southern States Land and Timber Co. et. al. v. Albert Gilchrist et. al.* settlement agreement. A draft dated January 21 does not have the provision; the final signature version drawn up ten days later does:

> (5) The Drainage Commissioners and Trustees shall employ J.O. Wright, Esq., now supervising Drainage Engineer of the United States, as Drainage Engineer, to have charge of such drainage work under the direction, supervision and control of the Drainage Commissioners and Trustees, and in case of inability to secure his services, or of his resignation or removal, the Drainage Commissioners and Trustees shall employ in such capacity a competent drainage engineer of known skill and experience.[7]

If this was a reward, it is difficult to pin down exactly what Wright did to receive it, and when. The most likely candidate is the Wright report extract prepared for Henry C. Hall in February 1910. As discussed earlier, William Ellis and William Jennings were under tremendous pressure to win the *Trustees v. Root* case, in which a homesteader carried out all the requirements of the 1883 Florida Settlers' Act and filed for a deed to his 80 acres near Davie, only to be refused by the Internal Improvement Fund. The trustees argued that their enabling legislation prohibited them from transferring any land necessary to carry out their mission to reclaim the Everglades, and because the sale of large blocks of land were necessary to finance the drainage project, every acre of land in the Everglades Drainage District fell under the definition of "necessary."

Root, on the other hand, argued that "necessary" meant lands directly needed for canals, locks, and other previously identified infrastructure. The trustees had a hard case to make, especially when they had no plan identifying where the infrastructure was supposed to go, or even what land was going to be drained. That's why getting the Wright report excerpt, especially the map, was so important; it gave General Ellis his map, but he still lost the case, in June 1911, as well as all the subsequent appeals.[8]

The Final Report of the Moss Committee took pains to point out that throwing together the Wright extract on short notice simply to satisfy a personal request was a particularly egregious example of poor decision-making, suggesting that the majority report authors may have had some reason to suspect that a *quid pro quo* was involved in its creation. The fact that Wright tenaciously clung to his assertion that the manuscript of the full report was finished on February 25, and that the excerpt was lifted out this manuscript, when everyone else involved recalled that the manuscript was not done until May, and that the excerpt was specially prepared for Mr. Hall well in advance of the manuscript, is highly suggestive. The strategic objections and obstructions raised by General Ellis, the Internal Improvement Fund's general counsel, whenever the subject of Wright's hiring by the state came up indicate that this was a topic that the Fund did not want the committee to delve into.

On the other hand, Wright had been on the scene in Florida since 1907, had become a friend of Napoleon Broward, and was, outwardly at least, sympathetic to the state's drainage program. He was experienced in dredging operations, having been part of the Chicago River Sanitary Canal project a decade earlier under Isham Randolph. He was, ostensibly, reasonably qualified for the job. Still, making his hiring part of a settlement agreement of a five-year, multi-million-dollar lawsuit was very odd indeed. Whether he would have been hired had Jennings and Governor Gilchrist known of his North Carolina activities is a question that will never be answered.

II

After the Final Report was released, the dominos fell in rapid order. On August 30, the indictments against Elliott, Morehouse, and two accountants within the Office of Experiment Stations, F.E. Singleton and R.P. Teele, were dropped by the United States Attorney General. Elliott and Morehouse were offered their jobs back at higher wages.[9] It is not known if Morehouse accepted the offer, but he was soon working for the Bureau of the Census, where he became an expert on business data. Elliott did return to his old job, albeit briefly. This was mostly ceremonial; at the Republican national convention in June, Theodore Roosevelt's bid to unseat his hand-picked successor, William Howard Taft, and secure the nomination for a third term failed. Roosevelt announced his candidacy as an independent, guaranteeing the election of Democrat Woodrow Wilson. This was the first Democratic administration to take over the White House in sixteen years; the personnel turnover in all departments would be extensive. The time from August 1912 to the inauguration in March 1913 was a period of suspended animation, punctuated occasionally by the growing threat of war in Europe.

George McCabe handed in his resignation on January 31 and announced that he was moving to Portland, Oregon. "I have no special offer or prospects there," he said. He chose it simply because he thought he would enjoy it there. He had trouble outrunning his reputation, however, as the *Journal of the Kansas Medical Society* reported in October 1913:

> The public generally will have no difficulty in recalling the Hon. George P. McCabe. He was that official of the Department of Agriculture under the Taft-Wilson regime whose steady hostility to the enforcement of the Pure Food Law, aided by a discreditable conspiracy which he engineered, finally forced Dr. Wiley out. Mr. McCabe is now ready to capitalize on his experience. This circular letter, sent from his office, now removed to Portland, Ore., tells its own story.[10]

The circular informed readers that "court cases, with attendant public notice of violation, are expensive and hurtful.... I am prepared to advise manufacturers and dealers on the legality of their labels, and if necessary represent them before the United States, various State Food Commissioners, and state and federal courts."

However, Portland was not a hotbed of regulatory law, and by 1915 he was in Chicago, working as a lobbyist for the meatpacking industry (where the first question asked him in one Washington hearing was: "are you the same McCabe who was involved in the Wiley-McCabe affair back in 1911?"). By 1933, he had returned to Washington, working as chief counsel for the American Brewers Association (by which time the Wiley-McCabe affair seems to have finally been forgotten).[11]

Elliott retired with the change in administration in March 1913 and worked as a consulting engineer, forming a partnership with the Peoria-based J.H. Harmon in 1916. Their firm, the Elliott and Harmon Engineering Company, was based in both Washington and Illinois. Elliott revised his best-known book, *Engineering for Land Drainage* in 1919. He died in Washington in 1926.[12]

Assistant Secretary Hays was already in Rome when the Final Report was issued, drafting the charter for the International Institute of Agriculture. After World War II it would become the United Nations Food and Agriculture Organization. From Rome, he traveled to Buenos Aires, where he helped organize the Argentina Department of Agriculture. Sailing back to the United States, his ship was taken into detention by the Germans and he and his wife spent several weeks in harsh conditions before being released to the Brazilian government. Upon his return he purchased a farm in West Chester, Pennsylvania. However, too ill to work it, he sold it in 1920 and moved to his brother's farm near Eldora, Iowa. He died in January 1928. His tenure with the Agriculture Department is now mostly forgotten, and of all the participants in the Wright Report Incident, he is the one with the most credible claim to have blundered into impropriety through misunderstanding and naiveté. Today, he is known as the father of American scientific plant breeding, especially of grains.[13] Beverly Galloway was promoted from Chief of the Bureau of Plant Industry to be his replacement as Assistant Secretary.

Secretary Wilson, as long promised, retired in March 1913 to the life of a gentleman farmer at his home in Traer, Iowa. He died in 1920. He was not only the longest-serving agriculture secretary, he has been the longest-serving cabinet officer in the nation's history–15 years, 363 days, a record that will probably never be broken. The Agriculture Department's new Mall building was not named for him when it was completed in 1930, as he had hoped. In 1936, as part of Harold Ickes's Public Works Administration program, the south building—for a few years at least, the largest office building in the world—was erected across Independence Avenue. It was connected to the Mall Building by two enclosed bridges, and the west bridge was named for Secretary Wilson in 1937.[14]

In 1916, the irrigation and drainage investigations divisions were moved out of the Office of Experiment Stations into a new bureau, the Office of Public Roads and Rural Engineering, where they were combined with other units sharing a focus on the application of civil and mechanical engineering to agriculture. These included the Bureau of Public Roads; the Divisions of Farm Machinery and Farm Structures of the Bureau of Plant Industry; and the Division of Rural Engineering of the Office of Experiment Stations. The Bureau of Public Roads grew tremendously in the 1920s, so in 1931 it was pulled out and given its own status as a bureau. The remaining units were renamed the Division of Agricultural Engineering.[15]

On April 28, 1919, former representative Ralph Moss died at his farm near Ashboro, Indiana, after being struck by a charging bull. His attention was distracted by a balky piece of farm equipment and he did not see or hear the bull until it was too late. He was injured on Thursday and died the following Saturday. He was 57.[16]

Leigh Hunt moved to Las Vegas about 1923, where he invested in mines and attempted to put together an investment group to construct an electric power plant in

Boulder Canyon a few miles southeast of Las Vegas by dynamiting the canyon walls into the canyon floor to form a dam. He was unsuccessful, but in 1928 Congress approved the Bureau of Reclamation's plan to construct a 726-foot-high concrete dam, 20 miles downstream in Black Canyon; it was nevertheless known as Boulder Dam.[17]

The Commissioner of the Bureau of Reclamation (BOR) overseeing the construction of the dam was Elwood Mead. After returning to the United States from Australia in 1916 he accepted a joint appointment as professor at the University of California–Berkeley and chairman of the California Land Settlement Board, which established the two model farming communities of Durham, in the Sacramento River Valley, in 1918, and Delhi, in the San Joaquin valley, two years later. Both failed within a few years due to overpriced land, low nationwide crop prices, insufficient water, and in the case of Delhi, bad planning.[18]

In 1924 President Hoover appointed him head of BOR, the agency Mead had once tried to talk Theodore Roosevelt out of creating. Three years earlier, Hugh MacRae, the developer of New Berne and other model immigrant communities near Wilmington, North Carolina, founded the Farm City Corporation in an attempt to establish a much

Directional sign for Penderlea, North Carolina. Based on Hugh MacRea's "Farm City" concept, Penderlea, built during the Great Depression by the U.S. Resettlement Administration, proved unsuccessful and the land was sold off after World War II to private owners. Photo 1938, by Ben Sahn and the U.S. Resettlement Administration (Library of Congress No. LC-USF33-006323M1 [P&P] LOT 1483).

larger town aimed primarily at giving (white) tenant farmers a chance to own their own farmsteads. It failed for lack of financing, but in 1924, Congress appropriated $15,000 to investigate the colonization of cut-over and overflowed lands of the South. MacRae and Mead, already friends, worked together on the panel examining the possibilities of such settlements. They kept the idea alive with occasional infusions of Congressional investigation funds for close to a decade, but by 1932 Mead, along with new Interior Secretary Ray Lyman Wilbur, agreed that the opposition of the Department of Agriculture and the need for the BOR to focus on its two signature projects, Boulder Dam and Grand Coulee Dam, made further participation impossible.[19]

MacRae did eventually build Farm City, under the name Penderlea, with assistance from the Division of Subsistence Homesteads (one of Franklin Roosevelt's "Alphabet Soup" agencies), but Interior Secretary Ickes was never in favor of the project (or the agency), as his agriculture priority was soil conservation, which emphasized farm consolidation, not dispersion. Penderlea topped out at 112 families in 1937, and the property was liquidated in 1946.[20]

Under Mead's direction Boulder Dam was built on budget and 20 months ahead of schedule. Lake Mead, the impoundment behind the dam, is named in his honor. Mead died in January 1936, four months after Boulder Dam was dedicated. In 1947 it was renamed Hoover Dam.[21]

In November 1913, the lawsuit brought against Richard J. Bolles and the Florida

Back row, left to right: John Whitting, Director, Shoshone Irrigation District; Wyoming Governor Frank Emerson; and Elwood Mead at a State Park in Wyoming, c. 1930, shortly after construction of Boulder Dam (Hoover Dam) had started. Photographer unknown (Wyoming State Archives No. P85-31/07).

Fruit Lands Company by the Progresso trustees was decided. The court found that Bolles had paid $360,000 for the land and $400,000 in commissions to sales agents to achieve projected gross proceeds of $2.9 million dollars. Of this, $1.4 had already been paid by purchasers and about $1.5 million was still owed by smallholders on time payments. The court found no legal grounds to demand the return of fully paid contracts but held that payments still due the firm should be held in abeyance until the land had been drained and surveyed by the state. The federal Department of Justice, having convened a grand jury months earlier, immediately indicted Bolles and seven other officials and agents of the Florida Fruit Lands Company on criminal charges of conspiracy to commit fraud.

A year later, in a parallel case, Dr. E.C. Chambers of the Chambers Land Company of Kansas City was found guilty of twelve counts of intent to commit mail fraud and sentenced to two years imprisonment and a fine of $6,000. One associate was sentenced to a year and retrials were ordered for three others. The indictment that had been brought against Bolles in Washington, D.C., was dismissed in a Jacksonville court in mid–1914, probably by a bribed magistrate. The Attorney General began anew, the case worked its way painfully through the system with massive infusions of legal ingenuity and effort pushing back the day of reckoning until the inevitable happened; Richard Bolles died of a heart attack in the berth of a Florida East Coast train near Palm Beach on March 17, 1917.

He left everything to his secretary, Agnes Cain Pepper, who used the money to start a private military school for boys in Jacksonville, the Bolles School, in 1933. In 1962 it dropped its military focus and began admitting girls and young women in 1971. Today it is an exclusive private co-ed K-12 school with about 1,100-day students and 100 boarding students, mostly international.[22]

On May 13, 1912, even before the hearings concluded, Thomas Will was writing his partners with second thoughts:

> I feel that a serious mistake has been made in selling Everglades lands on the plans hitherto employed, whether that of the auction or of selling direct from the map; for both plans overlooked the two fundamentals of association and transportation. It is interesting to note how, in the case of the Davie settlement, these two principles have asserted themselves. People owning land elsewhere felt impelled to leave those untouched and settle upon lands not their own, in order to be on a canal and among neighbors.[23]

Will thought that he could avoid the problems that had plagued Bolles, Chambers and the Tatums by building a compact townsite of one to two square miles on the rich "pond apple slough" lands rimming the south shore of Lake Okeechobee. He initially wanted to arrange a land swap with the big auction-style land sellers so that the owner of a trust certificate conveying (in theory) ownership of a ten-acre plot in one of the gigantic land company holdings could trade the certificate for a plot in his new town of Okeelanta. The landowners and the Internal Improvement Fund all threw cold water on this idea. "I recall our conversation in the matter of concentrated colonization," wrote Bolles, "I do not see any way for you to accomplish your object except by the owners of small tracts in the Florida Everglades Land Company exchanging with each other.... The only practical way that I can see for you to accomplish your purpose would be for you to purchase one or two sections, and colonize them with a townsite included."

The problem, as Bolles explained, was that most of these prospective villagers were still paying off the contract price on their scattered parcels to a variety of different sellers.

Even assuming Will's own Everglades Land Sales Company was willing to let its customers trade in parcels previously purchased in its 70,000 acres for a place in Okeelanta, there was no motivation for any other land company to do the same; they would be giving up a sale solely to allow the customer to buy a site in Will's non-profit cooperative. The best Will could hope for is that land values stayed high and the new Okeelanta buyers could sell their previously purchased parcels before the burden of making double payments broke them.[24]

Taking Bolles's advice, Will himself purchased a section of land southwest of Lake Okeechobee in February 1913. Eventually he bought 1,000 acres, about one and a half square miles. His son Lawrence and four others founded the town of Okeelanta in October 1913. Will joined him in 1916. A short dirt road connected it to Highway 25, the east-west highway from West Palm Beach to Fort Myers. In 1922, after a decade-long cycle of dry years, the North New River Canal, which ran beside the town, overflowed most of the land southeast of the lake as water draining off the land formed a dam that backed up the water being forced down the canal from the lake, just as C.G. Elliott predicted it would. Many years later, a nearby settler, R.H. Little, recalled that so much rain fell in 1922 and 1923 that it was possible to drive a boat out of the canal for miles across what had been farm fields.[25]

Thomas Will joined the exodus out of Okeelanta, moving to his daughter's home in Ft. Lauderdale in 1922. In 1925, an observer noted that "Okeelanta is just about deserted, there are still a few families in the community, but they're there principally because they do not have sufficient funds to get out."[26] The hurricanes of 1926 and 1928 finished it off. The 1939 *WPA Guide* to Florida noted only the turnoff from Highway 25 to "the former site of Okeelanta village."[27] By then, Will had been dead two years.

Very little is known about the life of J.O. Wright after he resigned from the State of Florida. He briefly worked for the Furst-Clark Company, the Everglades Drainage District's largest contractor, but soon left as money dried up, contracts were allowed to lapse, and new contracts were issued with the proviso that they would only be paid in bonds. The last record of his appearance before the Fund's trustees for the company is in late 1913. Arthur Morgan biographer Aaron D. Purcell believes he returned to Lake Mattamuskeet because he owned land in the area.[28] It is certainly possible, as his friend Lawrence Brett was chief engineer of New Holland Farms until 1917 and one of the problems with the Mattmuskeet Lake project was that its canals, dug across its shallow, soft lake bottom, silted in rapidly and required constant dredging, so a man of Wright's experience would have been useful. On the other hand, by 1914 Wright would have been 64 and may have been ready to retire.

Wright did carry through with his threat to sue John Seip for $7500 of the stock of the Provident Land Company. On September 29, 1916, a North Carolina circuit court ordered that he be issued 75 shares of the firm's regular, $100 par-value stock.[29] On November 10, stock certificate No. 75 was executed in his favor. Wright's lawyers sought an injunction against the execution of the judgment, asserting that the delivery was outside the ordered 60-day window, and that the stock was not the same as that owned by the other stockholders. This was probably a move by Wright's lawyers to try to convert an equity award (an order for specific performance to grant the shares) into an award of monetary damages for $7500. It was a smart move—to be a hostile, minority shareholder in one of John Seip's companies was an unpromising prospect. However, the North Carolina Supreme Court ruled in February 1917 that the delivery of Certificate No.75 was not tardy, and that the shares were acceptable. Wright did not attempt another lawsuit.

After this, Wright's trail all but ends. Part of the problem is that in contrast to the

Everglades, about which so much had been written since the 1940s, very little has been told about the other great wetlands of America: the potholes of Minnesota, the Louisiana bayous, the Okefenokee Swamp of Georgia, the Albemarle-Pamlico Peninsula of North Carolina and the Great Dismal Swamp of Virginia.[30] Despite being one of the largest, most extensive and costly drainage projects in American history (certainty the most expensive failed project) there are almost no archival records relating to the Lake Mattamuskeet—New Holland Farms project after 1912.

We do know one more thing. James Oliver Wright died in Columbia, South Carolina, on November 21, 1932. He was survived by his wife, Katherine Vinnedge Wright, a son from his first marriage, George, and a daughter from his second, Helen.

III

Lawrence Brett became Chief Engineer of the Southern Land Reclamation Company, the firm attempting to reclaim Lake Mattamuskeet, in 1911. By 1914 it had dredged 83 miles of canal. These were found inadequate and eventually 130 miles of canal were dug. The canals silted in rapidly and required constant re-dredging throughout their lives.[31] In 1915 the Southern Land Reclamation Company changed its name to New Holland Farms. By 1916 about 20,000 acres of the lake bottom had been successfully drained and New Holland started to develop an 850-acre town site surrounding the pump station. In March 1918 New Holland Farms sold the development to a group of investors named the North Carolina Farms Company, a subsidiary of a Columbus, Ohio, firm, the D.L. Dollings Company. Brett's firm was replaced with an in-house engineer from the Dollings firm.

Brett successfully re-established his engineering consultancy, the Lawrence Brett Engineering Company, in Wilson about 100 miles northwest of the lake. In 1912 he had married Mildred Roney, daughter of Julius Roney, a wealthy tobacco buyer. After Julius Roney died in 1919, Brett and wife moved into the family home, one of the finest in Wilson. Lawrence Brett died in 1937 at age 52. His widow Mildred continued to live there until her death in 1968, and their son Lawrence Brett, Jr., lived in the Roney-Brett house until his death in 2012.[32]

After investing $3.5 million, the R.L. Dollings Company entered receivership in 1923 and was taken over by the state for unpaid taxes. The lake refilled. A second New Holland Farms partnership purchased the property from the state in 1924. In 1933 this second New Holland company abandoned its efforts. The lake refilled again. In 1934 it was purchased by the National Audubon Society and given to the federal government as a wildlife refuge. The equipment was pulled out of the pumping station and it was turned into a hunting lodge. In 1974 the lodge, privately owned, closed. It was designated a national historic site in 1980 to prevent its destruction. It was subsequently turned over to the state, which transferred it to the National Park Service. It is in the process of being restored by a private foundation.

Of the other eastern North Carolina drainage districts that Wright had been involved with, only John Seip's Moyock was an out-and-out failure. At the time it was created in 1910, about three-quarters of the land in the Moyock Drainage District was owned by the Carolina Land and Timber Company. Most of it was already cut over. The remainder had been farmed for generations, in some cases over 75 years. By 1926, only 400 of the 14,000 acres within the district had been improved (not just drained, but actually reclaimed and put to use) since 1910. While some of the other districts the Agriculture Department surveyed between 1906 and 1910 were less than successful, Moyock was the only one in which no real progress was made.[33]

The Pungo Drainage District dredged the Pungo River, successfully draining land held by a number of different owners. However, the land of the single largest owner, the John L. Roper company, could not be drained without the addition of a series of lateral canals. In 1913, the firm formed a sub-district called the Washington County Drainage District No. 4 to cut laterals only on its own land. It was organized, let for bids, and the work contracted to a firm called the Eastern Home and Farm Association. Eastern Home then tried to back out, asserting that the new drainage district could not be overlaid on the old. The drainage district sued. The court rejected Eastern Home and Farm's argument, ordering both the issuance of bonds and specific performance by Eastern Home and Farm. Given this shaky beginning, the district made surprisingly good progress; by 1926 2,000 of its total 9,600 acres had been turned into farms or homes.[34]

Although the Roper company pulled out of the Pantego Drainage District, to the irritation of C.G. Elliott, the company did live up to a promise it made to undertake its share of the drainage burden privately. By 1926, 7,000 of Pantego's 8,000 acres were in use. In 1916, the Roper company sold 45,000 acres in Washington, Beaufort and Hyde

Reforestation on Norfolk Southern Farms, about 1916. Photo by Herbert H. Brimley (Brimley Collection, North Carolina State Archives, Neg. No. PhC-42-Bx13-Forest and Forest Industries-F51).

counties to the Carolina, Clinchfield and Ohio Railroad. It was on the north side of Terra Ceia, adjacent to both Washington District No. 4 and the Pantego Drainage District. Most of this tract, called the Norfolk Southern Farms, had already been surveyed during the Pungo and Pantago surveys of 1909–11. A new drainage district, Albemarle No. 1, was created on 31,000 acres of the land in 1917.

John A. Wilkinson was hired to manage the timbering operations and the dredging of about 175 miles in canals. Norfolk Southern Farms anticipated reclaiming 5,000 to 10,000 acres per year to sell as farmland, although it planned to retain 15–20,000 acres. In describing to a reporter what the firm planned to do with its retained parcel, Wilkinson was somewhat indefinite. It could be interpreted to mean they planned to run a corporate farm. On the other hand, he may have meant they planned to set up a large-scale tenant-farmer operation. The fate of Norfolk Southern Farms is unknown, but the drainage district itself was apparently successful, as it was "A" rated by Moody's seven years later, and a Department of Agriculture report in 1930 indicated that it was actively converting land to agricultural uses.[35]

In 1916 the Belhaven sawmill of the Roper Lumber Company burned and was not rebuilt. However, the economy of the town was converting by this time from saw milling to supporting farming and fishing, and by 1926 its population had increased to 2,600. A company making wooden barrels, boxes and casks, a subsidiary of the Standard Oil

Shipping strawberries to market, from St. Helena, North Carolina, about 1915. Photographer unknown (Hugh MacRae Trucking Development Co. Collection, North Carolina State Archives, No. PhC 150-087).

Company, was the largest single firm in town, but accounted for only about 12 percent of the town's economy. The town had 17 wharves on the river, including four owned by the railroad and one by the town.[36]

On December 1, 1922, the Roper sawmill in New Berne caught fire, creating a conflagration that destroyed over 20 square blocks, 500 homes and businesses and left 1,800 homeless. The Roper mill, which employed 300, was by now no longer operated by J.L. Roper, the firm having leased it out to the Rowland Lumber Company, who processed

Opening of the North New River Canal at Lake Okeechobee, April 24, 1912. Front, left to right: Prof. Rolfs, U.S. Department of Agriculture; unknown; Governor Gilchrist (with shovel); State Comptroller William V. Knott; State Drainage Engineer J.O. Wright. This ceremony was held about half-way through the Moss Committee hearings, soon after Wright admitted writing his partners in North Carolina that he did not think Everglades lands had any redeeming agricultural value. He would resign four months later. From brochure *Souvenir: Official Opening of the Gulf to Atlantic Waterway of the Everglades Drainage Canal, April 23–27, 1912.* Photographer unknown (Box 21, William Sherman Jennings Papers, P.K. Yonge Library of Florida History, Special and Area Studies Collections, George A. Smathers Libraries, University of Florida, Gainesville).

Roper lumber shipments under contract. Although most of Roper's holdings in the Pamlico Sound area were timbered out, the company continued in business in North Carolina until 1993, and is still an active corporation in Virginia under the name Roper Brothers Lumber Company.[37]

John Wilkinson was killed in a car accident in Raleigh in February 1932. He was 67. His mansion, Forest River Manor, was soon purchased for a hotel and marina, and it continues in that role today, recently restored, in a town now primarily dedicated to tourism.[38]

IV

In July 1912, as the Moss Committee headed into its final days, Vance Helm of the Everglades Land Sales Company retained a team of engineers to undertake a consulting project for his firm. Daniel Mead was professor of engineering at the University of Wisconsin; Leonard Metcalf was a consulting engineer specializing in water and sewage infrastructure based in Boston. Allen Hazen was a consulting engineer engaged in similar work out of Chicago. The Everglades Land Sales Company owned 70,000 acres of land along the Miami Canal and South New River Canal in what is now south Broward and north Dade counties west of U.S. Highway 27.[39] Assuming the State of Florida did not augment the work outlined in its current plans, Helm wrote Mead, what would be the condition of the firm's lands, and if not drained, what additional improvements would the firm need to make the land satisfactory for agricultural use?[40]

The three engineers convened in Jacksonville on August 3, where they were met by H.H. Ralston, a vice-president of the Everglades Land Sales Company, W.J. Kackley, the firm's drainage engineer, and J.O. Wright. The six men traveled to Fort Myers, then through the Everglades to Miami, returning to Jacksonville on August 12. Wright briefed the team on the status of the state's drainage plan. He noted that in *Senate Document No. 89* he had estimated that the canals would require an aggregate capacity of 3,938 cubic feet per second (cfs), but he had revised this figure downward to 3,200.[41] The consultants returned to their respective homes to prepare the report, which Daniel Mead estimated would be ready in November.

Two weeks later, J.O. Wright resigned. "When I accepted the position of Chief Engineer, two and one-half years ago, I thought the matter had been divorced from politics and was to be carried on as a business proposition. In this I was mistaken.... Finding it impossible to accomplish the results desired, I wish to be relieved of the duties of Chief Drainage Engineer as soon as you can secure some one to take the position."[42]

Coming on the heels of the Moss Committee report, it would be natural to assume that this was the reason Wright quit (or was fired). However, the Moss report contained nothing new. John Seip's startling revelations had come back in February, and John Wilkinson's and Wright's own corroboration of the North Carolina deals had come in early May. Not only had the Fund's trustees not fired him then, they had paid for thousands of copies of two brochures defending him.[43] It would be odd that the trustees supported him through the seven bruising months of the Moss Committee hearings, only to ask him to resign after the spotlight had been turned off.

But a careful reading of the minutes of the Internal Improvement Fund shows that the reason for the trustees' ire may have had little to do with the Moss Committee. It appears that Wright's penchant for bad engineering may have finally caught up with him. The locks and sluice gates for the North New River at Lake Okeechobee were ready for construction bids. On August 9, the trustees deemed it "advisable that the plans and specifications of locks to be constructed in the Everglades should be examined and passed upon by some well-known engineers before the contracts should be let."[44] Captain Slattery of the Corps of Engineers recommended two referees, and the plans were sent off through the Corps.

The first draft of their report was ready in late August, just days before Wright turned in his resignation. On September 26, a few days after he quit, the final report was formally presented to the Corps. Major Sewell and Captain Slattery met with the trustees, bringing a 20-page report. The proposed locks and sluiceways were fine. The canal was not. At high lake level, the locks and sluice gates would pass 1,400 cubic feet of water per second. The canal could only accept 871 cfs because of water stagnating or back-flowing up the canal after entering from the table-flat wetlands and farm fields downstream from the lock. The technical report concluded with this warning, in all caps:

> WE DESIRE TO EMPHASIZE AT THIS POINT THAT THE SLUICE GATES PROVIDED IN THE DAMS HAVE IN ALL CASES AND UNDER THE MOST UNFAVORABLE CONDITIONS A DISCHARGING CAPACITY GREATER THAN THE CARRYING CAPACITY OF THE CANAL WHEN RUNNING BANK FULL[45]

Translation: Your canals won't work.

On November 12, Mead, Hazen and Metcalf (MHM) presented their report to Vance Helm. Its tone was set in the opening: "In our judgment, the present system of canals as outlined by the State of Florida is not sufficient to take care of the runoff from the Upper Everglades as a whole … the work already done by the State, and at present definitely projected, is entirely inadequate for the drainage of the Everglades."[46]

The MHM Board noted that it was neither desirable nor possible for the Everglades Land Sales Company to underwrite a plan to reclaim the entire Everglades when its interests were limited to lands measuring only about four percent of the total upper Everglades, scattered across an area measuring about ten or twelve percent of the whole. However, the board found that the specific infrastructure needed to reclaim the firm's land was, to a significant extent, dependent on the state's future drainage efforts. Therefore, the MHM Board split the report into two parts: a detailed engineering analysis of what it would take to make the 70,000 acres of Everglades Land Sales Company land usable, and an overview of the drainage needs of the entire Everglades. In spite of this, the problem of Everglades drainage was so complex that the general overview was longer than the site-specific engineering analysis.

The consultants concluded:

1. Draining the Everglades was technically feasible, but so expensive that nobody, not even the State, would ever be able to do it as one big project. Thus, reclaiming the Everglades would be an incremental program, taking place over many decades, parcel-by-parcel, section-by-section.
2. Draining Lake Okeechobee and reclaiming the Upper Everglades were two separate things, largely unrelated to each other in terms of engineering. In practical application, this meant that canals built for one purpose had to be separate from canals built for the other.
3. As originally planned by J.O. Wright, the five canals intended to drain Lake Okeechobee and the Everglades were to have an aggregate capacity of 3,938 cubic feet per second, later revised to 3,200 cfs. Wright estimated that the Everglades below the lake drained at the rate of 90 cfs per township, or 2.5 cfs per square mile, roughly 7,800 cfs in total, although it does not appear that he factored this into his calculation of required canal capacity.[47] Wright believed he was dredging his canals to a specification of

3,200 cfs, but the MHM Board calculated that the theoretical maximum capacity of the five canals was actually 2,700 cfs, with a practical maximum of 1,877 cfs, mostly due to surface subsidence caused by the drying of the peat-based soils.[48]

4. The report prepared by J.O. Wright was "incomplete and inadequate" and ignored basic data that were easily available.[49] The report as modified by C.G. Elliott presented "a clearer conception of the magnitude and uncertainties of the problem." It also dealt with Lake Okeechobee drainage and Everglades drainage as two separate problems. (There is a typo in the calculations, carried over from the Moss Committee transcript, but it appears that Elliott estimated a capacity of 2,551 cfs to drain Lake Okeechobee alone.) Elliott calculated the canal capacity needed to drain the Everglades, exclusive of the lake, at 6.72 cfs per square mile, roughly 21,000 cfs.[50] However, in the opinion of the MHM Board, this was still low. "Cautious as the Elliott report is," the MHM board found, "we are of the opinion that it is still too optimistic, and that the capacities therein suggested are not as great as the available data indicate to be necessary."[51]

5. The MHM Board concluded that the required capacities for Everglades drainage, exclusive of the lake, were: 40 cfs per square mile on small tracts of 50 square miles or less; 21 cfs per square mile on tracts of around 200 sq. mi.; 14 cfs per square mile on tracts of 750 square mile or greater. For the Everglades as a whole, 7 cfs per square mile, or about 28,000 cfs.[52]

6. The capacity needed to handle peak flood load from Lake Okeechobee was 40,000 cfs. This required a separate canal, 1,000 feet wide by 15 feet deep, following the shortest possible route from the lake to the sea.[53]

Later, after measuring gages were installed, the typical-year peak contiguous 10-day inflow to the lake ("average 10-day peak period") was measured at 25,800 cfs. The highest measured contiguous 10-day period ("maximum 10-day peak period") was 51,600 cfs. Based on this, the greatest possible 10-day inflow ("theoretical maximum 10-day peak period") was estimated at 70,000 cfs. The typical 90-day rainy season inflow was measured at 8,300 cfs, with a measured high of 15,310 cfs. Note that these are inflows to the lake, not outflows. The lake acted as a buffer, absorbing spikes in inflow by rising, then draining. Its ability to do this depended on the pre-existing level and the length and volume of the peak period. Hence, the lake could absorb a much larger 10-day peak inflow than a 30- or 90-day peak period. Overall, based on these measured streamflows, the MHM estimate that an absolute maximum continuous outflow of 40,000 cfs was needed proved to be high, but not by much.[54]

7. Except for a small 2,000-acre parcel near Davie Farm, all of the lands of the Everglades Land Sales Company were periodically inundated. Utilization of these holdings would probably require a combination of subdivision, dikes, canals and at least some pumping. Except for Davie Farms, it would be advantageous for the firm to pursue a strategy of "blocking up" its holdings—removing the checkerboard pattern of state-owned sections—so the company's land could be contained within one or more sets of dikes.

The report seems to have made surprisingly little impact, at least in public. It was, after all, privately commissioned and privately printed. Arthur Morgan later wrote, "the report of Mead, Metcalf and Hazen was a straightforward attempt to look the facts in the face, but it was largely neutralized by the report of Randolph, Leighton and Perkins in 1913." There is no mention of it in the Thomas Will papers; it appears that Vance Helm never showed it to him. An extensive review of it appeared in *Engineering News*, but not until almost a year after its release. It noted that "the board concluded that in no case which it saw could the owners of land within the Everglades expect effective drainage … the problem is complicated by the absence of any drainage act under which the work can be carried out and by the policy of the State in selling alternative rather than contiguous sections. Both of these defects must be remedied, the board reported, before work can be properly carried on."[55]

This went to the heart of the Internal Improvement Fund's failures since the 1903 Jennings land patent from the federal government. The North Carolina drainage law permitted the creation of specific districts encompassing private and public land. These were defined, surveyed by drainage engineers who valued each acre of land on the basis of present value and benefit to be concurred, apportioned a tax, and floated a bond issue to pay for the improvements. The bonds, and the total tax projected for collection over a thirteen-year period, could be no higher than the "increment" (the increase in land value) estimated in the engineer's report.

Florida eschewed individual districts. Since 1905, it had relied upon a one-shot drainage plan for the entire Everglades, sold huge tracts of checkerboard lands at nominal prices, and levied a flat per-acre drainage tax that remained the same regardless of whether the land was actually improved, or by how much. It was the land sales that carried the financial load, sold by the state at sharply discounted prices in the hope that the money realized would pay for at least a limited amount of drainage. This would, in theory, be enough to raise the price of land for the state's interstitial sections to $60 to $100 per acre, which would allow the state to recoup the losses incurred from the sales to the initial large-block purchasers at one to ten dollars an acre.

Of course, the big-block buyers would reap a windfall, but it could be argued that they were the ones who assumed the most risk by putting their money on the table first. However, as we have seen, speculators such as R.J. Bolles were remarkably adept at risk-shifting to thousands of smallholders through the use of mail order sales and quasi-conveyance instruments such as clearance receipts and trust certificates, which gave the appearance of ownership, but it truth were only contingent options.[56]

The ultimate weakness in the state's plan was that it scattered private holdings, regardless of whether they were huge tracts owned by one landholder or small plots disbursed among thousands of mail-order buyers, over hundreds of square miles. Both committed the state to a massive drainage program to drain the scattershot pattern of private holdings and the public land interspersed between them. Jennings's "reversion" argument may have been tenuous at best, but there is no doubt that the thousands of contingent options, on lands sold by speculators like Bolles, Chambers, and others depended on the state draining the land sufficiently to permit someone—hopefully the federal government—to underwrite a detailed survey, which would permit the quasi-deeds to each parcel to be converted into genuine warranty deeds, effecting a permanent, irrefutable transfer of title.

At a meeting between the big landowners and the Internal Improvement Fund held in the Manhattan Hotel in New York City on September 12, 1912, far from the prying eyes and ears of the Florida press and public, with a copy of the Mead, Hazen and Metcalf report sitting on the conference table between them, the landowners and the Internal Improvement Fund debated the future of the Everglades Drainage District.[57]

Governor Gilchrist reported that the balance in the Internal Improvement Fund, depleted by delinquencies, was $23,950. The landowners told Gilchrist and incoming governor Park Trammell that they would not pay the District's five-cent-an-acre tax, nor would they attempt to make good on taxes now in arrears. There would be no further financial participation in the District until there was "some definite plans made by which they could see the final completion of this great work," which did not appear feasible. Gilchrist reported that there were no potential big-block purchasers on the horizon; in fact, there was a glut of private land on the market available for little more than the cost of back taxes. The idea of paying for Everglades drainage through massive, checker-boarded land sales was dead; the retail sale of those lands to smallholders by lottery prior to reclamation was now considered tantamount to fraud. The idea of bond financing was proposed. Gilchrist explained that legislation would be required. How much had been spent so far? About $2.1 million, mostly through the Internal Improvement Fund, paid to dredge 140 miles of canals. How much more would be needed? Gilchrist replied that would be up to Governor-elect Trammel, but his best estimate was six to seven million dollars. According to one participant, "the room became very quiet."[58]

10

Lamar's Crying Cow

> We couldn't hope to bury them all, so we resorted to fire. We broke up the wrecked buildings, and when that wasn't enough, we tore down what was left standing. The sky was black with smudge. The smell was unbelievable. It's not true that we buried the whites and burned the colored. You couldn't tell the difference; white, black, man, woman. What the water didn't despoil the sun did. There wasn't much left of them.
>
> —John Cottrell of Moore Haven, on the Hurricane of 1928[1]

In the spring of 1913, after taking the oath of office, new governor Park Trammel reorganized the Everglades Drainage District, hoping to give it more of the outward appearance of the statutory drainage districts used in other states. The Internal Improvement Fund was almost fully depleted, having spent $1.84 million since 1904. In 1912 the Fund's income had been $231,000 and its expenditures $564,000. It was losing about $25,000 per month. Trammel's solution was bond financing.[2]

The drainage district itself was given sovereign powers independent of the Internal Improvement District so it could create its own bonded indebtedness and enter into obligations separate from those of the Fund's trustees. The size of the district was expanded, and a map created, divided into graduated taxing zones. Initially, there were three zones: Red, Blue, and Uncolored. The closer to a canal a parcel was, the higher its tax, ranging from fifteen cents for adjacent land, to five for distant tracts. No attempt was made to actually link the tax assessment to value increment. Moreover, the district had no idea what its tax base—the aggregate value of the land in its jurisdiction—was worth. Based on the assessor's rolls of the various counties within its boundaries, it estimated $9.691 million, but admitted that this was little more than a guess.[3]

The revised act did permit local landowners to create "special districts," but the formation of a special district did not relieve private landowners of the burden of paying the Everglades Drainage District tax. There were two processes for formation, one through the circuit court or one through a county commission. The county commission process in particular was heavily weighted towards big landowners, who could impose their will on the minority if the county commission administered the special district.[4]

Asked at the E.C. Chambers fraud trial in 1914 why the state didn't just drain the Everglades, then sell parcels at market prices, Governor Trammel and General Ellis both replied that it was impossible; big buyers like Mr. Chambers paid the bill for the drainage efforts. As the Governor explained, "the Everglades are not a swamp, but a state in its own right, covered with saw grass and water, which needs draining."[5] But that was an effect masquerading as a cause. Whether it was Governor Jennings's "reversionary rights" argument that the Everglades would belong to the railroads if the drainage program halted, or his belief that Congress had reneged on its implied promise to Florida Senator Wescott in 1848 that the federal government would drain the Everglades before transferring the land to the State of Florida, the important thing was that almost everyone had become convinced that at some point, if enough land was sold, and enough drainage work accomplished, the federal government would step in and finish the project.[6]

Governor Trammel needed to both justify his proposed Everglades bonds and blunt the pessimism caused by the selective dissemination of the Mead, Hazen, Metcalf report. He responded in time-honored fashion: by digging down, getting together $35,000, and hiring an engineer of his own, the famous Isham Randolph of Chicago, to do another study. Randolph had impeccable credentials, having made his reputation on the Chicago Sanitary Canal project, which reversed to the flow of the Chicago River away from Lake Michigan into the Des Plains River, preventing the urban runoff of the city from polluting the lake. Wright had been a general manager for one of the dredging contractors on this job, but there were many contractors, the project had been completed almost fifteen years ago, and it was uncertain if Randolph even remembered him.[7]

Randolph was tasked with assembling and supervising his own board of engineers. He chose Marshall Leighton of the J.G. White Engineering Corporation and Edmund T. Perkins, consulting engineer. The White Engineering firm would handle support, payments and bookkeeping.

To some extent, the "problem statement" contained in Randolph's contract was more of a "solution statement." Any consideration of pumping was out. It had to provide for a lowering of the surface level of Lake Okeechobee by four feet but did not require this to be linked to Everglades drainage. In addition, the consultants should not "give out to any person, firm or corporation any information, facts or data concerning said work, or the plans to be submitted for the drainage area described herein, or the location and route of any canal, nor the estimated cost thereof."[8]

Former governor William Jennings wrote Gano Dunn, president of the J.G. White Engineering firm that during the contract negotiations there had been

> ...many difficulties encountered.... During the second day's conference there was published in one of our daily newspapers scare headlines of what appeared to be an authoritative publication ... by Messrs Meade, Metcalf and Hazen, estimating the cost of the drainage at $80,000,000, and also some information to the effect that some one of your corporation had placed high estimates upon the work under consideration and it evidently caused the Trustees to take an entirely different view of the proposed plan of having the having the work done by commission.[9]

Although Dunn replied: "we are not aware of any members of our organization having views as to the cost of draining the Everglades, although at various times during the course of the negotiations we have held different views as to the cost of the report," Jennings had gotten his point across: just the rumor that someone in the Randolph–J. G. White team had commented favorably on the quality of work in the Mead, Hazen and Metcalf report had been enough to cause at least some of the trustees to question whether the project should be done by independent consultants, or should instead be performed in-house, by state engineers, who would presumably be more tractable. The message to Dunn and Randolph was clear: we're not paying for another Mead, Hazen, and Metcalf report.

And that's not what they got. The report, issued in October, was only mildly critical of the Internal Improvement Fund's previous efforts. "The existing system of canals contemplates the reclamation of a greater portion of the Everglades in the immediate future than will probably be justified by the demand for new lands," the report stated. "It would have been much better to provide for an orderly progression of reclamation in accordance with the demand and in due regard to market conditions and transportation facilities."[10]

The report reasserted the almost century-old belief that draining the Everglades was primarily a matter of diverting the southern flow from Lake Okeechobee into the ocean, but then stated, "we have encountered an idea ... by a large number of intelligent citizens of Florida to the effect that the problem of draining the Everglades cannot be solved by progressive steps, but must forthwith be covered by a great interdependent system of canals. We believe this to be an erroneous idea, and that the Everglades can be reclaimed progressively."[11]

However, the Randolph commissioners never addressed the main point raised in the Mead, Hazen, Metcalf report that no such "progressive system" could be carried out without a system of dikes and pumps, because without them, the "undrained" land would just contribute to surface sheet flow, as it had done for eons. Ultimately, this sheet flow would either drain into an intercepting canal, thereby overfilling it and flooding "drained" lands, or it would continue overland until it spread across drained lands, reverting them to their original condition. To be drained, a selected parcel had to be physically separated from the surrounding areas and continually pumped dry, at least during the wet season.

The Randolph commission's answer was a widely expanded network of canals. The commissioners reached capacity figures for the then-currently planned network that were roughly comparable to those of Mead, Hazen and Metcalf. They estimated peak Everglades runoff at 16 cubic feet per second per square mile, but unlike the Mead, Hazen and Metcalf Report, did not provide a sliding scale depending on the size of the parcel being considered. (The estimates in the Mead, Hazen and Metcalf Report varied from 40 cfs per square mile for a 50-square mile parcel to 14 cfs for a 750 square-mile parcel to 7 cfs for the entire Everglades. The Randolph commission cautioned that its number was not usable on a region-wide scale.) The peak runoff into the lake was estimated at about 51,500 cfs total, not much less than Mead, Hazen and Metcalf.[12]

The Randolph commission proposed a deep, 200-foot wide Okechobee-St. Lucie River canal that was only a slightly downsized version of the 70,000 cfs version in the Mead, Hazen, Metcalf report. The St. Lucie canal would cost $2.3 million dollars. After this was completed, the Randolph commission recommended that the district start an incremental series of improvements that would widen 260 miles of existing canals (some still unfinished) and add 136 miles of new canals at an aggregate cost of $4.3 million. There would also be a new hydroelectric plant in the St. Lucie canal that was included, if you followed the fine print down far enough, less for the electricity it would produce than for the $900,000 in bonds it justified. The total bill for the plan: $24.6 million. In eight years, the estimated cost of draining the Everglades had ballooned over 1,200 percent.[13]

"In my judgment, the salvation of the Everglades hangs upon the digging of the Okeechobee-St. Lucie canal. Without that canal, the efforts now being expended are a sheer waste of money and effort," Randolph wrote a few months after the report was released.[14] In essence, the report was a roundabout version of the Mead, Hazen and Metcalf Report. It denied that draining the lake and draining the Upper Everglades were two different problems while creating an engineering solution that did just that. Rather than take an incremental "dike, ditch and pump" approach, it advocated a linear extension of the Wright report by continuing to dig canals until there was nothing left to pump, ignoring the problems of irrigation, that is, the desiccation of peat-based soils. Like Thomas Will and William Jennings's compendium of reports, Senator Fletcher managed to get an appropriation passed to have the Randolph report printed as a congressional document, *Senate Document No. 379.*

But the district could not sell its bonds. In 1915 it renegotiated its contract with the Furst-Clark company, requiring the dredging firm to accept two-thirds of its payments in 6 percent interest notes. William Jennings warned Isham Randolph that "the Trustees are practically out of available funds with which to prosecute the work of draining the Everglades. For this reason, they have not formally adopted your good report." Jennings asked for advice on how the trustees should proceed, assuming partial implementation, which would permit them to adopt the report, and would rescue the chances of going ahead with the bond issue. Randolph urged Jennings that "if there are not available funds for the St. Lucie Canal and the minor canals, work on the minor canals should cease and all effort and expenditures be concentrated on the St. Lucie Canal."[15]

The trustees heeded Randolph's advice. Work on everything except the uncompleted North New River and Hillsboro canals was halted. All the resources thereby released were shifted to the St. Lucie Canal, much of which had to be blasted through rock that extended almost to the surface. A Toledo firm, Spitzer, Rorick and Company, eventually bought the six million bond issue in two tranches, the first, $3.5 million, in January 1917 and the second, $2.5 million, in July 1920.[16]

By 1925 the graduated "Red-Blue-No Color" tax system had been expanded into six zones. The highest tax rate "Zone 1" lands were taxed at a rate of $1.25 per acre. Out of 4.1 million acres in the district, 186,000 acres, mostly adjacent to the lake or the outfalls of canals, qualified as "Zone 1." The lowest rate, "Zone 6," lands were taxed at $0.10 per acre. Half of the total acreage of the district fell into this category.[17] In 1913 the district claimed a total tax base (land value) of $66.650 million, this figure having been extrapolated from the sale price of a mere 10,634 acres out of the district's four million acres, or 0.25 percent. (In 1909, using a flat two dollars an acre estimate, the Internal Improvement Fund had reached an aggregate land value of $8.6 million. About the same time, a survey of county appraisers' office tax records had yielded an estimate of $9.7 million.)[18]

In 1912, under the old, pre–1913 law, the Everglades Drainage District had collected $210,000 in drainage taxes. In 1926 it collected $1.487 million. Where the district had been, at the time of its formation in 1905, a relatively useless appendage to the land sales of the Internal Improvement Fund, the situation was now reversed. There was now very little income from land sales; tax revenues drove Everglades drainage. On July 1, 1926, the district had $10.250 million in bonded indebtedness and $2.133 million in short-term debt, mostly notes given to contractors in lieu of cash payments, and discounted anywhere from five to seven percent.

The period since 1910 had been a dry climatic cycle. Its end came in 1922 when 30 days of rainy weather flooded most of the locks and canal dams on the south side of Lake Okeechobee. Many of these had been completed only two or three years earlier. Thomas Will's Okeelanta washed over and stayed inundated, except for the occasional drought, for the next 20 years. Ritta Island, just offshore in Lake Okeechobee where the Miami Canal entered the lake and the site of some of the earliest Okeechobee settlements, submerged.

This was only the beginning. In 1924, 95 days of almost continuous rain in late summer and fall raised Lake Okeechobee four and a half feet. Fred Cottrell was superintendent of the Disston Island Drainage District at Moore Haven, a subdistrict that operated two pumping stations. In the dry season, they were used to pump water out of the lake into irrigation canals. In the wet season, they pumped water out of the canals into the lake. In 1924, Cottrell said "we got 46 inches of rain in six weeks. I mean to tell you that is water." Farmer R.H. Little said, "we began to realize there was not much truth in the statements that were made after each flood that this would be the last one." Cottrell explained that when the farmlands flooded, the water in the canals began flowing north, and would have drained back into the lake but for the locks and gates. The Everglades Drainage District had attempted to install a levee around the south shore of the lake by digging a linear borrow pit and throwing up a spoil bank about five feet high. When the lake reached 19 feet in 1924 it broke through in several places. The district came back and raised it by digging another borrow pit on the lake side of the levee.[19]

On September 16, 1926, Cottrell and his assistant, Flanders, were standing atop the levee. The Disston Island Drainage District was running both their pumps southbound from the lake as fast as they could turn.[20] Despite their efforts, the lake was at 19 feet, about eighteen inches below the top of the dike, and coming up an inch every couple of days. Cottrell turned to Flanders and said, "If we have a blow, even just a gale, Moore Haven is going under water." Two days later, the hurricane of 1926 struck. It passed over

"People elsewhere in the state really don't care if the folks down there perish or not." An agricultural workers' shack near Canal Point on the south rim of Lake Okeechobee in the years immediately after the 1926 and 1928 hurricanes. Photo by Marion Post Wolcott and the U.S. Farm Security Administration, c. 1931 (Library of Congress No. LC-USF34-051157-D [P&P] Lot 1590).

downtown Miami, heading northwest. "When that hurricane really started the waves would break cleanly over the top," Cottrell recalled. "That sand dike melted, just exactly like you take a spoonful of sugar and put it in hot coffee. It disappeared before your eyes—it just melted." His wife and daughter were drowned in the ensuing flood.

The problem, said Cottrell, "is the fact that all these canals which have been dug are nothing but ditches. During the dry season they will carry water, plenty of it, and keep the lake down, which is a good thing, but in the flood season ... they will not carry a drop of water from Lake Okeechobee. In fact, in 1926 they carried water back into the lake."[21]

Florida's economy, which had been experiencing an irrational land boom during the early 1920s, started to sour just before the hurricane. Addison and Wilson Mizner, the developers of Boca Raton in Palm Beach County, had not only been stealing from their own Palm Beach National Bank, they had started using it as a front to borrow heavily from other financial institutions so they could embezzle their money. The Palm Beach National Bank belonged to the so-called "Manley-Anthony System," a consortium of 200 banks participating in a regional clearinghouse in Atlanta that cleared checks and provided overnight loans that allowed banks to rectify their short-term balances to each other without having to go to the Federal Reserve. Most of the loans propping up the Palm Beach National Bank came from other Manley-Anthony institutions.

On June 21, 1926, one of these banks, the Commercial Bank and Trust Company of West Palm Beach, went into receivership, citing delinquent loans to the Mizners' bank. The next day the doors of the Palm Beach National Bank never opened and contractors and materialmen found that the checks they held from the Mizner Development Corporation could not be cashed or deposited. A bank run ensued and within a week, 83 banks in Florida and Georgia, 25 in the Manley-Anthony system, closed. What started as a slow slump turned into an economic free-fall that only accelerated with the September 1926 hurricane. For all intents and purposes, the Great Depression hit Florida a full three years before the rest of the country. In January 1927, Charles Krom, manager of the swanky Flamingo Hotel on Miami Beach wrote the owner, Carl Fisher, "It will be two weeks tomorrow since the Flamingo opened and as far as business is concerned, there just hasn't been any." Between 1925 and 1929, regional bank deposits in south Florida fell 75 percent.[22]

The 1926 hurricane killed about 600, 250 in the Miami-Fort Lauderdale area and 350 on the south rim of Lake Okeechobee. Most of the latter were sugar cane laborers of Caribbean descent in Clewiston and Moore Haven. This was followed in September 1928 by an even stronger storm (probably a Category 4 on today's Saffir-Simpson Scale) that came ashore at Palm Beach and passed over the lake. Local law enforcement and the Red Cross counted 1,800 bodies, mostly south shore agricultural workers, but most locals, white and black alike, believed the death toll, based on those known to have been in the area and subsequently missing, to be closer to 3,000. Many of the dead were washed up into irrigation and drainage ditches that subsequently silted over and were forgotten, the skeletons uncovered when the route of the old ditches were re-dug for culverts or tile drains in the 1950s and 60s.[23]

After the 1928 storm, Fred Elliott, the state drainage engineer since the resignation of J.O. Wright (and no relation to Charles Elliott) blamed the Army Corps of Engineers for requiring the state to maintain a sufficiently high lake level to permit navigation between the St. Lucie and the Caloosahatchee Rivers. Governor Martin hesitated to activate the National Guard, afraid it would scare away tourists during the upcoming tourist season. But the day after the storm he decided to go to the south rim to gage the situation

Fred C. Elliott (right) as a young engineer in Florida, about 1907. Born in 1878, he was educated as a civil engineer at the Virginia Military Institute and was Florida State Drainage Engineer from 1912 until 1958. He was heavily criticized in the 1920s for keeping water levels in Lake Okeechobee high during the winter dry season, thus increasing the risk of overtopping the dikes during the wet season. Elliott countered that he was forced by the Army Corps of Engineers to provide sufficient water to the St. Lucie and Caloosahatchee Rivers to maintain a navigable cross-state waterway. The high lake contributed to the great south rim floods of 1926 and 1928, the latter resulting in 2,800 deaths. Elliott died in 1963. Photographer unknown (State Archives of Florida, No. MSC6374).

for himself. He took a powerboat from West Palm Beach, up the Palm Beach Canal to Canal Point, and caught a gladesboat across the lake to Belle Glade, the first place where the highway was passable. He counted 126 bodies beside the road over the six miles from Belle Glade to Pahokee. Upon his return he activated the Guard.

The Red Cross, the most visible relief organization in the weeks after the 1928 hurricane, told a group of farmers at a tent meeting in Belle Glade that they would continue to distribute tents and other temporary aid, but they would not assist in the rebuilding of homes, as they considered the south rim of the lake too dangerous for habitation. "That tent disgorged as angry an assemblage of ruined farmers as I ever hope to see," Lawrence Will (Thomas's son) wrote afterwards.[24]

Fred Elliott had proposed a new plan after the 1926 storm in the district's *1925–26 Annual Report*, released in January 1927. "That there will be other storms is certain," Elliott wrote. "The experience of last September makes clear the necessity of combating this danger ... in other words, dikes must be built along the shore of Lake Okeechobee."[25] Elliott believed that the best way for the district to finance both its new mission of flood/hurricane control and complete its long-standing drainage/reclamation goals was to greatly expand its boundaries and to place a 1-mill (0.1 percent) *ad valorum* tax on all land within the district, including lands already paying the drainage tax. Since much of the land proposed for inclusion, in the Kissimmee River Valley north of the lake, the Loxahatchee Valley area east of the lake, and the Caloosahatchee River Valley west of the lake, had a higher value than the Everglades to the south, a value-based tax would have greater potential for revenue than the existing zone-tax, based mostly on distance from a canal.

But, he noted, "the Legislature has twice declined, or at least failed, to enact the necessary law, for extending the boundaries of the district. Whether or not the desired legislation can be passed is a matter of conjecture." Therefore, Elliott proposed a back-up plan, which he called the "Restrictive Area Plan." No longer would the drainage district work towards a single, Everglades-wide goal. Instead, it would select twelve zones, starting with areas along the Palm Beach Canal, then move south to the Hillsboro and New River Canals, then to the south and west side of the lake. In most cases, the zones—which ran from 38,000 to 108,000 acres in size—would be drained through the enlargement of existing canals and the installation of control structures.

Over the course of eight years, 418,000 usable acres would be created at a cost of $3.107 million. In addition, $791,000 spent on Lake Okeechobee levees (with a matching contribution of $791,000 from the Internal Improvement Fund) would create an additional 75,000 acres in salable lands for the Fund. Finally, $4.6 million would widen and improve the St. Lucie Canal.[26] This was the first Everglades water management plan to place more emphasis on flood control than on reclamation.

At the time Elliott released the *1925–26 Annual Report*, the Everglades Drainage District had an annual income of about $1.5 million per year and a bonded indebtedness of $10.255 million. Elliott recommended that the bonded indebtedness of the district be increased by about 20 million dollars to pay for the revised plan. But this ran into much resistance, mostly from Miami and Ft. Lauderdale. Vance Helm, now representing landowners through the Miami Chamber of Commerce, protested several provisions in both Fred Elliott's plan and Governor Martin's financing scheme, which would tax rural Dade County landowners the heaviest to pay for work done far away. In March 1927 the commissioners of the Everglades Drainage District retained yet another group

Anson Marston. As a junior engineer, Marston wrote the two-page information flier for Charles Elliott that so enraged the Everglades land scammers, and that figured predominantly in the early days of the Moss Committee hearings. In the late 1920s, he was one of a three-engineer panel of experts that reviewed and approved the so-called Isham Randolph plan, which supported the basic assumptions of the original Wright Report, although the Randolph Report did acknowledge that the plan would be far more expensive than Wright estimated. Photo by Harris & Ewing (Library of Congress No. LC-H25-61626-F [P&P]).

of consulting engineers, the "Everglades Engineering Board of Review," to pass judgment on the Isham Randolph plan and Fred Elliott's financing plan.[27]

The board was comprised of Anson Marston of Iowa State University, George Hills, a consulting engineer and former employee of Isham Randolph who had taken over the Jacksonville headquarters of the Randolph consulting firm when Randolph retired, and Samuel McCrory, Chief of Agricultural Engineering, U.S. Department of Agriculture.[28]

In general, this "Everglades Engineering Board of Review" made only mild criticisms of the Isham Randolph plan, with the exception of soil subsidence, which the Randolph report had grossly underestimated. The board also recommended that further efforts be pursued in phases, as suggested by Fred Elliott. Governor Martin recommended a $20 million bond issue. In June the Everglades Drainage District, out of money and facing the reality that Martin's bond issue would take an extended period to approve, ordered all work suspended.[29]

In mid–1927, the Dade Drainage District, one of the subdistricts created under the 1913 state law, hired Arthur Morgan and his Dayton-Morgan Engineering Company to advise them as to whether they should support Governor Martin's proposed bond issue. Morgan was scathing in his evaluation of both the Isham Randolph report and its re-evaluation by the Marston-Hills-McCrory Everglades Engineering Board of Review the previous year. The original sin, of course, was the Wright report, and it was Randolph's refusal to categorically erase it and start over with a clean-slate analysis that had brought the Everglades Drainage District to its current grief.

"I believe that Mead, Metcalf and Hazen made a report which is sound in its technical engineering," Morgan wrote to Anson Marston in 1927, "When the original Randolph board was appointed by the Drainage Board shortly afterward, I remarked to my associates that it was not necessary to await their report. Knowing the personnel of the board, it was evident that they were the kind of men who would be appointed, not primarily for their engineering counsel, but to approve a policy. The report sustained my prediction, and was used to discredit the report of Mead, Metcalf and Hazen.... It is a report either of men unable to handle issues of that size, or it is a report of omissions and evasions."[30]

However, Morgan may not have been the most objective choice of referees. The most recent Everglades Engineering Board of Review included S.H. McCrory of the Office of Agricultural Engineering.[31] Morgan later recalled that:

> At the time Mr. [Charles] Elliott was removed from his position [in 1912], Mr. McCrory, one of the staff, expressed himself to me with great indignation concerning the treatment Mr. Elliott had received. When I said we of the staff should stand by him, Mr. McCrory replied that he intended to remain silent, as in that case he probably would be chosen as Mr. Elliott's successor. He did remain quiet and was so appointed, holding that or a higher position for many years.[32]

Samuel McCrory was the engineer who performed the survey of Lake Mattamuskeet under the supervision of J.O. Wright in 1909. Although never criticized by name during the Moss Committee, it was McCrory's survey that facilitated Wright's and Willett Hays's unsuccessful attempt to form a $100,000 corporation to drain and develop the lake with John Seip and John Wilkinson. There was no doubt that anyone associated with J.O. Wright's ventures in North Carolina was going to come under a cloud of suspicion from Arthur Morgan, even if Morgan didn't already think he was an opportunistic toady.

Morgan attempted to persuade Governor Martin that "at some time the Everglades Drainage District will have to recognize and liquidate past mismanagement, and begin over again. We believe it is better to do that now than when another ten or twenty million dollars have been spent." Martin replied that engineers had no place recommending policy. Morgan reported both to Helm and the prospective underwriters (Dillion, Reed and Company and Eldredge and Company) that the plan created wildly disparate tax burdens and needed to be managed locally instead of remotely from Tallahassee. As proposed by Martin, the plan couldn't be sold to the majority of landowners expected to carry the burden. The bonds were issued, but never sold. "It is embarrassing to record that so much of my relationship to the Florida Everglades consisted of disapproval of what was going on." Morgan recalled some two decades later.[33]

A new governor, Doyle Carlton, took office in January 1929 and sought federal aid. "There are now before the Congress of the United States certain measures looking to participation on the part of the Federal government in works of flood control for Lake Okeechobee," Fred Elliott wrote at the time Carlton became governor. "Participation in flood control on the part of the United States must be based on the assumption that the Federal government has an interest or interests in Lake Okeechobee."[34]

But the problem in going, hat in hand, to Congress, as even Fred Elliott admitted, was one of credibility: "no money has ever been appropriated by the State for drainage, no general State tax is imposed for such purpose, the bonds issued for carrying on the work are not an obligation of the State and no law authorizes the state, itself, to take a part in or have a hand in this drainage enterprise."[35]

This point was made painfully clear to Florida Attorney General Frederick Davis when the Everglades bill was introduced in the House Committee on Flood Control shortly after Governor Carlton's inauguration. Davis was asked about the source of the money utilized by the drainage district since 1913. Was from it from private funds? State money?

> *Mr. Davis*: The money was realized by the State from the sale of lands and from taxes and assessments on the lands.
>
> *The Chair*: How much from the sale of lands?
>
> *Mr. Davis*: I can't give you the exact figures, but I would say as much from the sale of land as from taxes.
>
> *The Chair*: Six million of the thirteen million spent?

Mr. Davis: Roughly, yes sir.

The Chair: From the patented lands in 1903?

Mr. Davis: Yes, almost all.

The Chair: Well, then the [federal] Government has donated six million and the private owners have donated six million?

Mr. Davis: I wouldn't consider the private owners to have donated it. They simply paid the assessment.

The Chair: But the State of Florida did not pay for it. You see, you are coming to us, asking the Federal Government for money. The question that will be handed us on the floor is: How much has the State of Florida paid on any of these enterprises to date?

Mr. Davis: The State of Florida, so far as spending money out of the general treasury to do this work, has not done it....

The Chair: Well, if we had the giving of money, we would give you five million dollars and send you back. We would have done that long ago. We wouldn't waste time. But we are up against the proposition that the Federal interest is not what you claim it is in this case. If it is charity you want, or relief, there isn't any use fooling this committee. Go to the Appropriations Committee, or the Red Cross. We have to base it upon the Federal interest as shown in the facts and figures.

Mr. Davis: The Federal interest is, as I see it, as long as we are forced to comply with certain requirements that the Federal Government imposes on us in order to preserve the navigability and commercial features of the lake, that any extra cost that is imposed on us is a proper charge against the Federal Government.

The Chair: Sure, we had that last year. That is not the rule and can not be and never will be, because every stream in the United States would be in there.

Mr. Davis: I personally would not object to the State becoming a party to this proposition, by amending the constitution or otherwise, but you must remember a vast number of the people that come down into this particular territory are people who come from other states and settle in this territory, and it is mighty hard to get people in other parts of the state interested in whether they perish or not.

The Chair: What did you say?

Mr. Davis: I say that it is mighty hard to get people in the other parts of the State interested in these people, as to whether they perish or not.

The Chair: You don't mean that, do you?

Mr. Davis: That is the natural condition, yes sir.

The Chair: You are saying that—

Mr. Davis: I have heard it advocated in certain districts of Florida that what the people ought to do is build a wall down there and keep the military there to keep the people from coming there.[36]

Instead, the committee recommended a plan submitted by the Army Corps of Engineers. In keeping with the Corps' jurisdiction, both reclamation and flood control gave way to inland navigation. The Corps recommended a levee around the entire lake, 16 feet high on the north, 31 feet on the south, combined with much enlarged St. Lucie and Caloosahatchee canals. The estimated cost was $10.7 million, of which the state was expected to pay $6.7 million. Governor Carlton went looking for a better deal. He got it. Because it was questionable whether the Everglades Drainage District could openly abandon its goal of reclamation in favor of flood control (especially with ten million dollars in bonds outstanding and property owners paying annual taxes in the expectation of dry land), the legislature created the Okeechobee Flood Control District, covering everything in Florida south of the north rim of Lake Okeechobee, the Keys excepted. In July 1930, as part of the federal Rivers and Harbors Act, a beefed-up version of the 1928 plan, pushed by President Hoover's over the reservations of a reluctant Corps of Engineers, was approved by Congress, with only a $2 million matching share. In 1935 this was reduced to $500,000.[37]

However, the Everglades and Okeechobee districts, burdened by overwhelming tax arrearages, were able to do little other than watch as the Corps of Engineers built the 35-foot-high Herbert Hoover Dike around the lake. By 1942, the Corps had spent $23 million on the project. The Hoover dike did little to reclaim the wetlands for productive use. In 1944 Everglades Drainage District engineer Lamar Johnson drew up a new plan. It widened and deepened the existing canals, but its most notable feature was the addition of three large "water conservation areas," essentially shallow, diked reservoirs, in west Dade, Broward and Palm Beach counties. Johnson asserted they were needed to impound downstream water from the lake during the wet season. Large landowners such as the Lykes and Collier families on the west coast and the Graham family dairy farmers of Hialeah, asserted that their only purpose was to relieve the state of the burden of paying drainage district taxes on its land. They sued to dissolve the Everglades and Okeechobee districts entirely.[38]

Then came the Great Flood of 1947. Following closely on the heels of another multi-day rainstorm three weeks earlier, 13 to 18 inches of rain fell in three days between October 9 and 11 almost uniformly over all of south Florida. Everything east of the Everglades from Palm Beach to Miami essentially reverted to its prehistoric condition, with scattered ancient hammocks sticking out of broad, intertwined stream channels flowing to the ocean. Johnson, now the Everglades district's chief engineer, quickly put together a largely pictorial report documenting the damage. The cover showed a drawing of a weeping cow stranded in water up to its neck. "Lamar's Crying Cow" (or "The Bawling Bovine") became the symbol of the state's timidity and incompetence in dealing with the danger of Everglades flooding.[39]

The flood drove the state back into the arms of the Army Corps of Engineers, which saw the Everglades as one big engineering project waiting to happen. The result was the creation of the Central and Southern Flood Control District (CSFCD), which replaced both the Everglades and the Okeechobee districts, and was, in turn, the precursor to the South Florida Water Management District. In a nutshell, the Corps built it, and the state district took care of it. Johnson's water conservation

Cover illustration for the infamous 1947 "Crying Cow" report *Tentative Report of Flood Damage—Florida Everglades Drainage District, 1947*. The report led to the creation of the Central and Southern Flood Control District and the takeover of Everglades water control by the U.S. Army Corps of Engineering. Drawing by Walter D. Church (State Archives of Florida, No. RC13588).

Harvesting sugar cane for U.S. Sugar Corp., Belle Glade, Florida, 1930s. As predicted by J.O. Wright, sugar cane became the only really viable crop in the Everglades, despite its high labor demands and staggering requirements for phosphate-based fertilizers, which rendered Lake Okeechobee all but sterile by the 1950s. Photograph by Marion Post (Wolcott and U.S. Farm Security Administration. Library of Congress No. USF33-030478-M1).

districts were retained and expanded. The use of gravity canals was largely abandoned in favor of pumping stations, locks, dams and gates. (By 1975, when the plan was closed out in favor of its successor, about 400 such "control structures" existed.[40])

Except for corporate sugar cane farms hugging the south rim of the lake, reclamation, colonization and utility became forgotten goals. Saving the exploding urban areas hugging the coastline from flooding and feeding their voracious demand for cheap, clean drinking water became the exclusive goals.[41] Broward County, which did not exist in 1912, had a population of two million in 2012, yet it extended hardly any farther inland than the Davie, Foreman or Graham farms of the early twentieth century due to the giant impoundment areas and massive dikes created to prevent floods and force water down into the freshwater aquifer that fed the municipal water wells of 31 cities.

In 1948, the Model Land Company, the real estate division of the Florida East Coast Railroad, sold its last 134,880 acres of Everglades land to the State of Florida, which was assembling land on behalf of the federal government for the new Everglades National Park. The price was $115,000, 83 cents an acre. The purchase agreement included a provision in which the railroad, and all the various corporate predecessors that Henry Flagler had brought together in the nineteenth century to create it, forever surrendered any rights they may have as a result of the failure of the state to drain and survey land as promised in agreements dating back to 1902. William Jennings's residuary rights argument, so tenuous, so contrived, never really went away.

At the time, close to two-thirds of the new park was made up of land still owned by the Internal Improvement Fund, who never had been able to sell it, or who had sold it to speculators who later defaulted on their installment payments or taxes. At the time of the purchase, J.W. Hoffman, president of the Model Land Company, said that between taxes, access roads, fire control and canal maintenance, the firm had probably lost somewhere around two dollars an acre on its almost 50-year ownership of Everglades land. Although widely derided, the land records of the state's acquisition agent bear him out—the company probably did expend between five to ten cents per acre, per year, to maintain the land it received for no cost. But it the end, it could sell almost none of it. All of the sales of the Model Land Company were outside the Everglades, on the coastal ridge or within growing urban areas.[42]

When the Everglades Drainage District was re-financed in 1929, Fred Elliot said, "there is but one difference between the Everglades as they originally were and the Everglades as they are now, or will be in the future. That one difference is drainage. Subtracting drainage, the Everglades would promptly return to their original condition of watery waste, uninhabitable by human beings and unfit for the general scheme of things for uses by man."[43] Fred Elliott was correct in one regard. Stop the work done up to 1929 and the Everglades would have reverted to a "watery waste." By then, the Everglades were so altered that simply walking away would have left the equivalent of a wetlands strip mine. But he was wrong, of course, to describe the Everglades of 1870 as wasteland. It was a complex, vibrant natural ecosystem. It was merely "unfit in the general scheme of things for man," a very, very short measuring stick.

The present Everglades, along with its adjacent wetlands such as the Corkscrew Swamp to the west and the Kissimmee River basin to the north, are not restored natural systems. They are carefully crafted and very closely managed engineering systems designed to outwardly resemble nature while performing a multitude of tasks, overlapping and often mutually contradictory, that the original pre-drainage ecosystem was never intended to handle. A team of geo-hydrologists summarized the 21st century Everglades this way:

> Present-day conditions differ greatly from predrainage conditions. More than half of the Everglades has been drained for more than a century, with a large northern portion farmed, and a large eastern portion urbanized.... Drainage, elevated influxes of nutrients, compartmentalization, and altered water depths have all affected the remaining Everglades.... Despite these problematic changes, a substantial portion of the of the remaining Everglades can be restored to close to original conditions, provided that that the original driving forces of hydrology and water chemistry are restored at the upstream border, and provided that surface water is once again allowed to flow slowly along the full length and breadth of the landscape.[44]

Unfortunately, these are all still big "ifs."

II

The Wright Report scandal is a reasonably well-known historical incident. It has appeared in several books on the history of the Everglades written since 1947.[45] However, it has always been narrowly viewed through in the context of *Everglades* history. The importance it played in North Carolina environmental history has been completely overlooked. Even more than this, however, the incident is much broader in significance and provides many important historical lessons.

It is an excellent example of the failure of a federal government department to respond to the technological demands of the first machine age of 1870–1910. The only real qualifications that Secretary "Tama Jim" Wilson held when he was appointed by President McKinley in 1897 were that he was a loyal Republican, a farmer, and had previously been a two-term U.S. Representative from Iowa. At the time, that was more than good enough. He came to a department housed in a modest, rather unattractive two-story Second Empire sandstone pile called the Cluss Building on the Mall near the Smithsonian Institution. In 1897, the USDA had 2,444 employees and a budget of $2.4 million. When he retired a few days shy of sixteen years later, his department had 13,858 employees, and a budget over $16 million.[46]

This was exactly the opposite of what Tama Jim expected and wanted when he came to Washington. Wilson told an audience in 1905: "when I came down here—with a good deal of reluctance—to do something in the Department of Agriculture, my prevailing thought was that I would try to make that institution subservient to the [state] stations of the country, and to help build them up."[47] Using the Hatch Act, passed in 1887, which created state cooperative extension and education institutions, Wilson believed many, if not most, of the research and development functions of the department could be delegated to the states.

Instead, the opposite happened. The Office of Road Inquiry, created by Congress in 1893 with a staff of two, had a budget of $202,150 in 1913, plus an appropriation of $500,000 for matching-share state road repair activities.[48] Theodore Roosevelt gave responsibility over the Pure Food and Drug Act of 1906 to the USDA because it alone had the scientific expertise. Wilson loathed the Act because it placed his department, which previously had always been a booster of what is today called "agribusiness," in an adversarial, regulatory capacity. Not only did Wilson dissuade Roosevelt from locating the new Bureau of Reclamation created in the Adams Act of 1902 in the Agriculture Department, he tried to move the Irrigation Investigations Division of the Office of Experiment Stations to the Department of the Interior to merge with it.

By 1912 the Department of Agriculture was primarily a research and technology organization. As much as a third of its budget went to research, science, and technological applications.[49] In this environment, James Wilson was an anachronism. He could have undertaken a modernization of his agency's management, structure, policies and rules, but he instead staked his reputation on one project: the construction of a new Department of Agriculture Building, at the time planned to be the largest office and laboratory complex in North America. It became both an obsession and a debacle. Two million dollars were appropriated by Congress in 1901, and the architects were selected in October 1901. What followed was eight years of chaos. Part of it was a conflict between House Speaker Cannon, who wanted to preserve the House's power of the purse, and the Senate, which had authority over the parks and planning commission for the Mall.

Characteristically, Wilson did not want to leave a paper trail recording his intense personal involvement in the project, so he delegated representation on the building commission to Dr. Beverly Galloway, Chief of the Bureau of Plant Industry, a quiet, reticent botanist without keen skills in negotiation or bureaucratic infighting whose qualifications were that he was loyal and circumspect. The first architects, Lord and Hewlett, quit in frustration. The second architects, Rankin, Kellogg and Crane, seemed to solve the varied problems by moving the building to the opposite, or north, side of the Mall, about where the Smithsonian Museum of American History now stands. However, Wilson, acting through Galloway, objected because the adjacent neighborhood was little better than a slum with no prospect of immediate improvement. The Mall commission approved a return to the south side.[50]

But the south side of the Mall was subject to the so-called "809 foot line," which did not permit any building closer into the mall than roughly the back of the Smithsonian Castle.[51] This meant the Agriculture Department site on the south side was only half as deep as the one on the north side because the Mall was skewed relative to the centerline drawn from the Capitol dome, through the Washington Monument, to the future site of the Lincoln memorial. With no more money for design left, Wilson had Rankin, Kellogg and Crane chop up the existing plans. Only the east and west wings could be built, because the existing Cluss building was where the new building's central administrative block would go, and the appropriation prohibited the use of rented quarters during construction. Therefore, the Cluss Building could not be torn down until the two wings were finished. Worse, the southward projections of the wings had to be cut in half because the lot was so shallow. The plan was to proceed to a Phase II where the Cluss Building would be razed, the new center block built in the yawning gap between the two laboratory wings, and extensions over Independence Avenue with underpasses for traffic would connect to a future South Building.

But Phase II was not approved, to some extent due to the Wiley-McCabe and Wright Report scandals. What resulted was an awkward grouping of the Cluss building with two large, disconnected wings slightly behind and to each side, each wing showing a blank, whitewashed brick wall to Independence Avenue to the south. In 1910 Representative James Mann of Illinois, a member of the Agriculture Committee, noted bitterly that "A future place will never be hot enough to properly singe the man responsible for the Agricultural Department building constructed as it is." The cure did not come until 1930, when the Cluss building was razed and the center block built, and 1936, when Harold Ickes's Public Works Administration (PWA) built the South Building.[52]

The story of the new Agriculture Department building would be an amusing digression, except it highlights three key elements that shaped the James Wilson administration. The first was Wilson's old-school thinking. His approach to the growth and modernization of his department was, literally, to put the concrete before the intangible. He focused on his really big building instead of putting any serious thought into management strategy, structure, and implementation. His organizational chart was often a fiction. His financial controls and recordkeeping were out of the mid-nineteenth century. In both the Wiley-McCabe and Wright report hearings, mid-level managers repeatedly said they had no idea what the official policies and procedures of the department were, or where they could be found. When it came to the procedure for authorizing publications, Joseph Arnold privately admitted to George McCabe that that each bureau made up its own policy, and that he could not locate most of them.[53] As a result, Wilson ended up with neither his grand building nor a well-functioning cabinet-level department. As for the building, many of the laboratories were soon outgrown and moved to the Arlington Farm (where the Pentagon is now) or to its successor in Beltsville, Maryland. By World War II many of the labs in the new mall building had been converted to offices.

Second, Wilson did not appreciate the need for ability and self-reliance in subordinates. Beverly Galloway was a highly skilled botanist, but he had no business negotiating with architects Daniel Burnham or Charles McKim of the Capitol Planning Commission, let alone Senator Newlands of Nevada, over the politics of the National Mall. Wilson picked him because he was faithful and loyal, traits he proved again in the Wright Report Incident when Galloway (probably) forged the technical review of the Elliott Report in the name of his subordinate, Prof. Charles Goodrich. In 1913 Galloway was rewarded by being appointed Willett Hays's successor as Assistant Secretary of Agriculture, a position he retained after the Woodrow Wilson administration took office in March 1913.

This brings us to Wilson's third flaw: a tendency to rely on men who were simply not up to the job, primarily George McCabe, whose bluster exceeded his skills. McCabe, who never distinguished himself in any way after leaving the department, gained a mastery over the minutiae of the obsolete, the trivial, and the contradictory to cajole, flatter or intimidate away controversy and adverse publicity. He had an uncanny knack for doing it in precisely the way best suited to blow up in his face.

When Wilson turned to McCabe to take care of his problems with the Pure Food and Drug Act, McCabe not only failed, he made things worse. McCabe's solutions—the three-man board of review stacked against Dr. Wiley and the Remsen Board of Review—might have worked, except that McCabe personalized the dispute by filing a frivolous charge against McCabe for his bad apples and a not-so-frivolous charge against Heinz Foods for their "India Relish." The Heinz family of Pittsburgh was too big to antagonize for mere caprice. He then tried to get rid of Wiley on a pretext that could not hold up to scrutiny. In trying to defend himself and Wilson, he lied to Chairman Moss about the abatement roster, thereby earning the enduring suspicion and enmity of the congressman who mattered the most to his department—the Chairman of the House Committee on Agriculture.

It is entirely possible that the Wright Report Incident may never have happened had George McCabe not tried to lie to Ralph Moss about the "Permanent Abatement Log" and been caught. Frank Clark of Florida and his allegations of suppressed reports was not that important to either Ralph Moss or the Committee on Agriculture. But when McCabe replicated his tactic during the Wiley-McCabe Affair of disposing of inconvenient employees by harassing them with dismissals and referrals to the attorney general, Moss could smell blood. Moss gave McCabe the rope he needed to hang himself, stood back and watched the inevitable unfold.

These cracked foundations of leadership were a direct cause of the Wright report scandal. Elwood Mead had been a strong and entrepreneurial leader of the Division of Irrigation and Drainage Investigations, something his immediate superior, A.C. True, was not. Mead's job was to sell the services of his division to states, counties and localities and in return receive cooperative funding and congressional appropriations. He had a competitor in the Interior Department's Geographic Survey, and after 1905 he had a new competitor in the Bureau of Reclamation. He first hoped to co-opt the Bureau of Reclamation by having it located within the Department of Agriculture, then, when Wilson let the Interior Department absorb it, realized that he would have to out-hustle it.

Elliott's overtures to candidate Broward, then Governor-elect Broward in 1904 and 1905, need to be viewed in this context. It was hopeless to survey the Everglades within the normal annual appropriation of the Office of Experiment Stations. Clearly, Mead's goal was to secure a special appropriation over $100,000. But two things happened: the appropriation did not go through, and Mead, frustrated over his adversary Frederick Newell's victory in securing the Bureau of Reclamation, and despairing of getting a full-time position at the University of California, left for Australia. He was not replaced; his responsibilities were merely re-assigned to existing personnel.

When J.O. Wright testified that Charles Elliott was not enthusiastic about an Everglades investigation, he was probably correct, but it wasn't because he was opposed to the idea of doing a study there. He had sold his boss, A.C. True, on the idea of doing a blockbuster investigation backed up with a $100,000 congressional appropriation secured by Florida state officials and federal representatives. But it never came through, and by the time it was clear the idea had blown up, Mead was on his way out the door, either to California or Australia. When Mead and his family stepped on the gangplank in San Francisco on that Honolulu-bound boat in mid–1907, the institutional conveyor belt leading to the Wright Report Incident creaked to a start.

III

The other enduring lesson of the Wright Report Incident is that the traditional way of thinking about America's wetlands, as separate and unique geographic, economic, political and environmental entities is wrong. While Lake Mattamuskeet and Lake Okeechobee may have been very different and separate places in terms of geology, hydrology, meteorology and the other Earth sciences, they were uniquely connected so far as economics, politics, public administration and the other social science factors are concerned. Some of the most important decisions that affected the future of the Everglades were influenced by simultaneous affairs occurring in the Albemarle-Pamlico Peninsula and the Great Dismal Swamp 1200 miles away.

Even if we ignore for a moment the illegalities or attempted illegalities of men like James Oliver Wright, John Seip and Dr. Willett Hays, it is still the case that by the early years of the twentieth century, wetlands were being surveyed, measured, evaluated and mapped for alteration by men like Charles Elliott, Arthur Morgan and Isham Randolph who moved from state to state applying established engineering yardsticks and recommended solutions arrived at through professional consensus; so-call "established best practices." And when the time came to implement these solutions, equally interstate firms, such as the Furst-Clark Construction Company of Baltimore, assembled the equipment and performed the work, often contributing to the financing of a project by accepting partial payment in notes or bonds.

The history of American land development has always been replete with men like Richard J. Bolles. Keep in mind that Bolles honed his tradecraft in the parched highlands of eastern Oregon and western Colorado, far from any wetlands. What is unique about the Wright controversy is both that it involved the misuse of professional expertise by a government servant for private gain, and, more importantly, it involved the misuse of such expertise at one location in the expectation of profit at another site in another state. The entire time that J.O. Wright was involved in the surveying and evaluation of Everglades land, his private correspondence expressed deep reservations about the ability to drain the land and the utility of those lands once drained. At times, he flatly disparaged the value of Everglades land and the worth of reclaiming them. Wright was never an Everglades believer. His Everglades exploits were always intended to advance his North Carolina land holdings, from which he anticipated large, if not stupendous, profits.

Whether he was correct or not, or even whether he was even acting rationally or not, is beside the point. What is important is that his public reports, statements, surveys and representations (or misrepresentations) as to one wetlands—the Everglades—were always colored by the gains he hoped to reap from other wetlands—Mattamuskeet, Pantago and Moyock. These wetlands did not have isolated histories. What happened at one place affected the other. The only reason we know about what happened in eastern North Carolina is because of the rather spectacular meltdown of the Wright-Elliott Report and the two-page circular issued by the Office of Experiment Stations in January 1910. In retrospect, these were trivial events, exacerbated by residual ill-will between members of Florida's congressional delegation and state officials and fueled by big-money, high-risk land investments carried out during the classical end game inherent to any speculative boom-bust cycle.

The Wright Report Incident, in other words, was a historical freak. What has yet to come to light is the mundane, the average, the ordinary, the norm: federal government drainage engineers traveling from swamp to swamp, writing up uniform reports and drawing up uniform plans; state bureaucrats or private consultants doing the same for landowners; followed by dredging, filling, ditching, terracing and construction by honest, hard-working contractors; then entrepreneurs and financial institutions shopping for land deals; real estate brokers looking to buy or sell; settlers clipping coupons, answering ads, each looking for their own little patch of the capitalistic blue sky. The result was not a string of wetland pearls across a high, dry nation. It was, instead, a network of human-made sites, either in the potential, the making, or the actual; one big place called "opportunity."

Chapter Notes

Introduction

1. "Majority Report," in *The Everglades of Florida: Expenditures in the Department of Agriculture: Final Report* (62nd Cong. 2nd Session, House Report No. 1207, August 22, 1912): 1.

2. The best examples are (in chronological order): Marjory Stoneman Douglas, *The Everglades: River of Grass* (New York: Rinehart and Co., 1947); Alfred Jackson Hanna and Kathryn Abbey Hanna, *Lake Okeechobee: Wellspring of the Everglades* (Indianapolis: Bobbs-Merrill, 1947); Nelson M. Blake, *Land Into Water, Water Into Land: A History of Water Management in Florida* (Tallahassee: University Presses of Florida, 1980); Mark Derr, *Some Kind of Paradise: A Chronicle of Man and the Land in Florida* (New York: William Morrow, 1989; Gainesville: University Press of Florida, 1998); David McCally, *The Everglades: An Environmental History* (Gainesville: University Press of Florida, 1999); Michael Grunwald, *The Swamp: The Everglades, Florida, and the Politics of Paradise* (New York: Simon & Schuster, 2006).

3. Curtis J. Richardson, *Pocosin Wetlands: An Integrated Analysis of Coastal Plan Freshwater Bogs in North Carolina.* (Only Chapter 1, "A History of Swamp Land Development in North Carolina," by J. Paul Lilly is historical.) Ann Vileisis, *Discovering the Unknown Landscape: A History of America's Wetlands* (Washington, D.C.: Island Press, 1997); Tycho de Boer, *Nature, Business and Community in North Carolina's Green Swamp* (Gainesville: University Press of Florida, 2008).

4. Vileisis, *Discovering the Unknown Landscape*: 163.

5. Homestead Act, P.L. 37–64, 12 Stat. 392 (May 20, 1862). A woman could not initiate a homestead, but a widow married to a "head of household" at the time of settlement was eligible for either purchase or grant.

6. See, for example, Richard J. Orsi, *Sunset Limited: The Southern Pacific Railroad and the Development of the American West, 1850–1930* (Berkeley: University of California Press, 2005), esp. Chapter 3. On the other hand, the Louisville and Nashville was apparently uninterested in retail land sales, selling 600,000 acres of its Florida holdings at one time in 1902, leaving only its port facilities at Pensacola: Maury Klein, *History of the Louisville and Nashville Railroad* (New York: Macmillian, 1972): 284–287.

7. Edward N. Akin, *Flagler: Rockefeller Partner and Florida Baron* (Gainesville: University Press of Florida, 1991 [1988]): 187. The Model Land Company collection at the University of Miami Libraries is an extensive archive of the Florida East Coast's efforts between 1899 and 1940 to sell retail land through local real estate agents in south Florida.

8. The Model Land Company Collection at the University of Miami's Richter Library, is actually the correspondence of the Morse and Pepper & Potter real estate agencies with their MLC counterparts, mostly in St. Augustine.

9. Orsi, *Sunset Limited: The Southern Pacific Railroad and the Development of the American West, 1850–1930*: 159–162. The railroad purchased a Portland magazine, *Pacific Monthly*, in 1912, and changed the name and format to *Sunset*. The railroad sold it to Lawrence Lane, former executive at *Better Homes and Gardens*, in 1930. It has been through several owners since.

10. For an explanation of "binders," which were option contracts based on the time lag between the sale of a parcel and the formal registration of the deed of sale with the county, see: Christopher Knowlton, *Bubble in the Sun: The Florida Boom of the 1920s, and How it Brought on the Great Depression* (New York, Simon & Schuster, 2020).

11. "Testimony of John Seip" in *Everglades of Florida: Hearings Before the Committee on Expenditures in the Department of Agriculture, Pt. 15* (March 4, 1912): 726.

12. Letter from John Matthew, Florida Fruit Lands Corp., to N.B. Broward, September 9, 1909, Napoleon Broward Papers, University of Florida Libraries Digital Collections: https://ufdc.ufl.edu//UF00102912/00076.

13. James R. Kluger, *Turning on Water with a Shovel: The Career of Elwood Mead* (Albuquerque: University of New Mexico Press, 1992): 123.

14. Bruce Epperson, *Roads Through the Everglades: The Building of the Ingraham Highway, the Tamiami Trail and Conners Highway, 1914–1931* (Jefferson, NC: McFarland, 2016): 211–223.

15. Curtis Richardson, Rhonda Evans and David Carr, "Pocosins: An Ecosystem in Transition,"

in Curtis J. Richardson (ed.) *Pocosin Wetlands* (Stroudsburg, PA: Hutchinson Ross Publishing): 13–14.

16. Christopher W. McVoy, *et. al.*, *Landscapes and Hydrology of the Predrainage Everglades* (Gainesville: University Press of Florida, 2011): *passim*; Nelson Blake, *Land Into Water, Water Into Land: A History of Water Management in Florida* (Tallahassee: University Presses of Florida, 1980): 254–266.

17. The Miami-Ft. Lauderdale Urbanized area, with a population of 5.5 million, is the fifth densest large urban area at 4,442 persons per square mile. (The other top five are Los Angeles (6,999); San Francisco (6,266); New York (5,319); and Las Vegas (4,524). Urban Areas, unlike Metropolitan Statistical Areas, do not follow county borders and net out areas of very low population, such as the Everglades, which make up two-thirds of western Dade and Broward Counties, or the San Gabriel or San Fernando Mountains in Los Angeles.

18. Charles C. Daniel III, "Hydrology, Geology and Soils of Pocosins: A Comparison of Natural and Altered Systems," in Curtis J. Richardson (ed.) *Pocosin Wetlands* (Stroudsburg, PA: Hutchinson Ross Publishing, 1981): 69–108.

Chapter 1

1. *Report of the Joint Commission Created by the Legislature of 1907, Chapter 5632, Session Laws of 1907, to Investigate the Acts and Doings of the Trustees of the Internal Improvement Fund: Appendix to the Senate Journal of April 14th, 1909* (Tallahassee, State of Florida, 1909) [Hereafter, *1909 Internal Improvement Fund Investigative Report*]: 292–293.

2. Daniel L. Schafer, "U.S. Territory and State," in Michael Gannon (ed.) *The History of Florida* (Gainesville: University Press of Florida, 2013): 220. The treaty was signed on Feb. 22 1819, ratified within a few days by the U.S. Senate, approved by the Spanish Government on Oct. 24, 1820, ratified again by the Senate in February 1821, and a governor appointed by President Adams and dispatched to Florida on March 12, 1821. Admission to the U.S.: "An Act for the Admission of the States of Iowa and Florida Into the Union (5 U.S. Stat. 742, October 7, 1844).

3. Act of May 26, 1824 (18th Congress, 1st Sess.); 1 Stat. 165.

4. Schaeffer, "U.S. Territory and State": 228.

5. The distinction between the two peoples are linguistic, not ethnic, or racial. See Patsy West, *The Enduring Seminoles: From Alligator Wrestling to Ecotourism* (Gainesville: University Press of Florida, 1998): 1–3. For the story of the Creek migration, 1700–1820, see: John Missall and Mary Lou Missall, *The Seminole Wars: America's Longest Indian Conflict* (Gainesville: University Press of Florida, 2003): Chapter 1.

6. Joe Knetsch and Paul S. George, "A Problematical Law: The Armed Occupation Act of 1842 and Its Impact on Southeast Florida," *Tequesta* 53 (1993): 63–80.

7. Knetsch and George, "A Problematical Law": 75; Schaeffer, "U.S. Territory and State": 231.

8. 5 U.S. Stat. 445 (Sept. 4, 1841). See also: *Everglades of Florida: Acts, Reports and Other Papers, State and National, Relating to the Everglades of the State of Florida and Their Reclamation* (62nd Congress, 1st. Session, Senate Document No. 89, 1911): 33. Hereafter, *Senate Document No. 89* (1911).

9. "An Act Supplemental to the Act for the Admission of Florida and Iowa into the Union," 5 Stat. 788 (March 3, 1845).

10. "Resolution by the Legislature of Florida," *Senate Document No. 89*: 34.

11. *Report to Accompany Bill S. No. 338* [*Report No. 242*] 30th Cong, 1st. Sess. (August 12, 1848) [The "Buckingham Smith Report"] An abridged version of this document can be found in *Senate Document No. 89*: 46–66.

12. Junius Elmore Dovell, *A History of the Everglades in Florida* (Ph.D. Dissertation, University of North Carolina—Chapel Hill, 1947): 84–85. In my opinion, this is the best account of human history in the Everglades up to the start of the "Central and Southern Florida" era (1949–present).

13. "Report of Buckingham Smith, Esq. on His Reconnaissance of the Everglades 1848," in *Senate Document No. 89*: 46–55; and appendices, 56–66.

14. "Report of Buckingham Smith, Appendix No. 5: Letter From Lieut. Col. S.H. Long, Topographical Engineers to J.D. Wescott, Jr., February 7, 1848," in *Senate Document No. 89*: 57–58; "Report of the Secretary of the Treasury to the Senate of the United States, August 10, 1848," in *Senate Document No. 89*: 39–40.

15. 9 U.S. Stat. 519 (Sept. 28, 1850), also known as the "Swamp Lands Act of 1850." The provision is in Section 2. See also *Senate Document No. 89*: 67 for excerpts.

16. Swap Lands Act of 1850, Sec. 4. Acreage conveyed: *1909 Internal Improvement Fund Investigative Report*: 272. It is also reported that 33,895,534 acres was conveyed as of 1908: *Senate Document No. 89*: 94. The discrepancy is probably due to the unclear methodology in the act for determining what was a wetland and for measuring their extent. See: Ann Vilesis, *Discovering the Unknown Landscape: A History of America's Wetlands* (Washington: Island Press, 1997): 77. The total land area of the state was 35.073 million acres. The fifteen states were Louisiana, Arkansas, Missouri, Mississippi, Alabama, Florida, Ohio, Indiana, Illinois, Michigan, Wisconsin, Iowa and California: Vilesis, *Discovering the Unknown Landscape*: 77.

17. *1909 Internal Improvement Fund Investigative Report*: 267.

18. *1909 Internal Improvement Fund Investigative Report*: 267.

19. Nelson Blake, *Land into Water—Water into Land: A History of Water Management in Florida* (Tallahassee: University Press of Florida, 1980):

43; Dovell, *A History of the Everglades of Florida*: 112–113.

20. *1909 Internal Improvement Fund Investigative Report*: 274.

21. *1909 Internal Improvement Fund Investigative Report*: 279–280.

22. *1909 Internal Improvement Fund Investigative Report*: 274.

23. *1909 Internal Improvement Fund Investigative Report*: 280.

24. Vose offered: *Minutes of the Internal Improvement Fund*, II: 92 (April 30, 1875); Dovell, *A History of the Everglades of Florida*: 114–116.

25. The deal: *Minutes of the Internal Improvement Fund*: II; 211–221 (September 22, 1877). The veto: *Minutes of the Internal Improvement Fund*: II: 236–237 (December 7, 1877).

26. *1909 Internal Improvement Fund Investigative Report*: 37

27. Alfred Jackson Hanna and Kathryn Abbey Hanna, *Lake Okeechobee: Wellspring of the Everglades* (New York: Bobbs-Merrell, 1948): 95.

28. Blake, *Land into Water, Water into Land*: 76–77.

29. Michael Grunwald, *The Swamp: The Everglades, Florida, and the Politics of Paradise* (New York: Simon & Schuster, 2006: 83–86; Hanna and Hanna, *Lake Okeechobee: Wellspring of the Everglades*: 91–104.

30. *Minutes of the Internal Improvement Fund*: II; 212–221 (September 22, 1877). Reed sale: Hanna and Hanna, *Lake Okeechobee: Wellspring of the Everglades*: 98. Reed was also supposed to pay $100,000 directly to Disston, but apparently never did.

31. "Abstract of Report by J.J. Daniel, W.H. Davidson, and John Bradford, Committee Appointed by the Governor on November 17, 1885," in *Senate Document No. 89*: 21–24.

32. The state investigators ultimately faulted the Internal Improvement Fund for not requiring Disston to drain Lake Okeechobee, beyond some channeling of the Caloosahatchee River, while at the same time accelerating the flow from the Kissimmee River into the lake. It is true that most of Disston's work was north and west of the lake, near Kissimmee and near today's Fort Myers. Dovell: *The Everglades of Florida*, 138–140.

33. Joe Knetsch has published about Disston in only one obscure source, "Hamilton Disston and the Development of Florida," *Sunniland Tribune* (January 24, 1998): 1–2. However, his research and sources are discussed and supported by Michael Grunwald: Grunwald, *The Swamp: The Everglades, Florida and the Politics of Paradise*: 96–97; 387n81–3; 390n96–5. There is no evidence that Disston was dissolute, an alcoholic or deranged, and he was not insolvent. However, he may have drowned in the bathtub after passing out from otherwise non-fatal angina attack.

34. Blake, *Land into Water, Water into Land*: 76–77.

35. *1909 Internal Improvement Fund Investigative Report*: 292.

36. Dovell, *The Everglades of Florida*: 177 n.6. The loophole is located in *Acts and Laws of Florida 1881*, Ch. 3226. This provision would cause headaches for decades, as arguably, every square mile of the Everglades was obligated under one trust or another, but nobody could tell for certain which one. *Trustees of the Internal Improvement District v. Root*, 58 So. 371 (Fla., 1912).

37. Dovell, *The Everglades of Florida*: 178–179.

38. *1909 Internal Improvement Fund Investigative Report*: 293–294.

39. Dovell: *The Everglades of Florida*, 178.

40. An example of one of these certificates can be found at: *1909 Internal Improvement Fund Investigative Report*: 293–294.

41. Daniel L. Schafer, "U. S. Territory and State," in Michael Gannon (ed) The History of Florida (Gainesville: University Press of Florida, 2013): 231–233; *1909 Internal Improvement Fund Investigative Report*: 292.

42. Sec. 620 and 621, Florida General Statutes. Joe Knetsch and Paul S. George, "To Settle the Land: Pre-Emption and the Withers Report in Early Twentieth Century Broward County," *Broward Legacy* 3, 4 (1990): 27–33. Out of 55 claims investigated by circuit rider I.N. Withers in two townships (32 square miles) around present Davie in 1905, only ten are on record as having proceeded all the way through to purchase and registration of deed.

43. Chapter 3451, Acts of Florida 1883, Sec. 1. *Trustees of the Internal Improvement District v. Root*, 51 So. 648 (Fla. 1910); *Trustees of the Internal Improvement District v. Root*, 58 So. 371 (Fla. 1912) Everglades subsequently excluded: Chapter 5908, Acts of Florida 1909 (June 5, 1909); Section 624, General Statutes of Florida, 1914.

44. Letter from W. S, Jennings to S.B. Rogers, July 8, 1909, Napoleon Broward Papers, University of Florida Special Collections: https://ufdc.ufl.edu/UF00102912/00074.

45. Dovell: *The Everglades of Florida*, 196; Minutes of the *Internal Improvement Fund*: V: 263–272 (November 21, 1904); *1909 Internal Improvement Fund Investigative Report*: 293–294. For the subsequent, eventful history of the Scott purchase, later known as the Archibold Hopkins tract, then as Chevelier, see: Bruce D. Epperson, *Roads Through the Everglades, The Building of the Ingraham Highway, the Tamiami Trail and Conners Highway, 1914–1931* (Jefferson, NC: McFarland, 2016).

46. *Minutes of the Internal Improvement Fund*: V, 263–272 (November 21, 1904). For the best historical overview of this situation, see: "Annual Report of the General Counsel Trustees Internal Improvement Fund, December 21, 1908," *Minutes of the Internal Improvement Fund*: VII, 519–550 (December 21, 1908), esp. 525–543.

47. Letter from W. S, Jennings to S.B. Rogers, July 8, 1909, Napoleon Broward Papers, University of Florida Special Collections: https://ufdc.ufl.edu/UF00102912/00074.

48. Jennings recalled: Letter from W. S, Jennings to S.B. Rogers, July 8, 1909, Napoleon Broward

Papers, University of Florida Special Collections: https://ufdc.ufl.edu/UF00102912/00074. Southern States and L&N suits: *Minutes of the Internal Improvement Fund*: VII, 133–137 (December 5, 1907).

49. Letter from William Jennings to N.B. Broward, January 21, 1905, in *Senate Document No. 89*: 25–26.

50. Chapter 5377, *Laws of Florida 1905*; Samuel Proctor, *Napoleon Bonaparte Broward: Florida's Fighting Democrat* (Gainesville, University of Florida Press, 1950): 223, 250; *Senate Document No. 89*: 15–16.

51. The Kreamer Report is reproduced in: "Message of Gov. N.B. Broward to the Legislature of Florida Relative to Reclamation of Everglades," in *Senate Report No. 89*: 99–101.

52. *Senate Report No. 89*: 14; Dovell, *The Everglades of Florida*: 210–211. One expert: Letter from C.G. Elliott, Division of Drainage Investigations, to Dr. Elwood Mead, Chief of Office of Experimental Stations, Department of Agriculture, January 6, 1905, Box 2, Exhibit E-2, Record Group 16.5.2 (Dept. of Agriculture, Office of the Solicitor, Agriculture Investigations 1912), NARA Archives II, College Park, MD.

53. Blake, *Land into Water, Water into Land*: 97.

54. Epperson, *Everglades Roadbuilding*: Chapter 1.

55. Blake, *Land into Water; Water into Land*: 98.

56. It was so used, and part of it still is, at Navy Wells Park southwest of Florida City. The water line originally ran under Flagler's Overseas Railroad, and now runs under the highway to the Keys.

57. "Settlement Agreement Between Board of Drainage Commissioners and Southern States Land and Timber Co. et. al., January 31, 1910," William Jennings Papers, University of Florida Special Collections: https://ufdc.ufl.edu/uf00094871/00004/; Blake, *Land into Water; Water into Land*: 100.

58. [Florida] *Senate Journal* 1909: 1605–1623. The same document, including the attached Florida legislative statement, can be found in *Senate Document No. 89*: 130–138.

59. "Memorandum of Understanding, Board Drainage Commissioners of the State of Florida and Southern States Land and Timber Co. et. al., January 31, 1910, William Jennings Papers, University of Florida Special Collections: https//ufdc.ufl.edu/uf00094871/00004; "Articles of Agreement Between the Trustees of the Internal Improvement Fund of the State of Florida and Richard J. Bolles, et. al., January 31, 1910, William Jennings Papers, University of Florida Special Collections: https//ufdc.ufl.edu/uf00094871/00004; Letter from J.C. Lunning, Secretary of the Trustees of the Internal Improvement Board to W.S. Jennings, April 8, 1910, William Jennings Papers, University of Florida Special Collections: https//ufdc.ufl.edu/uf00094871/00004.

60. Blake, *Land into Water, Water into Land*: 97.

61. George W. Hallam, *Bolles: The Standard Bearer* (Jacksonville: The Bolles School, 1983): 15–16. As far as is known, the diary itself no longer exists. It was probably destroyed.

62. Hanna and Hanna, *Lake Okeechobee: Wellspring of the Everglades*: 137.

63. Letter from John Matthew, Secretary, Florida Fruit Lands Co. to Napoleon Broward, September 9, 1909, Napoleon Broward Collection, University of Florida: https://ufdc.ufl.edu/UF00102912/00076.

64. Hanna and Hanna, *Lake Okeechobee: Wellspring of the Everglades*: 137; Grunwald, *The Swamp*: 141–142.

65. Harvey Duval was no known relation to William P. Duval, former governor of Florida (1822–26), for whom Duval County is named.

66. Letter from R.J. Bolles, Florida State Drainage Land Company, to W.S. Jennings, June 19, 1909, W.S. Jennings Collection, University of Florida Special Collections: https://ufdc.ufl.edu/UF00094873/00090; "How Broward As Governor Came to Own 27,000 Acres of Land," Miami *Metropolis* (April 4, 1910).

67. *Minutes of the Internal Improvement Fund*: VII, 485–489 (December 16, 1908); 502–519 (December 23, 1908); Hanna and Hanna, *Lake Okeechobee: Wellspring of the Everglades*: 137; Proctor, *Napoleon Bonaparte Broward: Florida's Fighting Democrat*: 361n19.

68. Rodney E. Dillon Jr., and Joe Knetsch, "The Florida Fiber Company, Duncan U. Fletcher, and the Middle River Enterprise," *Broward Legacy* (Summer/Fall 1998): 34–44.

69. "Duncan U. Fletcher," in *Florida Biographical Dictionary* (New York: Somerset Publishers): 135.

70. Rodney E. Dillon Jr., and Joe Knetsch, "The Florida Fiber Company, Duncan U. Fletcher, and the Middle River Enterprise," *Broward Legacy* (Summer/Fall 1998): 34–44.

71. But not necessarily paid in full: Philip Weidling and August Burgard, *Checkered Sunshine: The History of Fort Lauderdale, 1793–1955* (Ft. Lauderdale: Wake-Brook House, 1974): 38–40. Letter from John Matthew, Secretary, Florida Fruit Lands Co. to Napoleon Broward, September 9, 1909, Napoleon Broward Collection, University of Florida Special Collections: https://ufdc.ufl.edu/UF00102912/00076.

72. *Florida Biographical Dictionary* (New York: Somerset Publishers, 1995): q.v. Broward, Napoleon B.

73. Fund income: *Senate Document No. 89* (1911): 128–129. Dispensation of Fund lands: Senate Document No. 89: 120.

Chapter 2

1. Letter from Lawrence Brett to J.O. Wright, March 3, 1907, Box 2, Exhibit E-14, RG 16.5.2, Department of Agriculture, Office of the Solicitor, Everglades Investigation 1906–13, Archives II, College Park, MD.

2. Mary C. Robbin and U.S. Geological Survey, *A Brief History of the U.S. Geological Survey*

(Washington: Dept. of the Interior, 1975). Document No. USGS: INF-74-26.

3. Nathan Reingold, "Preliminary Inventory of the Records of the Bureau of Agricultural Engineering (Record Group 8)" (Washington: NARA, 1953). NARA Publication No. 53-21.

4. Hatch Act: 24 Stat. 440, Ch. 314; U.S. Office of Technology Assessment, *An Assessment of the United States Food and Agricultural Research System* (Washington, USGPO, December 1981): 35-36. NTIS Publication No. PB-82-170572.

5. *Annual Reports of the Department of Agriculture for the Fiscal Year Ended June 30, 1905* (Washington, USGPO, 1906): 130-131.

6. Unless otherwise cited, this biography of Elwood Mead is taken from: James R. Kluger, *Elwood Mead: Irrigation Engineer and Social Planner* (Ph.D. Dissertation, Univ. of Arizona, 1970): Chapters 1-3.

7. Pub.L 57-161, 32 Stat. 388 (June 13, 1902) (Signed June 17, 1902). Rev. 1939, Rev. 1982.

8. James R. Kluger, *Turning on Water with a Shovel: The Career of Elwood Mead* (Albuquerque: University of New Mexico Press, 1992): 27-40. They were wrong: *Kansas v. Colorado*, 206 U.S. 46 (1907).

9. Donald Pisani, *Water and American Government: The Reclamation Bureau, National Water Policy, and the West, 1902-1935* (Berkeley: University of California Press, 2002): 6, 25, 44-45; 48-49.

10. Pisani, *Water and American Government: The Reclamation Bureau, National Water Policy, and the West*: 46.

11. Kluger, *Turning on Water with a Shovel: The Career of Elwood Mead*: 33.

12. Pisani, *Water and American Government: The Reclamation Bureau, National Water Policy, and the West, 1902-1935*: 102-103.

13. Kluger, *Turning on Water with a Shovel: The Career of Elwood Mead*: 102.

14. "Testimony of Dr. Samuel Fortier," in *Everglades of Florida: Hearings Before the Committee on Expenditures in the Department of Agriculture, Pt. 37* (June 13, 1912): 1613.

15. "Testimony of Dr. Samuel Fortier," in *Everglades of Florida: Hearings Before the Committee on Expenditures in the Department of Agriculture, Pt. 37* (June 13, 1912): 1613. Fortier recalled: Samuel Fourtier, "Australia Wants an Irrigationist," *San Francisco Call* 106, 17 (June 17, 1909). Elliot received no raise: "Personnel Department Record: Charles G. Elliott," Record Group 16.5.2 (Department of Agriculture, Office of the Solicitor, Everglades Investigations Records) Box 7, no file no, Archives II, College Park Maryland.

16. Charles E. Rosenberg, "The Adams Act: The Adams Politics and the Cause of Scientific Research," *Agricultural History* 38, 1 (January 1964): 3-12.

17. "Testimony of Dr. A.C. True," in *Everglades of Florida: Hearings Before the Committee on Expenditures in the Department of Agriculture, Pt. 35* (June 10, 1912): 1258-1612.

18. Kluger, *Elwood Mead: Irrigation Engineer and Social Planner*: 63.

19. Mead's investments: Kluger, *Elwood Mead: Irrigation Engineer and Social Planner*: 62-63; Elliott:

Arthur Morgan, "The Florida Everglades Incident," (MS, Yellow Springs, Ohio, 1954, 46 pp); Arthur Morgan Papers, University of Florida: http://ufdc.ufl.edu./UF00103500/00001/.

20. Willi Hager, *Hydraulicians in the USA 1800-2001, A Biographical Dictionary of Leaders in Hydraulic Engineering and Fluid Mechanics* (London: Taylor and Francis, 2015): q.v. "Elliott, C. G."; *Who Was Who in America, Vol. 1 (1897-1942)* (Chicago: Marquis Who's Who, 1981 [1943]): q.v. Elliott, Charles Gleason; "Testimony of Mr. Charles G. Elliott," *Everglades of Florida: Hearings Before the Committee on Expenditures in the Department of Agriculture, Pt. 6* (March 7, 1912): 773; "Personnel Department Record: Charles G. Elliott, Record Group 16.5.2, Box 7, miscellaneous personnel records file, Department of Agriculture, Office of the Solicitor, Everglades Investigation 1906-13, Archives II, College Park, MD.

21. Letter from C.G. Elliott to Elwood Mead, January 6, 1905, RG 16.5.2, Box 2, Exhibit E-2, Department of Agriculture, Office of the Solicitor, Everglades Investigation 1906-13, Archives II, College Park, MD.

22. Samuel Proctor, *Napoleon Bonaparte Broward: Florida's Fighting Governor* (Gainesville: University of Florida Press, 1950): 210-211. One theory is this: the usual solution to low water in Lake Hicpochee was to throw together a cofferdam at its lower (west) end, let the water rise, and then tear down the cofferdam and float the boat on top of the resulting swell. After a dozen times, a rubble pile built up at the west end, which just made the problem worse for each succeeding boat.

23. Description of Elliott's August 1904 trip: "Report Upon Drainage Investigations in Florida," appended to "Testimony of Hon. Frank Clark," in *Everglades of Florida: Hearings Before the Committee on Expenditures in the Department of Agriculture, Pt. 18* (March 8, 1912): 864. Elliott's 1904 report: "Drainage Investigations, 1904, by C.G. Elliott, Engineer, U.S. Department of Agriculture, in Charge," in *Everglades of Florida: Acts Reports, and Other Papers, State and National, Relating to the Everglades," 62nd Congress, 1st Session, 1911, Document No 89*: 94-97 (Hereafter: *Senate Document No. 89, 1911*).

24. Letter from C.G. Elliott to Elwood Mead, January 6, 1905, Box 2, Exhibit E-2, RG 16.5.2, Department of Agriculture, Office of the Solicitor, Everglades Investigation 1906-13, Archives II, College Park, MD.

25. Letter from C.G. Elliott to N.B. Broward, March 24, 1906, Box 2, Exhibit D-?, RG 16.5.2 Department of Agriculture, Office of the Solicitor, Everglades Investigation 1906-13, Archives II, College Park, MD.

26. Letter from N.B. Broward to C.G. Elliott,

March 3, 1905, RG 16.5.2, Box 2, Exhibit D-001, Department of Agriculture, Office of the Solicitor, Everglades Investigation 1906–13, Archives II, College Park, MD.

27. Letters from N.B. Broward to Secretary James Wilson, January 16, 1906, Box 2, Exhibit D-4, and January 31, 1906, Box 2, Exhibit D-?, both RG 16.5.2, Department of Agriculture, Office of the Solicitor, Everglades Investigation 1906–13, Archives II, College Park, MD.

28. Letter from James Ingraham, vice-pres., Florida East Coast Railroad to W.H. Beardsley, pres., FEC RR, May 4, 1915, James Ingraham Papers, University of Florida Special Collections: https://ufdc.ufl.edu/UF00095314/000003. The expenses for Taliafero's 1905 campaign, apparently advanced by former FEC president Parrott based upon an agreement between the railroad and the Consolidated Land Co., were significant enough that Parrott's sudden death in 1913 created a debt to his family's estate that Ingraham and Walter Coachman of the Consolidated Co. were attempting to work out privately, lest it have to be discussed in open court. James P. Taliafero was a lawyer, appointed by Governor Broward to the U.S. Senate March 4, 1899 in recess appointment and subsequently elected, but defeated a third time in November 1910. He retired in 1920 and died November 6, 1934 in Jacksonville. *Florida Biographical Dictionary* (New York: Somerset Publishers, 1995).

29. All of this land, 45,000 acres and 330 building lots in Okeechobee City, was sold in one large sale to William J. Conners of Buffalo in 1923. He then built Conner's Highway through it: Bruce Epperson, *Roads Through the Everglades: The Building of the Ingraham Highway, the Tamiami Trail and Conners Highway, 1914–1931* (Jefferson, NC: McFarland, 2018): 220.

30. Letter from Gov. N.B. Broward to Rep. S.M. Sparkman, May 23, 1906; letter from Rep. S.M. Sparkman to Secy. James Wilson, May 28, 1906; letter from Secy. James Wilson to Rep. S.M. Sparkman, June 2, 1906, all appended to "Testimony of J.O. Wright," in *Everglades of Florida: Hearings Before the Committee on Expenditures in the Department of Agriculture, Pt. 5* (February 16, 1912): 210–211.

31. Letter from Elwood Mead to Rep. S.M. Sparkman, June 2, 1906, reproduced in *Everglades of Florida: Hearings Before the Committee on Expenditures in the Department of Agriculture, Pt. 5* (February 16, 1912): 210–211. Elliott estimated: "Testimony of "Mr. C.G. Elliott," in *Everglades of Florida: Hearings Before the Committee on Expenditures in the Department of Agriculture, Pt. 17* (March 7, 1912): 829.

32. Exchange of correspondence and Sparkman's involvement: Napoleon Broward to James Wilson, January 16, 1906; Wilson to Broward, January 26, 1906; Broward to Wilson, January 31, 1906; all reproduced in *Everglades of Florida: Hearings Before the Committee on Expenditures in the Department of Agriculture, Pt. 5* (February 16, 1912): 208–209.

33. Aaron D. Purcell, "Plumb Lines, Politics and Projections: The Florida Everglades and the Wright Report Controversy," *The Florida Historical Quarterly* 80, 2 (Fall 2001): 161–197.

34. "Testimony of Mr. J.O. Wright," in *Everglades of Florida: Hearings Before the Committee on Expenditures in the Department of Agriculture, Pt. 3* (February 14, 1912): 72–73.

35. Letter from C.G. Elliott to J.O. Wright, July 11. 1906, Box 2, Exhibit E-?, RG 16.5.2, Department of Agriculture, Office of the Solicitor, Everglades Investigation 1906–13, Archives II, College Park, MD.

36. Letter from Secretary James Wilson to Gov. N.B. Broward, July 7, 1906, Box 2, Exhibit D-8; "Office of Experimental Stations: J.O. Wright, February 1, 1906 to February 1910; Written Assignments and Authorizations Given Him; Requests for His Service; Daily Routine, Duties and Location," Box 8, Exhibit M, RG 16.5.2, Department of Agriculture, Office of the Solicitor, Everglades Investigation 1906–13, Archives II, College Park, MD; "Testimony of Mr. C.E. Elliott," in *Everglades of Florida: Hearings Before the Committee on Expenditures in the Department of Agriculture, Pt. 17* (March 7, 1912): 823. Mead was in California: Letter from J.O. Wright to Alonzo Church Croom, December 7, 1906, Box 2, Exhibit D-?, RG 16.5.2, Department of Agriculture, Office of the Solicitor, Everglades Investigation 1906–13, Archives II, College Park, MD.

37. Principal at 11th District and transferred to high school: *Indiana School Journal* 23, 10 (October 1878): 458. Assault on Fawkner: "City News," Indianapolis *News* (February 7, 1881): 3. "Professor" Wright continued to teach at Indianapolis High for another 18 months. Fawkner later became superintendent of mails for Indianapolis: "Indianapolis, Ind. Honors Veteran Carrier," *The Postal Record* 33, 1 (January 1920): 46. Centerville: "Indiana Department," *School Education* 3, 4 (April-May 1884): 51.

38. *Proceedings of the Indiana Society of Civil Engineers and Surveyors: Eighth Annual Meeting, Indianapolis, Jan. 17–19, 1888* (Indianapolis: Wm. B. Burford, 1888): ii; Appendix (list of members): 6.

39. E.R. Shinable, "The Chicago Sanitary District Canal," *Journal of the Association of Engineering Societies* 14, 6 (June 1895): 45–51; "Annual Report of the Clerical Department, March 26, 1902," *Proceedings of the Board of Trustees of the Sanitary District of Chicago, 1902* (Chicago, 1903): 7802. Marriage: "Untitled," Indianapolis *Journal* 50, 25 (January 25, 1900): 3.

40. Isham Randolph, "Novel Plant Employed in Transporting the Excavations on the Chicago Canal Works," *International Engineering Congress, Glasgow, 1901, Proceedings (Section II: Waterways and Maritime Works)* (London: William Clowes and Son, 1902): 24–38

41. "Address of Congressman Small," in Joseph Hyde Pratt (ed.), *Proceedings of a Drainage Convention Called by the Geological Board and Held at Newbern, N.C., Sept. 9–10, 1908* (Raleigh: E.M. Uzell, State Printers, 1908): 23. "Testimony of Mr. J.O. Wright," in *Everglades of Florida: Hearings Before*

the Committee on Expenditures in the Department of Agriculture, Pt. 3 (February 14, 1912): 70–74; *Pt. 6* (February 19, 1912): 238.

42. "Testimony of Mr. Arthur E. Morgan," in *Everglades of Florida: Hearings Before the Committee on Expenditures in the Department of Agriculture, Pt. 9* (February 26, 1912): 353; also, "Statement of Congressman Small," in *Everglades of Florida: Hearings Before the Committee on Expenditures in the Department of Agriculture, Pt. 3* (February 14, 1912): 100–104.

43. John A. Garraty and Mark C. Carnes (eds.) *American National Biography* (New York: Oxford Univ. Press, 1999): q.v. Morgan Arthur Ernest.

44. David Levering Lewis, *The Improbable Wendell Wilkie* (New York: Liveright, 2018): 70–76, 90–92; Aaron D. Purcell, *Arthur D. Morgan: A Progressive Vision for American Reform* (Nashville: University of Tennessee Press, 2014); David E. Lilienthal, *The Journals of David E. Lilienthal: Volume 1, The TVA Years* (New York: Harper and Row, 1963): 16–36. In the end, the Morgan-Lilienthal dispute was a power struggle, fostered by FDR. Ostensibly, the fight was over how TVA should deal with the giant Commonwealth and Southern (C&S) electric holding company, run by Wendell Willkie. Morgan wanted a power-sharing pool, in which TVA would sell electricity to C&S, who would distribute and sell it. Lilienthal wanted a takeover of C&S, paid for out of future power sales. FDR waffled, then came down on the side of Lilienthal when the TVA proved successful and FDR no longer needed a bailout option, but also because FDR and Willkie loathed each other. The C&S properties were sold to TVA under court order for $76.8 million in cash, close to the $95 million Willkie demanded all along. In the words of Lilienthal, Morgan was a "rag-garbed martyr looking for someone to ignite one of his threads." The description was not entirely unjustified.

45. "Mr. J.O. Wright, Written Assignments and Authorizations Given Him; Requests for His Service; Daily Routine, Duties and Location," Box 8, Exhibit M, RG 16.5.2, Department of Agriculture, Office of the Solicitor, Everglades Investigation 1906–13, Archives II, College Park, MD.

46. Joseph Hyde Pratt, "Drainage of North Carolina Swamp Lands," *Journal of the Elisha Mitchell Scientific Society* 25, 4 (December 1909): 158–163; "Address of Congressman Small" in Joseph Hyde Pratt (ed.), *Proceedings of a Drainage Convention Called by the Geological Board and Held at Newbern, N.C., Sept. 9–10, 1908* (Raleigh: E.M. Uzell, State Printers, 1908): 23. "Testimony of Mr. A.D. Morehouse," in *Everglades of Florida: Hearings Before the Committee on Expenditures in the Department of Agriculture, Pt. 12* (February 29, 1912): 513.

47. For a description of these informational tours, and how one man's "constituent service" can be another man's "political stumping on the public's dime," see: "Statement of Congressman Small, of North Carolina" in *Everglades of Florida: Hearings Before the Committee on Expenditures in the Department of Agriculture, Pt. 9* (February 26, 1912): 353, also: 100–104.

48. "Government Begins Work for Preliminary Survey of Glades," Tallahassee *Sun* (November 24, 1906).

49. Proctor, *Napoleon Bonaparte Broward: Florida's Fighting Democrat*: 250. The case bounced around between various appellate courts until it was mooted by the Spanish-American War in the spring of 1898.

50. Letter from C.G. Elliott to J.O. Wright, November 23, 1905, Box 2, Exhibit E-14, RG 16.5.2, Department of Agriculture, Office of the Solicitor, Records of the Everglades Investigation, 1906–1912, Archives II, College Park, MD.

51. "Drainage Operations at Lauderdale and Dania," Pensacola *Journal* (Florala Edition, September 9, 1906): II, 14.

52. "Testimony of Mr. J.O. Wright," in *Everglades of Florida: Hearings Before the Committee on Expenditures in the Department of Agriculture, Pt. 3* (February 14, 1912): 75.

53. "Mr. J.O. Wright, Written Assignments and Authorizations Given Him; Requests for His Service; Daily Routine, Duties and Location," Box 8, Exhibit M, RG 16.5.2, Department of Agriculture, Office of the Solicitor, Everglades Investigation 1906–13, Archives II, College Park, MD.

54. Willi Hager, *Hydraulicians in the USA, 1800–2000: A Biographical Dictionary* (London: CRC Press, 2015): q.v., Stewart, John Truesdell.

55. *History of North Carolina: North Carolina Biography, Vol 6* (New York: Lewis Publishing, 1919): 170.

56. Letter from C.G. Elliott to J.O. Wright, November 23, 1906, Box 2, Exhibit E-17; letter from C.G. Elliott to J.O. Wright, November 28, 1906, Box 2, Exhibit E-14, both RG 16.5.2, Department of Agriculture, Office of the Solicitor, Everglades Investigation 1906–13, Archives II, College Park, MD.

57. Letter from John T. Stewart to Elwood Mead, March 1, 1907, Box 2, Exhibit E-12, RG 16.5.2, Department of Agriculture, Office of the Solicitor, Everglades Investigation 1906–13, Archives II, College Park, MD.

58. Superintendent Ogden of Everglades National Park arranged for its transcription and distribution in 1988. The report, in its original handwritten state, as transcribed, and supporting documents, can be found at http://everglades.fiu.edu/reclaim/monographs/FI07081707.htm, or search "John T. Stewart"/ "Everglades journal and associated files."

59. "Testimony of Mr. J.O. Wright," in *Everglades of Florida: Hearings Before the Committee on Expenditures in the Department of Agriculture, Pt. 3* (February 14, 1912): 80–83; "Never Got Into the Everglades; Knows Nothing About Them," Miami *Metropolis* (April 10, 1912).

60. "Insert C, Progress Report on the Drainage of the Everglades, Florida, by C.G. Elliott, June 1907" and "Insert D, Letter of Transmittal" in *Everglades of*

Florida: Hearings Before the Committee on Expenditures in the Department of Agriculture, Pt. 12 (February 29, 1912): 564.

61. Stewart's journal: John T. Stewart, *Report on Everglades Drainage Project in Lee and Dade Counties, Florida, January to May 1907* ("Stewart Journals"). Letter from C.G. Elliott to A.C. True, August 15, 1907, in *Everglades of Florida: Hearings Before the Committee on Expenditures in the Department of Agriculture, Pt. 12* (February 29, 1912): 566.

62. Letter from Lawrence Brett to J.O. Wright, March 14, 1907, Box 2, Exhibit E-18, RG 16.5.2, Department of Agriculture, Office of the Solicitor, Everglades Investigation 1906–13, Archives II, College Park, MD.

63. Letter from Lawrence Brett to J.O. Wright, March 3, 1907, Box 2, Exhibit E-14, letter from J.O. Wright to J.T. Stewart, March 30, 1907, Box 2, Exhibit E-26, RG 16.5.2, Department of Agriculture, Office of the Solicitor, Everglades Investigation 1906–13, Archives II, College Park, MD.

64. Stewart, *Report on Everglades Drainage Project in Lee and Dade Counties*: 60, 73; "Never Got into the Everglades, Knows Nothing About Them," Miami *Metropolis* (April 10, 1912).

65. Letter from J.O. Wright to N.B. Broward, August 21, 1907 (Box 2, Exhibit D-?); letter from N.B. Broward to J.O. Wright, September 10, 1907 (Box 2, Exhibit D-?), RG 16.5.2, Department of Agriculture, Office of the Solicitor, Everglades Investigation 1906–13, Archives II, College Park, MD.

66. J.A. Dapray to N.B. Broward, November 8, 1907, Napoleon Broward Collection, University of Florida Special Collections: https://ufdc.ufl.edu/UF00102912/00048.

67. Letter from J.O. Wright to N.B. Broward, November 2, 1907, Box 2, Exhibit D-25; letter from N.B. Broward to J.O. Wright, November 7, 1907, Box 2, Exhibit D-26; letter from N.B. Broward to Secretary Wilson, November 13, 1907, Box 2, Exhibit D-28; letter from N.B. Broward to C.G. Elliott, November 18, 1907, Box 2, Exhibit D-29; all RG 16.5. 2, Department of Agriculture, Office of the Solicitor, Everglades Investigation 1906–13, Archives II, College Park, MD.

68. Letter from J.O. Wright to N.B. Broward, November 2, 1907, Box 2, Exhibit D-?; "Itinerary and Duties of J.O. Wright, February 1, 1906 to February 28, 1910," Box 9, Exhibit M-793 though M-801, all RG 16.5. 2, Department of Agriculture, Office of the Solicitor, Everglades Investigation 1906–13, Archives II, College Park, MD.

69. "Letter from J.O. Wright to C.G. Elliott, February 18, 1908, Box 3, Exhibit G-54, RG 16.5. 2, Department of Agriculture, Office of the Solicitor, Everglades Investigation 1906–13, Archives II, College Park, MD; Testimony of Mr. J.O. Wright," in *Everglades of Florida: Hearings Before the Committee on Expenditures in the Department of Agriculture, Pt. 3* (February 15, 1912): 88–91.

70. "Testimony of Mr. J.O. Wright," in *Everglades of Florida: Hearings Before the Committee on Expenditures in the Department of Agriculture, Pt. 3* (February 15, 1912): 88–91; letter from J. O Wright to C.G. Elliott, April 6, 1908, Exhibit G-65, Box 3; letter from J.O. Wright to N.B. Broward, April 18, 1908, Exhibit D-?, Box 2; letter from N.B. Broward to J.O. Wright, September 21, 1908, Exhibit D-35, Box 2; letter from J.O. Wright to N.B. Broward, September 28, 1908, Exhibit D-36, Box 2, all RG 16.5. 2, Department of Agriculture, Office of the Solicitor, Everglades Investigation 1906–13, Archives II, College Park, MD.

71. "It is Not a Difficult Task to Drain the Everglades, Said U.S. Govt. Expert Wright," Miami *Metropolis* (February 28, 1908).

72. Letter from J.P. Taliafero to James Wilson, March 12, 1908, Box 2, Exhibit K-4, RG 16.5. 2, Department of Agriculture, Office of the Solicitor, Everglades Investigation 1906–13, Archives II, College Park, MD.

73. Letter from James Wilson to Sen. J.P. Taliaferro, March 14, 1908, Box 2, Exhibit K-?, RG 16.5.2, Department of Agriculture, Office of the Solicitor, Everglades Investigation 1906–13, Archives II, College Park, MD.

74. "Testimony of Mr. J.O. Wright," in *Everglades of Florida: Hearings Before the Committee on Expenditures in the Department of Agriculture, Pt. 6* (February 19, 1912): 245; letter from J.O. Wright to C.G. Elliott, February 29, 1909 and unattributed newspaper article dated February 28, 1909, both in *Everglades of Florida: Hearings Before the Committee on Expenditures in the Department of Agriculture, Pt. 24* (March 27, 1912): 1205–1206. According to Elliott, Wright's letter was written later (as late as 1911) and antedated at the order of Secretary Wilson: "Testimony of Mr. C.G. Elliott, cont.," in *Everglades of Florida: Hearings Before the Committee on Expenditures in the Department of Agriculture, Pt. 20* (March 13, 1912): 1004–1005.

75. Letter from N.B. Broward to J.O. Wright, May 6, 1907, Box 2, Exhibit D-?; letter from J.O. Wright to N.B. Broward, May 10, 1907, Box 2, Exhibit D-15; letter from James Wilson to N.B. Broward, May 16, 1907, Box 2, Exhibit D-16, RG 16.5.2, Department of Agriculture, Office of the Solicitor, Everglades Investigation 1906–13, Archives II, College Park, MD.

76. Letter from C.G. Elliott to J.O. Wright, April 9, 1908, Box 2, Exhibit G-66; letter from J.O. Wright to C.G. Elliott, April 6, 1908, Box 3, Exhibit G-65; RG 16.5.2, Department of Agriculture, Office of the Solicitor, Everglades Investigation 1906–13, Archives II, College Park, MD. "Testimony of A. Zappone," in *Everglades of Florida: Hearings Before the Committee on Expenditures in the Department of Agriculture, Pt. 2* (February 13 13, 1912): 52.

Chapter 3

1. "Testimony of Mr. C.G. Elliott, cont.," in *Everglades of Florida: Hearings Before the Committee on Expenditures in the Department of Agriculture, Pt. 17* (March 7, 1912): 822.

2. "Testimony of Mr. C.G. Elliott, cont.," in *Everglades of Florida: Hearings Before the Committee on Expenditures in the Department of Agriculture, Pt. 20* (March 13, 1912): 1016; "Testimony of Mr. J.O. Wright," in *Everglades of Florida: Hearings Before the Committee on Expenditures in the Department of Agriculture, Pt.* 6 (February 19, 1912): 247.

3. "Itinerary and Duties of J.O. Wright, February 1, 1905 to February 28, 1910, Box 9, Exhibit M-793 through M-801; "Explanatory," Box 9, "Mattamuskeet File" Nos. 145–149; letter from J.H. Small to W.H. Hays, August 17, 1908, Box 9, "Mattamuskeet File," No. 92, letter from J.H. Small to Secretary of Agriculture, August 17, 1908, Box 9, "Mattamuskeet File," No. 151, letter from W.M. Hays to Rep. John Small, August 20, 1908, Box 9, "Mattamuskeet File," No. 93, letter from W.M. Hays to Rep. John Small, August 25, 1908, Box 9, "Mattamuskeet File," No. 153; letter from J.H. Small to W.H. Hays, August 31, 1908, Box 9, "Mattamuskeet File," No. 94, letter from Rep. Albert Douglas to Secretary James Wilson, September 25, 1908, Box 8 "Moyock File," No. 477, letter from P.J. McCumber to Secretary James Wilson, September 28, 1908, Box 8, "Moyock File," No. 478; letter from John Seip, Carolina Land and Lumber Co. to Office of Experimental Stations, October 5, 1908, Box 8 "Moyock File," No. 481, letter from C.G. Elliott to Rep. Albert Douglas, August 6, 1908, Box 8, "Moyock File," No. 483, letter from C.G. Elliott to John Seip, Carolina Land and Lumber Co., October 9, 1908, Box 8, "Moyock File" No. 485, all RG 16.5.2, Department of Agriculture, Office of the Solicitor, Everglades Investigation 1906–13, Archives II, College Park, MD.

4. "Testimony of Mr. J.O. Wright," in *Everglades of Florida: Hearings Before the Committee on Expenditures in the Department of Agriculture, Pt. 3* (February 15, 1912): 105. "Testimony of Mr. C.G. Elliott," in *Everglades of Florida: Hearings Before the Committee on Expenditures in the Department of Agriculture, Pt. 17* (March 7, 1912): 788; "Testimony of Mr. A.D. Morehouse," in *Everglades of Florida: Hearings Before the Committee on Expenditures in the Department of Agriculture, Pt. 12* (February 29, 1912): 506.

5. "Letter of John M. Rankin, February 14, 1912"; "Letter of Henry C. Hall, February 15, 1912," in *Everglades of Florida: Hearings Before the Committee on Expenditures in the Department of Agriculture, Pt. 26* (April 3, 1912): 1298–1301. "Testimony of Secretary James Wilson," in *Everglades of Florida: Hearings Before the Committee on Expenditures in the Department of Agriculture, Pt. 26* (April 3, 1912): 1298; Letter from Henry Hall to John M. Rankin, February 21, 1912, Box 6 (no file no.), RG 16.5.2, Department of Agriculture, Office of the Solicitor, Everglades Investigation 1906–13, Archives II, College Park, MD. For some reason, throughout the hearings, Henry Hall was referred to as "Henry Gray Hall" or "Henry Grey Hall" when his own stationary identified him as "Henry C. Hall." (See letter of February 15, 1912 above).

6. "Testimony of Mr. J.O. Wright," in *Everglades of Florida: Hearings Before the Committee on Expenditures in the Department of Agriculture, Pt. 3* (February 14, 1912): 104–106 and *Pt. 6* (February 19, 1912): 248–251.

7. "Testimony of Mr. C.G. Elliott," in *Everglades of Florida: Hearings Before the Committee on Expenditures in the Department of Agriculture, Pt. 17* (March 7, 1912): 788. The text of this excerpt can be found in *Everglades of Florida: Acts, Reports and Other Papers, State and National, Relating to the Everglades of the State of Florida and their Reclamation*, 62nd Congress, 1st Session, Senate Document No. 89 (Washington: Govt. Printing Office, 1911): 130–137. [hereafter, *Senate Document No. 89*]. The text of the entire "January 25" version can be found in Column 1 of *Everglades of Florida: Hearings Before the Committee on Expenditures in the Department of Agriculture*. In the Hathitrust digital version of the hearing's transcripts, this document is included as "Part 43."

8. Letter from R.J. Bolles to W.S. Jennings, June 19, 1909, William Jennings Papers, University of Florida Special Collections: https://ufdc.ufl.edu//UF00094873/00080; *Minutes of the Internal Improvement District* VIII: 199–204 (October 5, 1909).

9. Letter from J.S. Lunning, Secretary, Internal Improvement Fund to W.S. Jennings, March 9, 1910, W.S. Jennings Papers, University of Florida Special Collections: https://ufdc.ufl.edu//UF00094871/00004; letter from Park Trammel, Florida Attorney General, with attached draft agreement, March 22, 1910, W.S. Jennings Papers, University of Florida Special Collections: https://ufdc.ufl.edu//UF00094871/00004.

10. "Testimony of Mr. J.O. Wright," in *Everglades of Florida: Hearings Before the Committee on Expenditures in the Department of Agriculture, Pt. 3* (February 15, 1912): 115.

11. Letter from C.G. Elliott to Trustees of Internal Improvement District [*sic*], March 6, 1909, Box 2, Exhibit D-38; letter from Gov. Albert Gilchrist to Secretary of Agriculture, March 11, 1909, Box 2, Exhibit D-39; letter from Gov. Albert Gilchrist to James Wilson, April 2, 1909, Box 2, D-?, all RG 16.5.2, Department of Agriculture, Office of the Solicitor, Everglades Investigation 1906–13, Archives II, College Park, MD.

12. "Testimony of Mr. J.O. Wright," in *Everglades of Florida: Hearings Before the Committee on Expenditures in the Department of Agriculture, Pt. 3* (February 15, 1912): 115.

13. "Itinerary and Duties of J.O. Wright, February 1, 1906 to February 28, 1910," Box 9, Exhibit M-793 through M-801, RG 16.5.2, Records of the Department of Agriculture, Office of the Solicitor, Everglades Investigation, 1906–13, Archives II, College Park, MD; "Testimony of Mr. A. Zappone," in *Everglades of Florida: Hearings Before the Committee on Expenditures in the Department of Agriculture, Pt. 2* (February 13, 1912): 53.

14. "Testimony of Mr. Joseph Arnold," in *Everglades of Florida: Hearings Before the Committee on*

Expenditures in the Department of Agriculture, Pt. 22 (March 20 and 25, 1912): 1116–1117.

15. "Testimony of Mr. C.G. Elliott," in *Everglades of Florida: Hearings Before the Committee on Expenditures in the Department of Agriculture, Pt. 18* (March 8, 1912): 857; "Testimony of Walter H. Beal," in *Everglades of Florida: Hearings Before the Committee on Expenditures in the Department of Agriculture, Pt. 24* (March 27, 1912): 1246; *Everglades of Florida: Hearings Before the Committee on Expenditures in the Department of Agriculture: Exhibit B of No. 5.* [Hathitrust digital version file "Part 43"] [The unpublished June 25, 1909 Bulletin 218 version also appears in *Senate Document No. 89* at 140–180].

16. "Testimony of Mr. J.O. Wright," in *Everglades of Florida: Hearings Before the Committee on Expenditures in the Department of Agriculture, Pt.* (February 14, 1912): 111; "Testimony of Mr. C.G. Elliott," in *Everglades of Florida: Hearings Before the Committee on Expenditures in the Department of Agriculture, Pt. 18* (March 8, 1912): 857.

17. "Memo from Joseph Arnold to Mr. McCabe, March 15, 1912, Box 4 (no file no.), RG 16.5.2, Department of Agriculture, Office of the Solicitor, Records of the Everglades Investigation 1906–13, Archives II, College Park, MD. "Testimony of Mr. Joseph A. Arnold," in *Everglades of Florida: Hearings Before the Committee on Expenditures in the Department of Agriculture, Pt. 22* (March 20 and 25, 1912): 1121.

18. "Testimony of Mr. Arthur E. Morgan," in *Everglades of Florida: Hearings Before the Committee on Expenditures in the Department of Agriculture, Pt. 9* (February 26, 1912): 341–342; letter from Harold J. Bryant to V.W. Helm, February 27, 1912, Box 8 (no file no.) RG 16.5.2, Department of Agriculture, Office of the Solicitor, Records of the Everglades Investigation 1906–13, Archives II, College Park, MD.

19. Map of Kreamer plan: Christopher W. McVoy, *et. al. Landscapes and Hydrology of the Predrainage Everglades* (Gainesville: University Press of Florida, 2011): Plate 1 (p. 53)

20. Nelson Blake, *Land into Water—Water into Land: A History of Water Management in Florida* (Tallahassee: University Press of Florida, 1980): 106–107.

21. "Testimony of Mr. Arthur E. Morgan," in *Everglades of Florida: Hearings Before the Committee on Expenditures in the Department of Agriculture, Pt. 9* (February 26, 1912): 344. *Everglades of Florida: Hearings Before the Committee on Expenditures in the Department of Agriculture, Pt. 9* (February 26, 1912): 384–385. All of the Everglades canals were incredibly flat. To run a 35-mile, canal 22 feet downhill entails an average slope of 0.012 percent, or one foot vertical per 8,400 feet horizontal. A realistic minimum would be about 1:2000.

22. "Testimony of Mr. C.G. Elliott," in *Everglades of Florida: Hearings Before the Committee on Expenditures in the Department of Agriculture, Pt. 17* (March 7, 1912): 798. Morgan estimated that the capacity of Wright's canals were 55 percent of what Wright claimed, 2,200 cubic feet per second: "Testimony of Mr. Arthur E. Morgan," in *Everglades of Florida: Hearings Before the Committee on Expenditures in the Department of Agriculture, Pt. 9* (February 26, 1912): 344. The letters: *Pt. 9* (February 26, 1912): 359.

23. "Testimony of Mr. C.G. Elliott," in *Everglades of Florida: Hearings Before the Committee on Expenditures in the Department of Agriculture, Pt. 17* (March 7, 1912): 802.

24. "Testimony of Mr. C.G. Elliott," in *Everglades of Florida: Hearings Before the Committee on Expenditures in the Department of Agriculture, Pt. 17* (March 7, 1912): 804; "Memo: A Comparison of the Drainage Plan as Originally Outlined by Mr. J.O. Wright With That Outlined by Mr. Elliott In His Final Revision of the Proposed Bulletin on the Drainage of the Everglades," no date [c. February 1912], Box 4 (misc. working files), RG 16.5.2, Department of Agriculture, Office of the Solicitor, Everglades Investigation, 1906–13, Archives II, College Park, MD.

25. "Testimony of Mr. J.O. Wright," in *Everglades of Florida: Hearings Before the Committee on Expenditures in the Department of Agriculture, Pt. 5* (February 16, 1912): 203.

26. *Everglades of Florida: Hearings Before the Committee on Expenditures in the Department of Agriculture: Exhibit B of No. 5, Comparison of Report of February 25, 1909 (Wright Report Extract), Report of June 25, 1909 (Wright Report, unpublished Report 218), and Report of January 10, 1910 (unpublished Elliott Report)*: 35–38; "Memo: A Comparison of the Drainage Plan as Originally Outlined by Mr. J.O. Wright with That Outlined by Mr. Elliott in His Final Revision of the Proposed Bulletin on the Drainage of the Everglades," no date [c. February 1912], Box 4 (misc. working files), RG 16.5.2, Department of Agriculture, Office of the Solicitor, Everglades Investigation, 1906–13, Archives II, College Park, MD.

It is important to note that several of the figures ascribed to Elliott in this paragraph were imputed by me based on his data. Elliott did not attempt to precisely estimate how large an area of the Everglades below Lake Okeechobee the canals would drain, or the quantity of flow at the canal mouths. He only provided a figure of 242 cfs of drainage per township (6.75 per square mile) and a drainage infiltration extending one mile to ether side of a canal. He was interested only in reproducing the methodology for estimating the canal capacity needed to drain Lake Okeechobee, not in planning for the reclamation of the Everglades as a whole, which he believed there was not sufficient information to undertake. Some of the data I applied was taken from the Mead, Hazen and Metcalf report (see below).

27. Daniel Mead, Allen Hazen and Leonard Metcalf, "Report on the Draining of the Everglades [in the Vicinity of Miami]," (Miami: Everglades Land Sales Co., Everglade Land Co. and Everglades Sugar and Land Co., November 12, 1912). University of Florida Special collections: http://ufdc.ufl.

edu/aa00007549/00001. "Testimony of Hon. Frank Clark, Congressman of Florida," in *Everglades of Florida: Hearings Before the Committee on Expenditures in the Department of Agriculture, Pt. 18* (March 8, 1912): 858.

28. "Testimony of Mr. Arthur E. Morgan," in *Everglades of Florida: Hearings Before the Committee on Expenditures in the Department of Agriculture, Pt. 9* (February 26, 1912): 365.

29. "Testimony of Mr. C.G. Elliott," in *Everglades of Florida: Hearings Before the Committee on Expenditures in the Department of Agriculture, Pt. 17* (March 7, 1912): 802–803, 858.

30. Letter from William McIntosh, Secretary, Trustees of the Florida Internal Improvement Fund to the Office of the Secretary of Agriculture (requesting forthcoming bulletin), Box 2, Exhibit D-42, RG 16.5.2, Department of Agriculture, Office of the Solicitor, Everglades Investigation, 1906–13, Archives II, College Park, MD.

31. Clearance certificates: Philip Welding and August Burghardt, *Checkered Sunshine: The History of Fort Lauderdale, 1793–1955* (Ft. Lauderdale: Ft. Lauderdale Historical Society, 1974): 39. Fifteen hundred requests: "Testimony of Secretary James Wilson," in *Everglades of Florida: Hearings Before the Committee on Expenditures in the Department of Agriculture, Pt. 26* (April 3, 1912): 1320.

32. Junius Elmore Dovell, *A History of the Everglades in Florida* (Ph.D. Dissertation, University of North Carolina—Chapel Hill, 1947): 244–248. The extract is reproduced in: *Senate Document No. 89*: 130–137.

33. "Draft Memorandum of Agreement Board of Drainage Commissioners and Southern States Land and Timber Co. et. al., December 29, 1909," William Jennings Papers, University of Florida Special Collectiions: https://ufdc.ufl.edu/uf00094871/00004.

34. Letter from W.S. Jennings to Sen. J.P. Taliaferro, November 26, 1909, Letters from W.S. Jennings to Sen. J.P. Taliaferro, November 26, 1909, William Jennings Papers, University of Florida Special Collections: https://ufcd.ufl.edu/UF00094871/000007.

35. Letters from W.S. Jennings to Sen. J.P. Taliaferro, November 26, 1909 and December 9, 1909; both William Jennings Papers, University of Florida Special Collections: https://ufcd.ufl.edu/UF00094871/000007. Talieferro and the FEC-RR and Southern States: letter from James Ingraham, FEC Vice President, to W.H. Beardsley, President, FEC-RR, May 4, 1915, James Ingraham Papers, University of Florida Special Collections: https://ufdc.ufl.edu/UF00095314/00003.

36. Aaron D. Purcell, "Plumb Lines, Politics and Projections: The Florida Everglades and the Wright Report Controversy," *The Florida Historical Quarterly* 80, 2 (Fall 2001): 161–197.

37. "Testimony of Mr. J.O. Wright," in *Everglades of Florida: Hearings Before the Committee on Expenditures in the Department of Agriculture, Pt. 7* (February 20, 1912): 288.

38. For a detailed explanation by William Jennings, see: *Minutes of the Internal Improvement Fund*: VII, 545 (Annual Report, December 21, 1908). Be forewarned: I am a lawyer and I find his argument impenetrable.

39. Of the five big pre–1903 landowners, only two, the Louisville & Nashville and the Florida East Coast were actually railroads. The other three—the Consolidated Land and Timber Co., the Empire Land Co. and the Union Land Co. (the former Disston firm) were not. Most either dealt in timber or mining or sold big-blocks to speculators like Bolles. However, they were typically referred to as "the railroads."

40. "Report of the Special Joint Committee of the Florida Legislature for the Year 1909, on the Drainage of the Everglades," in *Senate Document No. 89*: 89–94.

41. "Testimony of Mr. C.G. Elliott," in *Everglades of Florida: Hearings Before the Committee on Expenditures in the Department of Agriculture, Pt. 17* (March 7, 1912): 772; 804; "Testimony of Mr. A.C. True," in *Everglades of Florida: Hearings Before the Committee on Expenditures in the Department of Agriculture, Pt. 24* (March 27, 1912): 1217.

42. "Testimony of C.G. Elliott," in *Everglades of Florida: Hearings Before the Committee on Expenditures in the Department of Agriculture, Pt. 17* (March 7, 1912): 803–804; "Testimony of A.C. True," in *Everglades of Florida: Hearings Before the Committee on Expenditures in the Department of Agriculture, Pt. 24* (March 27, 1912): 1235–1236; "Testimony of Walter H. Beal," in *Everglades of Florida: Hearings Before the Committee on Expenditures in the Department of Agriculture, Pt. 24* (March 27, 1912): 1249; "Memoranda in Regard to Everglades of Florida Bulletin," in "Testimony of Joseph Arnold," in *Everglades of Florida: Hearings Before the Committee on Expenditures in the Department of Agriculture, Pt. 24* (March 20 and 25, 1912): 1135.

43. "Testimony of Joseph Arnold," in *Everglades of Florida: Hearings Before the Committee on Expenditures in the Department of Agriculture, Pt. 24* (March 20 and 25, 1912): 1135.

44. Arnold had not seen: "Testimony of Joseph Arnold," in *Everglades of Florida: Hearings Before the Committee on Expenditures in the Department of Agriculture, Pt. 22* (March 20 and 25, 1912): 1134. Galloway did not review: "Testimony of Beverly T. Galloway," in *Everglades of Florida: Hearings Before the Committee on Expenditures in the Department of Agriculture, Pt. 25* (April 1, 1912): 1278. Galloway verbally told: *ibid.* at 1281. Goodrich edits: "Testimony of Dr. C.L. Goodrich," in *Everglades of Florida: Hearings Before the Committee on Expenditures in the Department of Agriculture, Pt. 23* (March 26, 1912): 1189–94.

45. "Drainage of the Everglades of Florida" (base text, January 28, 1910 version), in "Testimony of C.G. Elliott," in *Everglades of Florida: Hearings Before the Committee on Expenditures in the Department of Agriculture, Pt. 22* (March 20 and 25, 1912): 1061–1093. See also: "Exhibit B of No. 5 [3-column comparison of Feb. 25, 1909; June 25, 1909 and

January 28, 1910 versions of Wright/Elliott reports] *Everglades of Florida: Hearings Before the Committee on Expenditures in the Department of Agriculture.* [Hathitrust digital file "Part 43"] All of this was cautionary language was inserted, as scattered sentences, by Elliott, usually to open or conclude a paragraph in Wright's original text to introduce a note of sobriety into the original's sometime effusive language.

46. "Testimony of Joseph Arnold," in *Everglades of Florida: Hearings Before the Committee on Expenditures in the Department of Agriculture, Pt. 22* (March 20 and 25, 1912): 1135.

47. Letter from Prof. C.L. Goodrich to Dr. B.T. Galloway, June 4, 1910, Box 7, no file no.; letter from G.H. Powell to Joseph A. Arnold, June 6, 1910, Box 7, no file no., RG 16.5.2, Records of the Department of Agriculture, Office of the Solicitor, Everglades Investigation, 1906–13.

48. Junius Elmore Dovell, "Thomas Elmer Will, Twentieth Century Pioneer," *Tequesta* 8 (1948): 21–55.

49. Richard J. Bolles, Florida State Drainage Land Co. to W.S. Jennings, June 19, 1909, William Jennings Papers, University of Florida Special Collections: https://ufdc.ufl.edu/UF00094873/00090; Thomas Will to N.B. Broward, July 10, 1909, Napoleon Broward Papers, University of Florida Special Collections: https://ufdc.ufl.edu/UF00102912/00074.

50. Gifford biography: Michael Grunwald, *The Swamp: The Everglades, Florida and the Politics of Paradise* (New York: Simon & Schuster, 2006): 127–129. Gifford's article: John Clayton Gifford, "The Everglades and the Landes of France," *Conservation* (August 1909): 453–460.

51. Letter from V.W. Helm to Thomas Will, December 2, 1912; letter from Thomas Will to V.W. Helm, December 7, 1912; both "Correspondence, December 1912," Thomas Will Papers, University of Florida Special Collections: http://ufdc.ufl.ed/AA00000147/00007.

52. "Testimony of Mr. Thomas E. Will," in *Everglades of Florida: Hearings Before the Committee on Expenditures in the Department of Agriculture, Pt. 13* (March 1, 1912): 618–619

53. Letter from Thomas Will to V.W. Helm, December 15, 1911; Thomas Will Papers, University of Florida Special Collections": http://ufdc.ufl.ed/AA00000147/00007.

54. "Testimony of Mr. Thomas E. Will," in *Everglades of Florida: Hearings Before the Committee on Expenditures in the Department of Agriculture, Pt. 13* (March 1, 1912): 605. The employee was Samuel Copper: letter from Thomas Will to Rep. J. Mark Wilcox, January 19, 1935, Thomas Will Papers, University of Florida Special Collections: https://ufdc.ufl.edu/AA00000147/00197.

55. Letter from Richard J. Bolles to N.B. Broward, September 10, 1909, Napoleon Broward Papers, University of Florida Special Collections: https://ufdc.ufl.edu//UF00102912/00076.

56. "Testimony of Mr. Thomas E. Will," in *Everglades of Florida: Hearings Before the Committee on Expenditures in the Department of Agriculture, Pt. 13* (March 1, 1912): 642; "Testimony of C.G. Elliott," in *Everglades of Florida: Hearings Before the Committee on Expenditures in the Department of Agriculture, Pt. 17* (March 7, 1912): 779–780; "Testimony of A.D. Morehouse," in *Everglades of Florida: Hearings Before the Committee on Expenditures in the Department of Agriculture, Pt. 12* (February 29, 1912): 555. A copy of the flier is reproduced in: "Testimony of C.G. Elliott," in *Everglades of Florida: Hearings Before the Committee on Expenditures in the Department of Agriculture, Pt. 17* (March 7, 1912): 805, although Elliott testified that he never saw it. Fifteen hundred distributed: "Testimony of Agriculture Secretary Wilson," in *Everglades of Florida: Hearings Before the Committee on Expenditures in the Department of Agriculture, Pt. 26* (April 3, 1912): 1320. Arnold and Wilson met: Memo from Joseph Arnold to Solicitor McCabe, March 15, 1912, Box 4, no file no, RG 16.5.2, Department of Agriculture, Office of the Solicitor, Record of the Everglades Investigation, 1906–13, Archives II, College Park, MD.

57. "Agreement Between Albert W. Gilchrist, Governor, et. al and Southern States Land and Timber Co., et. al., January 10, 1910," William Jennings Papers, University of Florida Special Collections: https://ufdc.ufl.edu/uf00094871/00004/; "Drainage Work to be Completed in Less Than Three Years if Present Plans of Trustees Are Approved," Miami *Metropolis* (February 3, 1910).

58. "Testimony of Mr. Thomas E. Will," in *Everglades of Florida: Hearings Before the Committee on Expenditures in the Department of Agriculture, Pt. 13* (March 1, 1912): 618; Minutes of the Internal Improvement District VIII, 301–309 (see section 5) (January 31, 1910).

Chapter 4

1. Philip Weidling and August Burghard, *Checkered Sunshine: The History of Fort Lauderdale, 1793–1955* (Ft. Lauderdale, FL: Ft. Lauderdale Historical Society, 1974): 41.

2. Testimony of Rep. Frank Clark, in *Everglades of Florida: Hearings Before the Committee on Expenditures in the Department of Agriculture, Pt. 18* (March 8, 1912): 834. Others in the party date this meeting from December 1910: "Hardee Writes in Defense of Frank Clark," *Jacksonville Metropolis* (October 30, 1911).

3. "Letter from Thomas Will to V.W. Helm, April 26, 1911, Thomas Will Papers, University of Florida Special Collections: http://ufdc.ufl.edu/AA00000148/00002.

4. Samuel Proctor, *Napoleon Bonaparte Broward: Florida's Fighting Democrat* (Gainesville: University of Florida Press, 1950): 305–306. Although the 17th Amendment was not ratified until 1913, Florida, like several states, had already gone to the direct election of senators. Election was a two-stage process,

an open primary in May with a two-man runoff in July or August. The general election, with only Democratic and Republican candidates allowed, was, of course, pointless.

5. Weidling and Burghard, *Checkered Sunshine: The History of Fort Lauderdale*: 38–44. Bolles had purchased the Progresso subdivision from the Florida Fiber Company, partially owned by Sen. Duncan Fletcher: Rodney E. Dillion, J. and Joe Knetsch, "The Florida Fiber Company, Duncan U. Fletcher and the Middle River Enterprise," *Broward Legacy* 21, 3–4 (Summer-Fall 1998): 34–44.

6. This is probably the most famous quote in the history of the Everglades and has been attributed to many sources. The earliest I can find is from the *Palm Beach Weekly News*, March 22, 1912. Thus, there is some doubt as to whether it specifically refers to the Florida Fruit Lands Co. auction, although the Hannas believe the quote was taken at the Ft. Lauderdale auction. See: Alfred Jackson Hanna and Kathryn Abbey Hanna, *Lake Okeechobee: Wellspring of the Everglades* (New York: Bobbs-Merrill, 1948):134.

7. Weilding and Burghard, *Checkered Sunshine: The History of Fort Lauderdale*: 38–39; Hanna and Hanna, *Lake Okeechobee: Wellspring of the Everglades*: 136–150. Bolles contract: *Minutes of the Internal Improvement Fund*: VII, 502–510 (December 24, 1908). On March 4, 1911, Bolles owned free and clear title to only 141,750 of the 500,000 acres he purchased in 1908, and had paid $478,128, with $461,875 still owed on his mortgage to the IIF: *Minutes of the Internal Improvement Fund* IX: 33–36 (March 4, 1911).

8. Letter from V.W. Helm, Everglade Land Sales Co., to Thomas Will, December 5, 1911; Thomas Will Papers, University of Florida Special Collections: https://ufdc.ufl.edu//AA00000147/000012.

9. "Testimony of Dr. Beverly T. Galloway, Chief, Bureau of Plant Industry," in *Everglades of Florida: Hearings Before the Committee on Expenditures in the Department of Agriculture, Pt. 25* (April 1, 1912): 1270–1272.

10. Letter from F.L. Floyd, Cherrydale, VA to the Florida Everglades Land Co., July 15, 1911; letter from William F. Greenwood, Everglades Land Co. to Thomas Will, Everglades Home Builders Assn., July 17, 1911, both Thomas Will Papers, University of Florida Special Collections: https://ufdc.ufl.edu//AA00000147/00001. In September 1911 Will's firm was the agent for the Everglades Land Co.; the Everglades Sugar and Land Co.; the Miami Everglades Land Co.; and the R.P. Davie Land Co.

11. "Statement of General Ellis during the Testimony of Charles G. Elliott" in *Everglades of Florida: Hearings Before the Committee on Expenditures in the Department of Agriculture, Pt. 20* (March 13, 1912): 1019–1021.

12. Hanna and Hanna, *Lake Okeechobee: Wellspring of the Everglades*:138–146.

13. "H. N. Graham to Secretary Wilson, Oct. 1, 1910; Secretary Wilson to Dr. Allen, Oct. 7, 1910; 'Memorandum of Action and Correspondence, Office of Postmaster General, Oct. 19 to Nov. 26, 1910'" in *Everglades of Florida: Hearings Before the Committee on Expenditures in the Department of Agriculture, Pt. 25* (April 1, 1912): 1261–1266; John T. Stewart, *Report on Everglades Drainage Project in Dade and Lee Counties* (Washington: U.S. Dept. of Agriculture, Office of Experimental Stations, January to May 1907). Original, a 2008 transcription by A. Benitez, and associated documentation, Everglades Digital Library, Florida International University: http:/www.everglades.fiu.edu/reclaim/monographsF107081707.htm, or search "Everglades John T. Stewart report transcription."

14. The industrial division of the FEC actually had several land companies. The Okeechobee Land Co. marketed land between the lake and West Palm Beach. The Fort Dallas Land Co. sold town sites in Miami given to Flagler by the Tuttle family in exchange for extending the railroad to Miami in 1895. The Perrine Land Co. co-owned land with the Perrine family south of Miami that had unique legal issues. The Chulota Land Company sold home lots and small farms near Orlando. The Model Land Co. was the largest land holder and except for it, all the firms were short-lived. See: Bruce Epperson, *Roads Across the Everglades: The Ingraham Highway, the Tamiami Highway and the Conners Highway* (Jefferson, NC: McFarland Press, 2017).

15. Everglades Drainage District tax revenues were $214,600 in 1910 and $221,900 in 1911: Fred C. Elliott, *Everglades Drainage District: Biennial Report 1927–28* (Tallahassee, FL: Board of Drainage Commissioners, 1929): 68.

16. *Minutes of the Internal Improvement Fund*, IX: 390–395 (April 10, 1911). Tax revenue of $200K in 1910 and engineer's quote: Fred C. Elliott, *Everglades Drainage District: Biennial Report 1927–28* (Tallahassee: State of Florida, January 1929): 78. Fred Elliott, chief engineer of the Everglades Drainage District 1912–1948, was not related to Charles Elliott.

17. Letter from V.W. Helm to Secretary James Wilson, May 18, 1910, Box 4, Exhibit P-26, RG 16.5.2, Department of Agriculture, Office of the Solicitor, Records of the Everglades Investigation, 1906–13, Archives II, College Park, MD.

18. The Welliver article is reproduced in *Everglades of Florida: Hearings Before the Committee on Expenditures in the Department of Agriculture, Pt. 18* (March 8, 1912): 879–883. "Florida Drainage Report," Washington *Tribune* (October 19,1911).

19. Letter from W.S. Jennings to Sen. J.P. Taliaferro, November 26, 1909, Letters from W.S. Jennings to Sen J.P. Taliaferro, November 26, 1909, William Jennings Papers, University of Florida Special Collections: https://ufcd.ufl.edu/UF00094871/000007.

20. Letters from W.S. Jennings to Sen. J.P. Taliaferro, November 26, 1909 and December 9, 1909; both William Jennings Papers, University of Florida Special Collections: https://ufcd.ufl.edu/UF00094871/000007.

21. Aaron D. Purcell, "Plumb Lines, Politics and

Projections: The Florida Everglades and the Wright Report Controversy," *The Florida Historical Quarterly* 80, 2 (Fall 2001): 161–197; letter from W.S. Jennings to Duncan U. Fletcher, May 8, 1911, William Jennings Papers, University of Florida Special Collections: https://ufdc.ufl.edu/uf00094871/00004.

22. John C. Gifford, *The Everglades and Other Essays Relating to Southern Florida* (Miami: Everglade Land Sales Company, 1911, 1912); letter from Thomas Will to John Gifford, May 4, 1911, letter from V.W. Helm to Thomas Will, May 5, 1911, both Thomas Will Papers, University of Florida Special Collections: https://ufcd.ufl.edu/AA00000148/000007. Letter from Thomas Will to V.W. Helm, May 8, 1911, Thomas Will Papers, University of Florida Special Collections: https://ufcd.ufl.edu/AA00000148/000007.

23. Letter from Thomas Will to V.W. Helm, July 26, 1911, Thomas Will Papers, University of Florida Special Collections: https://ufcd.ufl.edu/AA00000148/000007.

24. "Testimony of Sen. Duncan U. Fletcher," in *Everglades of Florida: Hearings Before the Committee on Expenditures in the Department of Agriculture, Pt. 19* (March 11, 1912): 945.

25. "Testimony of Sen. Duncan U. Fletcher," in *Everglades of Florida: Hearings Before the Committee on Expenditures in the Department of Agriculture, Pt. 19* (March 11, 1912): 968. Will *was* asked about the circumstances under which he borrowed a copy of the report in January 1910, but he testified that he returned this copy in a day or two, implying that he secured a second copy for his work on *Senate Document No. 89*: "Testimony of Sen. Duncan U. Fletcher," in *Everglades of Florida: Hearings Before the Committee on Expenditures in the Department of Agriculture, Pt. 16* (March 6, 1912): 746.

26. Letters from Thomas Will to V.W. Helm, July 26, 1911; September 13, 1911; October 4, 1911, all Thomas Will Papers, University of Florida Special Collections: http://ufdc.ufl.edu/AA00000/00003.

27. "Exhibit B of No. 5 [3-column comparison of February 25, 1909; June 25, 1909 and January 28, 1910 versions of Wright/Elliott reports] *Everglades of Florida: Hearings Before the Committee on Expenditures in the Department of Agriculture* (February 16, 1912): [This is listed in the Hathitrust digital version as "Part 43"], "Letter from W, H. Beal to B.D. Stallings," in *Everglades of Florida: Hearings Before the Committee on Expenditures in the Department of Agriculture, Pt. 12* (February 29, 1912): 558–559.

28. The text of the inserts and the transmittal letters are contained in: "Testimony of A.D. Morehouse," in *Everglades of Florida: Hearings Before the Committee on Expenditures in the Department of Agriculture, Pt. 12* (February 29, 1912): 558–589. Transmittal letter: Mr. Stallings to Ansel Wold, September 1, 1911, Box 3, Exhibit I-22, RG 16.5.2, Department of Agriculture, Office of the Solicitor, Records of the Everglades Investigation, 1906–13, Archives II, College Park, MD.

29. "Testimony of Mr. Joseph A. Arnold," in *Everglades of Florida: Hearings Before the Committee on Expenditures in the Department of Agriculture, Pt. 23* (March 26, 1912): 1178.

30. Fletcher arrived home: "Testimony of Sen. Duncan Fletcher," in *Everglades of Florida: Hearings Before the Committee on Expenditures in the Department of Agriculture, Pt. 19* (March 11, 1912): 1178. Wright met with Jennings and Fletcher: "Testimony of J.O. Wright," in *Everglades of Florida: Hearings Before the Committee on Expenditures in the Department of Agriculture, Pt. 6* (February 19, 1912): 279–282.

31. Letter from Thomas Will to V.W. Helm, October 14, 1911, Thomas Will Papers, University of Florida Special Collections: http://ufdc.ufl.edu/AA00000.148/00003. For the inserted material," see: "Testimony of Mr. A.D. Morehouse," in *Everglades of Florida: Hearings Before the Committee on Expenditures in the Department of Agriculture, Pt. 12* (February 29, 1912): 560–589. For the text of the "Elliott Report," see column 3 of "Exhibit B of No. 5" [also known as "Part 43"] of *Everglades of Florida: Hearings Before the Committee on Expenditures in the Department of Agriculture.*

32. "Testimony of J.O. Wright," in *Everglades of Florida: Hearings Before the Committee on Expenditures in the Department of Agriculture, Pt. 6* (February 19, 1912): 267; letter from Thomas Will to V.W. Helm, September 13, 1911, Thomas Will Papers, University of Florida Special Collections: https://ufdc.ufl.edu//AA00000148/000013. *Minutes of the Trustees of the Internal Improvement Fund* IX: 200–201 (August 30, 1911).

33. "Testimony of C.G. Elliott," in *Everglades of Florida: Hearings Before the Committee on Expenditures in the Department of Agriculture, Pt. 21* (March 15, 1912): 1029.

34. "Additional Testimony of Mr. George H. Carter," in *Everglades of Florida: Hearings Before the Committee on Expenditures in the Department of Agriculture, Pt. 25* (April 1, 1912): 1267–1269.

35. This can be verified by comparing them in "Exhibit B of No. 5" [also known as "Part 43"] of *Everglades of Florida: Hearings Before the Committee on Expenditures in the Department of Agriculture.*

36. Carter's initial story is in: Judson Welliver, "Another Feud on Like Wiley Case," *Washington Times* (October 15, 1911).

37. Letter from V.W. Helm to Thomas Will, December 11, 1911; letter from Thomas Will to V.W. Helm, December 5, 1911, both Thomas Will Papers, University of Florida Special Collections: https://ufdc.ufl.edu//AA00000147/00002.

38. Hanna and Hanna, *Lake Okeechobee: Wellspring of the Everglades*: 153.

39. *Trustees of the Internal Improvement District v. Root,* 58 So. 371 (1912). The issue was whether the trustees had to honor an otherwise valid 80-acre homesteader's application made pursuant to the Settlers' Act of 1883, although Root's claim would obstruct the trustees' later sale of a big block of land. The supreme court said the trustees had to honor the Root application.

40. Letter from Thomas Will to Mr. Ralston and

Mr. Delany, September 1, 1911, Thomas Will Papers, University of Florida Special Collections: https://ufdc.ufl.edu//AA00000147/00001.

41. Letter from Thomas Will to Vance Helm, October 14, 1911, Thomas Will Papers, University of Florida Special Collections: https://ufdc.ufl.edu//AA00000148/00003.

42. Judson Welliver, "Another Feud on Like Wiley Case," *Washington Times* (October 15, 1911).

43. Proctor, *Napoleon Bonaparte Broward: Florida's Fighting Democrat*: 187–188, 207.

44. Letter from Rep. Frank Clark to Secretary James Wilson, October 20, 1911; letter from Secretary James Wilson to Frank Clark, October 24, 1911, both Box 7, no file no., RG 16.5.2, Department of Interior, Office of the Solicitor, Records of the Everglades Investigation, 1906–13, Archives II, College Park, MD.

45. Letter from Frank Clark to James Wilson, October 8, 1911; letter from James Wilson to Frank Clark, October 30, 1911, both Box 7, no file no., RG 16.5.2, Department of Interior, Office of the Solicitor, Records of the Everglades Investigation, 1906–13, Archives II, College Park, MD.

46. "Statement of George P. McCabe," in *Everglades of Florida: Hearings Before the Committee on Expenditures in the Department of Agriculture, Pt. 1* (February 12, 1912): 23–25. The three manuscript copies of the May 1909 manuscript were found in a storage room of the old Agriculture Department building. Only one copy: "Testimony of C.G. Elliott," in *Everglades of Florida: Hearings Before the Committee on Expenditures in the Department of Agriculture, Pt. 21* (March 15, 1912): 1033.

47. Letter from J.O. Wright to A.C. True, October 27, 1911, Box 5, Exhibit T-1; letter from A.C. True to J.O. Wright, November 1, 1911, Box 5, Exhibit T-2, RG 16.5.2, Department of Agriculture, Office of the Solicitor, Records of the Everglades Investigation, 1906–13, Archives II, College Park, MD.

48. Letter from C.G. Elliott to R.M. Reese, Office of the Secretary of Agriculture, August 16, 1909, Box 4 M-106/107; Hon. J.H. Small to Secretary James Wilson, August 21, 1909, Box 4, M-113; letter from Hon. J.H. Small to Assistant Secretary W.M. Hays, August 31, 1909, Box 4, M-122; RG 16.5.2, Department of Agriculture, Office of the Solicitor, Records of the Everglades Investigation 1906–13, Archives II, College Park, MD.

49. "Testimony of C.G. Wright," in *Everglades of Florida: Hearings Before the Committee on Expenditures in the Department of Agriculture, Pt. 22* (March 20 and 25, 1912): 1053, 1094, 1100; "Judson Wellliver articles, Oct. 8 and Oct. 15, 1911, in "Testimony of Rep. Frank Clark," in *Everglades of Florida: Hearings Before the Committee on Expenditures in the Department of Agriculture, Pt. 10* (March 8, 1912): 879–884.

50. "Hardee Writes in Defense of Frank Clark," *Jacksonville Metropolis* (October 30, 1911).

51. Clark recounted: Testimony of Rep. Frank Clark, in *Everglades of Florida: Hearings Before the Committee on Expenditures in the Department of Agriculture, Pt. 18* (March 8, 1912): 834. Clark recalled that this meeting was in January or February 1910. Will recalled: letter from Thomas Will to Vance Helm, November 14, 1911, Thomas Will Papers, University of Florida Special Collections: http://ufdc.ufl.edu/AA00000148/00003.

52. Letter from James Wilson to E.G. Baxter, November 3, 1911, Box 4, File O-22, RG 16.5.2, Department of Agriculture, Office of the Solicitor, Records of the Everglades Investigation, 1906–13, Archives II, College Park, MD.

53. Elliott's chronology: letter from C.G. Elliott to Secretary Wilson, November 21, 1911, in *Everglades of Florida: Hearings Before the Committee on Expenditures in the Department of Agriculture, Pt. 21* (March 15, 1912): 1039–1043. Clark blackmail: "Testimony of Rep. Frank Clark" in *Everglades of Florida: Hearings Before the Committee on Expenditures in the Department of Agriculture, Pt. 18* (March 8, 1912): 877. Asked if the land was really worth $300,000, Clark said yes, asked if he made the commission on the sale, Clark replied "I wish I had."

54. Judson C. Welliver, "Everglades Sales Before Committee," *Washington Times* (December 8, 1911).

55. "Testimony of C.G. Elliott, in *Everglades of Florida: Hearings Before the Committee on Expenditures in the Department of Agriculture, Pt. 21* (March 15, 1912): 1033.

56. Memo from C.G. Elliott to James Wilson, November 21, 1911, in *Everglades of Florida: Hearings Before the Committee on Expenditures in the Department of Agriculture, Pt. 18* (March 8, 1912): 856–861.

57. "Statement [of J.O. Wright], November 25, 1911," Box 6, No file no., RG 16.5.2, Department of Agriculture, Office of the Solicitor, Records of the Everglades Investigation, 1906–13, Archives II, College Park, MD.

58. *Minutes of the Internal Improvement Fund* IX: 368 (March 15, 1912); letter from Frank Clark to James Wilson, January 6, 1912, Box 4, No file no., RG 16.5.2, Department of Agriculture, Office of the Solicitor, Records of the Everglades Investigation, 1906–13, Archives II, College Park, MD. Text of the brochure: "Testimony of J.O. Wright, in *Everglades of Florida: Hearings Before the Committee on Expenditures in the Department of Agriculture, Pt. 5* (February 16, 1912): 186–192.

59. Frank Huffacker, "Ohio Congressman Will Push Demands for Investigation of Everglades Land Reforms," *Jacksonville Metropolis* (December 15, 1915). However, the *Metropolis*, unlike the Jacksonville *Florida Times Union*, was not owned by the Florida East Coast Railroad: Edward W. Akin, *Flagler: Rockefeller Partner and Florida Baron* (Gainesville, University Press of Florida, 1991 [1988]): 196.

60. "Testimony of C.G. Elliott, in *Everglades of Florida: Hearings Before the Committee on Expenditures in the Department of Agriculture, Pt. 22* (March 20 and 25, 1912): 1058.

61. "Testimony of C.G. Elliott, in *Everglades of Florida: Hearings Before the Committee on*

Expenditures in the Department of Agriculture, Pt. 22 (March 20 and 25, 1912): 1059; letter from A.C. True to C.G. Elliott, January 8, 1912, Box 8, misc. file; letter from C.G. Elliott to A.C. True, January 10, 1912, Box 8, misc. file, RG 16.5.2, Department of Agriculture, Office of the Solicitor, Records of the Everglades Investigation 1906–13, Archives II, College Park, MD.

62. "Testimony of J.O. Wright" in *Everglades of Florida: Hearings Before the Committee on Expenditures in the Department of Agriculture, Pt. 6* (February 19, 1912): 273. Morgan, however, did believe this to be true: letter from Charles G. Elliott to Arthur Morgan, March 11, 1912, Arthur Morgan Papers, University of Florida Special Collections: https://ufdc.ufl.edu/UF00103500/00002. The Hannas claimed that they had seen a "confidential" report that provided evidence of this, but nobody else has been able to find it. I believe they are referring to the committee [i.e. draft] print of the Moss Committee final report, which is marked "Confidential," but it does not substantively differ from the final version. Hanna and Hanna, *Lake Okeechobee: Wellspring of the Everglades*: 159.

63. Letter from Thomas Will to V.W. Helm, January 20, 1912; J.O. Wright to Everglades Land Sales Co., January 24, 1912, V.W. Helm to Thomas Will, January 29, 1912, Thomas Will to V.W. Helm, February 1, 1912, R.M. Price, Everglade Land Sales Co. to Bowen & Will, February 3, 1912, all Thomas Will Papers, University of Florida Special Collections: https://ufdc.ufl.edu/AA00000147/000003.

64. Letter from the Office of the Secretary to C.G. Elliott, February 3, 1912, Box 5, File L, "Personnel "Departmental Record: C.G. Elliott," Box 7, No. file no.; "Personnel Department Record: Alanson D. Morehouse," Box 7, No file no.RG 16.5.2, Department of Agriculture, Office of the Solicitor, Records of the Everglades Investigation, Archives II, College Park, MD.

65. "Florida Land Sale Inquiry," *New York Times* (February 7, 1912); "Florida Land Sales to be Investigated," *New York Times* (February 8, 1912); "Clark Again Assails Florida Land Sales," *New York Times* (February 9, 1912).

66. "Say Elliott Was A Foil For Wilson," *New York Times* (February 11, 1912); "Florida Land Row A Campaign Issue," *New York Times* (February 12, 1912).

67. "Morgan Defends Engineer Elliott; Declares Drainage Chief Blameless," *Daily Texarkanian* (February 9, 1912) Arthur Morgan Papers, University of Florida Special Collections, https://ufdc.ufl.edu/UF00103500/00009.].

Chapter 5

1. Henry T. Brooks, "The Month in Review," *Postgraduate: Journal of the New York Postgraduate Medical School and Hospital* 26, 9 (September 1911): 873–876.

2. Letter from James Wilson to Theodore Roosevelt, July 17, 1905, Library of Congress Manuscript Division and the Theodore Roosevelt Digital Collection, Dickinson State University: https://thetheodorerooseveltcenter.org/Research/Digital-Library/Record?libID=o50057.

3. Daniel P. Carpenter, *The Forging of Bureaucratic Autonomy: Reputations, Networks and Policy Innovation in Executive Agencies, 1862–1928* (Princeton: Princeton University Press, 2001): 282.

4. *Investigation of the Department of the Interior and of the Bureau of Forestry: Hearings Held Before the Joint Committee of Congress Relative to the Investigation of Interior and its Several Bureaus, Officers and Employees, and of the Bureau of Forestry, in the Department of Agriculture, and its Officers and Employees, Volume 1: Final Reports* (61st Congress, 2nd Session, Senate Document No. 719, Washington, USGPO, 1911): 41–42; 154 [hereafter, *Senate Document No. 719*]; Frank Moore Colby (ed.) *The New International Year Book for 1910* (New York: Dodd, Mead and Co., 1911): 768. For a well researched account more favorable to Ballinger, based on the premise that Pinchot and Reclamation Service director Newell had overreached their authorities and exercised poor decision-making, see: Donald Pisani, Water *and American Government: the Reclamation Bureau, National Water Policy and the West, 1902–1935* (Berkeley: University of California Press, 2002):106–110.

5. Doris Kerns Goodwin, *The Bully Pulpit: Theodore Roosevelt, William Howard Taft and the Golden Age of Journalism* (New York: Simon & Schuster, 2013): 606–627.

6. The committee was comprised of six senators (4 Rep.; 2 Dem.) and six congressmen (3 Rep.; 3 Dem.). They were: Sen. K. Nelson (R-Minn., Chair.); Rep. S. McCall (D-Mass., V-Chair.); Sen. F. Flint (R-Cal.); Sen. G. Sutherland (R-Utah); Sen. E. Root (R-N.Y.); Sen. T. Paynter (D-Ky.); Sen. D. Fletcher (D-Fla.); Rep. M. Olmsted (R-Penn.); Rep. E. Denby (R-Mich.); Rep. E. Madison (R-Wisc.); Rep. J. Graham (D-Ill.); Rep. O. James (D-Ky.).

7. Goodwin, *The Bully Pulpit: Theodore Roosevelt, William Howard Taft and the Golden Age of Journalism*: 606–627.

8. *Senate Document No. 719*: 53.

9. *Senate Document No. 719*: 192.

10. *Hearings into Expenditures in the Department of Agriculture, January 22–26, 1912* (62nd Congress, 2nd Session, House Report 249): 10–22.

11. Clayton A. Coppin and Jack High, *The Politics of Purity: Harvey Washington Wiley and the Origins of Federal Food Policy* (Ann Arbor: University of Michigan Press, 1999); "The Exoneration of Dr. Wiley," *New Outlook* 99 (September 23, 1911): 147–148; Arthur Wallace Dunn, "Dr. Wiley and Pure Food, Part 1," *World's Work* 22 (1911): 14958–14965; _____, "Dr. Wiley and Pure Food, Part 2," *World's Work* 23 (1912): 29–40; H. Parker Willis, "Secretary Wilson's Work, Part 3: Pure Food and Drug," *Colliers* 49,3 (May 6, 1912): 10–12. McCabe's bar admission: "New Admissions for 1902," *Washington Law Reporter* 30, 41 (October 9, 1902): 661.

12. Letter from Henry Martyn Hoyt to William Moody, July 20, 1905, Theodore Roosevelt Papers, Library of Congress and the Theodore Roosevelt Digital Collection, Dickinson State University: https://www.thetheodorerooseveltcenter.org/Research/Digital-Library/Record?libID=o502255.

13. "Testimony of Dr. D.L. Dunlap," in William Graham, Chairman, *Hearings Before the House Committee on Expenses in the Department on Agriculture, February 5, 1910* (61st Congress, 3rd Session, House Report No. 1780, Washington, Government Printing Office): 11. [hereafter, House Report No. 1780]

14. "Testimony of Mr. A. Zappone," in *House Report No. 1780*: 76. Besides Remsen, the board also included Constantin Fahlberg, who first synthesized the artificial sweetener saccharin (benzoic sufimide). Wiley publicly questioned its safety due to its benzene-ring base. In the 1970s it was listed as a Group 2B (low probability) carcinogen. It has since been de-listed but has also been replaced on the market with newer products due to its metallic aftertaste.

15. Willis, "Secretary Wilson's Work, Part 3: Pure Food and Drug": 10.

16. H. Parker Willis, "Secretary Wilson's Record: Part 1, Patent Medicines, *Collier's* 49, 1 (March 23, 1912): 10–12.

17. "Testimony of Solicitor George P. McCabe," in *House Report No. 1780*: 59.

18. Willis, "Secretary Wilson's Work, Part 3: Pure Food and Drug,": 10–12.

19. Coppin and High, *The Politics of Purity: Harvey Washington Wiley and the Origins of Federal Food Policy*: 106; Part of this decision was reversed in 1916 and Coca Cola did reduce the amount of caffeine in the drink sometime around 1916: *United States v. Forty Barrels and Twenty Kegs of Coca-Cola and the Coca Cola Co. of Atlanta, Georgia*, 241 U.S. 265 (1916). It appears that Coca-Cola reduced the level of caffeine by taking out the kola nut extract. Contrary to popular belief, the formula for Coca-Cola has changed frequently over the years, primarily because the components have changed. For example, cinnamon today is different from cinnamon in 1888. The two primary aroma contributors today are vanilla and cinnamon; in inventor John Pemberton's 1888 notebook the two primaries were vanilla and lime juice: Ira Glass, et. al. "The Recipe," *This American Life* (National Public Radio. No. 427, February 11, 2011): https//thisamericanlife.org/427/original-recipe. Today, Coca-Cola does add caffeine citrate; it is distilled from liquid coffee.

20. Coppin and High, *The Politics of Purity: Harvey Washington Wiley and the Origins of Federal Food Policy*: 121.

21. "The Exoneration of Dr. Wiley," *New Outlook* 99 (September 23, 1911): 147–148; Arthur Wallace Dunn, "Dr. Wiley and Pure Food, Part 1," *World's Work* 22 (1911): 14958–14965; _____, "Dr. Wiley and Pure Food, Part 2," *World's Work* 23 (1912): 29–40.

22. "The Hampering of Wiley," *The Literary Digest* 43, 9 (August 26, 1911): 299–301.

23. H. Parker Willis, "Secretary Wilson's Record: Part 1, Patent Medicines, *Collier's* 49, 1 (March 23, 1912): 10.

24. "Statement of Hon. R.E. Bathrick from Ohio" in *Everglades of Florida: Hearings Before the Committee on Expenditures in the Department of Agriculture, Pt. 1* (February 3 and 6, 1912): 3–6.

25. Another Wiley McCabe affair: "Florida Land Sale Inquiry," *New York Times* (February 7, 1912); "Statement of Hon. Frank Clark from Florida" in *Everglades of Florida: Hearings Before the Committee on Expenditures in the Department of Agriculture, Pt. 1* (February 3 and 6, 1912): 11.

26. Letter from J.O. Wright to Everglade Land Sales Company, January 24, 1912; memo from V.W. Helm to Thomas Will, January 29, 1912; letters from Thomas Will to V.W. Helm, February 1 and February 3, 1912, all Thomas Will Papers, University of Florida Special Collections: http://ufdc.ufl.edu//AA00000147/000003.

27. "Statement of Hon. Frank Clark from Florida" in *Everglades of Florida: Hearings Before the Committee on Expenditures in the Department of Agriculture, Pt. 2* (February 6, 1912): 14–45.

28. "Statement A. Zappone, Chief of the Division of Acccunts," in *Everglades of Florida: Hearings Before the Committee on Expenditures in the Department of Agriculture, Pt. 2* (February 6, 1912): 47–66.

29. *Everglades of Florida: Acts, Reports and Other Papers, State and National, Relating to the Everglades of the State of Florida and Their Reclamation* (62nd Congress, 1st. Session, Senate Document No. 89). [hereafter, *Senate Document No. 89*]

30. "Statement of Maj. J.O. Wright," in *Everglades of Florida: Hearings Before the Committee on Expenditures in the Department of Agriculture, Pt. 7* (February 20, 1912): 262, 281–283.

31. "Exhibit B of No. 5 [3-column comparison of February 25, 1909; June 25, 1909 and January 28, 1910 versions of Wright/Elliott reports] *Everglades of Florida: Hearings Before the Committee on Expenditures in the Department of Agriculture* (February 16, 1912). [This is listed in the Hathitrust digital version as "Part 43"],

32. Daniel Mead, Allen Hazen and Leonard Metcalf, *Report of the Drainage of the Everglades* (Miami: Everglades Land Sales Company, Nov. 12, 1912). One copy is in the Arthur Morgan Papers, and a second copy is in the Ernest "Cap" Graham Papers, both University of Florida Special Collections.

33. Testimony of Maj. J.O. Wright" in *Everglades of Florida: Hearings Before the Committee on Expenditures in the Department of Agriculture, Pt. 4* (February 15, 1912): 200.

34. Testimony of Maj. J.O. Wright" in *Everglades of Florida: Hearings Before the Committee on Expenditures in the Department of Agriculture, Pt. 4* (February 15, 1912): 127–129.

35. This is verified in his report, although he implies that his canals *will* drain the water generated by 2,061 square miles (1,318,912 acres) of land below the lake. *Senate Document No. 89*: 133–134.

36. "Testimony of Maj. J.O. Wright" in *Everglades*

of Florida: Hearings Before the Committee on Expenditures in the Department of Agriculture, Pt. 4 (February 15, 1912): 157.

37. "Accusers Accused in Florida Inquiry," *New York Times* (February 17, 1912).

38. "Testimony of Maj. J.O. Wright" in *Everglades of Florida: Hearings Before the Committee on Expenditures in the Department of Agriculture, Pt. 4* (February 15, 1912): 248–251; "Testimony of C.G. Elliott" in *Everglades of Florida: Hearings Before the Committee on Expenditures in the Department of Agriculture, Pt. 17* (March 7, 1912): 789–791, 822; "Testimony of A.D. Morehouse" in *Everglades of Florida: Hearings Before the Committee on Expenditures in the Department of Agriculture, Pt. 12* (February 29, 1912): 506–507.

39. "Testimony of Secretary James Wilson" in *Everglades of Florida: Hearings Before the Committee on Expenditures in the Department of Agriculture, Pt. 26* (April 3, 1912): 1302; Henry Hall to John M. Rankin, February 21, 1912, Box 6, No. file no., RG 16.5.2, Department of Agriculture, Office of the Solicitor, Records of the Everglades Investigation, 1906–13.

40. Testimony of A. Zappone" in *Everglades of Florida: Hearings Before the Committee on Expenditures in the Department of Agriculture, Pt. 6* (February 13, 1912): 50–60; "Itinerary and Duties of J.O. Wright: February 1, 1906 to February 28, 1910," Box 9, Exhibit M, RG 16.5.2, Department of Agriculture, Office of the Solicitor, Records of the Everglades Investigation, 1906–13.

41. Chapter 3451, Acts of 1883; after 1906, Sections 624–626, Florida General Statutes.

42. *Minutes of the Internal Improvement District* VIII: 19 (January 23, 1909).

43. *Root v. Cordner and the Trustees of the Internal Improvement District*, 59 Fla. 648, 51 So. 535 (Fla. 1910). In the *Southern Reporter* version, the case is mis-titled *Trustees of the Internal Improvement District v. Root.*

44. *Trustees of the Internal Improvement Fund v. Root*, 58 Fla. 371 (Fla., April 9, 1912). The statute involved was originally Chapter 3451, F.S., later revised to Secs. 624–626, F.G.S. "Important Decision Rendered by Supreme Court in Florida Everglades Land Matter," Miami *Metropolis* (April 15, 1912).

45. In the modern era, this had become a controversial topic. To what extent can the government forcibly purchase a parcel for the purpose of giving or selling it to another private party for, say, real estate development or urban revitalization, which are actually tax augmentation schemes.

46. Chapter 5908, Sec. 1, Acts of 1909, June 9, 1909 (Amending Sec. 624, Florida Compiled Laws). "The provisions of this section shall not apply to any lands in the Drainage District now created, or which may hereafter be created." There is no record of any settler after Root being granted land under the Settler's Act within the drainage district.

47. "Testimony of Maj. J.O. Wright" in *Everglades of Florida: Hearings Before the Committee on Expenditures in the Department of Agriculture, Pt. 6* (February 19, 1912): 244, 247, 250–252.

48. "Testimony of Maj. J.O. Wright" in *Everglades of Florida: Hearings Before the Committee on Expenditures in the Department of Agriculture, Pt. 6* (February 19, 1912): 271.

49. "Testimony of Maj. J.O. Wright" in *Everglades of Florida: Hearings Before the Committee on Expenditures in the Department of Agriculture, Pt. 6* (February 19, 1912): 273. Why Was Wright's Report Suppressed?": Part 5 (February 16, 1912): 186–192. "To the General Public: Facts Concerning the Employment of J.O. Wilson as Chief Engineer," n.d. (1912), Arthur Morgan Papers, University of Florida Special Collections: https://ufdc.ufl.edu/UF00103500/00005.

50. "Agreement Between the Board of Drainage Commissioners of the State of Florida, Made the 31st Day January, 1910," William Jennings Papers, University of Florida Special Collections: https://ufdc.ufl.edu/uf00094871/00004; "Say Elliott was A Foil for Wilson," *New York Times* (February 11, 1912).

51. "Testimony of Arthur E. Morgan" in *Everglades of Florida: Hearings Before the Committee on Expenditures in the Department of Agriculture, Pt. 10* (February 27, 1912): 410. This letter also appears in Arthur Morgan, "The Florida Everglades Incident," (manuscript, 46 pp, May 1954), Arthur Morgan Papers, University of Florida: http://ufdc.ufl.edu/uf00103500/00001. In this paper, Morgan asserts (p. 26) that three men were under the paid influence of an Everglades land company (or multiple companies): the son of Secretary Wilson, Solicitor McCabe and J.O. Wilson. The "son of Secretary Wilson" could mean Jasper Wilson, Secretary Wilson's son and private secretary, or it could be a garbled reference to Assistant Secretary Hays, who was indeed involved in North Carolina land dealings. There is no evidence that either James or Jasper Wilson, sons of the secretary, were involved in any of these affairs. While George McCabe may have been in the pay of firms subject to the Pure Food and Drug Act, there is no proof he had an interest in Florida land. Finally, beyond his somewhat extravagant salary with the State of Florida, there is still no proof that J.O. Wilson had a pecuniary interest in Florida land.

52. Does the Punishment Fit the Crime?" *Engineering News* 67, 10 (February 22, 1912): 359–360.

53. Arthur Morgan, "More Concerning Mr. Elliott's Dismissal: The Engineering Plans For Draining the Everglades," *Engineering News* 67, 13 (March 28, 1912): 601–602; "The Engineering Plans for Draining the Florida Everglades," *Engineering News* 67, 13 (March 28, 1912): 604; Isham Randolph, "The Charges Against Mr. Charles G. Elliott," *Engineering News*, 67, 15 (April 25, 1912): 799; letter from Isham Randolph, Isham Randolph & Co., to Secretary James Wilson, April 18, 1912, Box 6, no file no., RG 16.5.2, Department of Agriculture, Office of the Solicitor, Records of the Everglades Investigation, 1906–13. Several of these articles are also scattered throughout the files of the Arthur

Morgan Papers at the University of Florida, available on-line.

54. "Brief re: Author E. Morgan," (undated), Box 6 (et. al.), no file no., RG 16.5.2, Department of Agriculture, Office of the Solicitor, Records of the Everglades Investigation, 1906–13, Archives II, College Park, MD. Several carbon copies of this document are scattered among the various boxes, in working files.

55. "Testimony of Arthur E. Morgan" in *Everglades of Florida: Hearings Before the Committee on Expenditures in the Department of Agriculture, Pt. 9* (February 26, 1912): 338.

56. "Testimony of Arthur E. Morgan" in *Everglades of Florida: Hearings Before the Committee on Expenditures in the Department of Agriculture, Pt. 9* (February 26, 1912): 347.

57. "Comparison of the Drainage Plan as Originally Outlined by Mr. J.O. Wright with That Outlined by Mr. Elliott in His Final Revision of the Proposed Bulletin on the Everglades," Box 4, "Solicitor's Working Files," RG 16.5.3, Department of Agriculture, Office of the Solicitor, Records of the Everglades Investigation, 1906–13, Archives II, College Park, MD; "Testimony of Arthur E. Morgan" in *Everglades of Florida: Hearings Before the Committee on Expenditures in the Department of Agriculture, Pt. 9* (February 26, 1912): 355–365.

58. Mead, Hazen and Metcalf, *Report on the Drainage of the Everglades* (1912).

59. "Comparison of the Drainage Plan as Originally Outlined by Mr. J.O. Wright with That Outlined by Mr. Elliott in His Final Revision of the Proposed Bulletin on the Everglades," Box 4, "Solicitor's Working Files," RG 16.5.3, Department of Agriculture, Office of the Solicitor, Records of the Everglades Investigation, 1906–13, Archives II, College Park, MD.

60. "Comparison of the Drainage Plan as Originally Outlined by Mr. J.O. Wright with That Outlined by Mr. Elliott in His Final Revision of the Proposed Bulletin on the Everglades," Box 4, "Solicitor's Working Files," RG 16.5.3, Department of Agriculture, Office of the Solicitor, Records of the Everglades Investigation, 1906–13, Archives II, College Park, MD.

61. "Testimony of Arthur E. Morgan" in *Everglades of Florida: Hearings Before the Committee on Expenditures in the Department of Agriculture, Pt. 9* (February 26, 1912): 355.

62. "Testimony of Arthur E. Morgan" in *Everglades of Florida: Hearings Before the Committee on Expenditures in the Department of Agriculture, Pt. 9* (February 26, 1912): 365.

63. Arthur Morgan, "The Florida Everglades Incident," (ms, 46 pp, May 1954), Arthur Morgan Papers, University of Florida: http://ufdc.ufl.edu/uf00103500/00001.

64. "Testimony of Arthur E. Morgan" in *Everglades of Florida: Hearings Before the Committee on Expenditures in the Department of Agriculture, Pt. 9* (February 26, 1912): 363

65. "Testimony of Arthur E. Morgan" in *Everglades of Florida: Hearings Before the Committee on Expenditures in the Department of Agriculture, Pt. 9* (February 26, 1912): 419.

66. "Testimony of Arthur E. Morgan" in *Everglades of Florida: Hearings Before the Committee on Expenditures in the Department of Agriculture, Pt. 10* (February 27, 1912): 414–415.

67. "Testimony of Arthur E. Morgan" in *Everglades of Florida: Hearings Before the Committee on Expenditures in the Department of Agriculture, Pt. 10* (February 27, 1912): 377–378.

Chapter 6

1. "Affidavit of Mr. Wiley," *Tarault v. Seip* 74 S.E. 3 (N. C. 1912).

2. "Moss Strikes New Scandal," Greencastle (Ind.) *Star-Democrat* (March 1, 1912). This was the hometown weekly of Rep. Moss, who had a nearby farm.

3. "Itinerary and Duties of J.O. Wright: February 1, 1905 to February 28, 1910, Box 8, Exhibit M-793 through M-801; "Request for Services of J.O. Wright: February 1906 to February 1910 Inclusive," Box 9, Exhibit M-788 to M-792; "Statement of Expenses Incurred in Connection with the Lake Mattamuskeet, Moyock, and Angola Bay and Lake Phelps Projects, Box 2, Exhibit C-8 through C-30, all RG 16.5.2, Department of Agriculture, Office of the Solicitor, Records of the Everglades Investigation, 1906–13, Archives II, College Park, MD. Meets Wilkinson: "Testimony of Mr. John A, Wilkinson" in *Everglades of Florida: Hearings Before the Committee on Expenditures in the Department of Agriculture, Pt. 30* (May 3, 1912): 1429.

4. The Roper Co. built the mill: "Norfolk Newsletter," *St. Louis Lumberman* (October 15, 1908): 45. Wilkinson built the mill: "Building Up Belhaven," *Manufacturers' Record* 52 (November 28, 1907): 49.

5. William Stewart, *History of Norfolk County Virginia and Representative Citizens* (Chicago: Biographical Publications, 1902): 554.

6. *Eastern Land, Lumber and Mfg. Co. v. State Board of Education of North Carolina and W.G. Lewis*, 101 N.C. 35 (N.C., 1887); Tycho de Boer, *Nature, Business and Community in North Carolina's Green Swamp* (Gainesville: University Press of Florida, 2008): 140–141. By 1887, Baird and Roper had sold the land to Eastern Land and Lumber but was still timbering it.

7. "C. I. Millard Becomes President of the John L. Roper Lumber Co.," *St. Louis Lumberman* 46, 1 (July 1, 1910): 82D; "Norfolk Newsletter," *St. Louis Lumberman* (October 15, 1908): 45.

8. de Boer, *Nature, Business and Community in North Carolina's Green Swamp*: 100–102.

9. "Norfolk Southern Railroad," in *Decisions of the Interstate Commerce Commission (Valuation Reports)* (Washington: GPO, 1925): 84; 725–754. Sybil H. Arginter, "National Register of Historic Places: Belhaven Commercial District (National Park Service and North Carolina Dept. of Natural

Resources, December 19, 1984): NPS Form 10–900, p. 10.

10. *Standard and Poor's Manual of Railroads*, Volume 48 (1915): 1435–1437; J. Paul Lilly, "A History of Swamp Land Development in North Carolina," in Curtis J. Richardson (ed.) *Pocosin Wetlands: An Integrated Analysis of Coastal Freshwater Bogs in North Carolina* (Stroudsburg, PA: Hutchinson Ross Publishing, 1981): 20–39.

11. "Explanatory," [Mattamuskeet Project] Box 8, M-145 to M-146; letter from Rep. J.H. Small to Asst. Secy. W.M. Hays, August 17, 1908, Box 8, M-92; letter from Rep. J.H. Small to Secretary Wilson, August 17, 1908, Box 9, M-151; letter from W.M. Hays to Rep. J.H. Small, August 25, 1908, Box 8, M-153; letter from Rep. J.H. Small to W.M. Hays, Box 8, M-94; all RG 16.5.2, Department of Agriculture, Office of the Solicitor, Records of the Everglades Investigation, 1906–13, Archives II, College Park, MD.

12. Lake Mattamuskeet has exercised an almost mystic challenge to drainage engineers. Four times it was drained; four times it refilled. Today, much reduced by a highway and a railroad grade, it is a national wildlife refuge: Ann Vileisis, *Discovering the Unknown Landscape: A History of America's Wetlands* (Washington: Island Press, 1997): 97, 123; Lilly, "A History of Swamp Land Development in North Carolina": 26–27.

13. Vileisis, *Discovering the Unknown Landscape: A History of America's Wetlands*: 42; Lilly, "A History of Swamp Land Development in North Carolina": 20–39.

14. "Explanatory," [Mattamuskeet Project] Box 8, M-145 to M-146; letter from Rep. Albert Douglas to Secy. James Wilson, Box 8, M-477; letter from Rep. P.J. McCumber to Secy. James Wilson, September 28, 1908, Box 8, M-478; letter from James Wilson to Albert Douglas, September 29, 1908, Box 9, M-479; all RG 16.5.2, Department of Agriculture, Office of the Solicitor, Records of the Everglades Investigation, 1906–13, Archives II, College Park, MD.

15. Letter from John Seip to Office of Experimental Stations, October 5, 1908, Box 8, M-481; letter from Asst. Secy. W.M. Hays to Rep. P.J. McCumber, October 6, 1908, Box 8, M-482; both RG 16.5.2, Department of Agriculture, Office of the Solicitor, Records of the Everglades Investigation, 1906–13, Archives II, College Park, MD.

16. Letter from C.G. Elliott to Rep. Albert Douglas, October 6, 1908, Box 8, M-483; letter from Rep. Albert Douglas to C.G. Elliott, October 8, 1908, Box 9, M-484, letter from Rep. J.H. Small to Secy. James Wilson (with attached petition), November 2, 1908, Box 8, M-487, all RG 16.5.2, Department of Agriculture, Office of the Solicitor, Records of the Everglades Investigation, 1906–13, Archives II, College Park, MD.

17. Henry Holcumb Bennett (ed.), *The County of Ross: A History of Ross County, Ohio* (Madison, WI: Selwyn A. Brant, 1902): 678–679; *Dictionary of Ohio Historic Places, Vol 1.* (St. Clair Shores, MI: Somerset Publishers, 1999): 1223; "Loses in Case of Dismal Swamp," Richmond *Times Dispatch* (January 22, 1905): 1.

18. *Tarault v. Seip*, 158 N.C. 363, 74 S.E. 3 (N.C., Mar. 13, 1912).

19. "Explanatory," [Mattamuskeet Project] Box 9, M-145 through M-149; "Explanatory," [Moyock Project] Box 9, M-472 through M-475, letter from J.O. Wright to Joseph Hyde Pratt (N. C. State Geologist), February 6, 1909, Box 9, M-503; all RG 16.5.2, Department of Agriculture, Office of the Solicitor, Records of the Everglades Investigation, 1906–13, Archives II, College Park, MD.

20. "Itinerary and Duties and Duties of J.O. Wright: February 1, 1906 to February 28, 1910," Box 8, M-793 through M-801, RG 16.5.2, Department of Agriculture, Office of the Solicitor, Records of the Everglades Investigation, 1906–13, Archives II, College Park, MD. Law passed in March, 1909: Joseph Hyde Pratt, "Drainage of North Carolina Swamp Lands," *Journal of the Elisha Mitchell Scientific Society* 25, 4 (December 1909): 158–163.

21. Joseph Hyde Pratt (ed.), *Proceedings of a Drainage Convention Called by the Geological Board and Held at Newbern, N.C., Sept. 9–10, 1908* (Raleigh: E.M. Uzell, State Printers, 1908): 23.

22. Joseph Hyde Pratt, "Drainage of the North Carolina Swamp Lands," *Journal of the Elisha Mitchell Scientific Society* 25, 4 (December 1909): 158–163.

23. Met through Lukins: "Testimony of Mr. John E. Seip," in *Everglades of Florida: Hearings Before the Committee on Expenditures in the Department of Agriculture, Pt. 15* (March 4, 1912): 735; claimed Wright planned to leave: "Testimony of Mr. John E. Seip" in *Everglades of Florida: Hearings Before the Committee on Expenditures in the Department of Agriculture, Pt. 11* (February 27, 1912): 471. "My negotiations": "Testimony of Mr. John E. Seip," in *Everglades of Florida: Hearings Before the Committee on Expenditures in the Department of Agriculture, Pt. 15* (March 4, 1912): 735.

24. "Testimony of Mr. John E. Seip" in *Everglades of Florida: Hearings Before the Committee on Expenditures in the Department of Agriculture, Pt. 11* (February 27, 1912): 473.

25. "Testimony of Mr. John E. Seip," in *Everglades of Florida: Hearings Before the Committee on Expenditures in the Department of Agriculture, Pt. 14* (March 2, 1912): 654.

26. "Testimony of Mr. John E. Seip" in *Everglades of Florida: Hearings Before the Committee on Expenditures in the Department of Agriculture, Pt. 11* (February 27, 1912): 473.

27. Letter from J.O. Wright to Joseph Hyde Pratt, February 6, 1909, Box 8, M-503; letter from J.O. Wright to A.M. Simmons, November 26, 1909, Box 8, M-511 and M-512, RG 16.5.2, Department of Agriculture, Office of the Solicitor, Records of the Everglades Investigation 1906–13, Archives II, College Park, MD.

28. "Testimony of Mr. John A. Wilkinson" in *Everglades of Florida: Hearings Before the Committee*

on Expenditures in the Department of Agriculture, Pt. 30 (May 3, 1912): 1431.

29. Letter from J.O. Wright to John Seip, March 7, 1909, Box 9, "John Seip Letters" [envelope], RG 16.5.2, Department of Agriculture, Office of the Solicitor, Records of the Everglades Investigation, Archives II, College Park, MD.

30. "Testimony of Mr. John A. Wilkinson" in *Everglades of Florida: Hearings Before the Committee on Expenditures in the Department of Agriculture, Pt. 30* (May 3, 1912): 1433; letter from J.O. Wright to John Seip, March 17, 1909, Box 9, "John Seip Letters" [envelope], RG 16.5.2, Department of Agriculture, Office of the Solicitor, Records of the Everglades Investigation, Archives II, College Park, MD.

31. "Testimony of Mr. John A. Wilkinson" in *Everglades of Florida: Hearings Before the Committee on Expenditures in the Department of Agriculture, Pt. 31* (May 7, 1912): 1430.

32. "Testimony of Mr. John A. Wilkinson" in *Everglades of Florida: Hearings Before the Committee on Expenditures in the Department of Agriculture, Pt. 31* (May 7, 1912): 1433.

33. Verbal request: "Explanatory," [Pantego Drainage District], Box 9, File N-1 through N-4, RG 16.5.2, Department of Agriculture, Office of the Solicitor, Records of the Everglades Investigation, 1906–13, Archives II, College Park, MD. Included all of Albemarle and two stockholders: "Testimony of Mr. John A. Wilkinson" in *Everglades of Florida: Hearings Before the Committee on Expenditures in the Department of Agriculture, Pt. 31* (May 7, 1912): 1428. Roper and Norfolk Southern: *Poor's Manual of Railroads 1912*: 734–735.

34. "Memo from C. G Elliott to Omer Fairley re: Pantego Creek Drainage District, May 1, 1909," Box 9, N-5, Department of Agriculture, Office of the Solicitor, Records of the Everglades Investigation, 1906–13, Archives II, College Park MD.

35. Letter from Lawrence Brett to C.G. Elliott, November 1, 1909, Box 8, M-277, RG 16.5.2, Department of Agriculture, Office of the Solicitor, Records of the Everglades Investigation 1906–13, Archives II, College Park, MD. Wright and Brett went into business: "Testimony of Mr. John A. Wilkinson" in *Everglades of Florida: Hearings Before the Committee on Expenditures in the Department of Agriculture, Pt. 31* (May 7, 1912): 1432–1433; Wright and Brett like brothers: "Testimony of J.O. Wright," in *Everglades of Florida: Hearings Before the Committee on Expenditures in the Department of Agriculture, Pt. 32* (May 7, 1912): 1432–1433; 1490.

36. Letter from J.O. Wright to John Seip, March 5, 1910, Box 9, "John Seip Letters" [envelope], RG 16.5.2, Department of Agriculture, Office of the Solicitor, Records of the Everglades Investigation 1906–13, Archives II, College Park, MD; "Testimony of Mr. John Seip" in *Everglades of Florida: Hearings Before the Committee on Expenditures in the Department of Agriculture, Pt. 15* (March 4, 1912): 657, 712, 727.

37. "Testimony of Mr. John E. Seip" in *Everglades of Florida: Hearings Before the Committee on Expenditures in the Department of Agriculture, Pt. 11* (February 27, 1912): 478.

38. Letter from J.O. Wright to John Seip, March 17, 1909, Box 9 "John Seip Letters" [envelope]; J.O. Wright to John Seip, March 28, 1909, Box 9, "John Seip Letters" [envelope], RG 16.5.2, Department of Agriculture, Office of the Solicitor, Records of the Everglades Investigation, 1906–1913, Archives II, College Park, MD.

39. "Testimony of Mr. John A. Wilkinson" in *Everglades of Florida: Hearings Before the Committee on Expenditures in the Department of Agriculture, Pt. 30* (May 7, 1912): 1430.

40. Letter from J.O. Wright to John Seip, April 8, 1909, Box 9, "John Seip Letters" [envelope], RG 16.5.2, Department of Agriculture, Office of the Solicitor, Records of the Everglades Investigation, 1906–1913, Archives II, College Park, MD.

41. "Willett M. Hays," *The Annals of Iowa* 16 (1928): 477. Could not find a suitable candidate: letter from James Wilson to Theodore Roosevelt, July 9, 1904, Library of Congress Manuscript Division and the Theodore Roosevelt Digital Library, Dickinson State Library: https://www.thetheodorerooseveltcenter.org/Research/Digital-Library/Record?libID=o45974; Pinchot: letter from Theodore Roosevelt to Gilbert Pinchot, July 14, 1904, Library of Congress Manuscript Division and the Theodore Roosevelt Digital Library, Dickinson State Library: https://www.thetheodorerooseveltcenter.org/Research/Digital-Library/Record?libID=o188630; Davison: letter from Theodore Roosevelt to Thomas Collier Platt, August 2, 1904, Library of Congress Manuscript Division and the Theodore Roosevelt Digital Library, Dickinson State Library: https://www.thetheodorerooseveltcenter.org/Research/Digital-Library/Record?libID=o188749.

42. "Iowan Asks for Guards in Korea," Davenport *Daily Times* (February 29, 1904).

43. Donald C. Clark, *Living Dangerously in China: The Western Experience, 1900–1950* (no location: Eastbridge, 2003).

44. "Testimony of Mr. W.M. Hays," in *Everglades of Florida: Hearings Before the Committee on Expenditures in the Department of Agriculture, Pt. 28* (April 29, 1912): 1388, 1393; letter from Leigh Hunt to W.M. Hays, July 21, 1900, Box 8, M-100 and M-101, RG 16.5.2, Department of Agriculture, Office of the Solicitor, Records of the Everglades Investigation, 1906–1913, Archives II, College Park MD; letter from J.O. Wright to John Seip, July 1, 1900, Box 9, "John Seip Letters" [envelope], RG 16.5.2, Department of Agriculture, Office of the Solicitor, Records of the Everglades Investigation, 1906–1913, Archives II, College Park MD.

45. "Testimony of Mr. W.M. Hays," in *Everglades of Florida: Hearings Before the Committee on Expenditures in the Department of Agriculture, Pt. 29* (April 30, 1912): 1396. This same spreadsheet appears in multiple places throughout the transcript.

46. "Big Drainage Project in North Carolina With Rural-District Plan," and "Largest Pumping Plant is at Mattamuskeet," *Engineering News* 77, 9 (March 1, 1917): 346–348 and 348–351.

47. Letter from A.D. Morehouse to J.O. Wright, September 13, 1909, Box 9, N-88, RG 16.5.2, Department of Agriculture, Office of the Solicitor, Records of the Everglades Investigation, 1906–1913, Archives II, College Park MD.

48. "Testimony of Mr. John A. Wilkinson," in *Everglades of Florida: Hearings Before the Committee on Expenditures in the Department of Agriculture, Pt. 31* (May 7, 1912): 1434–1435; "Testimony of Mr. W.M. Hays," in *Everglades of Florida: Hearings Before the Committee on Expenditures in the Department of Agriculture, Pt. 28* (April 29, 1912): 1382. Land was sold: Letter from J.O. Wright to John Seip, September 4, 1909, Box 9, "John Seip Letters" [envelope], RG 16.5.2, Department of Agriculture, Office of the Solicitor, Records of the Everglades Investigation 1906–1913, Archives II, College Park, MD.

49. Seip had consulted: Letter from J.O. Wright to John Seip, July 29, 1909, Box 9, "John Seip Letters" [envelope], RG 16.5.2, Department of Agriculture, Office of the Solicitor, Records of the Everglades Investigation 1906–1913, Archives II, College Park, MD. Wright informed Seip in May: Letter from J.O. Wright to John Seip, May 14, 1909, Box 9, "John Seip Letters" [envelope], RG 16.5.2, Department of Agriculture, Office of the Solicitor, Records of the Everglades Investigation 1906–1913, Archives II, College Park, MD. Wilkinson told Seip: "Testimony of Mr. John A. Wilkinson," in *Everglades of Florida: Hearings Before the Committee on Expenditures in the Department of Agriculture, Pt. 31* (May 7, 1912): 1431.

50. Letter from J.O. Wright to John Seip, July 29, 1909, Box 9, "John Seip Letters" [envelope], RG 16.5.2, Department of Agriculture, Office of the Solicitor, Records of the Everglades Investigation 1906–1913, Archives II, College Park, MD.

51. "Testimony of W.M. Hayes, Assistant Secretary of Agriculture" in *Everglades of Florida: Hearings Before the Committee on Expenditures in the Department of Agriculture, Pt. 29* (April 30, 1912): 1392. Wright was earning a commission from school board: "Testimony of Mr. John E. Seip," in *Everglades of Florida: Hearings Before the Committee on Expenditures in the Department of Agriculture, Pt. 11* (February 28, 1912): 481. Sold to another party and Wright received $1,250: "Testimony of J.O. Wright," in *Everglades of Florida: Hearings Before the Committee on Expenditures in the Department of Agriculture, Pt. 32* (June 5, 1912): 1465.

52. Letter from J.O. Wright to A.M. Simmons, Box 8, M-511, RG 16.5.2, Department of Agriculture, Office of the Solicitor, Records of the Everglades Investigation 1906–1913, Archives II, College Park, MD.

53. Letter from J.A. Wilkinson to C.G. Elliott, December 15, 1909, Box 9, N-72; letter from C.G. Elliott to J.A. Wilkinson, December 17, 1909, Box 9, N-73; letter from J.A. Wilkinson to C.G. Elliott, December 20, 1909, Box 9, N-75; letter from Rep. J.N. Small to C.G. Elliott, December 20, 1909, Box 9, N-61, letter from Rep. J.N. Small to C.G. Elliott, December 29, 1909, Box 9, N-66, all RG 16.5.2, Department of Agriculture, Office of the Solicitor, Records of the Everglades Investigation 1906–1913, Archives II, College Park, MD; R.D. Marston and R.P. Teele, *Economic Status of Drainage Districts in the South* (Washington: U.S. Dept. of Agriculture, October, 1930, U.S.D.A. Technical Bulletin No. 194): 10–12.

54. J.O. Wright, "Report of a Conference at Norfolk, Va., Saturday, January 22, 1909, Box 9, N-86, RG 16.5.2, Department of Agriculture, Office of the Solicitor, Records of the Everglades Investigation 1906–1913, Archives II, College Park, MD; "Testimony of C.G. Elliott" in *Everglades of Florida: Hearings Before the Committee on Expenditures in the Department of Agriculture, Pt. 22* (March 20 and 25, 1912): 1094, 1099.

55. "Testimony of John Seip" in *Everglades of Florida: Hearings Before the Committee on Expenditures in the Department of Agriculture, Pt. 15* (March 4, 1912): 726. January 21–23 date: "Itinerary and Duties of J.O. Wright, February 1, 1905 to February 28, 1910, Box 8, M-793 through M-801, RG 16.5.2, Department of Agriculture, Office of the Solicitor, Records of the Everglades Investigation 1906–1913, Archives II, College Park, MD.

56. Letter from C.G. Elliott to J.Y. Joyner, January 2, 1910, Box 8, M-290, RG 16.5.2, Department of Agriculture, Office of the Solicitor, Records of the Everglades Investigation 1906–1913, Archives II, College Park, MD. "Itinerary and Duties of J.O. Wright, February 1, 1905 to February 28, 1910," Box 8, M-793 through M-801, RG 16.5.2, Department of Agriculture, Office of the Solicitor, Records of the Everglades Investigation 1906–1913, Archives II, College Park, MD.

57. "Testimony of John Wilkinson" in *Everglades of Florida: Hearings Before the Committee on Expenditures in the Department of Agriculture, Pt. 31* (June 5, 1912): 1456–1458; Letter from E.P. Crouch to C.G. Elliott, January 17, 1910, Box 9, N-17, RG 16.5.2, Department of Agriculture, Office of the Solicitor, Records of the Everglades Investigation 1906–1913, Archives II, College Park, MD; letter from C.G. Elliott to S.W. Wilkinson and Brothers Co., January 18, 1910, Box 9, N-80, RG 16.5.2, Department of Agriculture, Office of the Solicitor, Records of the Everglades Investigation 1906–1913, Archives II, College Park, MD.

58. "Testimony of C.G. Elliott" in *Everglades of Florida: Hearings Before the Committee on Expenditures in the Department of Agriculture, Pt. 22* (March 20 and 25, 1912): 1094, 1099.

59. Letter from J.O. Wright to John Seip, March 5, 1910, letter from J.O. Wright to John Seip, June 24, 1910, letter from J.O. Wright to Mr. Lukins, Carolina Land and Lumber Co., October 3, 1910, all Box 9, "John Seip Letters," RG 16.5.2, Department of Agriculture, Office of the Solicitor, Records of the Everglades Investigation 1906–1913, Archives II, College Park, MD.

60. Testimony of Mr. John Seip" in *Everglades of Florida: Hearings Before the Committee on Expenditures in the Department of Agriculture, Pt. 15* (March 3, 1912): 712, 727.

61. "Testimony of John Seip" in *Everglades of Florida: Hearings Before the Committee on Expenditures in the Department of Agriculture, Pt. 15* (March 4, 1912): 718–720.

Chapter 7

1. Alfred J. Hanna and Kathryn A. Hanna, *Lake Okeechobee: Wellspring of the Everglades* (Indianapolis: Bobbs-Merrill, 1947): 270–277.

2. Letter from Arthur Morgan to J.E. Dovell, May 22, 1946, Arthur Morgan Papers, University of Florida Special Collections: https://ufdc.ufl.edu/uf00103500/00005.

3. Letter from Charles Elliott to Arthur Morgan, March 11, 1912, Arthur Morgan Papers, University of Florida Special Collections: https://ufdc.ufl.edu/uf00103500/00002.

4. *Everglades of Florida: Acts, Reports and Other Papers, State and National, Relating to the Everglades of the State of Florida and their Reclamation* (62nd Congress, 1st Session, Senate Document No. 89, 1911). [hereafter *Senate Document No. 89*] The Wright report extract is at 129–138, and the Wright Report is at 140–180. Clark accused: letter from Rep. Frank Clark to Secy. James Wilson, October 28, 1911, Box 8, no file no; letter from Secy. James Wilson to Rep. Frank Clark, October 30, 1911, Box 4, no file no.; letter from Rep. Frank Clark to Secy James Wilson, January 6, 1912, Box 4, no file no.; letter from Secy. James Wilson to Rep. Frank Clark, January 18, 1912, Box 7, no file no., all RG 16.5.3, Department of Agriculture, Office of the Solicitor, Records of the Everglades Investigation 106–1913, Archives II, College Park, MD.

5. "Letter of R.D. Hardee," *Jacksonville Metropolis* (October 30, 1911), in *Everglades of Florida: Hearings Before the Committee on Expenditures in the Department of Agriculture, Pt. 26* (April 3, 1912): 1332–1333.The text of the flier can be found in: "Testimony of J.O. Wright," in *Everglades of Florida: Hearings Before the Committee on Expenditures in the Department of Agriculture, Pt. 4* (February 15, 1912): 140–141.

6. "Testimony of Hon. Frank Clark," in *Everglades of Florida: Hearings Before the Committee on Expenditures in the Department of Agriculture, Pt. 18* (March 8, 1912): 834, 865, 870–872.

7. Letter from C.G. Elliott to A.B. Collins, May 16, 1911, Box 5, R-1027, RG 16.5.2, Department of Agriculture, Office of the Solicitor, Records of the Everglades Investigation 1906–1913, Archives II, College Park, MD.

8. "Testimony of A.D. Morehouse," in *Everglades of Florida: Hearings Before the Committee on Expenditures in the Department of Agriculture, Pt. 12* (February 29, 1912): 526 "Testimony of C.G. Elliott," in *Everglades of Florida: Hearings Before the Committee on Expenditures in the Department of Agriculture, Pt. 17* (March 7, 1912): 782.

9. "Testimony of A.C. True," in *Everglades of Florida: Hearings Before the Committee on Expenditures in the Department of Agriculture, Pt. 24* (March 27, 1912): 1217; "Testimony of Walter Beal," in *Everglades of Florida: Hearings Before the Committee on Expenditures in the Department of Agriculture, Pt. 24* (March 27, 1912): 1242.

10. "Testimony of J.O. Wright," in *Everglades of Florida: Hearings Before the Committee on Expenditures in the Department of Agriculture, Pt. 4* (February 15, 1912): 140–141.

11. "Testimony of Joseph A. Arnold," in *Everglades of Florida: Hearings Before the Committee on Expenditures in the Department of Agriculture, Pt. 22* (March 20 and 25, 1912): 1108. "Memorandum for McCabe [from Joseph Arnold]," February 29, 1912, Box 4, no file no., RG 16.5.3, Department of Agriculture, Office of the Solicitor, Records of the Everglades Investigation, 1906–13, Archives II, College Park, MD.

12. Letter from James Wilson to N.B. Broward, May 16, 1907, Box 2, Exhibit D-16; letter from N.B. Broward to James Wilson, May 21, 1907, Box 2, Exhibit D-17, RG 16.5.3, Department of Agriculture, Office of the Solicitor, Records of the Everglades Investigation, 1906–13, Archives II, College Park, MD.

13. Letter from James Wilson to Theodore Roosevelt, December 12, 1903, Library of Congress Manuscript Division and Theodore Roosevelt Digital Collection, Dickinson State University: https://thetheodorerooseveltcenter.org/Research/Digital-Library/Record?libID=o43058; letter from James Wilson to Theodore Roosevelt, July 12, 1905, Library of Congress Manuscript Division and Theodore Roosevelt Digital Collection, Dickinson State University: https://thetheodorerooseveltcenter.org/Research/Digital-Library/Record?libID=o49977; letter from James Wilson to Theodore Roosevelt, July 17, 1905, Library of Congress Manuscript Division and Theodore Roosevelt Digital Collection, Dickinson State University: https://thetheodorerooseveltcenter.org/Research/Digital-Library/Record?libID=o50057.

14. Testimony of Secretary James Wilson," in *Everglades of Florida: Hearings Before the Committee on Expenditures in the Department of Agriculture, Pt. 26* (April 3, 1912): 1315–1316.

15. "Testimony of Sen. Duncan Fletcher" in *Everglades of Florida: Hearings Before the Committee on Expenditures in the Department of Agriculture, Pt. 19* (March 11, 1912): 927–928.

16. A copy of this flier is located at *Everglades of Florida: Hearings Before the Committee on Expenditures in the Department of Agriculture, Pt. 4* (February 15, 1912): 140–141.

17. "Testimony of Sen. Duncan Fletcher" in *Everglades of Florida: Hearings Before the Committee on Expenditures in the Department of Agriculture, Pt. 19* (March 11, 1912): 931. "I know it was not the Wright report, because I think all the Florida authorities,

including the governor, had been wanting to get that for some time."

18. "Testimony of Sen. Duncan Fletcher" in *Everglades of Florida: Hearings Before the Committee on Expenditures in the Department of Agriculture, Pt. 19* (March 11, 1912): 934.

19. "Testimony of Joseph A. Arnold" in *Everglades of Florida: Hearings Before the Committee on Expenditures in the Department of Agriculture, Pt. 22* (March 22 and 25, 1912): 1107.

20. "Testimony of Sen. Duncan Fletcher" in *Everglades of Florida: Hearings Before the Committee on Expenditures in the Department of Agriculture, Pt. 19* (March 11, 1912): 929.

21. "Testimony of Sen. Duncan Fletcher" in *Everglades of Florida: Hearings Before the Committee on Expenditures in the Department of Agriculture, Pt. 19* (March 11, 1912): 931.

22. Letter from Thomas Will to V.W. Helm, November 14, 1911, Thomas Will Papers, University of Florida Special Collections: http://ufdc.ufl.edu//AA00000148/00003.

23. "Testimony of A.D. Morehouse" in *Everglades of Florida: Hearings Before the Committee on Expenditures in the Department of Agriculture, Pt. 12* (February 29, 1912): 532–533.

24. These documents can be found at: "Testimony of A.D. Morehouse" in *Everglades of Florida: Hearings Before the Committee on Expenditures in the Department of Agriculture, Pt. 12* (February 29, 1912): 558–590. Only one copy of Elliott Report: "Testimony of C.G. Elliott" in *Everglades of Florida: Hearings Before the Committee on Expenditures in the Department of Agriculture, Pt. 21* (March 15, 1912): 1033. Difference between Elliott and Wright reports: "Testimony of C.G. Elliott" in *Everglades of Florida: Hearings Before the Committee on Expenditures in the Department of Agriculture, Pt. 21* (March 15, 1912): 1032.

25. "Testimony of Joseph A. Arnold" in *Everglades of Florida: Hearings Before the Committee on Expenditures in the Department of Agriculture, Pt. 22* (March 22 and 25, 1912): 1126.

26. Rep. Moss had earlier caught this in the testimony of Thomas Will: "Testimony of Thomas Will" in *Everglades of Florida: Hearings Before the Committee on Expenditures in the Department of Agriculture, Pt. 13* (March 1, 1912): 607.

27. "Testimony of Sen. Duncan Fletcher" in *Everglades of Florida: Hearings Before the Committee on Expenditures in the Department of Agriculture, Pt. 19* (March 11, 1912): 929.

The Chairman: Now, this telegram you received from Gov. Broward. Did you understand, when you were in the Secretary's office, that it related to the circular or a report? In the telegram it refers to it as a bulletin."

Sen. Fletcher: I did not know whether it meant this particular one or not, but I knew it meant some paper or statement. . . .I knew it was not the Wright report, because the I think all the Florida authorities, including the governor, had been wanting to get that report out for some time.

28. "Itinerary and Duties of J.O. Wright: February 1, 1906 to February 28, 1910," Box 9, M-793 to M-801, RG 16.5.3, Department of Agriculture, Office of the Solicitor, Records of the Everglades Investigation, 1906–13, Archives II, College Park, MD.

29. "Testimony of C.G. Elliott" in *Everglades of Florida: Hearings Before the Committee on Expenditures in the Department of Agriculture, Pt. 21* (March 15, 1912): 1033.

30. "Testimony of Sen. Duncan Fletcher" in *Everglades of Florida: Hearings Before the Committee on Expenditures in the Department of Agriculture, Pt. 19* (March 11, 1912): 945.

31. "Testimony of Sen. Duncan Fletcher" in *Everglades of Florida: Hearings Before the Committee on Expenditures in the Department of Agriculture, Pt. 19* (March 11, 1912): 949–952.

32. "Testimony of Sen. Duncan Fletcher" in *Everglades of Florida: Hearings Before the Committee on Expenditures in the Department of Agriculture, Pt. 19* (March 11, 1912): 950.

33. "Testimony of Maj. J.O. Wright" in *Everglades of Florida: Hearings Before the Committee on Expenditures in the Department of Agriculture, Pt. 6* (February 19, 1912): 262–263.

34. "Testimony of Mr. Joseph Arnold" in *Everglades of Florida: Hearings Before the Committee on Expenditures in the Department of Agriculture, Pt. 23* (March 26, 1912): 1178. "Testimony of Mr. George H. Carter" in *Everglades of Florida: Hearings Before the Committee on Expenditures in the Department of Agriculture, Pt. 19* (March 11, 1912): 981; "Testimony of Sen. Duncan Fletcher" in *Everglades of Florida: Hearings Before the Committee on Expenditures in the Department of Agriculture, Pt. 19* (March 11, 1912): 929.

35. "Testimony of Sen. Duncan Fletcher" in *Everglades of Florida: Hearings Before the Committee on Expenditures in the Department of Agriculture, Pt. 19* (March 11, 1912): 963.

36. Letter from Thomas Will to V.W. Helm, Everglades Land Sales Company, September 13, 1911, Thomas Will Papers, University of Florida: http://ufdc.ufl.edu/AA00000148/00003.

37. Letter from Thomas Will to V.W. Helm, Everglades Land Sales Company, October 4, 1911, Thomas Will Papers, University of Florida: http://ufdc.ufl.edu/AA00000148/00003.

38. Letter from Thomas Will to V.W. Helm, Everglades Land Sales Company, October 14, 1911, Thomas Will Papers, University of Florida: http://ufdc.ufl.edu/AA00000148/00003.

39. George Carter specifically said that he thought Elliott was "trying to put something over" on the committee, but the reliability of his testimony is open to question, as he was clearly covering for Fletcher: "Testimony of George C. Carter" in *Everglades of Florida: Hearings Before the Committee on Expenditures in the Department of Agriculture, Pt. 19* (March 11, 1912): 982.

40. Letter from Thomas Will to Rep. J. Mark Wilcox, January 19, 1935, Thomas Will Papers,

University of Florida Special Collections: http://ufdc.ufl.edu/AA00000147/00197.

41. Letter from C.G. Elliott to A.C. True, January 10, 1912, Box 8, no file no., RG 16.5.3, Department of Agriculture, Office of the Solicitor, Records of the Everglades Investigation 1906–13, Archives II, College Park, MD.

42. Testimony of C.G. Elliott" in *Everglades of Florida: Hearings Before the Committee on Expenditures in the Department of Agriculture, Pt. 17* (March 7, 1912): 822.

43. "Testimony of C.G. Elliott" in *Everglades of Florida: Hearings Before the Committee on Expenditures in the Department of Agriculture, Pt. 17* (March 7, 1912): 789.

44. "Testimony of C.G. Elliott" in *Everglades of Florida: Hearings Before the Committee on Expenditures in the Department of Agriculture, Pt. 17* (March 7, 1912): 829.

45. "Testimony of C.G. Elliott" in *Everglades of Florida: Hearings Before the Committee on Expenditures in the Department of Agriculture, Pt. 21* (March 15, 1912): 1029.

46. "Four Indicted in Everglades Inquiry," *New York Times* (April 2, 1912).

47. "Dr. Beverly Galloway" in *Everglades of Florida: Hearings Before the Committee on Expenditures in the Department of Agriculture, Pt. 25* (April 1, 1912): 1271.

48. "Testimony of Dr. Beverly Galloway," in *Everglades of Florida: Hearings Before the Committee on Expenditures in the Department of Agriculture, Pt. 25* (April 1, 1912): 1271.

49. Letter from Prof. C.L. Goodrich to Dr. B.T. Galloway, June 4, 1910, Box 7, no file no., RG 16.5.3, Department of Agriculture, Office of the Solicitor, Records of the Everglades Investigation, 1906–13, Archives II, College Park, MD.

50. "Testimony of Dr. Beverly Galloway," in *Everglades of Florida: Hearings Before the Committee on Expenditures in the Department of Agriculture, Pt. 25* (April 1, 1912): 1278.

51. "Testimony of Joseph A. Arnold," in *Everglades of Florida: Hearings Before the Committee on Expenditures in the Department of Agriculture, Pt. 13* (March 1, 1912): 1157.

52. Letter from Thomas Will to Rep. Mark Wilcox, January 19, 1935, Thomas Will Collection, University of Florida Special Collections: https//ufdc.ufl.edu//AA00000147/00197. Will confirmed this version of events, without naming Copper, in 1926: Dovell, *The Everglades of Florida*: 300n71, citing *Ft. Lauderdale Call* (June 12, 1926). The microform article Dovell cites is no longer legible due to progressive acetate degeneration.

53. "Testimony of Thomas Will," in *Everglades of Florida: Hearings Before the Committee on Expenditures in the Department of Agriculture, Pt. 13* (March 1, 1912): 605–639.

54. Letter from Thomas Will to Rep. Mark Wilcox, January 19, 1935, Thomas Will Papers, University of Florida Special Collections: https//ufdc.ufl.edu//AA00000147/00197.

55. George Carter also described the Jacksonville editing session in a letter he wrote in mid-October: "Testimony of George C. Arnold," in *Everglades of Florida: Hearings Before the Committee on Expenditures in the Department of Agriculture, Pt. 25* (April 1, 1912): 1267; letter from William Jennings to Duncan U. Fletcher, October 6, 1911, William Jennings Papers, University of Florida Special Collections: https://ufdc.ufl.edu/UF00094874/00002; letter from Thomas Will to V.W. Helm, October 14, 1911; letter from V.W. Helm to Thomas Will, December 11, 1911, both Thomas Will Collection, University of Florida Special Collections: http://ufdc.ufl.edu/AA00000147/00002.

Chapter 8

1. "Testimony of Dr. A.C. True, in *Everglades of Florida: Hearings Before the Committee on Expenditures in the Department of Agriculture, Pt. 40* (July 31, 1912): 1710.

2. "Explanatory," [introduction to Mattamuskeet file], Box 9, M-145, RG 16.5.3, Department of Agriculture, Office of the Solicitor, Records of the Everglades Investigation, 1906–13, Archives II, College Park, MD.

3. Letter from John Seip, Carolina Land and Timber Company to Director, Office of Experimental [sic] Stations, Box 8, M-481; letter from C.G. Elliott to Rep. Albert Douglas, October 6, 1908, Box 8, M-483; letter from C.G. Elliott to John Seip, October 9, 1908, all RG 16.5.3, Department of Agriculture, Office of the Solicitor, Records of the Everglades Investigation, 1906–13, Archives II, College Park, MD.

4. Letter from J.O. Wright to John Seip, February 6, 1909, Box 9, "John Seip Letters" [envelope]; Letter from J.O. Wright to John Seip, March 7, 1909, Box 9, "John Seip Letters" [envelope], both RG 16.5.3 Department of Agriculture, Office of the Solicitor, Records of the Everglades Investigation, 1906–13, Archives II, College Park, MD.

5. Letter from J.O. Wright to John Seip, March 28, 1909, Box 9, "John Seip Letters" [envelope], letter from J.C. Wright to John Seip, July 29, 1909, Box 9, "John Seip Letters" [envelope], RG 16.5.3 Department of Agriculture, Office of the Solicitor, Records of the Everglades Investigation, 1906–13, Archives II, College Park, MD "Testimony of Mr. John Wilkinson, in *Everglades of Florida: Hearings Before the Committee on Expenditures in the Department of Agriculture, Pt. 30* (May 3, 1912): 1430.

6. Letter from J.O. Wright to John Seip, April 8, 1909, Box 9, "John Seip Letters" [envelope], letter from Leigh Hunt to W. Hays, July 21, 1909, Box 4, M-100, RG 16.5.3 Department of Agriculture, Office of the Solicitor, Records of the Everglades Investigation, 1906–13, Archives II, College Park, MD; "Testimony of W.M. Hays," in *Everglades of Florida: Hearings Before the Committee on Expenditures in the Department of Agriculture, Pt. 29* (April 30, 1912): 1392.

7. "Testimony of W.M. Hays," in *Everglades of Florida: Hearings Before the Committee on Expenditures in the Department of Agriculture, Pt. 26* (April 3, 1912): 1336.

8. Letter from J.O. Wright to John Seip, April 8, 1909, Box 9, "John Seip Letters" [envelope], RG 16.5.3, Department of Agriculture, Office of the Solicitor, Records of the Everglades Investigation, 1906–13, Archives II, College Park, MD.

9. "Testimony of W.M. Hays," in *Everglades of Florida: Hearings Before the Committee on Expenditures in the Department of Agriculture, Pt. 26* (April 3, 1912): 1347.

10. Testimony of W.M. Hays," in *Everglades of Florida: Hearings Before the Committee on Expenditures in the Department of Agriculture, Pt. 26* (April 3, 1912): 1349–1352.

11. Letter from J.H. Small to Secretary of Agriculture, August 17, 1908, Box 4, Exhibit E-151; letter from W.M. Hays to J.H. Small, August 25, 1908, Box 4, Exhibit E-153; letter from Milton Whitney, Bureau of Soils, to Sen. F.M. Simmons, January 20, 1909, Box 4, Exhibit F-333; letter from W.M. Hays to W.E. Hearn, Assistant in Soil Survey, Box 4, Exhibit F-335; Milton Whitney to F.M. Simmons, January 25, 1909, Box 4, Exhibit F-339; "Statement of Expenses Incurred in Connection With the Lake Mattamuskeet, Moyock, Angola Bay and Lake Phelps Projects," Box 2, Exhibits C-8 through C-30, all RG 16.5.3, Department of Agriculture, Office of the Solicitor, Records of the Everglades Investigation, 1906–193, Archives II, College Park, MD. See also: "Testimony of W.M. Hays," in *Everglades of Florida: Hearings Before the Committee on Expenditures in the Department of Agriculture, Pt. 28* (April 29, 1912): 1367–1368.

12. "Testimony of John Wilkinson," in *Everglades of Florida: Hearings Before the Committee on Expenditures in the Department of Agriculture, Pt. 31* (May 7, 1912): 1435.

13. Letter from A.D. Morehouse to J.O. Wright, September 15, 1909, Box 9, N-84; "Statement of Expenses Incurred in Connection With the Lake Mattamuskeet, Moyock, Angola Bay and Lake Phelps Projects," Box 2, C-8 through C-30, all RG 16.5.3, Department of Agriculture, Office of the Solicitor, Records of the Everglades Investigation, 1906–193, Archives II, College Park, MD.

14. "Testimony of W.M. Hays," in *Everglades of Florida: Hearings Before the Committee on Expenditures in the Department of Agriculture, Pt. 29* (April 30, 1912): 1402.

15. Testimony of W.M. Hays," in *Everglades of Florida: Hearings Before the Committee on Expenditures in the Department of Agriculture, Pt. 29* (April 30, 1912): 1413

16. "Probers Say Department Erred on the Everglades," Jacksonville *Times Union* (August 20, 1912).

17. Thomas Luke Manget, *Hugh MacRae and the Idea of Farm City: Race Class, and Conservation in the New South, 1905–1935* (M.A. Thesis, Western Carolina University, 2012): 35, 54. Hugh MacRae has been implicated in an 1898 pogrom in Wilmington to drive out a race-progressive city government and install a strict Jim-Crow government. Twenty-five African Americans were killed. See: Wilmington Race Riot Commission, "1898 Wilmington Race Riot Report" (Raleigh: North Carolina Department of Cultural Resources, n.d.): http://www.history.neder.gov/1898-wrre/report/report.htm. None of his later progressive programs included blacks.

18. Paul Conklin, *Tomorrow a New World: The New Deal Community Program* (Ithaca: Cornell University Press, 1959): passim.

19. James R. Kugler, *Turning on Water with a Shovel: The Career of Elwood Mead* (Albuquerque: University of New Mexico Press, 1992): Chapter 6. Unlike the MacRae communities, Delhi and Durham were spectacular failures. Both were abandoned by 1928, costing the state over two million dollars.

20. Letter from C.G. Wright to Arthur Morgan, April 25, 1912, Arthur Morgan Papers, University of Florida Special Collections: https://ufdc.ufl.edu/UF00103500/00002.

21. Testimony of Maj. J.O. Wright," in *Everglades of Florida: Hearings Before the Committee on Expenditures in the Department of Agriculture, Pt. 32* (June 5, 1912): 1463–1465.

22. "Testimony of Maj. J.O. Wright," in *Everglades of Florida: Hearings Before the Committee on Expenditures in the Department of Agriculture, Pt. 32* (June 5, 1912): 1471.

23. "Testimony of Maj. J.O. Wright," in *Everglades of Florida: Hearings Before the Committee on Expenditures in the Department of Agriculture, Pt. 5* (February 19, 1912): 272.

24. "Testimony of J.O. Wright," in *Everglades of Florida: Hearings Before the Committee on Expenditures in the Department of Agriculture, Pt. 32* (June 5, 1912): 1473.

25. "Testimony of C.G. Elliott," in *Everglades of Florida: Hearings Before the Committee on Expenditures in the Department of Agriculture, Pt. 22* (March 20 and 25, 1912): 1053.

26. "Testimony of C.G. Wright," in *Everglades of Florida: Hearings Before the Committee on Expenditures in the Department of Agriculture, Pt. 33* (June 6, 1912): 1524.

27. Letter from George Boyd, Brett Engineering and Contracting, to C.G. Elliott, August 21, 1910, Box 9, M-294 and M-295, RG 16.5.3, Department of Agriculture, Office of the Solicitor, Records of the Everglades Investigation, 1906–13, Archives II, College Park, MD.

28. C.G. Elliott to Clerk of the Superior Court, Hyde County N.C., October 11, 1911, Box 9, M-298 and M-299, RG 16.5.3, Department of Agriculture, Office of the Solicitor, Records of the Everglades Investigation, 1906–13, Archives II, College Park, MD.

29. Office of the Clerk of the Superior Court, Hyde County N.C. to C.G. Elliott, October 26, 1911, Box 9, M-300, RG 16.5.3, Department of Agriculture, Office of the Solicitor, Records of the

Everglades Investigation, 1906–13, Archives II, College Park, MD.

30. "Largest Pumping Station is at Mattamuskeet," *Engineering News* 77, 9 (March 1, 1917): 348–351.

31. Letter from A.D. Morehouse to A.D. Watts, Office of Sen. Simmons., June 7, 1911, Box 9, M-311; letter from A.D. Morehouse to the Brindley Co., July 15, 1911, Box 9, M-314 and M-315, RG 16.5.3, Department of Agriculture, Office of the Solicitor, Records of the Everglades Investigation, 1906–13, Archives II, College Park, MD.

32. Letter from J.S. Mann to C.G. Elliott, December 20, 1911, Box 8, no file no., letter from J.P. Kerr to C.G. Elliott, December 22, 1911, Box 8, no file no., Department of Agriculture, Office of the Solicitor, Records of the Everglades Investigation, 1906–13, Archives II, College Park, MD.

33. Letter from J.H. Small to J.P. Kerr, January 3, 1912, Box 9, M-158; RG 16.5.3, Department of Agriculture, Office of the Solicitor, Records of the Everglades Investigation, 1906–13, Archives II, College Park, MD.

34. Letter from J.P. Kerr to C.G. Elliott, January 10, 1912, Box 8, no file no., RG 16.5.3, Department of Agriculture, Office of the Solicitor, Records of the Everglades Investigation, 1906–13, Archives II, College Park, MD.

35. Letter from C.G. Elliott to Charles Webb, December 28, 1911, Box 9, M-321, RG 16.5.3, Department of Agriculture, Office of the Solicitor, Records of the Everglades Investigation, 1906–13, Archives II, College Park, MD. See also "The Mattamuskeet Project," [solicitor's notes] Box 8, no file no., RG 16.5.3, Department of Agriculture, Office of the Solicitor, Records of the Everglades Investigation, 1906–13, Archives II, College Park, MD.

36. Letter from Charles Webb to C.G. Elliott, December 26, 1911, Box 9, M-318 and M-316, RG 16.5.3, Department of Agriculture, Office of the Solicitor, Records of the Everglades Investigation, 1906–13, Archives II, College Park, MD.

37. Letter from C.G. Elliott to J.P. Kerr, January 6, 1912, Box 9, M-326, letter from C.G. Elliott to J.P. Kerr, January 10, 1912, Box 8, no file no., Department of Agriculture, Office of the Solicitor, Records of the Everglades Investigation, 1906–13, Archives II, College Park, MD.

38. "Testimony of C.G. Wright," in *Everglades of Florida: Hearings Before the Committee on Expenditures in the Department of Agriculture, Pt. 33* (June 6, 1912): 1531, 1533, 1535.

39. Wright told the committee he met with Webb, Kerr and Graves, then Zappone and Ashley on "either the 19th or 20th." In his letter to Vance Helm of January 20, Will alludes to "steps to be taken to check the work of the drainage division," that Wright either did take or was about to take, with no details. On February 1, in reply to a brief, cryptic letter Wright sent to Vance Helm in Chicago, Will explained to Helm that he and Wright met for three hours on January 20 and describes Wright's accusations in brief detail, but stated that Wright said he communicated them to Rep. Moss. Wright did not mention Zappone and Ashley: Letter from Thomas Will to V.W. Helm, January 20, 1912; letter from J.O. Wright to Everglades Land Sales Company, Chicago, January 24, 1912; letter from V.W. Helm to Thomas Will, January 29, 1912; letter from Thomas Will to V.W. Helm, all Thomas Will Papers, University of Florida: http://ufdc.ufl.edu//AA00000147/00003.

40. Letter from Charles G. Elliott to Arthur Morgan, April 25, 1912, Arthur Morgan Papers, University of Florida Special Collections: https://ufdc.ufl.edu/UF00103500/00002.

41. "Statement of Chairman Moss," in *Everglades of Florida: Hearings Before the Committee on Expenditures in the Department of Agriculture, Pt. 35* (June 10, 1912): 1555–1561.

42. "Testimony of A. Zappone," in *Everglades of Florida: Hearings Before the Committee on Expenditures in the Department of Agriculture, Pt. 36* (June 11, 1912): 1573.

43. "Testimony of Dr. A.C. True," in *Everglades of Florida: Hearings Before the Committee on Expenditures in the Department of Agriculture, Pt. 40* (July 31, 1912): 1710.

44. To torment him: letter from George P. McCabe to A.C. True, June 24, 1912, Box 4, no file no., RG 16.5.3, Department of Agriculture, Office of the Solicitor, Records of the Everglades Investigation, 1906–13, Archives II, College Park, MD.

Chapter 9

1. Ralph Moss, et. al. "Majority Report" in *Everglades of Florida: Hearings Before the Committee on Expenditures in the Department of Agriculture: Final Reports* (62nd Congress, 2nd Session, House Document No. 1207, August 22, 1912): 1 [hereafter, *House Document No. 1207*]

2. "Majority Report," in *House Report No. 1207*: 1–11. See also: Confidential Committee Print [Draft Final Report]: *Expenditures in the Department of Agriculture, Final Reports*, Box 1, RG 16.5.3, Department of Agriculture, Office of the Solicitor, Records of the Everglades Investigation, 1906–13, Archives II, College Park, MD.

3. "Minority Views," in *House Document No. 1207*, 12–15.

4. Alfred J. Hanna and Kathryn A. Hanna, *Lake Okeechobee: Wellspring of the Everglades* (Indianapolis: Bobbs-Merrill, 1947): 159.

5. Confidential Committee Print [Draft Final Report]: *Expenditures in the Department of Agriculture, Final Reports*, Box 1, RG 16.5.3, Department of Agriculture, Office of the Solicitor, Records of the Everglades Investigation, 1906–13, Archives II, College Park, MD.

6. *Annual Reports of the Department of Agriculture for the Year Ended June 30, 1912* (Washington: Govt. Printing Office, 1913): 1089. Fred Elliott's assistant C.D. Curtis earned $1,800: *Minutes of the Internal Improvement District* X: 591, 596 (November 30, 1914).

7. "Agreement Between the Board of Drainage Commissioners and the Southern States Land and Timber Company et, al., January 31, 1910," William Jennings Papers, University of Florida Special Collections: https://ufdc.ufl.edu/uf00094871/00004.

8. *Minutes of the Internal Improvement Fund* IX: (August 26, 1911): 197. The trustees interpreted the *Trustees v. Root* opinion in the most draconian way possible, as a rejection of the Jennings Doctrine that no legislative conveyance of land (except a fee simple deed) is valid beyond the life of a sitting board of trustees. They reached this by asserting that the 1883 Settlers' Act was a legislative grant that preceded the Broward administration but that had continuing life. I don't see where that is stated or implied in either state court decision. My interpretation is more moderate: that the Settlers' Act is valid on any state land not previously designated and publicly identified as necessary to carry out a duly authorized public purpose. The problem for the Broward-era trustees was not that the Settler's Act was enacted by a prior legislature, it was that they, as an executive branch agency, had not formally designated and given public notice of those lands needed to carry out the 1855 Swamp and Overflowed Lands Act. The Settlers' Act was amended in 1909 to remove the Everglades from eligibility.

9. "Florida Land Report Condemns Officials," *New York Times* (August 20, 1912); "Everglades Charges Fail," *New York Times* (August 31, 1912).

10. "Where McCabe is Now," *Journal of the Kansas Medical Society* 13 (October 1913): 376.

11. *Government Control of the Meat-Packing Industry: Hearings Before the Committee on Agriculture and Forestry, United States Senate on S. 5305, Part 2* (February 6, 1919): 1624; *Tax on Intoxicating Liquor: Joint Hearings before the Committee on Ways and Means, House of Representatives and the Committee on Finance, United States Senate* (December 11 to 14, 1933): 400.

12. *Who Was Who in America, Vol. 1: 1897–1942* (Chicago, Marquis Who's Who, 1981 [1943]): q.v. "Elliott, Charles Gleason".

13. "Willett M. Hays," *Annals of Iowa* 16 (1928): 477; A.F. Troyer and H. Stoehr, Willet M. Hays, Great Benefactor to Plant Breeding and the Founder of Our Association," *Journal of Heredity* 94, 6 (2003): 435–441.

14. *Who Was Who in America, Vol. 1: 1897–1942* (Chicago, Marquis Who's Who, 1981 [1943]): q.v. "Wilson, James." The Pentagon, completed in 1942, eclipsed it in both size and number of persons housed.

15. Nathan Reingold, "Preliminary Inventory of the Records of the Bureau of Agricultural Engineering (Record Group 8) (Washington: National Archives and Records Administration, 1953): NARA Publication 53, 21. pp. 1–3. In 1966 the Bureau of Public Roads (by then the Federal Highway Administration) was moved to the new Department of Transportation. The units making up the Division of Agricultural Engineering in 1931 have since been through several reorganizations.

16. "Ex-Representative Moss is Dead rrom Injuries," Richmond *Palladium and Sun Telegram* (April 28, 1919): 3.

17. "Iowan Asks for Guards in Korea," Davenport *Daily Times* (February 29, 1904);

18. James Kluger, *Turning on Water with a Shovel: The Career of Elwood Mead* (Albuquerue: University of New Mexico Press, 1992): 85–101.

19. Kluger, *Turning on Water with a Shovel: The Career of Elwood Mead*: 123–126.

20. Thomas Luke Manget, *Hugh MacRae and the Idea of Farm City: Race Class and Conservation in the New South, 1905–1935* (Master's Thesis, Western Carolina University, 2012): 123–126.

21. Kluger, *Turning on Water with a Shovel: The Career of Elwood Mead*: 133–149.

22. "Florida Land Men Held," *New York Times* (November 21, 1913); "Everglades Land Speculator Bolles Dies in Florida Train," *New York Times* (March 27, 1917); Hanna and Hanna, *Lake Okeechobee: Wellspring of the Everglades*: 145–150; Junius Elmore Dovell, *A History of the Everglades of Florida* (Ph.D. dissertation, University of North Carolina-Chapel Hill, 1947): 318–324.

23. Letter from Thomas Will to V.W. Helm, May 13, 1912, Thomas Will Papers, University of Florida Special Collections: https://ufdc.ufl.edu//AA00000148/00002.

24. Letter from Richard J. Bolles to Thomas Will, May 11, 1912; letter from Henry C. Hall to Thomas Will, August 1, 1912, both Thomas Will Papers, University of Florida Special Collections: https://ufdc.ufl.edu//AA00000147/00005 (Bolles); https://ufdc.ufl.edu//AA00000147/00006 (Hall); *Minutes of the Internal Improvement Fund*: X: 36–40 (February 6, 1913).

25. R.H. Little, *Pioneering the Everglades* (Jacksonville: Works Progress Administration, 1938): 76; Junius Elmore Dovell, "Thomas Elmer Will, Twentieth Century Pioneer," *Tequesta* 8 (1948): 21–55.

26. Dovell, "Thomas Elmer Will, Twentieth Century Pioneer": 43.

27. Federal Writers Project, *Florida, A Guide to the Southernmost State* (New York: Oxford University Press, 1939): 475.

28. Aaron D. Purcell, "Plumb Lines, Politics and Projections: The Florida Everglades and the Wright Report Controversy," *Florida Historical Quarterly* 80, 2 (Fall 2001): 161–197.

29. *Seip v. Wright*, 173 N.C. 14, 91 S.E. 359 (N.C., Feb. 1, 1917).

30. The one exception to this is now twenty years old: Ann Vilesis, *Discovering the Unknown Landscape: A History of America's Wetlands* (Washington: Island Press, 1997). I give most of the credit for the extensive literature on the Everglades to two individuals: J.E. Dovell, who uncovered it, and Marjory Stoneman Douglass, who popularized it.

31. L.C. Forrest, *Images of America: Lake Mattamuskeet, New Holland and Hyde County* (Charleston, SC: Arcadia Publishing, 1999); Lake Mattamuskeet Foundation: "Lake Mattamuskeet Yesteryear," (multi-page website): www.mattamuskeet.org/history/drainage_district_htm.

32. Tom Butchko, "National Register of Historic Places, Old Wilson Historic District, Item #10A, Roundtree-Roney-Brett Home" (National Park Service and City of Wilson, June 29, 1984)

33. R.D. Marsden and R.P. Teele, *Economic Status of Drainage Districts in the South* (Washington: U.S. Dept. of Agriculture, October 1930, U.S.D.A. Technical Bulletin No. 194): 10–16.

34. Marsden and Teele, *Economic Status of Drainage Districts in the South (Bulletin 194)*: 10–16; *Drainage Commissioners of Washington County No. 4 v. Eastern Home and Farm Association, Inc.*, 165 N.C. 697; 81 S.E. 947 (N.C., 1914).

35. Howard L. Clark, "Broad Plans for Development of 45,000 acres of Wetlands in North Carolina," *Industrial Development and Manufacturers Record 70* (December 7, 1916): 716; *Moody's Government and Municipal Bonds 1924*: 1534; Marsden and Teele, *Economic Status of Drainage Districts in the South (Bulletin 194)*: 20.

36. "Belhaven Harbor, N.C.: Letter from Secretary of War, re: Report from the Acting Chief of Engineers on Preliminary Examination and Survey of Belhaven Harbor, N.C.," (69th Congress, 2nd Session, House Document No. 778, March 4, 1927). The firm was the International Cooperage Company. It accounted for about $1.2 million of the town's $8.1 million in commerce, but was the largest user of the docks, as it shipped almost everything by water.

37. "Worst Fire in History of New Berne," *Associated Press Wire Service* (December 1, 1922); Active in North Carolina: North Carolina Department of Corporations website. The Roper company is still an active entity in the State of New York as a Virginia foreign corporation.

38. Sybil H. Argintar, "National Register of Historic Places: Belhaven Commercial District" (National Park Service/North Carolina Dept. of Cultural Resources, December 19, 2014).

39. At this time, Broward County did not yet exist. Using today's landmarks, the firm owned 3 square miles in Davie near University Drive and Griffin Road, 25 square miles scattered in urban west Davie, Pembroke Pines, and Miramar, and another 80 square miles west of the urban development zone in uninhabited Water Conservation Area 3B.

40. Daniel Mead, Allen Hazen and Leonard Metcalf, *Report of the Drainage of the Everglades* (Miami: Everglades Land Sales Company, November 12, 1912): 11–12. There are two copies of this report; the first is in the Arthur Morgan Papers, University of Florida Special Collections and the second is in the Ernest "Cap" Graham Papers, University of Florida Special Collections. The Graham version is the easier to find: http://ufdc.ufl.edu/AA00007549/00001. Author: Mead, Daniel W. Title: "Report on the Drainage of the Everglades." Date: November 12, 1912.

41. Mead, Hazen and Metcalf, *Report of the Drainage of the Everglades*: 33.

42. *Minutes of the Internal Improvement Fund* X: 505–505 (September 2, 1912). In the printed version of the minutes, Wright's resignation letter begins with a paragraph that does not appear in the original, hand-written, contemporaneous minutes of the meeting: "When I made a report on the drainage of the Everglades four years ago, I was fully convinced as to the feasibility of their drainage and the value of the land when drained. I have not changed my opinion on this subject." It was presumably added by the trustees.

43. The first was: "To the General Public: Facts Concerning the Employment of J.O. Wright as Chief Drainage Engineer," (1 p) published by the IIF about March 15 The second was: "Why was Wright's Report Suppressed?" (8 pp), ostensibly published by Wright himself, dated December 28, 1911. The text is reproduced in "Testimony of Maj. J.O. Wright," in *Everglades of Florida: Hearings Before the Committee on Expenditures in the Department of Agriculture, Pt. 5* (February 16, 1912): 186–192. The Internal Improvement Fund paid to publish 3,000 copies of the brochure: *Minutes of the Internal Improvement District* IX: 368 (March 15, 1912). Wright's subsequent employment: *Minutes of the Internal Improvement District* X: 242 (August 26, 1913); 264 (September 23, 1913); 283 (October 23, 1913); 304 (November 22, 1913). It should be noted that Wright's successor, Fred C. Elliott (no relation to C.G. Elliott) earned $250 per month, as opposed to Wright's $416.

44. *Minutes of the Internal Improvement Fund* X: 490–491 (August 9, 1912).

45. *Minutes of the Internal Improvement Fund* X: 525–543 (September 28, 1912).

46. Mead, Hazen and Metcalf, *Report of the Drainage of the Everglades*: 12, 14.

47. *Everglades of Florida: Hearings Before the Committee on Expenditures in the Department of Agriculture:* "Exhibit B of No. 2" Column 1 [the "Wright manuscript"]: 37. It appears Wright assumed Everglades drainage below Lake Okeechobee would drop to near-zero once that lake drainage was controlled. In the Hathitrust digital version of the committee transcript, "Exhibit B of No. 2" is listed as "Part 43".

48. Mead, Hazen and Metcalf, *Report of the Drainage of the Everglades*: 35.

49. Mead, Hazen and Metcalf, *Report of the Drainage of the Everglades*: 56.

50. Upper Everglades two million acres (3,125 sq. mi.): "Patent to the Everglades, 1903" and "Official Map of the Everglades, 1905" in *Everglades of Florida, Acts, Reports and Other papers, State and National, Relating to the Everglades*, United States Senate, 62nd Congress, 2nd Session, Senate Document No. 89, 1911): 91–93, 98. Elliott's methodology, and that of the MHM Board, unlike that of Wright, did not pre-assume that all of the Everglades would be drained at once; hence, both used a calculation based on the sub-area, as measured in square miles, to be drained. Elliott's calculations: Mead, Hazen and Metcalf, *Report of the Drainage of the Everglades*: 53. Evaluation of Elliott's methodology: Mead, Hazen and Metcalf, *Report of the Drainage of the Everglades*:

57. The report states that Elliott's calculations result in a required capacity to drain Lake Okeechobee of "2.572 inches per second." This must be a typo as it makes no sense. To drain two-and-a-half inches of lake level in one second is roughly seven trillion cubic inches of water per second.

51. Mead, Hazen and Metcalf, *Report of the Drainage of the Everglades*: 58.

52. Mead, Hazen and Metcalf, *Report of the Drainage of the Everglades*: 84.

53. Mead, Hazen and Metcalf, *Report of the Drainage of the Everglades*: 87.

54. Fred Elliott, *Everglades Drainage District: Biennial Report 1927–28 to the Board of Commissioners* (Tallahassee: State of Florida, 1913): 44–45. Later analysis was closer to 34,000–36,000 cfs.

55. "Reclaiming the Everglades," *Engineering Record* 68,17 (October 25, 1913): 454–457. Morgan later wrote: Dovell, *The Everglades of Florida*: 330–331.

56. A contingent option is a contract or promise to sell some specified parcel of land at a specific price if some event occurs, or conversely, to sell if a period of time expires in which nothing occurs. In the case of the Florida Fruit Lands Corp., the individual buyers purchased an undivided 10/55,000 share in the Bolles Tract, which would they could then convert to a specific ten-acre plot of land upon the contingent occurrence that the state would reclaim the Bolles Tract sufficiently to permit his firm to subdivide it.

57. *Minutes of the Internal Improvement District* IX: 518 (September 12, 1912).

58. Hanna and Hanna, *Lake Okeechobee: Wellspring of the Everglades*: 164–165.

Chapter 10

1. "Testimony of John S. Cottrell, of Moore Haven, Fla.," in *Flood Control in Florida and Elsewhere: Hearings Before the Committee on Flood Control, House of Representatives, January 10 to February 1, 1929* (Washington: USGPO, 1929):87.

2. Nelson M. Blake, *Land Into Water, Water Into Land: A History of Water Management in Florida* (Tallahassee: University Presses of Florida, 1980): 121; *Minutes of the Internal Improvement Fund*: X, 619–620 (Annual Report for 1913).

3. *Minutes of the Internal Improvement Fund*: X, 138–141 (April 21, 1913); F. Elliott, *Everglades Drainage District: Biennial Report 1927–28*: 66.

4. Blake, *Land Into Water, Water Into Land: A History of Water Management in Florida*: 123–124. This process ended up being used more often in the following sixteen years to create road districts than drainage districts. When the Great Depression hit, collapsing federal highway funds, Florida counties collectively owed $161 million in bond obligations. Bruce Epperson: *Roads Across the Everglades: The Building of the Ingraham Highway, the Tamiami Trail and the Conners Highway, 1914–1931* (Jefferson, NC: McFarland, 2016): 197.

5. "Trammell Tells of Everglades Deal," *New York Times* (November 21, 1914).

6. Reversionary rights argument: *Minutes of the Internal Improvement Fund*: VII, 543–547 (December 21, 1908). Obligation to survey: letter from William Jennings to Sen. James Taliaferro, December 9, 1909; William Jennings Papers, University of Florida Special Collections, UFL: https://ufdc.ufl.edu/UF00094871/00007; letters from William Jennings to Sen. Duncan Fletcher, May 8 and May 15, 1911, William Jennings Papers University of Florida Special Collections, UFL: https://ufdc.ufl.edu/UF00094874/00002.

7. Isham Randolph, "Novel Plant Employed in Transporting the Excavations on the Chicago Canal Works," *International Engineering Congress, Glasgow, 1901, Proceedings (Section II: Waterways and Maritime Works)* (London: William Clowes and Son, 1902): 24–38.

8. "Everglades Engineering Commission Contract, April 30, 1913," William Jennings Papers, University of Florida Special Collections: https://ufdc.ufl.edu/uf00094874/00008.

9. Letter from William Jennings to Gano Dunn, J.G. White Engineering Corp., May 12, 1913, William Jennings Papers, University of Florida Special Collections: https://ufdc.ufl.edu/uf00094874/00008. Gano Sillick Dunn (1870–1953). B.S. City College of N.Y., 1889; M.A., Electrical Engineering, Columbia, 1891; M.S., Electrical Engineering, City College, 1897. President, J.G. White Engineering Co., 1913–1953. Elected National Academy of Sciences, 1919. Under Dunn's leadership the White Engineering firm became one of the first multinational design-build engineering companies in the world, responsible for the Muscle Shoals steam power station, AL; Langley Field, VA; Naval Ordinance Plant, Louisville, KY. Dunn was personal advisor to Secretary of State Edward Stettinius,1930s. Initially opposed Tennessee Valley Authority and participated as expert in lawsuits opposing TVA act; reversed course in 1940, vigorously defending TVA as necessary to national defense. Probably was to some degree involved in planning Oak Ridge, Tennessee atomic bomb facility, as it used huge amounts of TVA electricity. See: Vannevar Bush, *Ganno Sillick Dunn, 1870–1953, Biographical Memoir* (Washington: National Academy of Sciences, 1954).

10. Florida Everglades Engineering Commission, *Florida Everglades* (U. S. Senate 63rd Cong. 2nd Session, Senate Document No. 379, 1913): 12. [hereafter, *Isham Randolph Commission Report*].

11. *Isham Randolph Commission Report*: 7–8.

12. *Isham Randolph Commission Report*: 55.

13. *Isham Randolph Commission Report*: 15.

14. Letter from Isham Randolph to W.S. Jennings, March 2, 1914, William Jennings Papers, University of Florida Special Collections: https://ufdc.ufl.edu/uf00094874/00008.

15. Letter from W.S. Jennings to Isham Randolph, February 28, 1914, William Jennings Papers, University of Florida Special Collections: https://ufdc.ufl.edu/uf00094874/00008; letter from Isham

Randolph to W.S. Jennings, March 2, 1914, William Jennings Papers, University of Florida Special Collections: https://ufdc.ufl.edu/uf00094874/00008.

16. Junius Elmore Dovell, *A History of the Everglades in Florida* (Ph.D. Dissertation, University of North Carolina—Chapel Hill, 1947): 383.

17. Fred C. Elliott, *Everglades Drainage District: Biennial District 1925–1926* (Tallahassee: State of Florida, 1927): 71.

18. Elliott, *Everglades Drainage District: Biennial Report 1927–28*: 66–68.

19. "Testimony of John S. Cottrell, of Moore Haven, Fla.," in *Flood Control in Florida and Elsewhere: Hearings Before the Committee on Flood Control, House of Representatives, January 10 to February 1, 1929* (Washington: USGPO, 1929):87.

20. Cottrell reported that the capacity of the Disston Island District pump stations was 365,000 cubic feet per second, but this is impossible; that would have been a phenomenal figure. For example, the Lake Mattamuskeet pump station, with four 850-hp steam engines, each driving a 72-inch centrifugal pump, had a capacity of 2200 cfs. ("Big Drainage project in North Carolina with Rural District Plan," *Engineering News* 77, 9 (March 1, 1917): 346–352. Either Cottrell's pumps had a capacity of 365,000 cubic feet per *minute* (6083 cubic feet per second) or more likely, a capacity of 365,000 *gallons per minute* (315 cubic feet per second).

21. "Testimony of John S. Cottrell, of Moore Haven, Fla.," in *Flood Control in Florida and Elsewhere: Hearings Before the Committee on Flood Control, House of Representatives, January 10 to February 1, 1929* (Washington: USGPO, 1929): 91.

22. Epperson: *Roads Across the Everglades: The Building of the Ingraham Highway, the Tamiami Trail and the Conners Highway, 1914–1931*: 182–185; Raymond B. Vickers, *Panic in Paradise: Florida's Banking Crash of 1926* (Tuskaloosa: University of Alabama Press, 2004): 32–74.

23. *Flood Control in Florida and Elsewhere: Hearings Before the Committee on Flood Control, House of Representatives, January 10 to February 1, 1929*: 92–105.

24. Lawrence Will, *Okeechobee Hurricane and the Hoover Dike* (Fort Lauderdale: Great Outdoors Publishing, 1978): 168.

25. Elliott, *Everglades Drainage District: Biennial District 1925–1926*: 12.

26. Elliott, *Everglades Drainage District: Biennial District 1925–1926*: 53–70.

27. Fred C. Elliott, Everglades Drainage District: Biennial Report, 1927–28 (Tallahassee, State of Florida: January 1929): 17; Alfred J. Hanna and Kathryn Hanna, *Lake Okeechobee: Wellspring of the Everglades* (Indianapolis: Bobbs-Merrill Company, 1948): 260.

28. Dovell, *Everglades of Florida*, 432.

29. Dovell, *The Everglades of Florida*: 440.

30. Letter from Arthur E. Morgan to Anson Marston, August 1, 1927, Arthur Morgan Papers, University of Florida Special Collections: https://ufdc.ufl.edu//UF00103500/000002.

31. The Department of Transportation was not created until 1967.

32. Letter from Arthur E. Morgan to J.E. Dovell, May 22, 1946, Arthur E. Morgan Papers, Smathers Library, University of Florida: https://ufdc.ufl.edu/uf00103500/00005/. In this quote Morgan mistaken uses the name "S. H. McCurdy," but in the remainder of the letter and from the context, he clearly means "McCrory" and I have silently corrected this in the quote cited. From 1913–15, McCrary was Elliott's replacement at the Irrigation and Drainage Investigations Division. In 1915 this division was part in a new bureau, the Office of Public Roads and Rural Engineering and McCrary was in charge of it. In 1931 the Office of Public Roads was spun off into its own bureau, and the remainder was called the Bureau of Agricultural Engineering. From 1931 to 1939 McCrory was Chief of Agricultural Engineering. Nathan Reingold, "Preliminary Inventory of the Records of the Bureau of Agricultural Engineering," (Washington, National Archives and Records Administration, 1953): NARA Publication No. 53–21, pp. 1–3.

33. The district will have to recognize: Dovell, *Everglades of Florida*: 455. Letters from Thomas Morgan to J.E. Dovell, March 9, 1946 and May 22, 1946, all Arthur Morgan Papers, University of Florida: https://ufdc.ufl.edu/uf00103500/000005. Quote from May 22, 1946 letter. For a summary of the report turned in by Arthur Morgan; see Hanna and Hanna, *Lake Okeechobee*: 260–261.

34. Fred C. Elliott, *Everglades Drainage District: Biennial District 1927–1928* (Tallahassee: State of Florida, January 1929): 81.

35. Elliott, *Everglades Drainage District: Biennial District 1927–1928*: 78.

36. "Statement of Frederick H. Davis (cont.), in *Flood Control in Florida and Elsewhere: Hearings Before the Committee on Flood Control, House of Representatives, January 10 to February 1, 1929* (Washington: USGPO, 1929): 128–129, 145–146.

37. Blake, *Land into Water, Water into Land*: 145–147.

38. Blake, *Land into Water, Water into Land*: 176–180.

39. Lamar Johnson, *Tentative Report on Flood Damage, October 1947 Flood* (Ft. Lauderdale: Everglades Drainage District, December 12, 1947).

40. "Central and Southern Florida Flood Control Project: Map Updated to 1975 (South Florida Water Management District Digital Map Library.) The URL is not obtainable. Go to www.sfwmd.gov/science & data/GIS/featured map gallery/Central and Southern Flood Control Project (revised 1975).

41. Michael Grunwald, *The Swamp: The Everglades, Florida, and the Politics of Paradise* (New York: Simon & Schuster, 2006): 222.

42. Epperson, *Roads Through the Everglades: The Building of the Ingraham Highway, the Tamiami Trail and Conners Highway, 1914–1931*: 71–73.

43. Elliott, *Everglades Drainage District: Biennial District 1927–1928*: 78.

44. Christopher W. McVoy, et. al. *Landscapes and*

Hydrology of the Predrainage Everglades (Gainesville: University Press of Florida, 2011): 6–7.

45. These include: Alfred Jackson Hanna and Kathryn Abbey Hanna, *Lake Okeechobee: Wellspring of the Everglades* (Indianapolis: Bobbs-Merrill, 1947); Nelson M. Blake, *Land Into Water, Water Into Land: A History of Water Management in Florida* (Tallahasee: University Presses of Florida, 1980): 106–119; Mark Derr, *Some Kind of Paradise: A Chronicle of Man and the Land in Florida* (New York: William Morrow, 1989; Gainesville: University Press of Florida, 1998); David McCally, *The Everglades: An Environmental History* (Gainesville: University Press of Florida, 1999); and Michael Grunwald, *The Swamp: The Everglades, Florida, and the Politics of Paradise* (New York: Simon & Schuster, 2006).

46. *Annual Reports of the Department of Agriculture for the Fiscal Year Ended June 30, 1912* (Washington, U.S. Government Printing Office, 1913): 113; True, A.C. [Alfred Charles] *A History of Agricultural Experimentation and Research in the United States, 1907–1925* (Washington, U.S. Government Printing Office, June 1937) (U.S.D.A. Miscellaneous Publication No. 251).

47. James Wilson, "Address," *Proceedings of the Association of American Agricultural Colleges and Experimental Station, Nov. 14–16, 1905* (U.S. Govt. Printing Office, 1906) (U.S.D.A., Office of Experimental Stations, Bulletin No. 164).

48. *Annual Reports of the Department of Agriculture for the Fiscal Year Ended June 30, 1912* (Washington, U.S. Government Printing Office, 1913): 886.

49. *An Assessment of the United States Food and Agriculture Research System* (Washington: United States Congress, Office of Technology Assessment, December 1981) (NTIS No. PB-82–170572): Chapter 3.

50. Dana G. Dalrymple, *Designing the Nation's Capital: The 1901 Plan For Washington, D.C.: The Plan is Tested: Agriculture, Architects and the Mall, 1901–1905* (Washington, National Park Service): https:www.nps.gov/parkhistory/online_books/ncr/designing-capital/sec5.html. "Letter of B.T. Galloway," in *The Mall Parkway: Hearing Before the Committee on the District of Columbia, United States Senate, Re: Bill S. 4845, Regulating the Erection of Buildings on the Mall, March 12, 1904* (Washington, USGPO, 1904): 6. See also: "Letter of Secretary James Wilson," (p. 4); "Statement of B.T. Galloway," (pp 8–12).

51. The original plans were to tear down the Castle to enforce the 809-foot line. Construction started on the present Smithsonian Museum of Natural History with the intention that it would be the Castle's replacement.

52. James Mann: *Congressional Record*, 61st Congress, 2nd. Sess. (February 9, 1910): 1659.

53. Memo from Joseph A. Arnold to George P. McCabe, February 19, 1912, Box 4, no file no., RD 16.5.3, Department of Agriculture, Office of the Solicitor, Records of the Everglades Investigation, Archives II, College Park, MD.

Bibliography

Manuscript Collections

1) *National Archives and Records Administration (NARA)*

A) Archives II, College Park, Maryland

The records consulted at Archives II came from a single collection, Record Group 16.5.3 (Dept. of Agriculture/Office of the Solicitor/Records of the Everglades Investigation, 1906–1913). These were the files assembled by solicitor George McCabe in preparation for the Moss Committee hearings that took place from February 3 to August 20, 1912. There are nine containers measuring approximately four linear feet. Most of the material is comprised of correspondence and office records, with a few briefs prepared for cross-examinations and limited amounts of other legal material. There is no finding aid.

B) Southeast Division, Atlanta Georgia

The relevant documents are in Record Group 8 (Dept. of Agriculture/Office of Experiment Stations, Field Reports, 1888–1915). These records are primarily correspondence and field reports from projects conducted by the drainage investigations division in Alabama, Mississippi and Florida, arranged alphabetically by correspondent. There are four containers measuring about two linear feet. Approximately one-third of the material pertains to the 1906–1909 Everglades survey, beginning with C. G. Elliott's preliminary reconnaissance of 1905. However, most, if not all, of the letters relating to the Everglades work were copied (i.e. transcribed) by George McCabe's office and are filed in his records, the RG 16.5.3 series at the Archives II facility. Thus, most of the material here can be found at College Park, but in the form of transcribed copies.

2) *University of Florida, Department of Special and Area Studies, Florida History Section*

The following digital collections were used in preparing this book:

Napoleon B. Broward Papers
James E. Ingraham Papers
May Mann Jennings Papers
William S. Jennings Papers
Claude L'Engle Papers
Arthur E. Morgan Papers
Thomas Elmer Will Papers and Scrapbooks
David Levy Yulee Papers

Each of these collections has a finding aid. There is, in turn, a master finding aid listing and briefly describing all available finding aids. It can found at the following URL: www.library.ufl.edu/spec/browseu_flm.htm.

The search and retrieval functions of the George A. Smathers Library (the special collections facility) are excellent, but unless the user has an institutional affiliation, he or she can only print, not download, documents. Outside scholars may secure such permission without much difficulty.

The library system was also the source of Volume 1 of the *Everglades of Florida* (Moss Committee) hearing transcripts, Parts 1–28. It was a copy formerly owned by John T. Stewart. The existence of Volume 2 is unknown and may never have been donated. Volume 1 has been digitized and is available for downloading. It can be found through the University of Florida Library's central catalog and unlike materials in the George A. Smathers library, it can be downloaded as a PDF file.

3) *Everglades Digital Library/ Digital Collections Center, Florida International University*

The Everglades Digital Library is a cooperative effort of Florida International Library, the University of Miami, HistoryMiami (the South Florida History Museum), Everglades National Park, Florida PALMM, and the U. S. Geological Survey. It was the source of most of the state and federal government reports listed below, including the Minutes of the Trustees of the Internal Improvement Fund; *Senate Document No. 89* (1911); *Senate Report No. 242* (The Isham Randolph Report, 1848) and others. The retrieval functions can be difficult to use, so often it is best to use it as a search engine to locate documents at a specific institution, then re-locate it using the institution's own website. This search engine is excellent for searching images.

4) *New York Public Library, Main (42nd Street) Branch.*

This was the source for Volume 2 of the *Everglades of Florida* (Moss Committee) hearing transcripts, Parts 29–43. The document was stored digitally, but unlike Vol. 1 at the University of Florida, each part was maintained as a separate PDF document.

5) *Florida Collection, Miami Public Library, Downtown Branch.*

This was the source for several Florida newspaper articles. All source newspapers were maintained on microform, primarily the Miami *Herald*, the Miami *Metropolis/Daily News*, the Jacksonville *Florida Times Union* and the Jacksonville *Metropolis*. Many Miami newspapers are in the process being migrated to digital format due to progressive acetate degeneration (vinegar rot).

Federal Government Reports and Documents

"Abstract of Report by J.J. Daniel, W.H. Davidson, and John Bradford, Committee Appointed by the Governor on November 17, 1885." In *Everglades of Florida: Acts, Reports and Other Papers, State and National, Relating to the Everglades of the State of Florida and Their Reclamation* (62nd Congress, 1st Session, Senate Document No. 89, 1911).

Annual Reports of the Department of Agriculture for the Fiscal Year Ended June 30, 1905. Washington, D.C.: Government Printing Office, 1906.

Annual Reports of the Department of Agriculture for the Year Ended June 30, 1912. Washington, D.C.: Govt. Printing Office, 1913.

Sybil H. Arginter. *National Register of Historic Places: Belhaven Commercial District.* Raleigh: National Park Service and North Carolina Dept. of Natural Resources, December 19, 1984. NPS Form 10–900.

An Assessment of the United States Food and Agriculture Research System. Washington, D.C.: Congressional Office of Technology Assessment, December 1981. NTIS Report No. PB-82-170572.

Tom Butchko. *National Register of Historic Places, Old Wilson Historic District, Item #10A, Roundtree-Roney-Brett Home.* Raleigh, National Park Service, the City of Wilson and the North Carolina Dept. of Natural Resources, June 29, 1984. NPS Form 10–900.

Everglades of Florida: Acts, Reports and Other Papers, State and National, Relating to the Everglades of the State of Florida and Their Reclamation (62nd Congress, 1st Session, Senate Document No. 89, 1911).

The Everglades of Florida, Expenditures in the Department of Agriculture: Final Report and Minority Views (62nd Cong. 2nd Session, House Report No. 1207, August 22, 1912). [Moss Committee Final Report]

Everglades of Florida, Expenditures in the Department of Agriculture: Hearings Before the Committee on Expenditures in the Department of Agriculture. 1–42: Transcripts of Testimony, February 3 to August 6, 1912.

Exhibit B of No. 5, February 16, 1912. Part 43 [Side-by-side comparison of February 25, 1909 Wright manuscript, unpublished June 25, 1909 Bulletin 218, a.k.a. the "Wright Report" and January 28, 1910 "Elliott Report."]

Everglades of Florida: A Report to Accompany Bill S. No. 338 (30th Congress, 1st Session, September 1848, Senate Report No. 242). [The Buckingham Smith Report]

Flood Control in Florida and Elsewhere: Hearings Before the Committee on Flood Control, House of Representatives, January 10 to February 1, 1929 (70th Congress, 2nd Session, 1929).

Florida Everglades Engineering Commission, *Florida Everglades* (63rd Cong. 2nd Session, Senate Document No. 379, 1913). [The Isham Randolph Report]

Government Control of the Meat-Packing Industry: Hearings Before the Committee on Agriculture and Forestry, United States Senate, on S. 5305, Part 2 (65th Congress, 3rd Session, February 1919).

Hearings Before the House Committee on Expenses in the Department on Agriculture, February 5, 1910. (61st Congress, 3rd Session, House Report No. 1780, 1910). [The "Wiley-McCabe Affair" hearings]

Investigation of the Department of the Interior and of the Bureau of Forestry: Hearings Held Before the Joint Committee of Congress Relative to the Investigation of Interior and its Several Bureaus, Officers and Employees, and of the Bureau of Forestry, in the Department of Agriculture, and its Officers and Employees, Volume 1: Final Reports. (61st Congress, 2nd Session, Senate Document No. 719, 1911).

The Mall Parkway: Hearing Before the Committee on the District of Columbia, United States Senate on Bill S. 4845, Regulating the Erection of Buildings on the Mall, March 12, 1904. (1904).

R.D. Marston, and R.P. Teele. *Economic Status of Drainage Districts in the South.* Washington, D.C.: U. S. Dept. of Agriculture, October 1930. USDA Technical Bulletin No. 194.

"Norfolk Southern Railroad." In *Decisions of the Interstate Commerce Commission (Valuation Reports).* (Washington, D.C.: Govt. Printing Office, 1925): 84; 725–754.

Office of Technology Assessment. *An Assessment of the United States Food and Agricultural Research System.* Washington, D.C.: Government Printing Office, December 1981. NTIS Publication No. PB-82-170572.

Nathan Reingold. *Preliminary Inventory of the Records of the Bureau of Agricultural Engineering (Record Group 8).* Washington, D.C.: National Archives and Records Administration, 1953. NARA Publication No. 53-21.

Buckingham Smith. "Report of Buckingham Smith, Esq. on His Reconnaissance of the Everglades 1848." In *Everglades of Florida: Acts, Reports and Other Papers, State and National, Relating to the Everglades of the State of Florida and Their Reclamation* (62nd Congress, 1st Session, Senate Document No. 89, 1911): 46–55; and appendices, 56–66.
Tax on Intoxicating Liquor: Joint Hearings before the House Committee on Ways and Means, and the Senate Committee on Finance, United States Senate. (73rd Cong. Interim 1st and 2nd Session, December 11 to 14, 1933).
A.C. True. *A History of Agricultural Experimentation and Research in the United States, 1907–1925.* Washington, D.C.: Govt. Printing Office, June 1937. USDA Miscellaneous Publication No. 251.
James Wilson. "Address." In *Proceedings of the Association of American Agricultural Colleges and Experimental Stations, Nov. 14–16, 1905.* Washington, D.C.: Government Printing Office, 1906. USDA, Office of Experimental Stations, Bulletin No. 164.

Florida Government Reports and Documents

Fred C. Elliott. *Everglades Drainage District: Biennial District 1925–1926.* Tallahassee: Board of Drainage Commissioners, 1927.
Fred C. Elliott. *Everglades Drainage District: Biennial Report 1927–28.* Tallahassee: Board of Drainage Commissioners, 1929.
Minutes of the Trustees of the Internal Improvement Fund of the State of Florida (Tallahassee: State of Florida).

- Volume 1: February 1873–June 1881
- Volume 7: 1907–1908
- Volume 8: 1909–1910
- Volume 9: 1911–1912
- Volume 10: 1913–1914

Report of the Joint Commission Created by the Legislature of 1907, Chapter 5632, Session Laws of 1907, to Investigate the Acts and Doings of the Trustees of the Internal Improvement Fund: Appendix to the Senate Journal of April 14th, 1909. Tallahassee: State of Florida, 1909.

North Carolina Government Reports and Documents

Joseph Hyde Pratt (ed.). *Proceedings of a Drainage Convention Called by the Geological Board and Held at Newbern, N.C., Sept. 9–10, 1908.* Raleigh, NC: E.M. Uzell, State Printers, 1908.
Joseph Hyde Pratt (ed.). *Proceedings of the Fourth Annual Drainage Convention Held at Elizabeth City, North Carolina, November 15 and 16, 1911.* Raleigh: Edwards and Broughton, State Printers, 1912.
Joseph Hyde Pratt, and Miss H.M. Berry (eds.). *Proceedings of the Eighth Annual Drainage Convention Held at Belhaven, North Carolina, November 29, 30 and December 1, 1915.* Raleigh, NC: Edwards and Broughton, State Printers, 1917.

Federal Acts and Statutes (in Chronological Order)

An Act Concerning Pre-emption Rights in the Territory of Arkansas. (18th Congress, 1st Session, Ch. 154, 1 Stat. 165, May 26, 1824).
An Act to Provide for the Armed Occupation and Settlement of the Unsettled Part of the Peninsula of East Florida (27th Congress, 1st Session, Ch. 122, 5 Stat. 502, August 4, 1842). [The Armed Occupation Act]
An Act for the Admission of the States of Iowa and Florida into the Union. (28th Congress, 2nd Session, 5 Stat. 788, March 3, 1845).
Swamp Land Act of 1850. (31st Congress, 1st Session, Ch. 84, 9 U.S. Stat. 519, 43 U.S.C. 981, September 28, 1850). [Swamp and Overflowed Lands Act of 1850]
An Act to Secure Homesteads to Actual Settlers on the Public Domain. (37th Congress, 2nd Session, Ch. 75, 12 Stat. 392, May 20, 1862). [The Homestead Act]
Hatch Agricultural Experiment Stations Act of 1887. (49th Cong. 1st Session, Ch. 314, 24 Stat. 440, 7 U.S.C. 361 *et. seq.*, March 2, 1887).

Legal Cases (in Chronological Order)

Land, Lumber and Mfg. Co. v. State Board of Education of North Carolina and W. G. Lewis, 101 N.C. 35 (N.C., 1887).
Kansas v. Colorado, 206 U.S. 46 (1907).
Tarault v. Seip, 158 N.C. 363, 74 S.E. 3 (N.C., 1912).
Root v. Cordner and the Trustees of the Internal Improvement District, 59 Fla. 648, 51 So. 535 (Fla., 1910). Note: In the *Southern Reporter* version (51 So. 535), the case is improperly styled *Trustees of the Internal Improvement District v. Root.*
Trustees of the Internal Improvement District v. Charles Root, 58 So. 371 (Fla., 1912).
Drainage Commissioners of Washington County No. 4 v. Eastern Home and Farm Association, Inc., 165 N.C. 697; 81 S.E. 947 (N.C., 1914).
United States v. Forty Barrels and Twenty Kegs of Coca-Cola and the Coca Cola Co. of Atlanta, Georgia, 241 U.S. 265 (1916).
Seip v. Wright, 173 N.C. 14, 91 S.E. 359 (N.C., Feb. 1, 1917).

Books and Articles

"Accusers Accused in Florida Inquiry." *New York Times* (February 17, 1912).
"Another Wiley McCabe affair: Florida Land Sale Inquiry." *New York Times* (February 7, 1912);

"Annual Report of the Clerical Department, March 26, 1902." *Proceedings of the Board of Trustees of the Sanitary District of Chicago, 1902.* Chicago, Sanitary District of Chicago, 1903: 7802.

"Australia Wants an Irrigationist," *San Francisco Call* (June 17, 1909).

Edward N. Akin. *Flagler: Rockefeller Partner and Florida Baron.* Gainesville: University Press of Florida, 1991 [1988].

Henry Holcumb Bennett (ed.). *The County of Ross: A History of Ross County, Ohio.* Madison, WI: Selwyn A. Brant, 1902.

"Big Drainage Project in North Carolina With Rural-District Plan." *Engineering News* 77, 9 (March 1, 1917): 346–348.

Nelson M. Blake. *Land Into Water, Water Into Land: A History of Water Management in Florida.* Tallahassee: University Presses of Florida, 1980.

"Brett, Lawrence." In *History of North Carolina: North Carolina Biography, Vol. 6.* New York: Lewis Publishing, 1919: q.v.

Henry T. Brooks. "The Month in Review." *Postgraduate: Journal of the New York Postgraduate Medical School and Hospital* 26, 9 (September 1911): 873–876.

"Broward, Napoleon B." In *Florida Biographical Dictionary.* New York: Somerset Publishers, 1995: q.v.

"Building Up Belhaven." *Manufacturers' Record* 52 (November 28, 1907): 49.

Daniel P. Carpenter. *The Forging of Bureaucratic Autonomy: Reputations, Networks and Policy Innovation in Executive Agencies, 1862–1928.* Princeton, NJ: Princeton University Press, 2001.

"City News." *Indianapolis News* (February 7, 1881).

"Clark Again Assails Florida Land Sales." *New York Times* (February 9, 1912).

Donald C. Clark. *Living Dangerously in China: The Western Experience, 1900–1950.* No location: Eastbridge, 2003.

Howard L. Clark, "Broad Plans for Development of 45,000 acres of Wetlands in North Carolina." *Industrial Development and Manufacturers Record 70* (December 7, 1916): 716

Frank Moore Colby (ed.). *The New International Year Book for 1910.* New York: Dodd, Mead and Co., 1911.

Paul Conklin. *Tomorrow a New World: The New Deal Community Program.* Ithaca, NY: Cornell University Press, 1959.

Clayton A. Coppin, and Jack High. *The Politics of Purity: Harvey Washington Wiley and the Origins of Federal Food Policy.* Ann Arbor: University of Michigan Press, 1999.

Charles C. Daniel III. "Hydrology, Geology and Soils of Pocosins: A Comparison of Natural and Altered Systems." In Curtis J. Richardson (ed.) *Pocosin Wetlands: An Integrated Analysis of Coastal Plan Freshwater Bogs in North Carolina.* Stroudsburg, PA: Hutchinson Ross Publishing, 1981: 69–108.

Tycho de Boer. *Nature, Business and Community in North Carolina's Green Swamp.* Gainesville: University Press of Florida, 2008.

Mark Derr. *Some Kind of Paradise: A Chronicle of Man and the Land in Florida.* New York: William Morrow, 1989; Gainesville: University Press of Florida, 1998.

Dictionary of Ohio Historic Places, Vol 1. St. Clair Shores, MI: Somerset Publishers, 1999.

Rodney E. Dillon, Jr., and Joe Knetsch. "The Florida Fiber Company, Duncan U. Fletcher, and the Middle River Enterprise." *Broward Legacy* (Summer/Fall 1998): 34–44.

"Does the Punishment Fit the Crime?" *Engineering News* 67, 10 (February 22, 1912): 359–360.

Marjory Stoneman Douglas. *The Everglades: River of Grass.* New York: Rinehart and Co., 1947.

J.E. [Junius Elmore] Dovell. *A History of the Everglades in Florida.* Ph.D. Dissertation, University of North Carolina, Chapel Hill, 1947.

_____. "Thomas Elmer Will, Twentieth Century Pioneer." *Tequesta* 8 (1948): 21–55.

"Drainage Operations at Lauderdale and Dania." Pensacola *Journal* (Florida Edition) (September 9, 1906): II; 14.

"Drainage Work to Be Completed in Less Than Three Years if Present Plans of Trustees Are Approved." Miami *Metropolis* (February 3, 1910).

Arthur Wallace Dunn. "Dr. Wiley and Pure Food, Part 1," *World's Work* 22 (1911): 14958–14965.

_____, "Dr. Wiley and Pure Food, Part 2," *World's Work* 23 (1912): 29–40.

C.G. Elliott, in Willi Hager (ed.) *Hydraulicians in the USA 1800–2001, A Biographical Dictionary of Leaders in Hydraulic Engineering and Fluid Mechanics.* London: Taylor and Francis, 2015: q.v.

_____, in *Who Was Who in America, Vol. 1 (1897–1942).* Chicago: Marquis Who's Who, 1981 [1943]: q.v.

"The Engineering Plans for Draining the Florida Everglades." *Engineering News* 67, 13 (March 28, 1912): 604.

Bruce Epperson. *Roads Through the Everglades: The Building of the Ingraham Highway, the Tamiami Trail and Conners Highway, 1914–1931.* Jefferson, NC: Mcfarland, 2016.

"Everglades Charges Fail." *New York Times* (August 31, 1912).

"Everglades Land Speculator Bolles Dies in Florida Train." *New York Times* (March 27, 1917).

"Ex-Representative Moss Is Dead from Injuries." Richmond *Palladium and Sun Telegram* (April 28, 1919).

"The Exoneration of Dr. Wiley." *New Outlook* 99 (September 23, 1911): 147–148.

Federal Writers Project, Works Progress Administration. *Florida, A Guide to the Southernmost State.* New York: Oxford University Press, 1939.

Duncan U. Fletcher, in *Florida Biographical Dictionary.* New York: Somerset Publishers, 1995: q.v.

"Florida Drainage Report." *Washington Tribune* (October 19, 1911).

"Florida Land Men Held." *New York Times* (November 21, 1913).

"Florida Land Report Condemns Officials." *New York Times* (August 20, 1912).

"Florida Land Row a Campaign Issue." *New York Times* (February 12, 1912).

"Florida Land Sales to be Investigated." *New York Times* (February 8, 1912).
L.C. Forrest. *Images of America: Lake Mattamuskeet, New Holland and Hyde County.* (Charleston, SC: Arcadia Publishing, 1999).
John Clayton Gifford. *The Everglades and Other Essays Relating to Southern Florida.* Miami: Everglade Land Sales Company, 1911, 1912.
_____. "The Everglades and the Landes of France." *Conservation* (August 1909): 453–460.
Doris Kearns Goodwin. *The Bully Pulpit: Theodore Roosevelt, William Howard Taft and the Golden Age of Journalism.* New York: Simon & Schuster, 2013.
"Government Begins Work for Preliminary Survey of Glades." Tallahassee *Sun* (November 24, 1906).
Michael Grunwald. *The Swamp: The Everglades, Florida, and the Politics of Paradise.* New York: Simon & Schuster, 2006.
George W. Hallam. *Bolles: The Standard Bearer.* Jacksonville: The Bolles School, 1983.
"The Hampering of Wiley." *The Literary Digest* 43, 9 (August 26, 1911): 299–301.
Alfred Jackson Hanna and Kathryn Abbey Hanna. *Lake Okeechobee: Wellspring of the Everglades.* Indianapolis: Bobbs-Merrill, 1947.
"Hardee Writes in Defense of Frank Clark." *Jacksonville Metropolis* (October 30, 1911).
Willett M. Hays. *Annals of Iowa* 16 (1928): 477.
"How Broward as Governor Came to Own 27,000 Acres of Land." *Miami Metropolis* (April 4, 1910).
Frank Huffacker. "Ohio Congressman Will Push Demands for Investigation of Everglades Land Reforms," *Jacksonville Metropolis* (December 15, 1915).
"Indiana Department." *School Education* 3, 4 (April–May 1884): 51.
"Indianapolis, Ind. Honors Veteran Carrier." *The Postal Record* 33, 1 (January 1920): 46.
"Iowan Asks for Guards in Korea." *Davenport Daily Times* (February 29, 1904).
"It Is Not a Difficult Task to Drain the Everglades, Said U. S. Govt. Expert Wright." *Miami Metropolis* (February 28, 1908).
Joe Knetsch. "Hamilton Disston and the Development of Florida." *Sunniland Tribune* (January 24, 1998): 1–2.
Joe Knetsch and Paul S. George. "A Problematical Law: The Armed Occupation Act of 1842 and Its Impact on Southeast Florida." *Tequesta* 53 (1993): 63–80.
Joe Knetsch and Paul S. George. "To Settle the Land: Pre-Emption and the Withers Report in Early Twentieth Century Broward County." *Broward Legacy* 3, 4 (1990): 27–33.
Maury Klein. *History of the Louisville and Nashville Railroad.* New York: Macmillan, 1972.
James R. Kluger. *Elwood Mead: Irrigation Engineer and Social Planner* (Ph.D. Dissertation, Univ. of Arizona, 1970).
_____. *Turning on Water with a Shovel: The Career of Elwood Mead.* Albuquerque: University of New Mexico Press, 1992.
Christopher Knowlton. *Bubble in the Sun: The Florida Boom of the 1920s, and How it Brought on the Great Depression.* New York, Simon & Schuster, 2020.
"Largest Pumping Plant Is at Mattamuskeet." *Engineering News* 77, 9 (March 1, 1917): 348–351.
David Levering Lewis. *The Improbable Wendell Wilkie.* New York: Liveright, 2018.
David E. Lilienthal. *The Journals of David E. Lilienthal: Volume 1, The TVA Years.* New York: Harper and Row, 1963.
J. Paul Lilly, "A History of Swamp Land Development in North Carolina." In Curtis J. Richardson (ed.) *Pocosin Wetlands: An Integrated Analysis of Coastal Freshwater Bogs in North Carolina.* Stroudsburg, PA: Hutchinson Ross Publishing, 1981: 20–39.
R.H. Little. *Pioneering the Everglades.* Jacksonville, FL: Works Progress Administration, 1938.
"Loses in Case of Dismal Swamp." *Richmond Times Dispatch* (January 22, 1905): 1.
Thomas Luke Manget. *Hugh MacRae and the Idea of Farm City: Race Class, and Conservation in the New South, 1905–1935.* M.A. Thesis, Western Carolina University, 2012.
David McCally. *The Everglades: An Environmental History.* Gainesville: University Press of Florida, 1999.
Christopher W. McVoy, Winifred Park Said, Jayantha Obeysekera, Joel VanArman, and Thomas W. Dreschel. *Landscapes and Hydrology of the Predrainage Everglades.* Gainesville: University Press of Florida, 2011.
Daniel Mead, Allen Hazen, and Leonard Metcalf, *Report on the Draining of the Everglades.* Miami: Everglades Land Sales Co., Everglade Land Co. and Everglades Sugar and Land Co., November 12, 1912.
Christopher F. Meindl, Derek H. Alderman, and Peter Waylen. "On the Importance of Environmental Claims-Making: The Role of James O. Wright in Promoting Drainage of Florida's Everglades in the Early Twentieth Century." *Annals of the Association of American Geographers* 92, 4 (2002): 682–701.
"C.I. Millard Becomes President of the John L. Roper Lumber Co." *St. Louis Lumberman* 46, 1 (July 1, 1910): 82D.
John Missall, and Mary Lou Missall. *The Seminole Wars: America's Longest Indian Conflict.* Gainesville: University Press of Florida, 2003.
Arthur Morgan. "The Florida Everglades Incident." (46 pp manuscript, May 1954). Arthur Morgan Papers, University of Florida Special Collections: http://ufdc.ufl.edu/uf00103500/00001.
_____. "More Concerning Mr. Elliott's Dismissal: The Engineering Plans for Draining the Everglades.," *Engineering News* 67, 13 (March 28, 1912): 601–602.
Arthur Ernest Morgan, in John A. Garraty and Mark C. Carnes (eds.) *American National Biography.* New York: Oxford University Press, 1999: q.v.
"Morgan Defends Engineer Elliott; Declares Drainage Chief Blameless." *Daily Texarkanian* (February 9, 1912).
"Moss Strikes New Scandal." Greencastle (Ind.) *Star-Democrat* (March 1, 1912).

"Never Got into the Everglades; Knows Nothing About Them." *Miami Metropolis* (April 10, 1912).
"New Admissions for 1902." *Washington Law Reporter* 30, 41 (October 9, 1902): 661.
"Norfolk Newsletter." *St. Louis Lumberman* (October 15, 1908): 45.
"Norfolk Southern Railroad," in *Standard and Poor's Manual of Railroads*, 48 (1915): 445.
Richard J. Orsi. *Sunset Limited: The Southern Pacific Railroad and the Development of the American West, 1850–1930*. Berkeley: University of California Press, 2005.
Donald Pisani. *Water and American Government: The Reclamation Bureau, National Water Policy, and the West, 1902–1935*. Berkeley: University of California Press, 2002.
Joseph Hyde Pratt. "Drainage of North Carolina Swamp Lands." *Journal of the Elisha Mitchell Scientific Society* 25, 4 (December 1909).
Proceedings of the Indiana Society of Civil Engineers and Surveyors: Eighth Annual Meeting, Indianapolis, Jan. 17–19, 1888. Indianapolis: Wm. B. Burford, 1888.
Samuel Proctor. *Napoleon Bonaparte Broward: Florida's Fighting Democrat*. Gainesville: University of Florida Press, 1950.
Aaron D. Purcell. *Arthur D. Morgan: A Progressive Vision for American Reform*. Nashville: University of Tennessee Press, 2014.
_____. "Plumb Lines, Politics and Projections: The Florida Everglades and the Wright Report Controversy." *The Florida Historical Quarterly* 80, 2 (Fall 2001): 161–197.
Isham Randolph, "The Charges Against Mr. Charles G. Elliott," *Engineering News*, 67, 15 (April 25, 1912): 799.
_____. "Novel Plant Employed in Transporting the Excavations on the Chicago Canal Works." *International Engineering Congress, Glasgow, 1901, Proceedings, Section II: Waterways and Maritime Works*. London: William Clowes and Son, 1902: 24–38.
"Reclaiming the Everglades." *Engineering Record* 68, 17 (October 25, 1913): 454–457.
Curtis J. Richardson, Rhonda Evans, and David Carr, "Pocosins: An Ecosystem in Transition," In Curtis J. Richardson (ed.) *Pocosin Wetlands: An Integrated Analysis of Coastal Plan Freshwater Bogs in North Carolina*. Stroudsburg, PA: Hutchinson Ross Publishing: 3–19.
Mary C. Robbin. *A Brief History of the U. S. Geological Survey*. Washington, D.C.: Dept. of the Interior, Geological Survey, 1975. Document No. USGS: INF-74–26.
Charles E. Rosenberg. "The Adams Act: The Adams Politics and the Cause of Scientific Research." *Agricultural History* 38, 1 (January 1964): 3–12.
"Say Elliott Was a Foil for Wilson." *New York Times* (February 11, 1912).
Daniel L. Schafer, "U.S. Territory and State." In Michael Gannon (ed.) *The History of Florida*. (Gainesville: University Press of Florida, 2013).
E.R. Shinable. "The Chicago Sanitary District Canal." *Journal of the Association of Engineering Societies* 14, 6 (June 1895): 45–51.
"Stewart, John Truesdell," in Willi Hager, *Hydraulicians in the USA, 1800–2000: A Biographical Dictionary* (London: CRC Press, 2015): q.v.
William Stewart. *History of Norfolk County Virginia and Representative Citizens*. Chicago: Biographical Publications, 1902.
A.F. Troyer, and H. Stoehr. "Willet M. Hays, Great Benefactor to Plant Breeding and the Founder of Our Association," *Journal of Heredity* 94, 6 (2003): 435–441.
"Untitled." *Indiana School Journal* 23, 10 (October 1878): 458.
"Untitled." Indianapolis *Journal* 50, 25 (January 25, 1900): 3.
Raymond B. Vickers. *Panic in Paradise: Florida's Banking Crash of 1926*. Tuscaloosa: University of Alabama Press, 2004.
Ann Vileisis. *Discovering the Unknown Landscape: A History of America's Wetlands*. Washington, D.C.: Island Press, 1997.
Philip Weidling, and August Burgard. *Checkered Sunshine: The History of Fort Lauderdale, 1793–1955*. Ft. Lauderdale: Wake-Brook House/Ft. Lauderdale Historical Society, 1974.
Patsy West. *The Enduring Seminoles: From Alligator Wrestling to Ecotourism*. Gainesville: University Press of Florida, 1998.
Judson Welliver. "Another Feud on Like Wiley Case." *Washington Times* (October 15, 1911).
_____. "Everglades Sales Before Committee." *Washington Times* (December 8, 1911).
H. Parker Willis. "Secretary Wilson's Record: Part 1, Patent Medicines." *Collier's* 49, 1 (March 23, 1912): 10–13.
_____. "Secretary Wilson's Work, Part 3: Pure Food and Drug." *Colliers* 49, 3 (May 6, 1912): 10–12.
"Where McCabe Is Now." *Journal of the Kansas Medical Society* 13 (October 1913): 376.
Lawrence Will. *Okeechobee Hurricane and the Hoover Dike*. Fort Lauderdale, FL: Great Outdoors Publishing, 1978.
"Wilson, James." In *Who Was Who in America, Vol. 1: 1897–1942*. Chicago: Marquis Who's Who, 1981 [1943]: q.v.
"Worst Fire in History of New Berne." *Associated Press Wire Service* (December 1, 1922).

Internet Resources

Dana G. Dalrymple. *Designing the Nation's Capital: The 1901 Plan For Washington, D.C: The Plan is Tested: Agriculture, Architects and the Mall, 1901–1905*. Washington, Department of the Interior, National Park Service: https:www.nps.gov/parkhistory/online_books/ncr/designing-capital/sec5.html. (text, maps, photographs)
Ira Glass, et al. "The Recipe," *This American Life* (National Public Radio. No. 427, February 11, 2011): https//thisamericanlife.org/427/original-recipe (archived radio broadcast).
Lake Mattamuskeet Foundation. *Lake Mattamuskeet Yesteryear*: www.mattamuskeet.org/history/drainage_district_htm (multi-page website).

Daniel Mead, Allen Hazen, and Leonard Metcalf. "Report on the Draining of the Everglades." Miami: Everglades Land Sales Co., Everglade Land Co. and Everglades Sugar and Land Co., November 12, 1912. University of Florida Special collections: http://ufdc.ufl.edu/aa00007549/00001 (two copies, in the Arthur Morgan Papers and Ernest "Cap" Graham Papers, University of Florida Special Collections, digitized manuscript document).

John T. Stewart. *Report on Everglades Drainage Project in Lee and Dade Counties, Florida, January to May 1907*: http://www.everglades.fiu/reclaim/monographs/F107081707.htm (digitized handwritten manuscript, transcribed typewritten version of manuscript, and separate interpretative notes and comments).

LeRae Umfleet, 1898 Wilmington Race Riot Commission, et al. *1898 Wilmington Race Riot Report*. Raleigh: North Carolina Department of Cultural Resources, 2006: https://digital.ncdcr.gov/digital/collection/p249901coll22/id/5842 (digitized published document). Note: the URL for this item has shifted frequently, but it has never gone dead. The above URL was verified on May 15, 2020.

Index

Adams Act of 1906 (U.S.) 35
Adams-Onis Treaty (1819) 13
Agriculture Dept. Mall Building (1908–1930) 152
Albemarle Development Co. 6, 10, 110, 111, 148, 150; *see also* Terra Ceia; Wilkinson, John
Albemarle-Pamlico Peninsula 105, 107, 133, 141
Albemarle-Pantego Railroad 105, 106; *see also* Norfolk Southern Railroad
Albemarle Sound 105
American Forestry Assn. 62
American Steel Dredge Co. 110, 112
Apalachicola River 13
Armed Occupation Act of 1842 (U.S.) 14, 22
Army Corps of Engineers 6, 30, 162, 176, 177; *see also* Central and Southern Flood Control District
Arnold, Joseph 4, 51–52, 55, 60–61, 63, 65, 122, 127, 131, 132; and *Senate Document No. 89* 72-74, 124–126, 129
Ashley, J. 78–80, 92, 96
Artesia, NC *see* MacRae Villages

Baird and Roper Lumber Co. 103–104; *see also* Roper, John L.
Ballinger, Richard 81, 82, 83, 85
Ballinger-Pinchot Scandal 81–85
Barrs, J.M. 75
Bathrick, Ellsworth 5, 90
Beal, Walter 49, 51–52, 55, 60, 93, 98, 121–122; and *Senate Document No. 89* 72-74, 92, 124
Beauford County, NC 103
Belhaven, NC 6, 10, 103, 105, 159
Belhaven Lumber Co. 106, 116, 159–161
Belle Glade, FL 173
Blount Tract (John Blount) (NC) 103–104
Bloxham, William D. 13, 20, 21–22; and Disston purchase 18–20
Boca Raton, FL 171
Bolles, Richard J. 3, 27–29, 50, 51, 53, 58, 59, 62, 65, 66, 67, 68, 69, 77, 93, 154, 155–156, 164; death 155; early life 27; *see also* Florida Fruit Lands Co.
Borland, William P. 68
Boulder Dam (Hoover Dam) 154
Boyd, George 142
Brandeis, Louis 84
Brett, Lawrence 30, 69, 112, 156, 157; early life 43–44; Lawrence Brett Engineering Co. 112, 118, 142–144, 157; 1906–1908 Everglades expeditions 43–48, 91
Bright, D.R. 145–146
Brooks, Henry T. 81
Broward, Napoleon B. 3, 10, 13, 23–26, 27–28, 48, 49–50, 58, 63, 65, 70, 75, 122, 123, 125, 126, 151; death of 66; and 1906–1908 Everglades survey expeditions 36–40, 45
Broward County, FL 14, 28, 94, 177, 178
Brown's Landing (Brown's Store) 44–46, 53, 54
Bryan, Nathan P. 66
Bryan, William James 29, 66
Bryan, William Jennings 23, 53
Bryant, F.E. 27
Buckingham Smith Report *see* Smith, Buckingham
Bulletin 218 (1909) 4–5, 52, 60–61, 72–74, 76, 90, 92, 126, 127, 129, 132; *see also Senate Document No. 89*; Wright Report
Bureau of Plant Industry (USDA) 60–61, 90, 122, 133
Bureau of Reclamation (U.S. Dept. of the Interior) 6, 140, 180
Burr, Gus 43

California Water and Forest Association 33
Caloosahatchee (dredge) 59
Caloosahatchee River 18–20 37, 44–45, 47, 51, 173, 176
Cannon, Joseph 84, 180
Carlton, Doyle 175, 176
Carolina Land and Timber Co. 50, 108, 110, 112, 118, 134, 135, 150, 156; *see also* Moyock; Seip, John
Carter, George 72–74, 91, 124, 126–127, 129, 130, 131, 132
Castle Hayne, NC *see* MacRae Villages
Central and Southern Flood Control District (FL) 6, 177–178; *see also* Army Corps of Engineers
Chadwick, E.W. 44–47
Chambers, E.C. (Chambers Land Co.) 3, 62, 69, 155, 164, 166
Chicago *Examiner* 77
Chicago River Sanitary Canal 41, 43, 151, 167
Clark, Frank 5, 43, 65, 75–80, 90, 91, 120–121, 132, 146
Cluss Building 180–181
Coca-Cola Co. 88, 201n19
Coleman, J.F. 143–144
Collier's magazine 83–84, 140
Comfort, Walter R. 29
Consolidated Land Co. 65, 70
Copper, Samuel 63, 129, 130
Corkscrew Swamp 179
Cottrell, John 166, 169–170
Cunningham, Clarence 83, 84
Curritick County, NC 110, 116

Dade County, FL 14, 173
Dapray, Maj. J.A. 45, 46
Davie, R.P. 28, 59, 62, 69
Davie Farms 94
Davis, Frederick 175–176
Davis, Henry 89, 93, 95, 96, 126–127, 128–129
Davison, G. Howard 113
Disston, Hamilton 18–21, 29, 50
Disston, Henry 18
Disston Island Drainage District 170–172
Disston Land Co. 21, 25, 52
Dollings, R.L. Company *see* New Holland Farms
Donation Act of 1824 (U.S.) 13–14
Doughton, R.L. 148
Douglas, Albert 50, 108
Douglas, Marjory Stoneman 2
Drainage Investigations Division (USDA) 1, 2, 3, 5–6, 26, 35, 42, 51, 73, 91, 92, 113, 146–147, 149, 152; created (1902) 31–33
Drew, John 17, 20
Dunlap, F.L. 86–88
Dunn, Gano 167
Duval, Harvey 27, 50

Eastern Home and Farm Assn. 158
Eastern Land v. State Board of Education (NC, 1887) 103–104
Elliott, Charles G. 1, 3, 4, 5, 6, 35, 36–37 43, 45, 49, 50, 51, 52, 55, 63–64, 65, 69, 72, 90, 91, 92, 93, 95, 98–100, 102, 107, 108, 112, 116, 118, 120, 126, 134, 137, 140, 141, 142, 146, 148, 149, 151, 158; early history 36; fired by Secretary Wilson 74–80; late career and death 152; orders first version of Wright Report suspended 55–58; proposes Everglades survey to Gov. Broward 38–40; and *Senate Document No. 89* 124, 125, 130
"Elliott Circular" *see* "Mimeographed Circular"
Elliott Report (Jan. 1910) 4, 60–61, 70–74, 76, 92, 124–126, 129, 130, 131–132, 133, 148
Ellis, William 69, 150–151, 166
Engineering News 45, 96–97, 163
Everglades (dredge) 25–26, 29, 43, 59
Everglades Drainage District 6, 13, 22, 25–26, 28, 29, 39, 42–43, 50, 60, 64, 69, 92, 93, 94–95, 99, 150, 164, 169, 170, 173, 174, 176, 177, 179; becomes independent of Internal Improvement Fund 164–165, 166; created 24–25; replaced by Central and Southern District 177
Everglades Engineering Board of Review Report 173–174
Everglades Land Sales Co. 55, 58, 62, 63, 67, 68, 74, 77, 123, 155, 161–162
Everglades National Park 178–179
Everglades Survey (Drainage Investigations Division, 1906–1908) 36–37, 39–40, 42–48

Fairey, Omer 111, 117
Fassett, J. Sloat 114
Federal Rivers and Harbors Act of 1930 (U.S.) 176
Fisheating Creek (FL) 53
Fisher, Carl 171
Fitts, Thomas 104
Flagler, Henry 18
Fletcher, Duncan 4, 29, 59, 63, 70, 75, 76, 78, 123–124; and *Senate Document No. 89* 71–74, 91, 92, 120–121, 124–132; testimony before Moss Committee 120, 126–132
Florida Coast Line Canal and Transportation Co. 29
Florida East Coast Railroad 26, 29, 39, 47, 65, 69, 70, 155; Model Land Co. subsidiary 69, 178
Florida East Coast Sugar and Drainage Co. 52
Florida Fiber Co. 29
Florida Fruit Lands Co, 28, 51, 58, 66–67, 69, 77, 154–155; *see also* Bolles, Richard
Florida Railroad 16
Florida, State of: admission to union 13, 14; creates Internal Improvement Fund 15–16
Floyd, J.C. 59, 110, 118–119, 136, 148
Fort Lauderdale 25, 26, 29, 43, 47, 66
Fort Myers 18–20, 30, 37, 43, 44, 47, 48, 59, 156
Fortier, Samuel 35
Fry, John 17
Funderhide, Paul 44–47
Furst-Clark Construction Co. 156, 169

Galloway, Beverly 4, 60, 61, 131–132, 152, 180
Garfield, James R. 33
Geological Survey (U.S. Dept. of the Interior) 14, 30, 31, 33
Gifford, John Clayton 62, 71
Gilchrist, Albert 29, 46, 49, 51, 53, 58, 69, 75, 120, 151, 160, 164–165
Glavis, L.R. 83–85
Gleason, William H. 17
Goodrich, C.L. 60–61, 90, 131–132
Government Land Office (U.S. Dept. of the Interior) 6, 14
Government Printing Office 60, 63
Graham, H.N. 69
Grand Coulee Dam 154
Graves, Douglas 145
Great Dismal Swamp (VA/NC) 5, 48, 102, 108, 110, 133
Great Flood of 1947 (FL) 177–178
Green Swamp (NC) 48

Hall, Henry C. 4, 50–52, 55, 70, 75, 76, 92, 94, 123, 130, 150–151
Hanna, A.K. 2, 74, 120, 149
Hanna, K.A. 2, 74, 120, 149
Hansborough, Henry 33
Hardee, W.R. 77
Harmon, J.H. 152
Harrison, William H. 17
Hays, Willett 2, 6, 50, 77, 102, 107, 108, 113, 114, 115, 118, 134, 137, 148, 149, 150, 175; later life and death 152; testimony before Moss Committee 135–138
Hazen, Allen 161; *see also* Mead, Hazen and Metcalf Report
Hearn, W.E. 137
Heinz Foods 88
Helm, Vance 62, 67, 69–70, 71, 72, 73, 74, 77, 79, 129, 161, 162, 163, 173, 175; *see also* Everglades Land Sales Co.
"Henry Hall Extract" *see* "Wright Report Extract"
Hepburn, William 89
Higgins, Edwin W. 51, 93, 136, 149
Hills, George 174
Hillsboro Canal 53, 173
Hoffman, J.W. 179
Holloway, Hampton 25–26
Holloway, Scott 25
Holmes, Edwin 123
Homestead Act of 1863 (U.S.) 6
Hoover, Herbert 153, 176
Hoover Dam 154
Hoover Dike (FL) 177
Hosier, H.G. 109
Howe, E.C. 62–64, 92
Huffaker, Frank 79, 95–96, 141
Hunt, Leigh 6, 113–114, 135, 137, 140
Hurricane of 1926 (FL) 170–171
Hurricane of 1928 (FL) 166, 171, 172, 173
Hyde County, NC 107, 137, 142–143

Ickes, Harold C. 152, 154
Ingraham, James 21, 25
Internal Improvement Act of 1855 (FL) 15–16, 20
Internal Improvement Fund (FL) 15–25, 67, 69, 70, 72, 73, 74, 78, 96, 151, 156, 163, 164, 166, 167, 169, 179; begins dredging 25; created 15–16; 1903 federal land patent 23–25; rescued by Disston purchase 18–20
Irrigation Investigations Division (USDA) 30–33, 35, 91; *see also* Office of Experiment Stations

Jacksonville *Metropolis* 77, 78, 79, 95, 141
Jennings, Bryan 53
Jennings, Douglas 66
Jennings, May Mann 53
Jennings, William S. 3, 10, 22, 27–28, 36–37, 58–59, 64, 70, 78, 92, 104, 150, 151, 167, 169, 178; lawyer for Richard Bolles 68–69; 1903 federal land patent 23–26, 163; *Senate Document No. 89* 71, 72, 73, 76, 80, 91, 92, 120, 126–127, 130
Johnson, Lamar 177

Kackley, W.J. 161
Kerr, John P. 144, 145
Keystone Saw and Tool Works 18, 19
Kipp, H.A. 44–46
Kissimmee River 18–20, 173, 179
Kreamer, James 25, 52
Krom, Charles 171

Lake Drummond (VA) 108
Lake Hicpochee (FL) 18–20, 37, 43, 53
Lake Kissimmee (FL) 18–20
Lake Mattamuskeet (NC) 6, 10, 49, 50, 107, 108, 109, 111, 112–116, 117, 118, 134–135, 136, 137, 140, 141–143, 144, 146, 149, 156, 157, 175; New Holland Farms 115, 116
Lake Monroe (FL) 13, 18
Lake Worth (FL) 25, 53
Lake Okeechobee (FL) 6, 15,

18–20, 25, 28, 37, 44–46, 47, 53, 93, 99, 107, 122, 155, 167, 168, 169, 175; Disston drainage plan 18–20; estimates of drainage requirements (1910–1923) 55–56, 93, 98–99; hurricanes of 1926 and 1928 169–172; levees built 170, 173
Lake Worth (FL) 25, 53
Legislative Land Grants (from Fla.) 13, 20–25
Leighton, Marshall 167; *see also* Randolph, Leighton and Peters Report
Lewis, Sinclair 85
Lilienthal, David 42
Lion Swamp (NC) 111, 112
Literary Digest magazine 89
Little, R.H. 156
Long, S.H. 15
Louisville and Nashville Railroad 24, 25, 26, 58
Loxahatchee River (FL) 173
Lukens, A.B. 109, 110
Lynde, H.M 109, 110
Lyons, Leslie J. 68

Mackey's Ferry, NC 105
MacRae, Donald 138
MacRae, Hugh 138–140, 153, 210 n17
MacRae Villages 138, 139, 140, 153–154, 160
Madden, Martin B. 149
Madison, Edwin 84
Mallory, Stephen 29, 39, 40
Manley-Anthony System 171
Mann, J.S. 145
Marathon, NC *see* MacRae Villages
Marston, Anson 2, 60, 122, 123, 174–175
Marston-Hills-McCrory (Everglades Engineering Board) Report 173–174
Martin, John W. 171, 173, 175
Martyn, Henry, Henry 85
Marvin, Frank 43
Mason, Webb and Kerr 6, 116, 142–143
McCabe, George 1, 49, 78–80, 92, 93, 98, 118, 121, 126, 130, 132, 133, 146, 147, 150; early career 85; later career 151–152; and Wiley-McCabe scandal 85–90
McCrory, Samuel H. 109, 134, 142, 144, 146, 174–175
McCumber, P.J. 108
McKay, George 14
McKinley, William 30, 180
Mead, Daniel 161; *see also* Mead, Hazen and Metcalf Report
Mead, Elwood 3, 32–34, 36, 38, 41, 43, 99, 140, 151, 152, 154; allocates $11,000 for Everglades survey (1906–1908) 39–40; early life and career 31; moves to Australia 35; selects Wright to lead Everglades survey 40; work for California and Bureau of Reclamation 152–154
Mead, Hazen and Metcalf (MHM) Report 55, 161, 162, 164, 167, 168, 174
Merchant, Clyve 47
Merriam, C. Hart 81
Metcalf, Leonard 161; *see also* Mead, Hazen and Metcalf Report
Miami (dredge) 60
Miami Board of Trade 47, 173
Miami *Metropolis* 63
Miami River Canal 26, 43, 53, 60, 161, 169
Milton, William 29
"Mimeographed Circular" 58, 60, 70 75, 77, 78, 90, 92, 120–124, 133, 148, 149
Missouri Pacific Railroad 45
Mizner, Addison and Wilson 171
Mollie Gibson Mine 27
Moody, William 85
Moore, Willis 150
Moore Haven, FL 170, 171
Morehouse, A.D. 1, 5, 42, 52, 55, 60, 63, 71, 72, 73, 74, 78, 79, 90, 93, 98, 99–100, 102, 121–122, 126, 130, 132, 134, 144, 145, 146, 149, 151; *Senate Document No. 89* 124–127
Morgan, Arthur 2, 4, 36, 41, 45, 51, 52, 60, 71, 80, 93, 95, 120, 126, 140, 156, 163; critical of 1927 Marston-Hills-McCrory Plan 174–175; early life and career 41–42; finds errors in Wright Report (Bulletin 218) 52–57, 97–100; testifies before Moss Committee 96–101
Morse, James 114
Moss, Ralph 1, 6, 80, 90, 92, 93, 96, 99, 102, 119, 120, 126, 134, 141, 146, 147, 148; death of 152; Wiley-McCabe Pure Food and Drug hearings 89–90
Moyock, NC 5, 6, 50, 108, 109, 110, 111, 112, 116, 118, 134, 135, 150, 157, 158; *see also* Carolina Land and Timber Co.

Neosho River survey (KS) 40, 43, 57
New Berlin, NC *see* MacRae Villages
New Berne drainage conference (NC) 109–110, 141
New River (North New River) Canal 25, 47, 53, 59, 156, 160, 173
Newell, Frederick Haynes 31–34, 140
Newlands, Francis 32–33
Newlands Reclamation Act (1902) 33
Newman, John 25–26, 47, 53, 59
Newport Shipbuilding and Drydock Corp. 106
Norfolk Southern Farms 159
Norfolk Southern Railroad 105–106, 111, 116, 159
Norris, George 84
North Carolina Board of Education 104, 108, 111, 113, 117, 135, 137, 150
Norton, Richard 109

Office of Experiment Stations (USDA) 1, 3, 5, 35, 50, 52, 55, 63, 72, 73, 91, 99, 108, 111, 121, 134, 137, 146–147, 149, 151, 180; creation of 30–31; run by Elwood Mead 32–33; *see also* Drainage Investigation Division
Okeechobee (dredge) 25–26, 29, 43, 59
Okeechobee City 39, 53
Okeechobee Flood Control District 176, 177
Okeechobee Land Co. (Disston Land Co.) 19–20, 22, 39; *see also* United Land Co.
Okeelanta, FL 132, 155–156, 169
Oregon Valley Land Co. 27

Palm Beach Canal 173
Palm Beach County, FL 14, 47, 171, 177
Pamlico Sound (NC) 2, 103, 143
Pantego Drainage District (NC) 111, 112, 116, 117, 158–159
Pantego River (NC) 103, 112
Parrott, Joseph 47
Patented lands 3, 14, 15–16, 22
Penderlea, NC 153
Pensacola, FL 13, 17
Pepper, Agnes Cain 155
Perkins, Edmund T. 167; *see also* Randolph, Leighton and Peters Report
Perry, Edward 19, 21
Phillips, J.V. 111, 117
Pinchot, Gifford 32, 33, 62, 113; and Pinchot-Ballinger Scandal 81–85
Plant, Henry 18
Plummer, Frank 77
Pocosin Wetlands 2
Powell, John Wesley 32
Pratt, Joseph Hyde 42, 141
Pre-Emption Act of 1881 (FL) 22
Price, O.W. 83–84
Progresso, FL 28–29, 66–67, 155
Provident Land Co. 5, 110, 112, 150, 156–157; *see also* Seip, John
Pungo River Drainage District 117, 158, 159
Purcell, Aaron 156
Pure Food and Drug Act of 1906 (U.S.) 85–88

"Railroad" lawsuits 24–26, 50, 58, 64, 150
Ralston, H.H. 161
Randolph, Isham 41, 97–98, 151, 167–169, 174

Randolph, Leighton and Peters Report 163, 167–169, 174
Rankin, John 50
Reclamation Act of 1902 (U.S.) 32–33
Reclamation Service (U.S. Dept. of the Interior) 3, 33; *see also* Bureau of Reclamation
Reid, Robert 15
Remsen, Ira 86–90
Reversion (legal theory) 22, 24, 59, 164, 166, 178
Roney-Brett house 157
Roosevelt, Franklin D. 42, 154
Roosevelt, Theodore 32, 33, 81, 85, 89, 113, 123, 151, 153, 180
Root, Charles 94, 150
Root v. Cordner and Trustees (1910) 94, 95, 150; *see also Trustees v. Root* (1912)
Roper, John L. (Lumber Co.) 103–104, 105, 106, 111, 116, 159–161
Rose, Rufus 19–21, 36–37, 52
Rowland Lumber Co. 160
Rusby, Henry 88–90
Russo-Japanese War 114

St. Augustine, FL 13, 14, 15
St. Cloud Canal (FL) 19–20
St. Helena, NC *see* MacRae Villages
St. Lucie Canal (FL) 25, 47, 163, 168, 169, 173, 176
Sanford, Henry 13, 18
Scott, Charles 23
Seip, John 5, 6 108–109, 110–119, 134, 135, 136, 137, 150, 161, 175; early history 108–109; sued by J.O. Wright 156–157; testifies before Moss Committee 102, 110–119
Seminole Wars 14
Senate Document No. 89 (1910) 4–5, 70–80, 91–92, 120, 123–132, 161
Senate Report No. 242 (1848) 58, 70; *see also* Smith, Buckingham
Senate Report No. 379 (1927) *see* Randolph, Leighton and Peters Report
Settlers' Act of 1883 (FL) 22, 94–95, 150
Shaw, A.C. 83
Simmons, F.M. 137
Singletary, I.F. 44–48
Singleton, F.E. 79
Skilder, E.S. 109
Sloan, Charles H. 149
Smith, Buckingham 15, 26, 58–59, 70, 74
Small, John N. 5, 49, 95, 103, 104, 107, 109, 116, 134, 135, 137, 141, 142, 143, 144
Smoot, Reed 126
South Florida Railroad 13
South Florida Water Management District 177
South New River Canal (FL) 28, 47, 53, 59, 67, 161
Southern Inland Navigation and Improvement Co. 17
Southern Land Reclamation Co. 143, 144, 145, 157; *see also* Mason, Webb and Kerr
Southern States Land and Timber Co. 25, 27–28, 58, 64, 150
Sparkman, Stephen 39–40
Spitzer, Rorick and Co. 169
Stallings, B.D. 72, 73, 124
Stewart, John T. 2, 50, 69, 72; early history 43; 1906 Everglades survey 43–48, 91
Swamp and Overflowed Lands Act of 1850 (U.S.) 15–16, 22, 58, 70, 95

Taft, William H. 82–85, 151
Taliafero, James P. 39, 47, 48, 58–59, 65, 70, 71
Tallahassee, FL 14, 43, 79, 93, 96, 126, 175
Tarault Tract 102, 109
Tarbell, Ida 85
Tatum Bros. Land Co. 26, 29, 59, 69
Taylor's Creek (FL) 53
Teele, R.P. 151
Teller, Henry M. 81
Tennessee Valley Authority 6, 41
Terra Ceia, NC 106, 110, 111, 112, 149, 160
Thompson, FL (Citrus Center) 30
Tidewater Power and Transit Co. 138–139
Trammell, Park 164, 166, 167
True, A.C. 33, 34, 35, 36, 42, 44, 48, 50, 60, 63, 65, 76–77, 79, 93, 95, 103, 116, 117, 122, 130, 134, 141, 144, 146–147
Trustees v. Root (1912) 74, 94–95, 150; *see also Root v. Cordner and Trustees*

United Land Co. 2; *see also* Disston Land Co.
University of California 34, 35
University of Kansas 43

Vinnedge, Katarine 41, 157
Virginia Land and Lumber Co. 109
Vose, Francis 16–18
Vose and Livingston 16

Wade, Neil 23–24
Walker, R.J. 15
Washington, George 108
Washington *Times* 70, 74–76, 141
Webb, Charles 144, 145
Welliver, Judson 70, 74–77, 95, 141
Westcott, James D. 15, 58–59, 70, 167
Wheeler, Harold 4, 52, 71, 93, 95, 96, 98
White, J.G. Engineering Co. 167
Wikersham, George 68, 69, 77, 84, 88, 93
Wilbur, Ray Lyman 154
Wiley, Harvey W. 81, 85–90, 91, 93, 128
Wilkinson, John 5, 6, 10, 91, 103, 105, 106, 110, 111, 112, 113, 115, 116, 117, 135, 137, 159, 160, 161, 175; death 161; early life 103–104
Wilkinson, Samuel 106
Will, Lawrence 156, 173
Will, Thomas 5, 63–64, 65, 67, 69, 73, 74, 76, 79, 92, 120, 123, 124, 127, 145–146, 155–156, 163, 169; arranges theft of Bulletin 218 (Wright Report) 63–64, 129–132; early life and career 61–62; edits *Senate Document No. 89* 70–76, 126–133; founds town of Okeelanta 155–156
Williams, Arthur 27–28
Williams, L.S. 135, 137
Wilson, James 1, 3, 4, 5, 30–31, 33, 35, 39, 40, 45, 47–48, 49, 50, 51, 60, 63, 65, 69, 70, 72, 75–80, 96, 107, 108, 113, 121, 122–124, 134, 137, 148, 149; mimeographed circular 120–123; new Agriculture Dept. Building 180–181; Pinchot-Ballinger affair 81–85; retirement and death 152; *Senate Report No. 89* 123–133; Wiley-McCabe scandal 85–90
Wilson, Jasper 85–86
Wilson, Woodrow 89, 151
Wilson, NC 111, 112
Wright, J.O. (James Oliver) 2, 3, 5, 6, 10, 26, 30, 50, 51, 52, 60, 61, 62, 69, 76, 77, 78, 79, 80, 90, 136, 148, 149, 161–163, 175; accepts job with State of Florida 64, 78, 92–93, 96, 150, 161–162; early life and career 40–41; edits Senate Document No. 89 72–74, 78, 91–92; late life and death 156–157; prepares Wright Report extract 50–52; surveys Everglades (1906–1908) 3, 40, 42–48, 91; testifies before Moss Committee 91–96, 127, 140–147; work in North Carolina 49, 50 103, 107, 108, 110, 111, 112, 114, 116, 135, 137, 140–146
Wright Report 1, 4, 49, 50–52, 60–63, 70, 75, 77, 78, 79, 92, 129, 133, 148, 149; Elliott revised version cancelled 60–62; Morgan and Wright find flaws in 52–59; used in *Senate Document No. 89* 70–74, 123–132; *see also Bulletin No. 218*
Wright Report extract (Henry Hall extract) 4, 26, 50–52, 70, 75, 77, 93, 148, 150
Wysocking Bay 108

Yulee, David Levy 14, 16

Zappone, A. 5, 91, 96, 141, 145, 146–147

www.ingramcontent.com/pod-product-compliance
Ingram Content Group UK Ltd.
Pitfield, Milton Keynes, MK11 3LW, UK
UKHW051930100926
8556IPUK00022B/1470

9 781476 684